BULGARIA

Kărdžali

Edirne

BLACK SEA

TURKEY

MACEDONIA AND THRACE

Xánthi

Komotiní

Keşan

İstanbul

Kavála

Liménas

Alexandroúpoli

Marmara Denizi

trymonikós Kólpos

Thásos

Kavákköy

Bandırma

Bursa

erissos

Athos

Athos 2033

Samothráki

Fengári 1611

Thermá (Loutrá)

Gökçeada

Çanakkale

Sithonía

Thrakikón Pélagos

Abide

Myrina

Límnos

Ayvaçık

Edremit

Balıkesir

Ágios Evstrátios

THE NORTHEAST AEGEAN

Mólyvos

Kyrá anagiá

Giourá

Pipéri

Mytilíni

TURKEY

Alónissos

Sporádes

Lésvos

Plomári

Skýros

SPORADES AND EVVIA

Psará

Akhisar

ymi

A

Híos

Híos

Úrla

İzmir

E

G

Pyrgí

Çeşme

Karystos

E

Ándros

A

Ándros

Aydın

Kéa

N

Tínos

Sámos

Vathý (Sámos)

Giáros

Tínos

Karlóvassi

Ikaría

Foúrni

Agathonísi

Kýthnos

S

Ermoúpoli

Ág. Kírykos

Arkí

Milâs

Muğla

Sérifos

Síros

E

Mýkonos

Lipsí

ands

Páros

Náxos

Pátmos

THE CYCLADES

Náxos

Léros

Bodrum

Kálymnos

Sífnos

Andíparos

Kímolos

Síkinos

Íos

Amorgós

Kós

Kós

Kéfalos

Mílos

Folégandros

THE DODECANESE

ni

Ródos

Santoríni (Thíra)

Anáfi

Astypálea

Tílos

D

Mt Atávyros 1215

RHODES

Sýrna

o

d

Hálki

Líndos

e

c

a

n

e

s

e

Ródos (Rhodes)

Kritikó Pélagos

Kárpathos

Haniá

CRETE

Réthymno (Rethimno)

Iráklio (Heráklion)

Kríti (Crete)

Kásos

Samariá Gorge

annes 2452

Ída (Psilorítis) 2456

Ágios Nikólaos

itía

Hóra Sfakion

Arkádi Plakiás

Knossós

Zákros

Ag. Galíni

Ierápetra

Gávdos

CALGARY PUBLIC LIBRARY

INSIGHT ⊙ GUIDES

GREECE

www.insightguides.com/Greece

⊙ Walking Eye App

YOUR FREE DESTINATION CONTENT AND EBOOK AVAILABLE THROUGH THE WALKING EYE APP

Your guide now includes a free eBook and destination content for your chosen destination, all for the same great price as before. Simply download the Walking Eye App from the App Store or Google Play to access your free eBook and destination content.

HOW THE WALKING EYE APP WORKS

Through the Walking Eye App, you can purchase a range of eBooks and destination content. However, when you buy this book, you can download the corresponding eBook and destination content for free. Just see below in the grey panels where to find your free content and then scan the QR code at the bottom of this page.

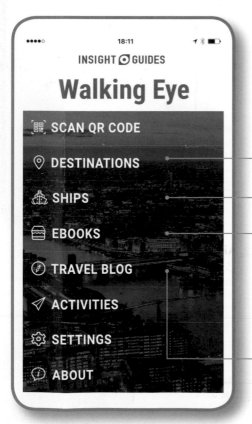

Destinations: Download your corresponding essential destination content from here, featuring recommended sights and attractions, restaurants, hotels and an A–Z of practical information, all for free. Other destinations are available for purchase.

Ships: Interested in ship reviews? Find independent reviews of river and ocean ships in this section, all available for purchase.

eBooks: You can download your free accompanying digital version of this guide here. You will also find a whole range of other eBooks, all available for purchase.

Free access to travel-related blog articles about different destinations, updated on a daily basis.

HOW THE DESTINATION CONTENT WORKS

Each destination includes a short introduction, an A–Z of practical information and recommended points of interest, split into 4 different categories:
• Highlights
• Accommodation
• Eating out
• What to do
You can view the location of every point of interest and save it by adding it to your Favourites. In the 'Around Me' section you can view all the points of interest within 5km.

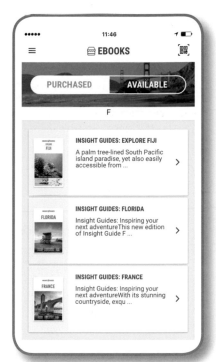

HOW THE EBOOKS WORK

The eBooks are provided in EPUB file format. Please note that you will need an eBook reader installed on your device to open the file. Many devices come with this as standard, but you may still need to install one manually from Google Play.

The eBook content is identical to the content in the printed guide.

HOW TO DOWNLOAD THE WALKING EYE APP

1. Download the Walking Eye App from the App Store or Google Play.
2. Open the app and select the scanning function from the main menu.
3. Scan the QR code on this page – you will then be asked a security question to verify ownership of the book.
4. Once this has been verified, you will see your eBook and destination content in the purchased ebook and destination sections, where you will be able to download them.

Other destination apps and eBooks are available for purchase separately or are free with the purchase of the Insight Guide book.

Contents

Introduction

The Best of Greece 6
An Ancient Story 19
A Diverse Land 21

History

Decisive Dates 26
Ancient Greece 31
Byzantine Greece 41
Ottoman Greece 47
Independent Greece 52
Greeks Today 64

Features

People and Identities 71
Literature 81
Music and Dance 89
Food and Drink 98
Art and Architecture 105
Flora and Fauna 115

Insights

MINI FEATURES

Coping with the Crisis 63
New Immigrants – and
    Extremist Reactions 74
Athens' New Museums
    and Galleries 152
Pápingo Trail 200

The Cycladic Bronze Age 244
Ancient Delos 255
Rhodes through the Ages 272

PHOTO FEATURES

Religious Festivals 96
A National Treasure Trove 156
The Palace of Knossos 268
Greece in Bloom 310

Places

Introduction 129
The Mainland 133
Athens 137
The Peloponnese 159
Central Greece 179
Epirus 191
Thessaloníki 205
Macedonia and Thrace 212
The Islands 227
Islands of the Saronic Gulf 229
The Cyclades 237
Crete 257
Rhodes 271
The Dodecanese 279
The Northeast Aegean 293
The Sporades and Évvia 313
Corfu 321
The Ionian Islands 327

Travel Tips

TRANSPORT

Getting There 336
Getting Around......................337

A – Z

Accommodation 343
Admission Charges 343
Budgeting for Your Trip 344
Business Travellers 344
Children................................344
Climate.................................344
Crime and Safety..................344
Customs Regulations.............344
Disabled Travellers 345
Embassies and Consulates ..345
Entry Requirements 345
Etiquette 346
Gay and Lesbian Travellers ...346
Health and Medical Care 346
Insurance..............................347
Internet 347
Media 347
Money 348
Opening Hours......................348
Photography 348
Postal Services.....................348
Religious Services.................349
Student Travellers.................349
Telecoms..............................349
Tipping..................................349
Toilets..................................349
Tourist Information 349

Websites 350
Weights and Measures 350
What to Bring........................350
Women Travellers 350

LANGUAGE

The Greek Language 351
Communication 351
Telephone Calls 352
In the Hotel 352
At a Bar or Café....................352
In a Restaurant.....................352
Food 352
Sightseeing...........................353
Travelling..............................354
Times and Dates...................354
Health...................................354

FURTHER READING

Ancient History
    and Culture 355
Byzantine History and
    Culture 355
Anthropology and Culture 355
Cuisine 355
Modern History 355
Modern Greek Literature.......356
Foreign Writers in/
    on Greece 356
Regional and
    Archaeological Guides 357
Botanical Field Guides 357
Other Insight Guides 357

Maps

Greece...................................130
Athens...................................134
Acropolis 138
Peloponnese..........................160
Central Greece......................180
Epirus...................................192
Thessaloníki..........................206
Macedonia and Thrace 214
Argo-Saronic Islands 230
The Cyclades.........................238
Iráklio 258
Crete (Kríti) 262
Rhodes Town 274
Rhodes...................................276
Dodecanese...........................282
Thásos, Samothráki
    and Límnos........................296
Lésvos, Híos, Ikaría,Foúrni
    and Sámos 300
Sporades...............................314
Evvia (Euboea)......................318
Corfu Town 322
Corfu.....................................324
Southern Ionian Islands........328

Inside front cover Greece

Inside back cover Athens metro
    & tramway; Greece: Physical
    and Main Ferry Routes

THE BEST OF GREECE: TOP ATTRACTIONS

From ancient sites steeped in history and sun-bleached islands or cool mountain villages to Venetian forts and cliffside monasteries.

△ **The Parthenon, Athens.** Although still partly covered in scaffolding and studded with cranes, this treasure of the Classical city never fails to impress. See page 139.

△ **Kérkyra Old Town, Corfu.** Venetian flair, domesticity and town planning at the far end of the Adriatic, bracketed by two imposing castles with eye-popping views. See page 321.

△ **Mystrás.** At the base of Mount Taýgettos, the capital of the Morea Despotate – with frescoed palaces and monasteries – saw out the Byzantine twilight until 1460. See page 169.

◁ **Metéora, Thessaly.** Half-a-dozen-plus frescoed monasteries and convents perch bizarrely on sheer rock pinnacles in the Píndos foothills. See page 188.

△ **Zagorohória.** Two score or so of handsome, stone-built villages in the shadow of lofty Mount Gamíla, with top-notch lodging and all adventure sports to hand in the canyons nearby. See page 198.

△ **Ýdra port town.** No cars, meticulously preserved architecture, cool marble flagstones under foot and compulsive people-watching make this a winner. See page 233.

▷ **Mt Pílio (Pelion).** The surprise of mainland Greece, with dense forests, cobbled hiking paths, tottering old villages and Caribbean-quality beaches all in one package. See page 187.

◁ **Delphi Sanctuary.** With its striking setting at the base of Mount Parnassós, the ancients reckoned this oracle the centre of the world. See page 181.

◁ **Haniá Venetian quarter.** Touristy and plenty of touts, yet exquisite and unbeatable for strolling, popping into small museums, in old buildings or just having a drink. See page 266.

▽ **Santoríni caldera view.** Commercialised to within an inch of its life but still a must-see, especially at sunset or sunrise from a bar terrace in Firostefáni, Firá or Ía. See page 252.

THE BEST OF GREECE: EDITOR'S CHOICE

Blonde crescent beaches, stunning monasteries, a castle or two, hikes through river gorges, food, music and folklore – here, at a glance, are our recommendations to help you plan your journey.

Byzantine mosaic inside Ósios Loukás monastery, Híos.

BEST MONASTERIES

Ósios Loukás monastery. Some of the best 11th-century mosaics on view in Greece. See page 181.

Néa Moní monastery. And the rest of the best 11th-century mosaics are here, on the distant island of Híos. See page 305.

Hozoviótissa monastery. The setting on Amorgós intrigued Le Corbusier on his 1911 visit. See page 252.

Loúsios gorge monasteries. Several cliffside eyries with gorgeous medieval frescoes. See page 167.

Panagía Parigorítissa, Árta. Fine dome mosaic and Renaissance-influenced architecture. See page 195.

Hóra and Monastery of St John, Pátmos. When the cruise-ship groups have left, enjoy this stunningly atmospheric hilltop village set around a labyrinthine monastery. See page 291.

The improbably perched Hozoviótissa monastery, Amorgós.

BEST CASTLES

Acrocorinth, Peloponnese. A soaring rock with an ancient acropolis stippled with Ottoman monuments, wrapped in Byzantine, Frankish and Venetian walls. See page 161.

Methóni, Peloponnese. Venetian stronghold and way-station for pilgrims, with a moat, gates, and a causeway to the remote Boúrtzi tower. See page 174.

Palamídi, Návplio. Venetian citadel critical in the War of Independence and reached via hundreds of steps. See page 164.

Knights of St John Castle, Kós Town. Well preserved, easy to visit example of the crusading order's Dodecanese strongholds. See page 287.

The watchtower at Methóni castle, surrounded by the sea.

Mólyvos, Lesvos. Medieval castle with great views over town and to Turkey. See page 301.

Monemvasiá, Peloponnese. First a Byzantine, later a Venetian, stronghold washed by the sea on three sides, and its lower town still inhabited. See page 170.

Hiking through the pristine Víkos Gorge, Zagória.

BEST BEACHES

Karavostási. The best on the Epirot coast, with views to Corfu and thick fluffy sand. See page 193.

Símos, Elafoníssi. Really broad sands at the easternmost tip of the Peloponnese. See page 267.

Hrysí (Gaïdouronísi) islet. Enact Crusoe fantasies on this day-trip islet reached from Ierá-

petra. See page 263.

Seïtáni beaches. Small pebble beaches and huge sandy bays are monk-seal refuges on Sámos. See page 309.

Levkáda, southwest coast Pórto Katsíki, Egremní and Gialós. Fabulous beaches all in a row. See page 329.

Velanió. Cleanest, longest, nudest beach on Skópelos. See page 315.

Stunning Pórto Katsíki beach, Levkáda.

BEST HIKES

Northern Kárpathos. A maintained network of trails links local settlements to occupy keen hikers for a week – the route from Trístomo to Diafáni is the most spectacular. See page 280.

Ascent of Mt Ólympos, Macedonia. Challenging climb of Greece's highest point, and home of the ancient gods. See page 216.

Hiking in the Píndos, Epirus. From day walks to five-day hiking loops, the North Píndos offers fabulous scenery for the adventurous. See page 202.

Víkos Gorge, Zagóri. Beats Crete's Samarian Gorge for its unspoilt, riverine environment and the height of its cliffs. See page 199.

Dimosári Gorge,

southern **Évvia.** Another canyon walk, mostly along an old and shady cobbled trail, emerging at a beach hamlet where pickup transport should be arranged. See page 319.

Mount Áthos, southern tip. The route through the "hermit's desert", between Megístis Lávras and Osíou Grigoríou monasteries on the Holy Mountain, will hopefully survive the bulldozers. See page 219.

Mount Pílio trails. Partly cobbled paths, from Xouríhti to Kalá Nerá via Miliés, descend from forested glades to seaside olive groves. See page 187.

Egiáli to Hóra, Amorgós. Trekkers come to this island specially for this spectacular five-hour traverse with the sea on both sides. See page 252.

BEST OLD TOWNS AND VILLAGES

Mastic villages, Híos. Fortified settlements with gates, arcaded passageways, keep-towers and sombre-hued houses. See page 304.

Rhodes Old Town. Among the best preserved medieval townscapes in the Mediterranean, a legacy of the crusading Knights of St John and the Ottomans. See page 271.

Tower-house villages, the Máni. Stone-built mini-fortresses pierce the sky in the Peloponnese's extreme, wild south cape. See page 171.

Réthymno Old Town. A delightful confection of Venetian and Ottoman architecture, overawed by a huge fortress. See page 264.

Thessaloníki upper town. Surrounded by massive walls and crammed full of old houses and places to eat. See page 210.

The medieval Street of the Knights, Rhodes Old Town.

BEST WINES

Límnos, Ároma Ínou Drýinos. Oak-aged, smokey-dry white.
Sámos, Samos Nectar or Anthemis. Best in a series of fortified, muscat-based dessert wines.
Thessaly/Macedonia border, Tsantali Rapsáni. Easy-drinking red from foot hills of Mt Ólympos.
Lésvos, Methymneos

red. Velvety red born of a volcanic terrain.
Epirus, Zítsa Cooperative white wines. Reliably light, dry, semi-sparkling.
Dráma region, Château Lazaridi. Red or white high-quality blends.
Neméa, Ktima Papaïoannou. Rich dark red, a medium-priced taverna staple.

Grapes for easy-drinking wines.

BEST MUSEUMS

Acropolis Museum, Athens. Though functionally designed, it does justice to its extraordinary exhibits. See page 140.
Sámos Archaeological Museum, Vathý. One of the country's best collections of the Archaic era, with exquisite small objects from the Hera sanctuary, culminating in

an enormous *kouros* (statue of a man). See page 308.
Theophilos and Theriade Museums, Variá, Lésvos. Two galleries in an olive grove: the first with over 50 works by naïve local artist Theophilos (1873–1934); the second, a fine modern art collection amassed by Theriade, Theophilos'

patron. See page 301.
Asian Art Museum, Corfu. Highly eclectic but never less than top-drawer collection assembled by two keen Greek diplomats – everything from Gandhara reliefs to Chinese vases. See page 323.
Benáki Museum, Athens. Arguably Athens' best museum, spanning

the whole of Greek history. See page 148.
Delphi Museum. The best of everything supplicants brought to the oracle here, in revamped premises. See page 183.
Olympia Museum. Superb statuary and a fine collection of Archaic bronzes make this a must. See page 176.

Fascinating finds at the Acropolis Museum.

BEST FESTIVALS

Athens Festival. Going for well over half a century now, with big-name international artists from June to August. Most performances at Herodeio and Epidauros theatres.
Pátra Carnival. The liveliest and most organised of Greece's pre-Lenten events: floats, outrageous costumes and parades.

Easter on Ýdra or Corfu. Fishermen at Ýdra carry the Epitáfios (shrine) into the water to bless the boats and ensure calm seas; on Corfu, brass bands leave not a dry eye with their funeral hymns, and showers of old crockery thrown from windows bring luck.
Thessaloníki International Film Festival. This star-studded November event, premiering both Greek and foreign works, is one of the most prestigious in Europe.
Levkáda International Folklore Festival. The largest folk-dance festival in Greece, with

troupes from all over the world. Last full week of August.
Sani Festival. The best provincial mainland festival, July–August, with jazz, classical and world acts.

Athens Festival performance at Herod Atticus theatre.

BEST LOCAL SPECIALITIES

Pickled caper greens, Nísyros, Léros, Angístri. The "national shrub" of these islands gets the vinegar treatment, thorns and all.
Soumáda, Levkáda. A white syrup from bitter almonds, drunk diluted with cold water – this island's is the best.
Lakérda, Aegean-wide. Bonito fillet slices soaked, pressed, then cured in salt – the finest oúzo partner.
Tsípouro, Thessaly or

Sporades. If you find oúzo too cloying, try this clean grape-mash spirit.
Kalatháki féta, Límnos. Small drum-shaped sheep-milk cheese.
Genuine thyme honey. Bare islands like Kálymnos make for the purest honey – dark and strongly aromatic.
Tsitsíravla, Pílio or Sporades. Pickled wild pistachio shoots, gathered in spring, are good on their own or as a salad topping.

The sandy Gomáti dunes, Límnos.

OFF THE BEATEN TRACK

Préspa Lakes, west Macedonia. Eerily scenic upland basin on the borders with Macedonia and Albania, with sleepy villages and good birdwatching. See page 214.
Mathráki. Most vegetated but depopulated of the isolated Diapóndia islets northwest of Corfu, with a fine, long beach and basic facilities. See page 325.
Mt Smólikas. Greece's second highest mountain range, separating Epirus and Macedonia, with two

small lakes and excellent hiking. See page 202.
Néda Gorge, Peloponnese. From the modern village of Figalía, below the temple of Vassae, a track threads through ancient Phigaleia to the River Néda where it thunders underground. See page 168.
Gomáti dunes, Límnos. Protected environment in the far north of the island with shallow waters, September sea lilies... and a proliferation of sun-loungers. See page 298.

Fun in the water, Benítses.

AN ANCIENT STORY

A heady mix of sun, sea and ancient sites
bathed in brilliant Aegean light, Greece
has enchanted travellers for centuries.

Minoan fresco, Crete.

Modern Greece, which emerged during the 19th century from 500 years of Ottoman rule, occupies a rocky pile of peninsulas and islands at the bottom of the Balkans in the eastern Mediterranean, with a language and landscape redolent of its pre-eminent place in the development of the western world. History, drama, politics and philosophy: the words as well as the concepts have their roots here. Around its rugged terrain are the names of the city-states which vied for supremacy in this region 2,000 years ago: Corinth, Sparta, Mycenae, Rhodes, Athens. And here too are Delphi, the Parthenon and Mount Olympos, forever associated with the ancient gods.

Whether you arrive in Greece by boat, plane or overland, your first impression as you stretch your legs is likely to be of the sun. Glimmering on the water, reflecting off metal and glass, casting shadows, the Mediterranean sun is omnipresent. Like the flash of a hidden camera, the brilliant light catches you unawares and transfixes you.

From that minute, you seem effortlessly to become a part of the Greek landscape – blue sky above, white sand below, ancient ruins, olive groves, a hillside vineyard… It is easy to fall in love with this radiant country, not least because so many of its over 11 million people are emotionally open, unafraid of shedding a tear, either in sorrow or in joy. Many travellers first experience this passion in the warmth of the welcome they receive, and they may even feel a little uneasy at the exuberance of their hosts. Yet those travellers tend to return time after time – for the mirror-smooth Aegean Sea shimmering in the still of the morning, for the *kafenía* with their wooden, thatched chairs and

The Fishermen's Memorial, Sámi.

rickety tables offering some shade from the blistering afternoon heat, and for the silvery green olive groves where the cicadas drone at evening time.

The country's membership of the European Union and its capital's hosting of the 2004 Olympic Games have done much to accelerate modernisation. But modern is less a synonym for homogeneous than it is in many other rapidly changing countries. A sense of history and a respect for tradition remain powerful, and most Greeks are proud to share their culture with visitors. The Greek word *xénos* means not only "stranger" or "foreigner" but also "guest", and a fortunate *xénos* will be invited into a Greek family's house to be lavishly supplied with food and drink and questioned with genuine curiosity. The aim of this book is both to guide visitors around Greece and its islands and to preview what is likely to be an entirely captivating experience.

The rugged, unspoilt coastline of Ydra.

A DIVERSE LAND

Mountains and caves, salt marshes and cloud-forest, blazing summers and snow in winter – few countries have such varied landscape and climate.

People perceive Greece as a land where people eat oranges and the sun shines all the time, but it is equally accurate (if not more so) to describe it as a place where it rains buckets and apples figure largely in the diet. Greece is actually the most varied country in the Mediterranean, with habitats ranging from near-deserts to temperate cloud-forests, from salt marshes to alpine peaks.

The splintered outline of the southeastern Balkan peninsula is the result of the flooding of the Mediterranean basin, which occurred when a debris dam at the future Strait of Gibraltar gave way. Waters from the Atlantic surged in and gradually submerged the mountain ranges, which segmented the deep, hot depression – a process completed only after the last Ice Age, and probably the basis of the Biblical flood account. Isolated, exposed summits became the Greek islands, Crete being the highest and largest. If the Mediterranean could be re-drained, the coastal ranges of former Yugoslavia, the Albano-Greek Píndos, the Peloponnesian mountains, Crete and the Turkish Toros would form one unbroken system. This mountainous arc has a core of karstic limestone, sensitive to erosion by rain and thus peppered with caves, sinkholes and subterranean rivers. Glaciers of the last Ice Age also had a role in shaping the mountains as far south as the present-day Gulf of Corinth.

Earthquake zone

Greece remains an active subduction zone, where the African tectonic plate burrows under the European plate. This means numerous faults, frequent – often destructive – earthquakes and a significant level of geothermal activity. Over 100 thermal spas are scattered across both the mainland and the islands. This geothermalism is

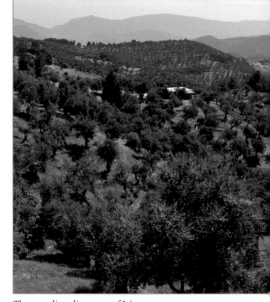

The sprawling olive groves of Lésvos.

predictably accompanied by vulcanism: you can trace the boundary of the plate collision zone by "joining up" the extinct or dormant volcanic islands of Méthana (now a peninsula), Póros, the submerged calderas of Mílos and Santoríni, and Nísyros, which has erupted within historical memory. In the northeast Aegean, Lésvos, Límnos and Aï Strátis islands are also of volcanic origin.

Only about one quarter of Greece's surface area is cultivable, principally in Thessaly and Macedonia. Much of the farmland occupies low-lying plains or upland plateaux, often the beds of former lakes drained to reclaim the land for agriculture or eliminate malarial mosquitoes. Only a few perennial freshwater lakes survive on the mainland north of the Gulf of Corinth: they tend to be shallow and murky, more suited to irrigation, fishing and wildlife conservation than recreation. The largest and most scenic is Lake Trihonída in Étolo-Akarnanía; runners-up include Vegoritída, Mikrí Préspa and Kastoriá in western Macedonia, plus Pamvótida in Epirus. The Epirote Píndos Mountains have a few glacial tarns, but lakes are almost entirely absent from the large islands owing to overly porous rock strata; Koúrna, near Haniá on Crete, is the largest.

Stony or partly forested mountains make up three-quarters of the country – and as Henry Miller put it, nowhere has God been so lavish

> *Greece has long made a modest profit from its minerals – bauxite, nickel and chromite on the central mainland, assorted volcanic substances on Mílos and Nísyros – and is set to become Europe's largest gold producer when new mines in the Halkidikí region are completed.*

coast of the Pílio peninsula with its lush "jungle" – in general precipitation is highest in the Ionian Islands (particularly Corfu and Zákynthos) and the western mainland, where the Píndos moun-

High-perched villages in central Greece witness harsh winters.

with rocks as in Greece. The hills are often bonily naked; the country's forests have been under steady attack since ancient times, and the rate of deforestation has accelerated alarmingly since World War I. Fires, usually deliberately started, are the main cause: under current climatic conditions, it takes a Greek pine wood more than 50 years to recover completely from a blaze.

Hot summers, cold winters

Greece's stereotypical "Mediterranean" climate and vegetation is in fact limited to the coastal areas; "modified continental" is a more accurate tag for the weather elsewhere, with hot, muggy summers and cold winters. Although there are numerous microclimates – such as the northeast

tain range forces moisture-laden air from the Ionian Sea to disgorge its load as rain or snow.

The rest of the country lies effectively in a "rain shadow", although the directional pattern is reversed at Mt Olympos near Thessaloníki, rising 2,917 metres (9,568ft) in the space of a few kilometres inland from the moist Thermaic Gulf, which sends wet air masses west to be trapped on the summit of the ancient gods. Olympos is the highest of a score of peaks over 2,300 metres (7,550ft), home to about a dozen ski resorts. While nobody is likely to fly in from northern Europe especially to ski – snowfall patterns are too unreliable – the resorts have long been popular with the Greeks themselves.

Greece's fabled, convoluted coast is claimed

to cover a distance equal to that of France, a country four times larger. But, despite figuring prominently on tourist posters, beaches are the exception rather than the rule. Much of the shoreline is inhospitable cliff, providing neither satisfaction for sand-seekers, nor anchorage for mariners. In fact, the most likely visitors are birds, as Greece lies under major migratory paths linking north-central Europe and Africa. When it is not cliff or beach, the Greek littoral is peppered with lagoons, estuaries and salt marshes that serve as important wildlife refuges. Some of the most important of these are at Kalógria near Pátra, Kalloní on Lésvos,

II, most rivers north of the Gulf of Corinth have been dammed, usually for irrigation and flood control rather than for hydroelectric power. Such projects, evidence of a non-accountable, central-planning mentality which has waned almost everywhere else in Europe, remain highly controversial – none more so than the Mesohóra dam on the Ahelóös, which has been declared illegal by the Greek Council of State, and had its funding revoked by the European Union. If ever filled, this massive reservoir – intended to irrigate the Thessalian plain – would doom already threatened fisheries and wetlands at the Ahelóös delta.

The bridge at Árta, on coastal Epirus.

the delta of the Évros river in Thrace, the Korission lagoon on Corfu, the Alykí marsh on Kós and the vast lagoon complex at Mesolóngi.

Controversial dams

No point in Greece is more than 100km (62 miles) from the sea, so the numerous rivers are not only short, but swift, as they lose altitude quickly, to the delight of local kayakers and rafters. The only major rivers to flow lazily along as in northern Europe, in their lower reaches anyway, are the Aliákmonas, the Pínios, the Ahelóös and the Árakhthos; the Áxios and Strymónas and Évros in Macedonia and Thrace also conform to people's idea of a continental river, but have their sources in other Balkan states. Since World War

A more positive outcome of damming is the artificial wetland at Kerkíni on the Strymónas, a mecca for birds.

Greece's rugged terrain, and its high proportion of territory as islands, encourages separate regional development. For such a small country, there are numerous dialects, in contrast to, say, far vaster Russia, which has little variation in its speech. Land communications were late in coming; well into the 20th century, it was easier to sail from Athens to the eastern Peloponnesian coast, or from Haniá to Crete's southern shore, than to go overland. Geographical determinism is an easy trap to fall into, but the mutual isolation of the provinces has undoubtedly been a dominant factor in shaping Greek identity, for better or worse.

LA GRECIA
VNIVERSALE ANTICA
Paragonata con la Moderna da
Giacomo Cantelli da Vignola
Con le direttioni delle Carte Migliori, è dè piu accre-
ditati Scrittori di Geografia data in luce da Gio:
Giacomo Rossi in Roma alla Pace l'anno 1683
con Priu. del S. Pont.

MARE DI SAPIENZA

DECISIVE DATES

Cycladic and Early Bronze Ages: c.3000–1450 BC

3000–2100 BC
Cyclades settled from Asia Minor; colonists introduce metal-working to these islands and to the mainland.

2100–1500 BC
Minoan culture, noted for its great cities and palaces, and sophisticated art, reaches its zenith on Crete.

c.1650–1610 BC
The settlement at Santoríni Akrotiri on Thera is annihilated by a volcanic eruption.

c.1450 BC
Most Minoan centres on Crete are devastated by fire, possibly during a revolt caused by social and environmental

Minoan figurine, Iráklio Archaeological Museum, Crete.

instability following the Thera cataclysm.

Mycenaean and Dorian Period: 1400–750 BC

1400 BC
A Peloponnesian tribe, the Myceneans, rise to promi-nence, building grand citadels at Mycenae and Tiryns.

c.1150 BC
"Sea Peoples" from Eurasian steppes, later dubbed the Dorians, invade large areas of Greece.

776 BC
The Dorians hold the first Olympic Games, in honour of Zeus and Hera.

Archaic Period: 750–500 BC

750 BC onwards
City-states, including Athens, Sparta, Thebes and Corinth, compete for supremacy.

550 BC
Sparta forms Peloponnesian League with neighbouring states. Rivalry with Athens increases.

500 BC
The Greek city-states control large parts of the Mediterr-anean and Black Sea coast.

Classical Period: 500–338 BC

490 BC
The Persian king, Darius, attempts to conquer Greece but is convincingly defeated by the Athenian army at Marathon.

481–479 BC
Xerxes, Darius's son, invades. Athens is captured, but then in a surprise attack, Greek boats sink the Persian fleet off Salamis.

431–404 BC
The Peloponnesian Wars, with Sparta and Athens the main protagonists. Athens capitulates; Sparta takes control of much of Greece.

338 BC
Philip II of Macedonia defeats Athens and Thebes at the Battle of Chaironeia and unites all Greek cities except Sparta.

Hellenistic and Roman Period: 338 BC–AD 395

336 BC
Philip II of Macedonia assassinated. His son, Alexander the Great, develops Greece (or rather, Macedonia) into an imperial power.

323 BC
Alexander's huge empire is divided on his death amongst his successors, the Diadokhi; centres of political power consequently shift from Greece to the Middle East and Egypt.

320–275 BC
The Diadokhi war among themselves; Rome emerges as a major power.

146 BC
Rome annexes Greece as a province of the Roman republic, and subsequently empire.

Byzantine Period: AD 395–1453

395
The Roman Empire is divided into East and West, with Greek-speakers dominant in the East.

1204
The Fourth Crusade, directed by the Venetians, attacks, plunders and briefly occupies Constantinople. Frankish Crusaders and Venetians divide Greek territory among themselves. Fortified harbours and land fortresses are built across the mainland, especially on the Peloponnese, and on many islands, particularly Rhodes, the east Aegean ones and Crete.

1453
Ottoman Turks under Sultan Mehmet II capture Constantinople; final

Count Ioannis Kapodistrias, Greek president from 1827 until his assassination in 1831.

disappearance of Byzantine Empire.

Ottoman Period: 1453–1821

1453
Communal administration of the Greek Orthodox population left to its own clergy, upon payment of taxes.

1500–1600s
Life in rural Greek territories is not congenial, with arbitrary taxation and venal governors.

Late 1700s
Living conditions improve throughout the Ottoman Empire; a wealthy, often educated Greek Orthodox gentry emerges in places like Mount Pílio, Zagóri, Lésvos, Híos and Pátmos.

1821
The Greek War of Independence breaks out almost simultaneously on the islands and the Peloponnese, where Archbishop Germanos blesses the revolutionary standard at Agía Lávra monastery.

Bishop Germanos blessing the flag.

The Emerging State: 1821–1922

1821–31

Three major European powers intervene in the Greek War of Independence. Their military assistance and diplomatic pressure ensure the emergence of an autonomous Greek state.

1832–33

Russia, France and Great Britain stipulate "final" borders of Greece and install Prince Otto of Bavaria as first king of Greece.

1863–64

Danish prince King George I succeeds the ousted Otto. Ionian Islands ceded to Greece.

1910

The Liberal Party under Eleftherios Venizelos comes to power and governs until 1920.

1912–13

The Balkan Wars erupt. Greece wrests southern Macedonia, Epirus, Crete and the east

German artillery shelling the Metaxas Line fortifications on the border with Bulgaria.

Aegean Islands from the Ottomans.

1916–17

Greece enters World War I on the Allied side.

1919–22

Encouraged by the Allies, Greek troops land at Smyrna, attempt to occupy much of Anatolia, but are defeated by Atatürk's Turkey. King

King Constantine I at Eskisehir, during the war between Greece and Turkey.

Constantine I goes into exile; a republic is established.

Refugees, Occupation, Civil War: 1923–49

1923

The borders between Greece and Turkey are settled and in a traumatic population exchange, 1.2 million Orthodox Greeks quit Asia Minor and 380,000 Muslims leave Greece for Turkey.

1928–33

Venizelos returns to office after alternating parliamentary and military rule.

1935

The monarchy is restored after an unsuccessful republican coup.

1936–41

Quasi-fascist dictatorship under General Ioannis Metaxas. When World War II is declared, Greece is initially neutral.

1940

Mussolini's invasion repulsed.

1941–44
Joint German, Bulgarian and Italian occupation of Greece. Resistance groups base themselves in the mountains.

1944–49
Germans and Bulgarians retreat; Allies attempt to reimpose royalist regime, prompting a three-year civil war between conservative forces and Communist rebels.

Postwar Politics: 1950–Present

1950s
Conservative parties rule, mostly under Constantine Karamanlis; Communist Party is outlawed.

1963–64
First free post-war elections return centrist governments under Georgios Papandreou.

1967
A junta of army officers under Georgios Papadopoulos seize control of the country.

1974
The junta attempts to take over Cyprus, fails and collapses. A referendum abolishes the monarchy; Greece is once again a republic.

1981–89
The Greek Socialist Party, PASOK, governs with Andreas Papandreou as prime minister until brought down by scandals.

1989–1993
Néa Dimokratía (Conservative) party regime until PASOK regains power.

1996–2004
Kostas Simitis succeeds Andreas Papandreou as PASOK prime minister.

2002
Greece adopts the euro as its currency.

2004
Néa Dimokratía wins elections under Kostas Karamanlis, nephew of Constantine. Athens hosts the Olympic Games.

2007
Criticised over its handling of devastating forest fires, Néa Dimokratía still wins snap elections.

2009
George Papandreou, son of Andreas, leads PASOK to electoral victory.

2010–11
Greece's finances revealed as insolvent. Papandreou resigns. Two bailout packages are offered by a troïka of European lenders.

2014
Greece records economic growth for the first time in six years.

2015
SYRIZA wins parliamentary elections; Alexis Tsipras becomes prime minister and enters coalition with the Independent Greeks Party. Greeks vote no to austerity measures in a July referendum.

2015–16
The number of refugees coming by sea to Greece rapidly increases as a consequence of the Syrian Civil War. Greece negotiates further bailout deals with its lenders, including a debt relief package.

Protesting against austerity measures enforced on Greece by the European Union.

ANCIENT GREECE

The rich civilisations that rose and fell in the Aegean have left a precious inheritance that is still relevant today.

The basis for the modern way of life in Greece was laid around 5500 BC, when settlers moved down from the north to the plains of Thessaly, then on to rockier land in the Peloponnese (Pelopónnisos), and began to cultivate olives and vines, as well as the cereals they had originally grown. Seaborne trade with the islands – particularly for obsidian from Melos, vital for weaponry – also commenced. Some three millennia later, a prosperous Bronze Age civilisation arose on Crete (Kríti), and influenced the entire Aegean.

Minoan and Mycenaean cultures

The Minoans, whose rituals have filtered down to us through the legend of Theseus and his labyrinthine struggle with the Minotaur, left proof of their architectural genius in the ruined palaces of Knossos and Phaistos (Festós). Adventurous sailors, they preferred commerce to agriculture. The 5th-century BC historian Thucydides reports that King Minos of Crete established his sons as governors in the Cyclades and cleared the Aegean of pirates. The Minoans also established a number of outposts in the Peloponnese and made contact with the Egyptians.

By 1550 BC, their civilisation had reached its zenith. Yet barely a century later, for reasons that remain unexplained, most Minoan settlements were destroyed by fire and abandoned. Akrotíri, on Thera (Santoríni), had been annihilated by a volcanic eruption in about 1630 BC, which also damaged Crete. But the causes of the wider disintegration of Minoan control remain a mystery. Only Knossos continued to be inhabited as Cretan dominance in the Aegean ended.

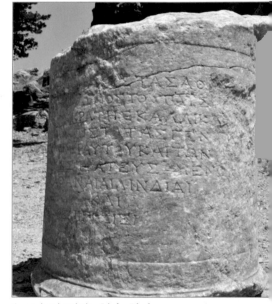

An ancient inscription, Líndos, Rhodes.

The Minoans' place was taken by Mycenaeans, inhabitants of Mycenae (Mykínes), a bleak citadel in the Peloponnese. We do not know whether the rulers of Mycenae exerted direct power over the remainder of the mainland. But in the *Iliad,* Homer portrays their king, Agamemnon, as the most powerful figure in the Greek forces, which suggests that Mycenae had achieved some sort of overall authority.

In its heyday, the Mycenaean world contained men rich enough to commission massive stone tombs and delicate gold work. Rulers were served by a complex array of palace scribes and administrators who controlled the economic life of the state, exacting tribute, collecting taxes and allocating rations of scarce metals.

Invasion of the Sea Peoples

Starting in the 12th century BC, this society, like the Cretan one before it, began to wither away. Classical myth connects the end of the Mycenaean age with the arrival of Dorian tribes, more properly known as the "Sea Peoples". In fact, there was no clear connection between the two events. Mycenaean power had declined irreversibly by the time the Sea Peoples entered Greece. These invaders, like later ones, entered Greece from the north and northeast. They were probably nomads from beyond the Black Sea, which would explain their incli-

civilised life suffered. Trade dwindled and communities became isolated from one another. Building in stone seems to have been too great an effort for the small pastoral settlements that had replaced the Mycenaean centres. Homer's *Odyssey* is set in a simple society where even the rulers busy themselves with menial tasks, and where wealth is measured in flocks and herds.

The Geometric Period

In the 8th century BC, there were signs of revival as trade expanded. There were contacts

Minoan vase.

nation to travel and account for their lower level of culture.

They also brought their own form of the Greek language. In areas where they settled densely, we find West Greek dialects, while Attica, the Aegean Islands and the Ionian colonies continued to use East Greek forms. The hostility, at a later date, between Athens and Sparta (Spárti) was based in part on this division between Ionian and Dorian peoples.

The Dorian migration, from about 1120 BC onwards, shortly preceded the onset of the Iron Age, and that of the Geometric period (named after its pottery decoration). Historical evidence for the period between the 11th and 9th centuries BC is patchy, but evidently

> By the 13th century BC, the Mycenaeans had adapted the Minoan Linear B script into the first written Greek. However, a proper alphabet only emerged with the modification of the Phoenician script during the 9th century BC.

with civilised peoples such as the Etruscans in the west, and the Phoenicians and Egyptians in the east. Artistic influence from the east was increasingly evident in metalwork and pottery. With the adoption of the Phoenician alphabet, writing revived among a much larger circle than before.

Another, equally important Greek concept was borrowed from the Phoenicians; the notion of the *polis* (city-state). In the Geometric era, small, isolated settlements were loosely grouped into large kingdoms. This system survived in both western and northern Greece into Classical times when Thucydides described how "the Aetolian nation, although numerous and warlike, yet dwell in unwalled villages scattered far apart".

Elsewhere, however, a network of small independent states grew up. At first, these were based around clusters of villages rather than

now a further distinction. Some states, mostly in the Dorian parts of the country, were reliant on a population of slaves who were excluded from power, such as Sparta, a major *polis*, and Thessaly, an *ethnos*. Other states, such as Athens, although not unfamiliar with slavery, had a more broadly based citizen body that included Greeks from outside the city.

Kings, aristocrats and tyrants

In general, Homer's kings must have surrendered power towards the end of the Geometric period and beginning of the Archaic era, giving

The theatre at Epidauros.

one large urban centre. But with the population explosion of the mid-8th century, large conurbations evolved and expanded as surplus population moved from the country to the town. Land became more intensively cultivated and highly priced. In the early Geometric era, the slump in population had caused arable land to fall into disuse. Farmers turned from sowing cereals to stock-breeding; now this process was reversed. Available land could not support such a rapidly growing population. (There is a clear parallel with the Peloponnese in the 19th century, and in both cases the outcome was the same: emigration on a massive scale.)

Together with the division between the new *polis* and the older *ethnos* (kingdom), there was

way to an aristocratic form of rule. But this too became entrenched in power and increasingly resistant to change. As commoners settled on land and amassed wealth, pressure grew for constitutional reform. Aristotle correctly identified the connection between the demand for reform and changes in military technique, saying "when states began to increase in size, and infantry forces acquired a greater degree of strength, more persons were admitted to the enjoyment of political rights". Just as the shift from monarchy to aristocracy had been reflected in the move from chariots to horseback fighting, the emphasis now switched from cavalry to infantry; aristocracy lost ground to democratic pressure. Men would only fight in the new larger armies if the aristocrats granted them political rights.

Military power swung away from the traditional horse-breeding aristocracies of Chalkis, Eretria and Thessaly to new powers: Corinth, Argos and, above all, Sparta, where the state was protected by an army of heavily armed foot-soldiers known as hoplites, whose core was a body of citizens trained as infantrymen from birth.

Often the demand for radical reform met with resistance from the upper classes, but some individuals, more far-sighted, recognised the need for change. One such was Solon, nick-

it. In the 6th century, tyrants seized power in a number of states. Usually they were dissident aristocrats, who gained the support of the lower classes with promises of radical change – promises which were often kept, as it was in the new ruler's interest to weaken the power of his peers. In the mid-7th century, for example, Kypselos of Corinth was supposed to have redistributed land belonging to his fellow aristocrats.

But it would be wrong to regard the tyrants as great innovators. They were symptoms of social change rather than causes of it. Conscious of

Theseus and Prokrustes portrayed on a vase painting from around 470 BC.

named "the Law-Giver", who was elected in early 6th-century Athens to introduce sweeping constitutional changes. Realising that the city's strength would depend upon the organisation of the citizen body, he opened up the Assembly to the poorest citizens and in other ways loosened the grip of the aristocracy.

Inevitably, these changes were attacked from both sides, as Solon himself complains in a number of his poems. But they did lay the foundations for the tremendous expansion of Athenian power throughout the next century.

Another result of these political tensions was tyranny. For the ancient Greeks, "tyrant" was not a pejorative; it simply meant a ruler who had usurped power instead of inheriting

their own vulnerability, they resorted to various propaganda expedients to stay in power. The most potent of these was the religious cult, and it is from the time of the tyrants that religion came directly to serve state purposes.

Religion was not only important to the state as propaganda; it was also a major economic factor. While the popular religious festivals and games earned revenues – enormous in some cases – for the city that staged them, temples, sacrifices and other rituals were very costly. Apart from waging wars, temple-building was probably the greatest drain on a city-state's resources. Thus the scale of its religious activities provided some measure of the wealth of a community.

Greeks versus the Persian Empire

Alongside the rise of an artistic culture shared across state boundaries, a process of political unification began. People in different cities started to become aware of a common Hellenic culture. The historian Herodotos was a keen promoter of the idea of one Greece, and asserted that the Greeks were "a single race because of common blood, common customs, common language and common religion". This shared cultural identity was reinforced by increasing numbers of religious festivals and

This victory did more than save Attica; it also confirmed Athens as the standard-bearer for the Greek military effort against the Persians. This explains why a frieze displaying the warriors killed at Marathon (situated just over 23km/15 miles from Athens) was placed in a prominent and highly unusual position around the Parthenon in the 440s BC. Only then was Athens becoming a power to be reckoned with. The silver mines at Laurion (modern Lávrion) in Attica began producing enough wealth to finance a major shipbuilding programme from early in the 5th century.

The Siphian frieze inside the Delphi Museum depicts scenes from the Trojan War.

athletic competitions that attracted participants from numerous Greek states.

But the sharpest spur to unity was an outside threat: the rise of the Persian Empire. Midway through the 6th century, King Cyrus had conquered the Ionian Greek cities on the Asia Minor coast, and Persian aspirations were further encouraged by his son Darius (521–486 BC) who conquered Thrace, subdued Macedonia and, after quashing an Ionian revolt in Asia Minor, sent a massive expeditionary force westwards into Greece. Athens appealed for help from Sparta, militarily the strongest Greek city, but succeeded in defeating the Persians at Marathon in 490 BC before the Spartan forces actually arrived.

Even so, for two generations after that, Aegina (Égina) remained superior to Athens as a Saronic Gulf trading force.

Athens and Sparta

A decade after the battle of Marathon, when Darius's son Xerxes organised a second attack on Greece, the city-states rallied around Sparta. Spartan king Leonidas and his Three Hundred (actually 2,300, including Thespians, Thebans and Spartan helots) valiantly sacrificed themselves trying to halt the Persian advance at Thermopylae. While Athens had the largest navy, the Spartans controlled the Peloponnesian League, with its considerable combined land forces. Both the crucial naval victory at Salamis in 480

BC and the land victory at Plataea the following year were won under Spartan leadership.

But no sooner had the Persian menace been banished than the Greek alliance broke up. There was intense suspicion among the rival city-states, especially between Sparta and Athens. Thucydides described how, as soon as the Persians withdrew, the Athenians rebuilt their city walls for fear that the Spartans would try to stop them.

The development of a Classical "cold war" became obvious as Athens extended its control over the Aegean with the help of the Delian League. Significantly, the Persian threat had receded long before peace was officially declared in 449 BC. Moreover, between 460 and 446 BC, Athens warred with its neighbours in an effort to assert its supremacy. Naval rivals such as Aegina were singled out for attack. There was even small-scale fighting between Athens and Sparta (the First Peloponnesian War), until the so-called "Thirty Years' Treaty" brought an uneasy truce in 445 BC.

In 433 BC, Athens allied itself with Corcyra, a strategically important colony of Corinth. Fighting ensued, and the Athenians took

The Caryatids of the Erechtheion, built on the Acropolis at the peak of Athens' glory.

THE RISE OF ATHENS

The Athenian Empire owed much to the Delian League, a naval alliance formed in 478 BC to liberate the Asia Minor Greeks and continue the struggle against the Persians. It was also underpinned by much anti-Spartan sentiment. Sparta's own version of the alliance, the Peloponnesian League, consisted of land forces, requiring minimum financing. But the creation of a navy called for long-term planning and central coordination – a crucial difference. Athens' smaller allies found it increasingly difficult to equip their own ships, and instead sent money to the Athenians. Thus Athens grew in strength as its allies became impoverished.

steps that explicitly violated the Thirty Years' Treaty. Sparta and its allies accused Athens of aggression and threatened war. On the advice of Pericles, its most influential leader, Athens refused to back down. Diplomatic efforts to resolve the dispute failed. Finally, in the spring of 431 BC, a Spartan ally, Thebes, attacked an Athenian ally, Plataea, and open war broke out between the two superpowers.

The Second Peloponnesian War dragged on for years since neither side was able to deal a deathblow to the other. The Peace of Nikias in 421 BC gave both sides breathing space, but lasted just six years.

The uncertain peace was finally shattered when the Athenians launched a massive assault against Syracuse in Sicily. Aided by a force of Spartans, Syracuse was able to break an Athenian blockade. Even after gaining reinforcements in 413 BC, the Athenian army was defeated again. Soon afterward, the navy was also beaten, and the Athenians were utterly destroyed as they tried to retreat.

But even the Sicilian disaster did not end hostilities – although it had a huge impact on Athenian domestic politics. By 411 BC Athens was in political turmoil: democracy was overthrown by an oligarchical party, which was in turn replaced by the more moderate regime

> One reason the Greek city-states failed as imperial powers, the Roman Emperor Claudius observed, was because they "treated their subjects as foreigners".

of the Five Thousand. At the end of 411 BC the rebuilt Athenian navy, fresh from several victories, acted to restore democratic rule. But the democratic leaders refused Spartan peace offerings, and the war continued at sea, with the Spartan and Athenian fleets exchanging costly victories. The end came in 405 BC when the Athenian navy was destroyed at Aegospotami by the Spartan fleet under Lysander, who had received much aid from the Persians. The next year, starved by an impenetrable blockade, Athens capitulated. Athens' defeat was perhaps the worst casualty in a war that crippled Greek military strength. The most culturally advanced Greek state had been sent into final eclipse.

Civic breakdown

Literature and art both flourished even during these incessant periods of fighting, but economic activity did not. A world where each tiny *polis* was determined to safeguard its independence at any cost carried within it the seeds of its own destruction.

The paradox was that city-states with imperial pretensions chose not to take the steps that might have brought success. Unlike Rome, Greek city-states did not extend citizenship to their subject territories. Nor could the military strength of Athens keep pace with its imperial commitments, which explains the permanent cycle of conquest and revolt. The Spartans had

the additional headache of a large slave population, the helots, often prone to revolt in their own province.

The first half of the 4th century continued this pattern. On the one hand, there were long wars between cities; on the other, evidence of prolonged economic difficulties as Corinth fell into irreversible decline, and Athens struggled in vain to recapture its previous prominence. Spartan power remained supreme until 371 BC when Thebes defeated the Spartan army at Leuktra.

The city-state system was gradually starting to

Alexander the Great's campaigns dramatically extended the boundaries of the Greek world.

fall apart. The old model of a citizen army was superseded by a more professional force, relying upon trained mercenaries. Aristotle noted that "when the Spartans were alone in their strenuous military discipline they were superior to everybody, but now they are beaten by everybody; the reason is that in former times they trained and others did not".

The spread of mercenaries, in fact, reflects the economic problems of the 4th century. Mercenary service, like emigration or piracy, was a demographic safety valve, and whereas in Archaic Greece of the 8th to the 6th centuries mercenaries had come from just a few backward areas; during the 4th century they were increasingly recruited from major cities as well, which points to economic difficulties over an increasingly wide area.

As in earlier times, military changes were connected with political ones. The decline of the citizen armies coincided with a trend away from democracy in favour of more autocratic government. Power shifted from the city-states towards Thessaly, an *ethnos* regime, and later still, towards Macedonia, which had been another old-fashioned kingdom.

Both regions had the advantage over Attica in that they were fertile and not short of

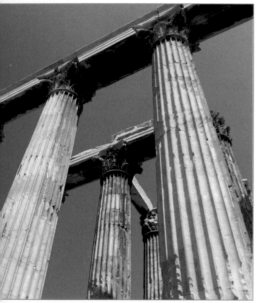

The temple of Olympian Zeus in Athens was completed by the Roman emperor Hadrian.

land. More rural than the city-states to their south, they managed to avoid the domestic political turmoil that periodically erupted in the latter. The military successes of the Thessalian tyrant, Jason of Pherae, in the early 4th century, indicated the confidence of these newcomers.

A little later, King Philip II of Macedonia moved southwards, secured the vital Thermopylae (Thermopýles) Pass and, after gaining control of Thessaly, defeated an alliance of Thebes and Athens at Chaeroneia in 338 BC. Banded together in the League of Corinth, the Greek city-states were compelled to recognise a new centre of power, Macedonia.

Alexander's Empire

In the *Republic*, Plato writes: "We shall speak of war when Greeks fight with barbarians, whom we may call their natural enemies. But Greeks are by nature friends of Greeks, and when they fight, it means that Hellas is afflicted by dissension which ought to be called civil strife".

This passage reflects three sentiments that were becoming widespread in the 4th century: first, that the Greeks were all of one race; second, which warfare between city-states was undesirable; third, that it was natural for the Greeks to fight their enemies in the east. It is ironic in this regard that a successful concerted effort against the Persians was made only under the leadership of Macedonia, traditionally a marginal power in the Greek world.

Philip's son Alexander mopped up any remaining resistance in Greece, then led a Greek-Macedonian army on a brilliant rampaging campaign to the east and south. In just over 10 years, he systematically swallowed up the ancient Persian Empire, reaching as far as the Indus Valley (in modern Pakistan). He even found time to conquer Egypt, where he founded Alexandria.

Alexander the Great's overseas empire drastically altered the boundaries of the Greek world. The city-states of mainland Greece no longer occupied centre stage. The mainland was drained of manpower as soldiers, settlers and administrators moved eastwards to consolidate Greek rule. At the same time, the intellectual and religious world of the Greeks opened up to new influences.

But there were limits to this process, for although the city-states gave up their political

ALEXANDER'S RULE

The Greek-speaking world not only expanded, it was also coming together: under the rule of Alexander the Great, inhabitants began to speak the same language, as *koine* or "common" Greek replaced local dialects in most areas. In 3rd-century Macedonia, for example, local culture was "Hellenised", and the native gods were replaced by Olympian deities. For the first time, coinage became widely used in trade – something which had been impossible so long as each city had its own currency. Now the Attic drachma became acceptable in an area ranging from Athens to the Black Sea, from Cappadocia to Italy.

freedom, they clung to self-determination in other spheres such as local taxation and customs duties. Likewise the calendar: in Athens, the year began in July, in Sparta in October, on the island of Delos, January.

Philosophers were debating ideas of communal loyalties that transcended the old civic boundaries. Perhaps this reflected the way in which these were being absorbed within larger units, such as the Hellenistic kingdoms, the Greek federal leagues and, eventually, the Roman Empire. Whatever the cause, the most influential philosophical school, Stoicism, emphasised the concept of universal brotherhood and talked of a world state ruled by one supreme power.

Roman expansion

Gradually but inexorably, Macedonian expansion curtailed the political autonomy of the city-states. In the 3rd century, they formed federations, and tried to exploit disputes between the Diadokhi, or successor-generals, who had inherited Alexander's empire. This policy had only limited success, mainly because of the paltry military resources available to the Greek leagues.

Early in the 2nd century, disputes among the city-states brought about Roman intervention for the first time in Greek history. Within 20 years, Rome had defeated first Macedonia, and then the Achaean League which had organised a desperate Greek resistance to Roman rule. The Roman consul Lucius Mummius marked his victory over the League by razing Corinth in 146 BC, killing the entire male population, and selling its women and children into slavery. As a deterrent to further resistance, this was brutal but effective. Conservative factions were confirmed in power in the cities and Greece became a Roman protectorate. In 27 BC, when the Roman Empire was proclaimed, the protectorate became the province of Achaea.

Greece – a Roman backwater?

By the 1st century AD, Greece was no longer the centre of the civilised world. Athens and Corinth could not rival Alexandria or Antioch, let alone Rome. The main routes to the east went overland through Macedonia; to the south, by sea to Egypt. But while Greece was certainly a commercial backwater, its decline was only relative: along the coast, cities flourished. The *polis* remained much as it had been

in Hellenistic times, and the Roman authorities permitted a degree of political self-rule. Philhellenic emperors such as Hadrian even encouraged groups of cities to federate in an effort to encourage a pan-Hellenic spirit.

But the *polis* was no longer a political force. Hellenistic rulers had feared the Greek cities' power; the Roman and later the Byzantine emperors feared their weakness and did what they could to keep them alive. They were vital administrative cogs in the imperial machine; if they failed, the machine would not function.

Two centuries of relative tranquillity were

The Arch of Galerius, Thessaloníki, completed in AD 303.

shattered by the invasions of the Goths in AD 255–270. They were successfully repelled, but the shock led to a loss of confidence and economic deterioration. Civic building programmes continued on a much reduced scale. The wealthy classes became increasingly reluctant benefactors, and two centuries passed before imperial authorities and the church revived the demand for architectural skills.

By that time, much had changed. In AD 330, Emperor Constantine had designated Constantinople an imperial co-capital on a par with Rome. By the late 4th century, Christianity had been made the official religion of the empire. The transition from Rome to Byzantium had begun.

BYZANTINE GREECE

The legendary wealth of Rome's eastern empire
attracted many potential invaders, from the
Franks and Venetians to the Ottomans.

The Byzantine Empire was established with the foundation of Constantinople, but the final separation of the eastern and western empires was not complete until the late 5th century, when Rome was taken by the Ostrogoths. With its political structure anchored in Roman tradition and a new religion triumphant over paganism, the Byzantine Empire survived a millennium of triumphs and declines until Constantinople fell to the Ottoman Turks in 1453.

A revealing incident occurred in the capital Constantinople in AD 968. Legates from the western Holy Roman Empire brought a letter for Nikephoros Phokas, the Byzantine Emperor, in which he was simply addressed as "Emperor of the Greeks" while the Holy Roman Emperor, Otto, was termed "august Emperor of the Romans". The Byzantine courtiers were scandalised. The audacity of it – to call the universal emperor of the Romans, the one and only Nikephoros Phokas, the great, the august, "Emperor of the Greeks" and to style a poor barbaric creature "Emperor of the Romans!"

Greek and Byzantine identity

Behind this reaction lies the curious cultural fusion which made up Byzantine identity. From the Hellenistic era came the belief in the superiority of the Greek world, and the summary dismissal of outsiders as barbarians. From Rome came a strong sense of loyalty to empire and emperor. And in the fervour that marked their belief in the moral superiority of *their empire* – which they regarded not as the "Eastern Roman Empire" but as the only true empire – is the stamp of evangelical Christianity.

The inhabitants of this empire did not call themselves Greeks or Byzantines: they were Romans, "Roméï". But the mark of a *Roméos* was

The well-restored medieval monastery of Filérimos, Rhodes.

that he spoke Greek and followed the rite of the Orthodox Church. Thus three elements of identity – Greek culture and language, Roman laws and regulations, and Christian morality – became intermingled.

Invasions by barbarian Huns, Visigoths and Ostrogoths during the 5th century helped shape the Greek part of the empire. Constantinople avoided the fate of Rome, which fell to similar onslaughts, by a combination of skilful bribery and a strong army. Thus, as the West was carved into minor kingdoms, the East remained largely intact, and the balance of power in the former Roman Empire moved conclusively to the East.

The Emperor Justinian (ruled AD 527–65) laid the foundations on which the Byzantine

Empire would rest for nearly a century. An ambitious and dynamic leader, he greatly expanded the empire's territory by conquering the southern Levant, northern Africa and Italy, in an effort to re-create the old Roman Empire. Justinian's administrative reforms created a centralised bureaucracy, a new fiscal system, and a provincial administration. The codes of Roman law were revised and unified in the Corpus Iuris Civilis, which remains to this day a cornerstone of European jurisprudence. These reforms greatly advanced the unification of the diverse peoples of the empire in a Hellenic context. In

northward and westward, taking Egypt, Syria, Iraq, Iran and Afghanistan. Portions of Asia Minor were wrested from the Byzantine Empire, and twice between AD 668 and 725, Constantinople was nearly overrun by Muslim forces.

The real break with Greek antiquity came late in the 6th century when Greece was first attacked and then settled by Slavic-speaking tribes from the north. Major cities such as Athens, Thebes and Thessaloníki were safe behind defensible walls. But much of the indigenous population of the Balkans, Greeks included, fled, especially to Calabria on the southern tip

The road to Maráthi's ancient quarries, Páros.

the end, Justinian's institutional reforms proved far more lasting than his military conquests.

The end of antiquity

Justinian's wars brought the empire to the verge of bankruptcy and left it militarily vulnerable. Threats from both East and West plunged the empire into a spiral of decline that lasted for nearly 300 years. The first menace to the Empire from the East came from the Persian Sassanid Empire. Zoroastrian Sassanid forces took control of Palestine, Syria and Egypt, and even threatened the capital, Constantinople, at one point. A more serious threat soon developed with the advent of Islamic expansionism. Erupting out of the Arabian Peninsula, Muslim forces swept

of Italy, or relocated their settlements to higher, more secure regions of the Balkans. The invasions marked the end of the Classical tradition in Greece, destroying the urban civilisation of the *polis*, and with it Roman and Greek culture.

But the Slavic arrivals failed to preserve their own distinct cultural identities, and quickly became Hellenised. Greek remained the mother tongue of the region, and Christianity remained the dominant faith. Although the Slavic invasions and Islamic conquests of the 7th and 8th centuries reduced the extent of the Byzantine state, it survived as a recognisable entity grounded more firmly than ever in the Balkans and Asia Minor.

The Greek language may have survived, but the old urban culture did not. The disappearance

In AD 841, Greece's most famous ancient temple, the Parthenon, became the Orthodox cathedral church of Our Lady of Athens.

of the city-states is shown by the way in which the word *pólis* came to refer exclusively to Constantinople as though there were no other cities. A small urban elite studied and wrote in *koine* Greek but had little impact on the mass of the population; their books were probably read by less than 300 people at any one time. Ancient

prosperity and a cultural renaissance. Agriculture flourished as conditions stabilised and, as emperors increasingly used land grants to reward military service, the area under cultivation expanded. The prosperity of improved agricultural conditions and the export of woven silk and other craft articles allowed the population to grow. Expanding commercial opportunities increased the influence of the nearby Italian maritime republics of Venice, Genoa and Amalfi, which eventually gained control of the Mediterranean trade routes into Greece.

But Byzantium's period of renewed glory was

Mosaic of Byzantine Emperor Justinian.

monuments were avoided because peasants thought that they were inhabited by demons.

Byzantine revival

When a new dynasty, which came to be called Macedonian, took the throne of the Byzantine Empire in 867 in the person of Basil I, its forces began to roll back the tide of Islamic expansion. Antioch, Syria, Georgia and Armenia were reconquered. The Byzantine fleet regained Crete in 961 and drove Muslim pirates from the Aegean Sea, reopening it to commercial traffic. Consolidation of the Balkans was completed with the defeat of the First Bulgarian Empire by Basil II in 1018.

The military gains of the Macedonian dynasty initiated a period of economic growth and

short-lived, lasting from the mid-9th to mid-11th centuries. The empire lacked the resources to maintain tight control over its territories. It was beset on all sides – by the Italian city-states to the west, the Slav kingdoms to the north, the Persians and Arabs in the east. The Greek peninsular and island provinces, being less vital than Anatolia, which supplied Constantinople with corn, were ceded more readily to other powers.

In 1071, a new enemy, the Seljuk Turks from central Asia, crushed a Byzantine army at Manzikert in Anatolia, capturing the emperor. In the late 11th century, a Norman army, allied with the Pope and commanded by Robert Guiscard, arrived from the west to ravage parts of Greece, including Thebes and Corinth. Civil war among rival military factions impaired the empire's ability to respond to such incursions, so Byzantium gave Venice trading rights in Greece in return for protection against the Normans. But before long, the Byzantines needed to counter Venetian power by encouraging the Genoese.

Crusaders and Venetians

When the Muslims seized Jerusalem, some European kings, claiming Christian ideology as their motive, but in fact seeing political and commercial advantages too, sailed east to recover the Christian holy places from Muslim

Venice was a powerful naval power, with boundless ambition for trade and territory. As a pay-off for the assistance given to the Crusaders, after the sack of Constantinople Venetians were allowed to take control of many of the Greek islands that had been part of the Byzantine Empire. The Ionian Islands were divided into fiefdoms among noble Venetian families (and remained under Venetian control until 1797); other Venetian aristocrats helped themselves to islands in the Aegean – notably Marco Sanudo, a nephew of the Doge, who claimed Náxos, founded a duchy and effectively ruled

Seventeenth-century iconostasis, Zákynthos Museum.

control. In the process, they gained footholds in territories that had been part of the Byzantine Empire – Cyprus, for example, taken by Richard I of England during the Third Crusade.

This was only a foretaste of still worse misfortune. In 1204, Constantinople itself was sacked by the Crusader forces en route to the Holy Land for the Fourth Crusade – diverted there by the Venetians under Doge Enrico Dandolo. The empire was fragmented. Successor states arose in Epirus, Nicaea and Trebizond. Greece itself was divided into small kingdoms ruled by Western princes – the Duchy of Athens under the Burgundian Othon de la Roche, the west coast and various islands by Italians – particularly the Venetians.

> The Venetian-, Genoese- or Crusader-held Aegean islands resisted longest against the Ottomans. Tínos only fell in 1715 – over 250 years after the Greek mainland.

the whole of the Cyclades from there. Even Crete, "the Great Island", became a Venetian territory, sold to Venice for a nominal sum by Prince Boniface of Montferrat, the titular leader of the Fourth Crusade, in return for its assistance in the conquest of Constantinople. Thus by the mid-13th century, Venice had control of the shipping routes to the Black Sea and Asian Minor, Egypt and North Africa.

Byzantium fights back

Only the resolute resistance of the Palaeologos Dynasty (1261–1453) prevented the Byzantine Empire from collapsing completely. The Palaeologi fought back into mainland Greece, recaptured Constantinople and most of the southern Balkans. But there was considerable confusion in western Greece, which briefly came under Serbian control, and in Thessaly, where the Vlachs established a separate principality.

Southern Greece and the islands remained under the control of the Venetians, the Geno-strongholds at Bursa, Nicomedia (Izmit) and Nicea. Leadership subsequently passed to his son, Osman I, the eponymous founder of a dynasty – the Osmanlı, better known in the West as the Ottomans – that was to endure for 600 years.

Towards the end of the 14th century, Asia Minor and the Balkans had fallen to the Ottoman Turks, and by 1400 the Byzantine Empire had shrunk to just Constantinople, eastern Thrace, Thessaloníki, Trebizond and part of the Peloponnese. In April 1453, Mehmet II ("the Conqueror") besieged Constantinople and

Mystrás on the Peloponnese.

ese, various other Italian adventurers and, in the case of Rhodes and most of its surrounding islands, the Knights of St John, a military order which had arisen during the Crusades – although in the 14th century the Palaeologi re-established a Byzantine presence at Mystrás. One of the results of this political confusion was ethnically and religiously mixed populations.

A threat from the east

According to semi-legendary accounts, Ertuğrul, khan of the Kayı tribe of the Öğüz Turks, fled from Persia in the mid-13th century to escape Genghis Khan's Mongol hordes. He was granted territory – if he could seize and hold it – in Bithynia, facing the Byzantine took it within two months. Eight years later, Trebizond and Mystrás had succumbed, too.

The fall of "The City" reverberated throughout Europe: with it had fallen the last descendants of the Roman Empire itself. Before long, Constantinople would again be the capital of a Mediterranean empire stretching from Budapest to the Caspian Sea and from the Persian Gulf to Algeria – but now it would be a Muslim city in the Ottoman Empire. The great Greek Byzantine Empire had come to an end. Although in the West this seemed the inevitable result of Byzantine decline, to the Greeks it was a more traumatic moment. They had passed under the rule of an alien creed, which however was preferable for many to domination by Catholic powers.

OTTOMAN GREECE

Greek nationalism grew slowly as the Ottoman Empire declined – until in the 19th century a bloody struggle for independence was launched.

The Ottoman Turks who now controlled the Balkans were the latest in a series of nomadic tribes who had moved westwards from central Asia. They were highly mobile, and their devotion to conquest made up for their initially scant numbers.

News of the fall of Constantinople was received with horror in Europe, but as an isolated military action it did not critically affect European security. To the Ottoman Empire, however, the capture of the imperial capital was of supreme symbolic importance. Sultan Mehmet II, a man of culture and learning as well as a superb warrior, regarded himself as the direct successor of the Byzantine emperors. He made Constantinople the capital of the Ottoman Empire as it had been of the Byzantine Empire and he set about rebuilding and repopulating the city. The cathedral of Agia Sofia was converted to a mosque, and Constantinople – which the Turks called Istanbul (from the Greek phrase *eis tin pólin*, "at/in the city") – replaced Baghdad as the centre of Sunni Islam.

But Constantinople also remained the ecclesiastical centre of the Greek church. Ottoman religious tolerance was reflected in the imperial government system. The sultan recognised minority religions, and permitted each *millet*, or religious community, a measure of self-government. Thus Mehmet II proclaimed himself the protector of the Greek Orthodox Church, and appointed a new patriarch after the custom of the Byzantine emperors. Patriarch Gennadios II Skholarios guaranteed loyalty and taxes to the Turks, in return for a degree of self-government for the Greeks. The church came to exert both religious and civil powers over Ottoman Greeks.

Under their new masters, the Greeks lived much as they had done earlier. Their houses,

Ottoman inscription on a Muslim tomb in Ioánnina.

like those of the Muslims, tended to be miniature fortresses, built on two or three floors around a central courtyard. The restored merchant's mansions in Kastoriá give a good idea of the effect. However, under Ottoman influence, Greek cuisine changed for the better – *garum* (fermented fish sauce) on everything was out, while *moussakás*, elaborate pastries and thick "oriental" coffee – which Ali Pasha, the "Lion of Ioánnina", found helpful in poisoning his rival, the Pasha of Vallona – was in.

Restricted rights

Although the Orthodox Greeks were allowed to conduct their religious affairs without too much interference from the Ottoman hierarchy, they nevertheless suffered several disabilities that did not apply to Muslims. Christians were not allowed to bear arms and were thus exempt from military service. But in return, they had to pay a special head tax, the *haratçh*.

In a court of law, a Muslim's word was always taken over that of a Christian, although disputes between Greeks were usually settled in Greek religious courts. A Christian man could not marry a Muslim woman without converting, though the opposite configuration was common, with the wife keeping her

relatives or home villages, but the levy was still resented. It was formally abandoned by the late 17th century – largely because of rampant success by Muslims in enrolling their children.

A long-drawn-out conquest

Although the Turks had firm control of Constantinople/Istanbul after 1453, it took more than two centuries for them to establish control over Albania, and all of Balkan Greece and its islands (indeed, except for Levkáda, the Ionian Islands, with the Venetians well entrenched,

A water colour of Thessaloníki by the great traveller and artist Edward Lear, clearly showing the city's minarets.

religion. Christians who adopted Islam but then reverted to Christianity were invariably punished for such apostasy by death. These "neomartyrs", however, helped to sustain the faith of the Orthodox populations under the Ottoman rule.

The most feared imposition on (mostly Slavic) Orthodox Christians was the janissary levy or *devşirme*: Christian villages were required, at irregular intervals, to surrender a quota of their fittest, most intelligent male children to the Ottomans. These conscripts were forcibly converted to Islam and trained to serve as praetorian guards (janissaries) or civil servants. Some janissaries rose to high office and were sometimes able to help their

never succumbed to the Ottomans). Albania, resisting under Skanderberg, was only pacified late in the 15th century.

Lésvos, for example, fell to the Turks in 1462, but it was not until the conquest of Genoese Híos in 1566 that all the islands of the northeast Aegean were under Ottoman control. Similarly, the Dodecanese, with its motley population of Greeks, Jews, pirates and Latin adventurers, resisted until late 1522, when the Knights of St John on Rhodes finally yielded to an imperial force numbering 100,000 after a six-month siege. With the fall of Rhodes, the position of neighbouring islands became untenable, and within five years they had all surrendered as well.

Crete took even longer to subdue. Since the early 13th century, the "Great Island" had been Venice's stronghold in the eastern Mediterranean, and its strategic value encouraged the Venetians to reinforce the major cities – Iráklio, Haniá and Réthymno – with solid fortresses that can still be seen today. An attack on an Ottoman convoy in 1645 provided the excuse for an assault on Crete. The Turks took Haniá after a bloody battle, then Réthymno, and soon had control over the whole island except the capital, Iráklio. It was not until 1669, after a gruelling 22-year siege,

Athens, controlled by Crusaders and their descendants since 1204, had declined to a minor provincial town when the Ottomans arrived in 1456, and remained so until the 1830s.

European powers – which provided opportunities for Greeks to stage optimistic but vain uprisings against the empire. In the aftermath of the defeat inflicted on the Ottoman navy at Lepanto by the Catholic Holy League in 1571,

that the Ottomans took the city and finally ruled all of Crete (except for three Venetian-fortified offshore islets: Spinalónga, Soúda and Gramvoúsa).

Attempts at revolt

Powerful enemies continually threatened the sultans' grip on Greece. The Venetians (and later the Russians) were thorns in the Ottoman flesh. The resulting conflicts left Greece much weaker. In 1537, for instance, an Ottoman fleet carried off half the population of Corfu after an attack on the Venetian garrison there, leaving the island with barely one-sixth of the numbers it had had in antiquity.

The expansionist ambitions of the Ottomans brought them into conflict with other

revolts broke out on the Greek mainland and the Aegean Islands, but were promptly crushed by the Ottomans. A similar fate befell the short-lived revolt launched by Dionysios Skylosofos in Epirus in 1611.

The Peloponnese was also caught in a bloody tug-of-war between Ottomans and their enemies. During the Russo-Turkish war of 1768–74, Greeks in the Máni region attempted to revolt, with devastating results. Their uprising was initially supported by Alexei and Fyodor Grigoryevich Orlov, members of an aristocratic Russian family, who brought their fleet to Greece in 1770 and raided the Peloponnese with little permanent outcome other than exposing the Greeks to Ottoman reprisals. They were more successful in the Aegean, destroying the Turkish fleet at Çeşme and occupying many islands until 1774.

Resistance to the Ottomans

In truth, the Ottomans never established total control over the Greek mainland; in the mountains, groups of brigands known as *kléftes* (klephts) had formed. They were essentially bandits, equally likely to plunder a Greek village as a Muslim estate but, thanks to their attacks on Ottoman officials such as tax collectors, in folklore they came to symbolise the spirit of Greek resistance to the Ottoman

More important for the development of Greek nationalism was the growth of a Greek merchant community. Commercial links with Europe introduced wealthy Greeks to European life-styles, and also to European cultural and political ideas. This mercantile middle class funded the intellectual revival which characterised the late 18th century in Greece, endowing schools and libraries, and sponsoring higher education.

The struggle for independence

In 1814, three Greek merchants in Odessa formed a secret organisation called "The

Ermoúpoli on Sýros.

authorities. They are certainly viewed in this light in the klephtic ballads that emerged, extolling the bravery and military prowess of the *kléftes* and their heroic resistance to the Turkish oppressors.

In an effort to counter klephtic depredations and to control the mountain passes, the Ottomans established a militia of *armatolí*. Like the *kléftes*, these were Christians – and the distinction between *kléftes* and *armatolí* was highly fluid, with roles easily exchanged. However, the existence of these armed bands meant that, when the struggle for Greek independence broke out in the early 19th century, there was a record of military experience.

GREEK SCHOLARS IN THE WEST

Economic success in 18th-century Greece was a significant factor in the development of its culture and identity. Large numbers of school teachers, with the backing of rich merchant benefactors, studied in the universities of Europe, notably in Italy and Germany. There they encountered the heady nationalist doctrines inspired by the French Revolution – and also discovered the reverence in which the language and culture of Ancient Greece were held throughout Europe. By the end of the 18th century, nationalism had found a fertile ground among young educated Greeks.

Friendly Society" (*Filikí Etería*) devoted to "the betterment of the nation", which rapidly acquired a network of sympathisers throughout the Ottoman lands. A number of vain attempts to secure themselves powerful backing were finally rewarded when their members organised an uprising against Ottoman rule in 1821.

Scattered violent incidents merged into a major revolt in the Peloponnese. The Ottomans found themselves initially outnumbered and were forced to retreat to their coastal fortresses, while atrocities were committed by both sides. Greeks slaughtered Turkish and Jewish civilians in Trípoli; Turks slaughtered the Greek inhabitants of Híos. Later, Egyptian troops, under Ibrahim Ali, laid waste most of the Peloponnese.

The struggle for Greek independence, which lasted from 1821 to 1832, was not a straightforward affair. Opposing the Ottomans was an ill-assorted band of *kléftes, armatolí*, merchants, landowners, intellectual theorists and aristocratic families known as Phanariots – all as keen to further their own interests as to advance the cause of Greek nationalism. When they were not fighting their Muslim opponents – mostly Egyptian or Albanian troops rather than "Turks" – they turned on each other.

Soon after the 1821 uprising, no fewer than three provisional Greek governments proclaimed themselves, each poised to take control of the liberated territories. A democratic constitution was drawn up in 1822, then revised in 1823, by which time the three factions were unified in a central authority. But the following year, feuding between rival groups culminated in outright civil war (prompting one chieftain, Makrygiannis, to protest that he had not taken up arms against the Turks to end up fighting Greeks).

Foreign support

Ironically, the belief that this was a national struggle was held with greatest conviction by the foreign philhellenes – Lord Byron among them – who came to help the Greeks. These men were influential in getting Western public opinion behind Greece. Thus Britain, France and Russia, all initially unsympathetic to the Hellenic dream, eventually put military and diplomatic pressure on the Ottomans to acknowledge Greek independence – a policy of "peaceful interference", as the British Prime

Minister Stratford Canning described it. The turning point came with the almost accidental destruction of the Ottoman fleet by an allied armada at Navarino in 1827. This intervention by the three Great Powers ensured that some form of independent Greece came into being, although its precise borders took several years to negotiate.

Count Ioannis Kapodistrias, a Greek diplomat formerly in the service of the Russian tsar, was elected the first president of independent Greece by a National Assembly in 1827. He encouraged Greek forces to push north into

Ioannis Kapodistrias, who some feared was aiming for dictatorship, was assassinated.

the central mainland, and his efforts were rewarded when the 1830 Protocol of London fixed the new state's northern boundary to run roughly from Árta to Vólos, including the Sporades.

Although well-liked by the peasantry, the more traditional Greek elites (whom Kapodistrias loathed) were alarmed by his high-handed administrative style, suspecting him of aiming at one-man rule. On 9 October 1831, he was shot by two chieftains of the Máni as he entered a church at Návplio. With the threat of anarchy and renewed civil war looming, Britain, France and Russia set about finding another suitable candidate to lead the new country.

INDEPENDENT GREECE

Independence did not guarantee peace and stability:
enemy occupation, civil war and a military junta
have all marked the path to today's democracy.

The new state was desperately poor, overrun by armed brigands and beset by political factionalism. In 1834, Maniot rebels defeated government troops and sent them home stripped of their equipment. There were few good harbours or roads; Athens remained a poor, dusty, provincial town. Internally, conditions were worse than they had been under Ottoman rule.

Bavarian absolutism was partly to blame. Some months after Kapodistrias's death, Greece was declared a kingdom and the crown given to Otto, son of Ludwig I of Bavaria, who arrived at Návplio in 1833 on a British man-of-war.

Widespread calls for a constitution were ignored until, in 1843, a bloodless coup in Athens forced Otto to accept constitutional rule and parliamentary government for Greece. Consecutive 1844 and 1864 constitutions endowed the country with democratic trappings, especially after Otto was deposed by a more forceful coup in 1862.

The "Great Idea"

The new kingdom was home to less than one-third of the Greeks around the Aegean. The prospect of "liberating" those Greeks still under Ottoman rule, of creating a new Byzantium by recapturing Constantinople and avenging the humiliation of 1453, was known as the "Great Idea" (*Megáli Idéa* in Greek) and aroused enormous enthusiasm. When King George I succeeded King Otto in 1863, he tellingly assumed the title of "King of the Hellenes" rather than simply "King of Greece". But irredentism (the annexation of a neighbouring state on the grounds of ethnicity or prior historical possession) was never a realistic policy since, without allies, the Greek army was no match for the Ottomans; yet the *Megáli Idéa* survived repeated setbacks. Only after the catastrophic 1922 defeat

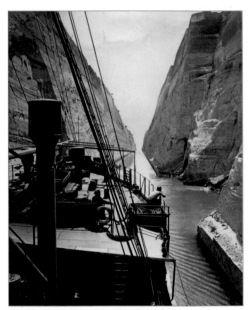

The Corinth Canal, completed in 1893, separates the Peloponnesian peninsula from the Greek mainland.

at the hands of the Turkish nationalists did this irredentist vision finally collapse.

The prominent late-19th century populist Theodoros Deligiannis encouraged foolhardy irredentist expeditions to Thessaly and Crete. His more far-sighted rival, Harilaos Trikoupis, realised that such adventures were unwise so long as Greece was dependent on foreign loans, which gave its creditors veto power over foreign policy initiatives. Trikoupis set out to reduce this dependency by development. Roads were improved, railways constructed, Piraeus became Greece's busiest port, and the Corinth Canal dug.

But despite the appearance of a few textile and food-processing factories, industry remained rudimentary; Greece was a rural nation of peasant smallholders. The lack of large estates (except in Thessaly) minimised social inequalities but it also meant that most farmers remained too miserably poor to adopt modern farming methods. The export of currants brought brief prosperity, but the global 1893 depression hit the entire economy. Greece went bankrupt, and hunger drove many peasants to emigrate.

A new government

Domestic problems only increased enthusiasm for the Great Idea. Thessaly and southeastern

A naïve depiction of Eleftherios Venizelos.

Epirus had been acquired in 1881, without any fighting, through the Congress of Berlin. When troubles on Ottoman Crete in 1897 provoked a wave of sympathy on the mainland, Greek naval forces were sent to the island while the army marched northwards – only to be humiliatingly defeated by Ottoman forces.

On Crete and in Macedonia, Ottoman rule was steadily crumbling. But the emergence of the new Balkan nations Bulgaria and Serbia complicated Greek foreign policy, for both countries shared Greece's aspiration for territory in Macedonia.

A precedent for military intervention in politics had been set with the coups of 1843 and 1862. In 1909, junior army officers revolted

and invited a radical new politician, Eleftherios Venizelos, to come over from Crete and form a government in 1910. A consummate tactician, Venizelos channelled the energies of the Greek middle class into his own Liberal Party, a dominant force in politics for the next 25 years.

A decade of wars

When the Balkan Wars erupted in 1912–13, Greece was strong enough to first wrest Epirus and southern Macedonia from the Ottoman forces and then to defend its gains, in alliance with Serbia and Romania, from a hostile

The notorious Dillesi gang who terrorised central Greece.

Bulgaria. The full gains from the fighting included – in addition to Macedonia – Epirus, Crete and the east Aegean Islands. Greece's area and population were nearly doubled at a stroke.

There was barely time to assimilate these new territories before the country was embroiled in World War I. Venizelos and the new king, Constantine I, quarrelled over whether to bring Greece into the conflict. The prime minister wanted Greece to give the Entente active support, while Constantine, brother-in-law of Germany's Kaiser Wilhelm II, insisted on keeping the country neutral. Who would have the final say over foreign policy – the king or parliament? The dispute attained the pitch of civil war by 1916, when Venizelist Corfu violated neutrality by hosting the Serbian army and government in exile, and Thessaloníki served as the "rebel" capital. In June 1917, Constantine was forced to leave the country and Greece entered the war on the side of the Entente, helping precipitate the final Central collapse in autumn 1918 with attacks across the Macedonian front.

Venizelos hoped that the Entente powers would reward Greece for its support with new territories. The annexation by Greece of Smyrna (Izmir), with its rich hinterland and large ethnic Greek population, had long been a basic tenet of the Great Idea. When, in May 1919, the Brit-

European allies changing to a "neutralist" position and refusing to sell them arms – and even selling some to the Turks. Kemal gradually forced the Greek army back behind long defensive lines ever closer to the coast. After a year-long stalemate, Kemal overran the Greek positions in late August 1922; the Greek army abandoned Smyrna a few days later. The Turkish army entered the city on 9 September, burning both the Armenian and Greek quarters and killing an estimated 30,000 of the Christian inhabitants in the process.

The 1923 Treaty of Lausanne, which definitively ended the Greco-Turkish war, fixed the

Victorious troops returning from Bulgaria during World War I.

ish, French and Americans approved the landing of Greek troops in Smyrna, it began to look as though the dream might at last be realised.

The Asia Minor Disaster

In late 1920, the pendulum of Greek political sentiment swung back, removing Venizelos from office and returning King Constantine I from exile. Army morale was damaged by politically motivated changes in command, but the revival of Turkish national fervour sparked by the Greek advance and galvanised by the emerging Turkish leader, Mustafa Kemal (subsequently Atatürk), was far more dangerous. Greek forces advanced to within 80km (50 miles) of Ankara in August 1921, but were hampered by their former

two countries' boundaries which hold today (with the exception of the Dodecanese islands, occupied by the Italians until after World War II). In addition, a massive population transfer, based on religion rather than language, was stipulated: 380,000 Muslim inhabitants of Greece moved to Turkey in exchange for 1.3 million Orthodox Christians (in fact 1 million of these had already left Anatolia since 1914). Except for a dwindling population in Istanbul and on the islands of Imbros and Tenedos, this ended a 2,500-year Hellenic presence in Asia Minor. The Greeks refer to these events as "the Asia Minor Disaster", and they remain a defining factor in the Greek perception of both themselves and of the Turks.

In the early 20th century, many Greek villages depended heavily on money sent home by young men, who had emigrated, particularly to the United States.

Republican interlude

Exhausted by 10 years of war, the Greek state now faced the huge problem of absorbing indigent newcomers into a country that had difficulty in sustaining its existing population. The economy benefited from the cheap labour, and

Greece finally began to industrialise. But the refugees also increased social tensions. Almost a million of them settled in squalid shanty towns outside the city centres.

After the disaster, King Constantine was forced to abdicate for good after a military coup, six high-ranking officers and royalist ministers were court-martialled and executed, and a parliamentary republic was established. It lasted only 13 years and was characterised by political intrigues and a brief military dictatorship under Theodoros Pangalos. The only period of stability – Venizelos's return to power from 1928 to 1932 – was terminated by the shock of international economic depression. In 1933, the Liberals were succeeded by

the royalist People's Party, whose leaders only half-heartedly supported the republic. An abortive Venizelist coup in 1935 resulted in Venizelos himself going into exile in Paris.

Return of the monarchy

The politicians' feuding rendered parliamentary government vulnerable to military pressure. The failed 1935 coup quickly resulted in a renewed mandate for the People's Party, and shortly after, the army backed restoration of the king, Constantine's son George II. In 1936, he offered the premiership to an extreme right-wing politician, Ioannis Metaxas, a former senior army officer and fervent royalist – despite his party having few parliamentary seats – to avoid more numerous Communist MPs exercising the balance of power. Soon afterwards, Metaxas responded to a wave of Communist-inspired strikes by declaring martial law and abolishing parliament. But self-styled "First Peasant" Metaxas never managed to firmly implement his so-called "Third Hellenic Civilisation". Despite imitating some of the characteristics of Fascist regimes, he regarded Britain as Greece's traditional patron in foreign affairs. But Germany's increasing dominance in the Balkans, as against Britain's naval strength in the Mediterranean, dictated a stance of neutrality.

But Germany was not the only power with designs on the Balkans. In April 1939, Mussolini invaded Albania and in October 1940 he prepared to cross the Albanian border into Greece. Metaxas could no longer hope to keep Greece neutral. Receiving the Italian ambassador in his dressing gown early on 28 October, he listened to a recital of trumped-up charges and responded to the ultimatum for free passage of Italian troops into Greece with a curt "This means war". *Óhi* or "No" Day is now a national holiday.

World War II and the Occupation

Fighting alone in the mountains of Epirus, the Greek forces surprised onlookers by pushing the Makaronádes ("Spaghetti Eaters", as the Italians were quickly dubbed) deep back into Albania. But in the spring of 1941, Hitler sent German troops south to pacify the Balkans in preparation for his attack on the Soviet Union. Victory was swift: the Nazi invasion of Greece began on 6 April, and by the end of the month they had appointed General Georgios Tsolakoglou as the first quisling prime minister.

Greece was occupied by German, Italian and Bulgarian forces, each with their designated zones. While their hold over the countryside was often tenuous, it was firm in the towns, which suffered most from food shortages, notably in the terrible famine of winter 1941–42 when over 100,000 perished. From the towns also the Germans deported and exterminated Greece's long-established Jewish communities during 1943–44. King George and the legal

German officers on top of the Acropolis, Athens.

government had left the country in 1941 and passed the war in British Egypt.

Yet in the mountains, organised resistance emerged, drawing on the klephtic tradition and making forays down into the plains. Much the largest of these groups was the Greek Popular Liberation Army (the Greek initials being ELAS), organised by the Communist-dominated National Liberation Front (Greek acronym EAM), but commanding broad support. Clashes between the three main rival resistance groups – there were also royalist EDES and centrist-Venizelist EKKA – were common, while the Germans and their new stooge, Greek Prime Minister Ioannis Rallis, established the collaborationist Security Battalions.

The dominance of EAM meant that when the British first contacted resistance groups in 1942, they found that military considerations collided with political ones. ELAS, with perhaps 60,000 fighters, was well placed to pin down German troops. But the British, suspecting that EAM intended to set up a Communist state in Greece after the war, also armed the other groups as a counterweight. EAM/ELAS, for its part, was annoyed that Churchill wished to restore the monarchy without consulting the Greek people. In turn, Churchill had little sympathy for ELAS guerrillas, whom he described as "miserable banditti".

Into the Cold War

In October 1944, the German forces abandoned Greece, replaced by Greek and British troops. In December 1944, bitter fighting erupted in Athens between ELAS fighters and British troops. Inflation continued to soar, the black market still flourished and violence erupted country-wide between the Security Battalions and their opponents.

The December 1944 fighting marked a decisive turning point in the slide towards the civil war that subsequently broke out between the national government and Communist insurgents, raging from October 1946 until October 1949. King George had returned to Greece in September 1946 following an apparently rigged plebiscite on the monarchy.

Greece during the late 1940s became a key battleground in the developing Cold War. In March 1947, the United States took over

IMPERIALISM IN ACTION

Italy occupied Rhodes and the Dodecanese from 1912 to 1943. During the years of Mussolini's rule, the islanders lived under the strictures of a totalitarian regime intent on "Italianising" the islands. A secret police network guarded against nationalist activity; the supremacy of Roman Catholicism was mandated; the blue and white colours of the Greek flag were prohibited in public; all shop signs had to be in Italian, with slogans such as "*Viva il Duce, viva la nuova Italia imperiale!*" daubed on the walls of recalcitrant shopkeepers. During the 1930s, under the harsh governorship of ardent Fascist Cesare Maria de Vecchi, many islanders emigrated.

from Britain as Greece's principal external patron. American military and economic aid flooded in, enabling the central government, at times very hard-pressed, to defeat the rebel Democratic Army in the mountains of northwest Greece by October 1949. But the victory entailed the incarceration of suspected left-wingers on desolate prison-islands like Makrónisos, Gyáros and Paleó Tríkeri and the forcible evacuation of entire villages.

Violation of civil rights and the emergence of a powerful security apparatus did not end in 1950. Politics continued to be polarised,

system designed to exclude small parties from parliament.

Greece had joined NATO in 1951, and the pro-Western orientation of its foreign policy secured continued support from the United States. However, the relationship was not straightforward: when the Cyprus dispute flared up in 1954, Greece refused to take part in NATO manoeuvres, and relations with putative ally Turkey soured. This foreshadowed problems later governments would have defining Greece's role in Europe. Nonetheless, the Cyprus issue was resolved – temporarily

British troops liberate Athens in 1944.

although the royalist-republican divide had become one between the royalist Right and the far Left; the banned Communists participated in the electoral system behind a front party, United Democratic Left (UDL).

Greece looks West

Democracy had weathered the civil war – but only just, with women finally granted the vote in 1952. In the following decade, a degree of stability was achieved, with only two conservative prime ministers in power between 1952 and 1963 – from 1955, the redoubtable Constantine Karamanlis. Yet this stability was precarious, relying as it did on restricted civil liberties, and a first-past-the-post electoral

– when that island became an independent republic in 1960.

The "economic miracle"

During the 1950s and 1960s, Greece, like Italy and Spain, experienced an "economic miracle" which transformed the country. Malaria was wiped out through anti-mosquito spraying, electric power reached many remote areas and communications improved. Athens mushroomed until it contained more than one-third of the country's entire population – as it still does.

Old forms of political control, which had operated best in small rural communities, began to erode. A new urban middle class arose which regarded the conservative elite as lacking a vision of Greece as a modern state.

The bitterly fought 1961 elections saw the resurgence of the political centre under the leadership of former Venizelist Georgios Papandreou. When the results were announced in favour of Karamanlis and his National Radical Union, Papandreou alleged that they were fraudulent.

Public disquiet at possible links between the palace, the ruling party and extreme right-wing violence increased in May 1963 when a prominent UDL deputy, Grigoris Lambrakis, was assassinated at a rally in Thessaloníki. Shortly

conservative opposition to hold elections in May 1967, Constantine was faced with the prospect of a third Centre Union victory.

However, schemes hatched between the king and senior army officers for military intervention were dramatically pre-empted when a group of junior army officers, working according to a NATO contingency plan, executed a swift coup d'état early on the morning of 21 April 1967. Martial law was proclaimed; all political parties were dissolved. The so-called Colonels (only two junta officers actually held this rank) were in power.

Women fought with the Resistance during the civil war.

afterwards, Karamanlis resigned and in the two successive elections that followed, Papandreou's Centre Union Party won power, the first centrist ruling party in Greece for over a decade. With conservative politicians prepared to surrender power – and Karamanlis gone into voluntary exile in Paris – an extended period of centrist rule now seemed possible, although right-wingers in the military and the palace saw this as a threat.

When Papandreou demanded a reshuffle of senior army officers, he found himself opposed by his defence minister and the new young king, Constantine II. The king tried clumsily to bring down the Centre Union government, but when Papandreou agreed with the main

The military junta

The military junta was motivated by self-interest, anti-Communism and ultra-nationalism. This combination was certainly not new: on various occasions in the interwar period, army officers had used the rhetoric of national salvation to avert being dismissed in politically motivated purges. In their attitudes, too, the new junta's officers drew on earlier examples. They claimed that they wanted the country to "radiate civilisation in all directions" by establishing a "Greece of the Christian Greeks" which would make it once again "a pole of ideological and spiritual attraction". This was an old dream, an escape from the modern world into a chimaeric fusion of classical Athens and Byzantium.

The first signs of widespread discontent coincided with the 1973 economic downturn. The protest leaders were students, whose occupations of university buildings in March and November were brutally broken up. After the November student occupation of the Athens Polytechnic, Colonel Georgios Papadopoulos, the regime's figurehead, was replaced by the even more sinister Brigadier Dimitrios Ioannides, previously commander of the military police.

In the end, the Cyprus problem toppled the junta. A foolhardy Greek nationalist

coup, prompted by Athens, against Cypriot president Archbishop Makarios led the Turks to invade northern Cyprus. Ioannides ordered Greek forces to retaliate by invading Turkey, but mobilisation was so chaotic and the disparity of forces so obvious that local commanders mutinied. On 24 July 1974, Constantine Karamanlis made a triumphant return from exile to supervise the restoration of parliamentary democracy.

Karamanlis's "New Democracy"

The transition to democracy proceeded remarkably smoothly considering the enormous problems that Karamanlis faced. Aware of his own vulnerability, he moved slowly in dismissing

junta collaborators and for some time never slept in the same quarters two nights running to forestall attempts by junta diehards to abduct him. At the elections held in November 1974, Karamanlis's New Democracy (Néa Dimokratía or ND) party won an overwhelming victory, though many people seemed to have voted for ND simply as a guarantor of stability.

Karamanlis was in theory able to proceed with necessary reforms, since a December 1974 referendum produced a decisive vote for the abolition of the monarchy, compromised by the king's actions before and during the junta. To replace it, Karamanlis created a presidency with sweeping powers. In the event of a swing to the Left, Karamanlis could simply resign his parliamentary seat and become president.

A move to the Left

Signs of such a swing were evident after the 1977 elections in which Andreas Papandreou's Panhellenic Socialist Movement (PASOK) made large gains. The younger Papandreou, Georgios's son, represented a new post-war generation; with his background as a professor of economics in the US, he seemed the ideal candidate to lead a technocratic party. Yet he still cultivated his 1960s reputation as a radical, vehemently attacking Karamanlis's policies, taking a belligerent stand over relations with Turkey, and threatening that a PASOK government would take Greece out of both NATO and the EEC, subject to a referendum. Support for PASOK grew, until, in 1980, Karamanlis resigned as prime minister and was voted in as president by parliament.

A TOTALITARIAN APPROACH

With their peasant or lower-middle-class backgrounds, the junta officers symbolised a provincial reaction to the new world of urban consumers brought about by Greece's economic "miracle" of the 1950s and 1960s. They stressed the need for a return to traditional morality and religion, and set about this with a fanatical attention to detail. Not only did they close the frontiers to bearded or mini-skirted foreigners (at least until the tourist trade was hit), they also prevented Greeks from reading "subversive" literature – much ancient drama included. This grim period of Greek history was marked by torture and internal exile of opponents.

Papandreou and PASOK

After PASOK's victory in the October 1981 elections, based on the simple campaign slogan of *Allagí* ("Change"), Papandreou formed Greece's first notionally socialist government. His significance lies not in his socialism – though the regime was manifestly anti-big-business – but in his remarkable success in articulating populist views, and engaging in no- or low-cost gestures such as instituting civil marriage and recognising the ELAS wartime resistance for the first time.

PASOK rhetoric carried the party until the three successive elections of 1989 and 1990,

Tank patrols Athens' streets during the failed military coup by King Constantine against Greece's junta, December 1967.

when accumulated scandals returned the New Democracy party to power. This proved to be only a short interregnum, for – helped by a fatal split within ND – PASOK won early elections in October 1993, returning Andreas Papandreou to office until ill health forced him to step down two years later. PASOK chose as his successor the relatively uncharismatic Kostas Simitis, who contrasted markedly with the flamboyant style of his predecessor.

As prime minister, Simitis had to oblige a population long accustomed to government largesse to accept economic reality. After Andreas Papandreou's death in June 1996, the government followed a tighter economic policy so as to allow Greece to join the European Monetary Union (EMU). This was not easy, since many PASOK deputies and labour unions strenuously opposed such attempts.

FYROM and Turkey

In foreign affairs, the emergence of an independent Macedonian state from the ruins of ex-Yugoslavia in 1991 acted as a red flag before a bull to the more nationalist fringe of Greeks. In 1993, Antonis Samaras pulled the plug on the ND government by defecting with other deputies to form the short-lived Politikí Ánixi party, whose main platform was intransigence on the Macedonia issue. But by the late 1990s, Greece was reconciled to the existence of an independent Macedonian state on her northern border, although agreement has yet to be reached on its name – Former Yugoslav Republic of Macedonia (FYROM), or the more disparaging Ta Skópia (The Skopje Things), are the only labels permitted in Greek public discourse.

Traditionally poor relations with Turkey improved markedly late in 1999 when there was an upsurge of public sympathy in each country for the other when both were afflicted by severe earthquakes. Helped by good personal rapport between the Greek and Turkish foreign ministers, one result was Greece dropping opposition to Turkish EU candidacy.

On the domestic front, Simitis secured a very narrow victory over nephew-of-Constantine Kostas Karamanlis's ND party in spring 2000 elections. Simitis continued with austerity measures aimed at controlling public expenditure and curbing inflation. These enabled Greece to join the eurozone in 2001 and it adopted the euro in early 2002 – abandoning Europe's oldest currency, the drachma. Despite Simitis' nickname of *O Logistís* (The Accountant), it eventually became evident that the books had been cooked under his watch to allow Greece to join the EMU, so Simitis now languishes in enforced retirement, persona non grata for any sinecure post with the EU.

The visit of Pope John Paul II to Athens in May 2002 demonstrated how long historical memories are in Greece when the Pope formally apologised for the sack of Constantinople following the diversion of the Fourth Crusade in 1204.

Just two months later, *Dekaeftá Noemvríou* ("17 November"), Europe's longest lived far-left terrorist group, which had operated with seeming impunity (and 23 fatalities) since 1974, was abruptly liquidated. By late 2003, trials saw most of its members convicted and jailed.

The 2004 Olympics

Simitis resigned before the elections of March 2004, leaving his polished foreign minister, George Papandreou (son of Andreas), as PASOK party leader. Despite 17 November having been wound up during PASOK's term, a decisive victory was won by ND under Kostas Karamanlis. He appointed himself minister of culture as well as premier to oversee the behind-schedule construction of the Olympic Games venues. Basic urban infrastructure, such as the new international airport at Spáta and the Athens metro, had been in place since 2001. In the event, Greece staged memorable games that confounded the most cynical critics – but left huge cost overruns and crumbling facilities with no compelling future role.

In 2007, Karamanlis called early elections for September and won almost as easily as in 2004. The new parliament only sat for half its statutory term of four years; "Kostakis" ("Charlie" or "Chuck" approximately), as the younger Karamanlis was derisively dubbed, unwisely called another snap election in October 2009, resulting in a resounding defeat for his party; and "Georgakis" ("Georgie" as George Papandreou the younger was equally disparagingly nicknamed) finally realised his dream of becoming prime minister.

The crisis unfolds

Although PASOK had clearly benefitted from public disgust at ND inaction and corruption since 2004, there was to be no honeymoon period for them. State finances turned out to be in far worse condition than anticipated, such that Greece's ability to pay its public payroll and meet its periodic obligations for bond maturities and debts to both domestic and foreign lenders was in doubt. Total debt eventually approached 400 billion euros. Greece was obliged to beg for a bailout from international lending agencies.

In May 2010, a €110 billion loan was offered by the so-called troïka, comprising the IMF, the European Union and the European Central

Bank, subject to conditions. These were the implementation of the harshest austerity measures ever imposed by any civilian government: the privatisation of most government assets and enterprises; an effective crackdown on rampant tax evasion by freelance professionals; depriving state coffers of half their expected revenue, along with sharp hikes in taxes; and the implementation of so-called structural reforms to make the Greek economy more competitive and spur growth.

These proposals sparked vehement opposition from those worst affected within Greece,

Andreas Papandreou in 1994 in Washington, DC, during an official visit to the US.

up to and including repeated civil disturbances in Athens which merely frightened off potential tourists, clients of Greece's only reliably functioning enterprise. The economy instead shrunk so precipitously that a second bailout of €130 billion had to be secured in late 2011, with a two-year extension on the implementation of reforms negotiated in late 2012.

The street-level effects of all these measures have been massive unemployment, in particular the dismissal of many civil servants and the cutting of most salaries and pensions to Third World levels. Many businesses, small and large, have failed, evidenced in the vast number of boarded-up shop fronts in Athens, Thessaloníki and other large towns, and the growing number of homeless.

In 2015, Greece renegotiated bailout terms with the troïka, and the new government, headed by SYRIZA's Alexis Tsipras, finally agreed to introduce the lenders' harsh economic measures. However, in a referendum held in July, the public opposed these measures, resulting in the finance minister's resignation, numerous strikes and protests, growing fears of Grexit and the renegotiation of the relief programme. In May 2016, a new compromise was reached, whereby the lenders

Alexis Tsipras, the current and 185th Prime Minster of Greece.

agreed to the major restructuring of Greece's debt, on the strict condition that the country remains on the path to radical political and economic reform.

Political meltdown

Politically, the effects of the crisis have been equally cataclysmic, effectively disintegrating the party duopoly which had run Greece since 1974. Papandreou resigned as prime minister in November 2011, deferring to a unity government led by European banker Lucas Papademos, whose brief was to negotiate effectively with the troika. Despite appreciable headway in this, and widespread feeling that he, albeit unelected, should be left in

place longer, inexorable pressure built up for spring 2012 elections.

These, on 6 May, returned a hung, unprecedentedly splintered parliament, with seven parties taking seats, and support for both PASOK and ND plunging below 20 percent nationwide. After futile negotiations to form a viable coalition, further elections took place on 17 June. Their results were broadly similar, with the same seven parties represented, and ND again the top poller, this time at 29.66 percent, fractionally ahead of SYRIZA at 26.9 percent. Even with 50 bonus seats for the front-running party, ND had to cobble together a coalition with all-but-extinguished PASOK and DIMAR (Democratic Left). SYRIZA, originally a leftist umbrella for old PASOK cadres, assorted activists and MPs expelled from other parties for failing to vote for austerity measures, benefitted mightily from the evaporation of both the PASOK and the hardline Communist vote, as noncooperative Communist behaviour since May convinced many that another ballot cast for them would be wasted.

The worst surprise from both balloting rounds was the emergence of the neo-Nazi, violently xenophobic Hrysí Avgí (Golden Dawn), which fed on the collapse of rival far-right party LAOS – and the public's disgust with dynastic-dinosaur politics. A noxious stew of ex-military commandos, Orthodox fanatics, common criminals, black-clad body-builders, heavy metal fans and bikers, their symbol is a swastika-like adaptation of the ancient Greek meander. They function as Greece's id, doing and saying things that "respectable" burghers only think about.

In early elections following the Greek parliament's failure to elect a president in January 2015, SYRIZA won for the first time and Alexis Tsipras was elected prime minister. In August 2015, Tsipras resigned in the aftermath of problems related to passing the long-negotiated bailout agreement through parliament. However, the September 2015 snap elections only reinforced SYRIZA's position, with the party winning 149 seats in the 300-strong parliament and falling just a few seats short of an absolute majority. On 21 September, Tsipras was once again sworn in as prime minister, heading a government formed by SYRIZA and the Independent Greeks Party (ANEL).

Coping with the Crisis

Greeks have been coping with their extended economic crisis in a number of creative ways.

Not a month goes by in Greece without a "back to the land" newspaper feature – young people, not just retirees, re-occupying old family property, rent-free, in their ancestral village. Here they can grow their own food, raise children in a bucolic environment, and perhaps even ply the trade they did back in town, if they weren't unemployed. Young people who can't leave the cities move back in with their parents (many never left) or occupy a spare flat owned by the family.

Failing internal migration, there's outright emigration; Australia, Canada, the UK, Germany and the Netherlands are favourite destinations. There are simply no well-paying jobs for recent graduates in Greece, with thousands applying for any vacancy; engineers in particular are fairly sure of positions overseas.

Greek banks, thanks to huge portfolios of non-performing loans, are dangerously undercapitalised. Since 2010, they have lost nearly 40 percent of their deposits as customers, fearful of a sudden changeover to a rapidly devaluating "new" drachma, withdraw euros as banknotes for keeping under mattresses.

Many small businesses have shut down. Others vacate commercial premises but continue to operate out of sitting rooms or converted garages at home. Pawnshops are burgeoning, as "we buy gold" signs and flyers in every town indicate. House calls are available for those not wanting to publically parade their circumstances.

As insurance, fuel and road tax costs soar, up to 40 percent of vehicles circulate without insurance coverage, and many cars are for sale, or abandoned illegally, sans number plates, on public thoroughfares. Bicycling as a means of transport is big, and cycling shops are one of the few flourishing retail sectors.

Winter heating has become a major issue, with massive conversion to energy-efficient wood stoves (especially to avoid punitive new taxes on heating oil). With unfiltered chimneys puffing everywhere, it's become a major air-quality issue and the government is being urged to rescind the taxes.

Make do and Mend

Second-hand goods, including formerly disdained clothing, are now socially acceptable, as is rubbish and roadside-scavenging. Anybody involved in fixing things – eg, tailors, seamstresses, shoe repairmen, auto mechanics – has a huge backlog of work.

Little is bought new unless heavily discounted, so shops hold sales continually. Middleman-free street markets are emerging, with farmers selling produce direct to consumers. Barter networks (using websites and/or open-air markets) have appeared in Athens, Vólos and other towns. One accrues credits through jobs done or voucher systems.

Seeing the state as effectively useless, people take far more independent initiative. Parents may hire a whole island bar for a benefit party to fix the local,

Farmers selling potato sacks at cost price in Thessaloníki in March 2012. Similar 'solidarity' actions take place throughout the country.

structurally unsafe school. Or taverna owners in a seaside resort sponsor divers at summer's end to retrieve all the junk submerged in the adjacent picturesque fishing harbour, knowing that the local *limenikó sóma* (harbour corps) will never do anything.

Leisure spending is way down – people eat out perhaps once a week, not two or three times as before. Many *tavérnes* only open on certain peak nights in winter. Those that offer real value or *prix fixe* menus (a recent novelty) are full to bursting, while fancy places struggle. Smarter live-music venues, recognising that some money is better than none, have moderated cover prices to attract customers, say from a formerly untenable €30 down to €15.

GREEKS TODAY

In many ways, Greece has become a modern European country. But there are other facets of the national character that have not changed in centuries.

s the phrase "modern Greece" an oxymoron? A Greek might well pose this question to Western visitors, given the history of the past 200 years: to claim a place among the Western European family of nations, Greeks have been obliged to prove themselves more like their 2,500-year-old forebears than their peasant grandparents. This is perhaps to say that notions of "modernity" are always in the eye of the beholder, and that contemporary Greece, more so than many parts of the world, is rife with contradictions.

The spread of Westernisation

Anyone who has been a regular visitor to Greece over the past 40 years cannot help but be aware of the rampant Westernisation of consumption and behaviour patterns – not just in Athens but also in small villages. During the 1970s, most Greek young women were, to not put too fine a point on it, dumpy, spotty, cultivating lank-and-greasy hairdos, and dressed in such styles (or lack thereof) as to make East Germans of the time look positively glamorous. Fast forward to the Noughties and the look is quite different – women in their twenties dressed to the nines and expensively quiffed even in the throes of the current crisis, and a good head taller than their peers of three decades before. In a country that until recently associated thinness with illness or meanness, one can now find ubiquitous slimming centres and beauty salons hawking the latest dietary and depilation secrets to anxious young women. Gyms, runners and cyclists have multiplied too, especially after the 2004 Olympics, surfing a wave of shame provoked by the sight of sleek, fit athletes – Greeks of both genders have long been among the most

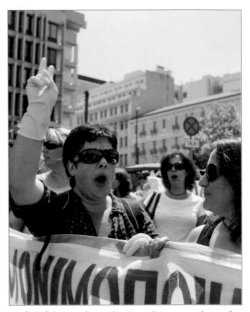

Workers demonstrating against austerity measures imposed on them by the government.

obese in the EU, along with the British and the Maltese.

Striking changes are also manifest in national politics, as election campaigns – the subject of tremendous passion throughout the 1970s and 1980s – have been met increasingly with contempt reflected in a startlingly high abstention rate (over one-third) for a country where violators of the compulsory-voting law were until recently punished with fines. Politicians as a class now enjoy an estimation on a par with heinous criminals, regarded as universally corrupt and self-serving. Many Greeks now prefer to make their views known on the street, in demonstrations peaceful or otherwise.

A strong national identity

Yet there is another side to contemporary Greece that stands firm against the tide of Westernisation and homogenisation, epitomised by the public protest over a proposed law in the mid-1990s which would have forced tavernas and bars to close at 2am rather than 4am. This was supposedly to increase worker efficiency. The widespread and continued outcry over this proposal eventually led to it being shelved or at worst applied week nights only. An attempt to re-introduce the measure more recently met with near-identical results. Amidst the often acrimonious

again reigns supreme as shops revert to the only rhythm sensible in the roasting heat.

Localism and homeland

Another facet of contemporary Greece that stresses the local can also be found in the unusual relationship that exists between villages and the large urban centres of Athens and Thessaloníki. While certainly not free of the snobbery that urban dwellers commonly express for the "backwardness" of their rural cousins, most of Greece is somewhat unusual in having a comparatively short urban memory. There are few Athe-

Celebrating the anniversary of the victory over invading Italian troops in 1940.

exchange of abuse between Germany and Greece during the current crisis, mediated in great part by each country's gutter press, a recurrent motif by Greek partisans was "they (the dreary northern Europeans) envy us our lifestyle.

Greece's working day, with its ostensibly inefficient split every Tuesday, Thursday and Friday into morning and early-evening work shifts (producing two sets of daily commutes in towns as people go to and from a siesta at home – or the beach), has also come under heavy attack from overseas creditors and eurocrats. The compromise solution, for many shops in Athens at least, is north-European style *synéhies óres* (a single shift) from October to April. But come summer, the *mikrós ypnos* or siesta

> The population of Greece is currently around 11,030,000, of whom almost 3.75 million live in Athens. Thanks to a century of emigration, there are also around 6 million Greeks living overseas.

nians whose grandparents were born in that city. Thus, a Greek who answers the question "Where are you from?" with "Athens" will invariably be asked "Yes, but where is your village?"

What seems an unusual query for anyone from a city such as London, Paris or New York makes perfect sense to the Athenian. These rural loyalties are manifested in the enormous flows of people out of the cities for Easter, most of August, and at election times, when many who have grown up in the largest towns still retain voting privileges in their family's ancestral village – where, indeed, their vote will numerically have more effect. Many city-dwellers – a rapidly increasing proportion of the population – will wax lyrical about the virtues of the food, the air and the water in their village; about an uncle's freshly pressed olive oil, a grandmother's cheese, an aunt's fig or pomegranate tree.

Regional pride is often more a matter of friendly rivalries, with differences in traditional costumes and wedding rituals, or whether Easter lamb (or goat) is prepared on a spit or in a clay oven, becoming topics of lengthy discussion. Such localism should not be surprising given that, in Greek, the word "homeland" (patrída) is used to refer as equally to one's country and to one's village or region of birth. Hence the condition of xenitiá, or "longing for homeland", experienced by many in the far-flung Greek diaspora is inherently equivocal: is one primarily nostalgic for the sight of the Parthenon or for the view across the valley to the mountains?

The women's sphere

Perhaps nowhere are the paradoxes of contemporary Greece more evident than in shifting gender relations. Gender in Greece has always been more complicated than the stereotype of Mediterranean male dominance. Men have certainly dominated the public sphere of politics, but women have always dominated in their own public sphere of the church and religious life (this in spite of the all-male church leadership).

In many parts of Greece, particularly the Aegean Islands, dowry and house ownership have given women resources not available to their husbands (although there is also property passed down through the male line). With the tourist boom, many of these houses have been turned into lodgings, providing women with a source of ready cash as well. This meant that despite the rhetoric of male power, women have often been able to control things from behind the scenes.

As one woman from the island of Kálymnos put it: "Women would make the pretence of consulting their husbands, but more often they would simply make decisions for the family in their husbands' absence. My mother sold the family house while my father was away fishing for several months and then found ways to sugar-coat the news to him when he returned". This notion of female power is perhaps best captured by Lainie Kazan in the Hollywood film *My Big, Fat Greek Wedding* (2002): "Yes the man is the head of the family, but the woman is the neck – she can turn him in any direction she wants". All this, mind, in a culture where "Re Kopeliá! (Hey girlie!)" is still considered an acceptable form of public address in shops or tavernas by certain older men to younger women.

The hip crowd at a café in Ermoúpoli in Sýros.

KÓS VERSUS KÁLYMNOS

What Greece may have, until recently, lacked in ethnic diversity, it certainly made up for in the multitude of claims to regional diversity. Residents of villages, towns and cities are eager to discuss the myriad differences in manners and customs of their nearby neighbours. Often this may lead to hyperbole: "The Kalymniots are all crazy!" insisted a taxi driver on the neighbouring island of Kós. "The Koans are all lazy", a Kalymniot shoots back, calling them – for good measure – kótes (a pun on the island-name Kós, and extreme insult in Greek, meaning "hens", reserved usually for frivolous women).

The early 1980s coming to power of the first PASOK government brought legal changes improving women's position in relation to property ownership and pensions, as well as mandating civil marriage – a church ceremony by itself was no longer sufficient. And women moved into national politics in increasing numbers. The two Greek Communist parties have been led by women in recent years (Aleka Papariga and, briefly, Maria Damanaki before she became an EU Maritime Affairs and Fisheries Commissioner), and ex-Prime Minister Constantine Mitsotakis' daughter Dora Bakogianni has long been a figure to be reckoned with in the centre-right ND party, having served as foreign minister and mayor of Athens. Women, however, remain under-represented in the Greek Parliament as a whole, at fewer than 20 percent of the 300 MPs.

Loosened family bonds

While these changes in the public sphere have been substantial, in everyday life it might be more accurate to think less in terms of a shift in power from men to women than as a shift from the older to the younger generation. As Greece has moved away from agriculture and other "traditional" occupations into a more anonymous urban society, parents and other relatives no longer have the crucial technical knowledge that will determine their children's future work lives. Their control over the personal lives of the younger generation has also largely withered away. No longer can parents "keep their daughters locked up in their houses", as many claimed to do in the old days – most parents cease trying when the girl is about 15. It is now common, even in smaller towns, for couples to cohabit for extended periods in Holy Bedlock rather than get married, and even have children out of wedlock – something unheard of in the 1980s. Perhaps the most prominent example of this is Alexis Tsipras, currently head of the opposition centre-left SYRIZA party, who has neither married his long-term partner nor had their two children baptised.

Women in the men's world

The traditional Greek *kafeníon*, serving just Greek coffee, brandy and *oúzo* to an all-male clientele, is an increasingly endangered species. Such establishments are now vastly outnumbered by the so-called frappádika, which serve

cold or hot cappuccino and espresso, *Nes-frappé* and other exotic drinks to a young, mixed-sex crowd glued to their mobiles or tapping on tablet devices. Ironically, recent years have seen the simultaneous increase in coffee shops that pride themselves on making Greek coffee the old-fashioned way, heated ever-so-slowly over a bed of ember-heated sand: kafés sti hóvoli.

In late-night bars, it is no longer uncommon to see women engaged in dances that were once the sole preserve of men, like the *zeïbékiko*, the swaying, eagle-like solo dance which had long been a particular expression of Greek male pas-

Generations old and new in Náousa on Páros.

sion and pain. And the dowry, a source of economic security to an older generation of women, is shunned by the daughters of these women as an insult to ideas about romantic love.

While older Greeks tend to see a struggle for power between the sexes, many younger people embrace at least a notion of "equality". Fathers now take a large share of childcare, and that extends to pushing the pram and changing the odd nappy – something unthinkaxble four decades ago. Also, in a marked contrast to Anglo-Saxon practice, if the parents go their separate ways, unless the father has behaved monstrously towards them, it is considered normal and expected that he will continue to have a close relationship with any offspring.

Fresh fish from the back of the truck, Lésvos.

Olive farmer from Páros.

PEOPLE AND IDENTITIES

The population of Greece is more diverse today than it has been for centuries, but Greek character is still defined by ancient traditions.

U ntil the early 1990s, Greece was unusual in the remarkable homogeneity of the ethnic and religious identifications of its population. This apparent homogeneity was itself a historically recent development – the preceding Byzantine and Ottoman empires were remarkably multicultural by today's standards – which was due in large part to events such as the population exchanges between Greece and Turkey in 1923 and the near-total extermination of Greek Jewry by the Nazis during World War II. This relative homogeneity has meant that Greek citizenship and "Greek" ethnicity have been seen as almost synonymous.

Post-war populations

In the post-war period, upwards of 97 percent of the population identified themselves by ethnicity as Greek and by religion as members of the Greek Orthodox Church. This still left room for some different identifications, including a sizeable Muslim Turkish minority in Thrace, plus much smaller ones on Rhodes and Kos; a Slav/Macedonian minority in Greek Macedonia; small Vlach villages throughout west-central Greece; the Pomaks, a separate Muslim group which claims ancestry from the aboriginal Thracians; the remaining Jewish population in Thessaloníki, Lárissa, Ioánnina, Corfu, Halkída, Vólos and Rhodes; Greek Catholics largely on the islands of Tínos and Sýros; Roma and Jehovah's Witnesses throughout the country. However, all of these minorities are regarded with varying degrees of suspicion or outright dislike by "mainstream" Greeks.

There are also ethnically identified Greeks who distinguish themselves in terms of origins, including the Greeks from the Pontic region and Caucausus around the Black Sea, Greeks

Waiting for custom in Líndos.

from northern Epirus (today in Albania), Asia Minor Greeks from west/central Anatolia, ethnic Greeks from Bulgaria or Romania, plus Arvanites, whose ancestors migrated to Greece in the Middle Ages and who spoke until recently a medieval dialect of Albanian.

Asia Minor refugees

An interesting case of borderline "ethnic" difference is the Greek refugees from Asia Minor who came to Greece during the Greek-Turkish population exchange of 1922 (in fact, the majority had arrived gradually, beginning in 1914, when the Ottomans moved against many Anatolian Greek Orthodox communities in revenge for the sufferings inflicted on Muslim communities in the

Balkans by the victors of the two Balkan wars). Although relatively indistinguishable from mainland Greeks in physical features and religion, the refugees, most of whom settled around Piraeus, Athens and Thessaloníki, still hold onto a separate identity several generations after their uprooting.

So what set this group apart from mainland Greeks? They brought with them a shared heritage and historical experience distinct from that of metropolitan Greece, a cosmopolitan outlook, a sense of grievance and dispossession (many refugees joined the Greek Communist Party in the 1930s), and a distinctive tradition in

and Karamania, deep in the Asia Minor interior, didn't speak a word of Greek upon arrival; Turkish was their first language, written somewhat awkwardly in the Greek alphabet. Many of these karamanlídiki manuscripts and books still exist. Such "Turkish" habits earned them contempt from "real" Greeks who called them tourkóspori (seeds of the Turk) and giaourtovaptisméni (baptised in yoghurt, after that foodstuff hitherto little known in metropolitan Greece).

Coastal Asia Minor Greeks also brought with them a sense of class superiority: many of them had been well educated or were wildly success-

Classroom on the beach in Páros.

food and music – indeed, the once underground, now popular *rebétika* music traces its roots to the Asia Minor refugees.

Being under the Ottoman Empire for a century longer than Greece proper, they felt a particular tie to Byzantium and the legacy of Constantinople. Their experience of major cosmopolitan cities, particularly Smyrna and Istanbul (or Constantinople as they refer to it), gave a sense of multiculturalism and high culture which didn't exist on the Greek mainland. Indeed, most Asia Minor refugees have positive memories of Greek-Turkish relations, claiming that it was the machinations of politicians and the "Great Powers" which caused problems between them. Thousands of such refugees from Cappadocia

ful merchants (or both) and felt themselves superior to what they saw as the "peasants" of Balkan Greece, even if they no longer enjoyed the financial advantages they once had. As refugees, the only possessions most were able to bring with them were the skulls of ancestors, a handful of earth from home and religious icons sewn into clothing. These icons were closely guarded, and passed down to children and grandchildren.

Often completely overlooked in the fixation on Asia Minor Greeks are the 300,000-plus ethnic Greeks who arrived, mostly from Bulgaria, but also Romania and what today is FYROM (former Yugoslav Republic of Macedonia. Because they came gradually over a long period (1913–28), they were able to bring considerable wealth with them, usually selling their real property and not just abandoning it as the Anatolian Orthodox did. This migration, though mediated by treaties, was effectively voluntary – all the Greeks of the Black Sea had to do to stay in their home countries was espouse that nationality and adhere to the national church. A surprising number did, and these days many Bulgarians are happy to admit to an ethnic Greek grandparent (or even two).

Food for thought

A Greek saying goes: "Eat, in order to remember!" In this straightforward, Proustian injunction lies a whole social and moral philosophy. Indeed, if anything unites all the diverse regions, classes, rural and urban dwellers, ethnic groups and both genders that make up modern Greece, it is perhaps best found in an attitude towards food as an embodiment of the good life, in which friends, family and community are all blended. It is striking to the outsider that Greek food, which does not rank among the world's haute cuisines, can be such a focus of everyday life, conversation and memory.

So what makes Greek food Greek? No doubt a cookbook writer will speak of ingredients and preparations. But equally key is the context of eating, that food be shared among friends, neighbours, even strangers and fortunate tourists, that people dip their forks into collective bowls, with one man spearing a particularly juicy tomato or nicely done bit of fish and force-feeding it to his friend; that there be music and boisterous conversation. That one should always have a full plate: there is no clearer symbol of the good life in Greece. At the same time, convention dictates that glasses are only to be filled two-thirds full at most; topping up is considered boorish.

Eating with the dead

Kóllyva made from boiled, sugared winter wheat kernels, supplemented by some or all of the following ingredients – pomegranate seeds, sesame seeds, almonds, sugared almonds, walnuts, parsley, breadcrumbs, currants, pistachios and raisins – is the food that living women offer in memory of the dead, or that the dead symbolically consume as part of their ongoing participation in the community of the Greek Orthodox faithful. It is obligatorily prepared for the two annual *Psyhosávvata* (Soul Saturdays, one before Lenten Sunday, the other preceding Pentecost Sunday),

when the dead are collectively remembered.

When preparing this dish, the entire family gathers and sprinkles a handful of it into a plate in the shape of a cross, asking God to forgive the deceased (indeed, the standard polite way to refer to a departed person is o *synhoriménos/i synhoriméni*, the "forgiven one"). Once the *kóllyva* is ready, the female head-of-house takes it to the church to be blessed. After the service, the priest reads each family's list of the named dead relatives who they wish to be remembered. Once the liturgy is over, the women retrieve their lists and plates and, on the steps of the church,

Cretan shepherds.

HOME FROM HOME

The refugees were not able to bring much to Greece, but they did carry their memories with them, and often preserved their spatial maps of life in Asia Minor by renaming their new Athenian neighbourhoods or towns after the places they had known (invariably prefixed by "Néa/Néos" (new), for example Néos Marmarás). One man in his twenties, whose grandparents were refugees, notes: "It's hard to forget about Asia Minor, they are always reminding us. My grandmother has made me promise to go back to her home village just to see it, and to bring back some water and some soil. Even if she is no longer alive, she wants me to pour it onto her grave".

New Immigrants – and Extremist Reactions

Since 1990, over a million immigrants have entered Greece, producing a huge ratio (1:10) of foreign-born to native in a once-homogeneous culture.

In 2005, an Athens newspaper ran a cartoon encapsulating Greece's demographics. An elderly man

Golden Dawn supporter.

stops a little boy and asks, "Can you help me find the Kafenio Orea Ellas (Café Beautiful Greece)?" The boy replies, "Sure! Go straight past the Kurdish Culture Club, turn right at the Bengali halal butcher, it's between the African cheap-call shop and the bar with the Russian floozies, you can't miss it!" Most new arrivals are Albanian or central European, but also come from a dozen other states. Racist (re-) actions are now commonplace; as one NGO leaflet put it, "Our grandfathers refugees, our parents emigrants, and we – xenophobes and racists?"

Greece has responded to its refugee crisis in substandard fashion, contravening various UN and EU rules (except the Dublin Regulation, which requires refugees to remain in the first European state of landfall – a hosting Greece can ill afford). As part of the Schengen Group, it sees itself, as in past ages, as first line of defence against barbarian hordes. Barbed-wire fencing on the Greek-Turkish land frontier helps stem traffic approaching 80,000 persons annually; east Aegean islands are also prime landing spots. After brief detention, most refugees disappear into the immigrant underground.

In 2001, legal status was offered to the (then) 500,000 illegals who could prove two years' residency and make social insurance contributions. But barely 350,000 applied, and irksome red tape meant that subsequent amnesties netted scarcely any more applicants.

2015 and 2016 saw a sharp increase in the number of refugees travelling to Greece by sea, with many fleeing the Syrian Civil War to the east. In 2015 alone, more than 850,000 people arrived, which was a fivefold increase on the previous year. Many treat Greece solely as a gateway to the Schengen Area. The current situation has had a predominantly negative impact on the country, facilitating the growth of organized crime and terrorism.

The rise of Golden Dawn

But since the crisis began, migrants found themselves surplus to employment requirements. Many took their savings and headed home. Others, unable or unwilling to leave, are targeted for attack by the overtly nationalist, neo-Nazi Hrysí Avgí (Golden Dawn) Party. Widespread resentment of immigrants – especially after violent crimes committed by Pakistanis and Afghans – was instrumental in GD's recent rise.

Golden Dawn thugs frequently undertake vigilante action against immigrants legal or otherwise: raiding street markets, demanding trading licenses from "obviously" non-Greek sellers, and trashing their stalls where none were forthcoming. Motorcycle-riding GD activists have smashed the windows of cars driven by foreigners in Athens, and three Asians have been killed to date. Cadres have also set up soup kitchens for the numerous new poor, but only serve food to "real" Greeks with identity documents. The police stand accused of actively cooperating with Golden Dawn, and of casting up to half their votes for them.

Accordingly, immigrants who complain about abuse often suffer sustained beatings and torture at police stations. The government panders to anti-immigrant sentiment lest it lose more votes to Golden Dawn. During late 2012, repeat roundups of immigrants were conducted by the Athens police, in an operation ironically named Zeus Xenios (Hospitable Zeus). Of 60,000 people detained, nearly 5,000 were deported after their documents were found to be wanting.

feed spoonfuls of *kóllyva* to each other, in a true moment of reciprocity and shared memory.

Any *kóllyva* left over from this communal act is offered to passers-by, perhaps even to tourists, as the women make their way home. But the ritual is not definitively over until that evening, when a plate of *kóllyva* is left out on the dining room table, with the front door open, so that the dead can also come and partake.

Honouring the departed

Kóllyva plays a key role not just in the two annual collective rituals of eating with/ remembering the dead, but at the regular memorial ceremonies that must be held for each deceased person three, nine and 40 days after death, and then three, six and nine months after, and finally every year on the anniversary of the death. These memorials begin in church with a liturgy in honour of the dead, and are followed by a reception, sometimes in the church courtyard, sometimes in a nearby reception hall, or, more intimately, in people's homes. Coffee and assorted baked goods are served, but *kóllyva* is the centrepiece. A photograph of the deceased is often placed near the plate of

Christmas family dinner, Athens.

GREECE AND FETA CHEESE

Féta (the word just means "slice") as a national symbol? It is certainly true that this pungent, delicately textured cheese has been embraced by tourists ever since they discovered slices of it sprinkled with olive oil and oregano complementing the motley flavours and colours of a Greek salad. *Féta* is made from variable mixes of goat's and ewe's milk (*egopróvio* says the label in Greek), and variations are found across the lower Balkans and Turkey. But in the mid-1990s, in the wake of challenges by Denmark to the EU calling for the right to produce a cheese called "feta", this humble staple took on new ethnic significance. In this case, it was the whiteness of *féta* produced from *egopróvio* milk, compared to what Greeks claimed was the yellower Danish "feta" produced predominantly from cow's milk, which seemed to stand for the purity of Greek *féta* – a tasty reflection of the whiteness of those eternal symbols of Greekness themselves, the Parthenon Marbles.

But if *féta* seems simple from the outside, that is not the experience of the Greeks themselves who will discuss the fine distinctions of taste, smell, texture and provenance between different types of tomato, olive oil, fig, or spring water. In talking about food, Greeks are not wallowing in the mundane, but rather recognising the key role that it plays in creating social/ family relations.

kóllyva, as if he or she were offering it to the assembled mourners. Indeed, the living are not just offering *kóllyva* to the dead, but on behalf of the dead; in other words, the soul of the dead person will be relieved of its sins by these acts of generosity on their behalf.

The custom of preparing *kóllyva* has a long history, resembling practices carried out in ancient Athens of *panspermia* – offerings of boiled grains to the dead or to Hermes, the god who guided the dead down to the underworld. The use of pomegranate seeds is another link to the ancient Greek symbolism of death.

to faithfully observe the fast. If they prove unable to keep it up, the women will at least fast in their place during the 40 days of Lent that culminate in the Easter feast and other fasts throughout the year, including the "Little Lents" before Christmas and 15 August.

If you attend a Greek liturgy, you will notice the predominance of women and children inside the church. Men, when they come to church, tend to sit outside and talk with their friends. It is not that Greek men are not religious, but they do tend to have a long-standing distrust of priests and of women's spaces –

Al fresco lunch in Ýdra.

In the Christian tradition (the practice was proclaimed canonical by the patriarch of Alexandria in the 7th century), the symbolism is clearly one of death and rebirth, as the grain or seed which falls to the ground must rot before it yields new life.

Food and faith

Food plays an important role in Greek Orthodox Christianity, most notably in the cycle of fasting and feasting throughout the year that sets the daily and seasonal rhythms of life for numbers of Greek rural and urban dwellers. As in many aspects of Greek religion, women are the caretakers of the observance, coaxing husbands, children and other family members

some even refer to the church as the woman's coffee shop. Absence from church is further mitigated for men by the fact that women bring consecrated bread, incense, basil and other items associated with the church home with them.

Women also prepare the appropriate foods for the different saints' days celebrations, which function like birthdays in Greece. This religious devotion gives women a particular power within the family. As one woman noted when her husband half-jokingly threatened to leave her and move back to his village for some peace and quiet, "If you leave, you won't have anyone to light a candle for you in church. If you leave, who will tend to your soul then?"

Name days

The great majority of Greeks are named after Orthodox saints, according to a system in which parents name children typically after the children's grandparents. A special bond tends to exist between a child and their eponymous grandparent, and in some cases that child will be favoured in property inheritance from that grandparent. Exceptions to this rule include naming a child after a recently deceased relative, after a protector saint (especially if the pregnancy or birth was difficult) or after an ancient Greek name – but even people with a resolutely "pagan" name will also have an alternate baptismal name (eg, a woman named Kyveli, the savage oriental goddess Cybele, may officially be Maria Kyveli). But this basic pattern ensures that there are relatively few names circulating through the system at any one time.

Everyone named Katerina will celebrate their name-day on 25 November, the date associated with the martyrdom of Agía Ekateríni of Alexandria. Name-day celebrations do not involve receiving presents or throwing a party, but rather opening one's house to family and neighbours who wish to come by and give you their good wishes, while you provide them with

> Traditionally, Greeks did not celebrate on their birthdays (birthday parties for children are a recent Western importation), but rather on the feast-day of the saint after whom they are named.

sweets and coffee. Name days thus have a collective aspect absent in birthdays, tying individual Greeks to their community, to grandparents and ancestors who have shared that name, and to the history of Greek Orthodoxy.

A common act of religious devotion in Greece is to build a chapel for one's saint (or for a miracle-working saint who helped you) and to hold liturgies in the saint's honour. Saints are protectors and intercessors between humans and God and are seen as responding to people's prayers if they show proper devotion.

Ritual as sensory experience

Entering a church or chapel in Greece can be an overpowering sensory experience. From the scents of myrrh and frankincense which are spread by priests, swinging censers rhythmically back and forth, to the flicker of candles which each person lights and places in a sand-filled brazier when entering, or again to the reverberating pitch of the liturgy being sung by the psáltes (cantors), often projected via loudspeaker throughout the town or village. And of course there is the sight of the multicoloured icons, illustrating key stories from the Bible, and the taste of communion bread and wine mixed to the consistency of gruel and presented by the priest on a spoon. This sensory aspect of Greek Orthodoxy is part of official doctrine as

Boarding the ferry at Skiáthos.

well, an expression of the notion of the "deification of matter", the idea that humans manifest the spiritual not in opposition to the material but in and through the material world.

Explosive Easter

Local differences come in many hues, from the typical colours used for house-painting, to the different dialects – such as Cretan, where the sound "k" is replaced by a more ancient "tch" found also in Cyprus – to the matrilineal inheritance patterns that characterise many of the Aegean Islands. On the island of Kálymnos, difference takes the form of a sonic assault every Easter.

In most of Greece, Easter is celebrated with the setting off of fireworks, an index of the heavenly activity that Easter commemorates. On Kálymnos, fireworks are replaced by dynamite – several thousand euros' worth, formed into projectiles and hurled from the courtyards of churches, from the two clifftops that bracket the harbour town, or in a "friendly" exchange across neighbouring back yards. No mere firecracker barrage can quite compare to the sound of dynamite going off around you, and Kálymnos's Easter celebrations have been known to both attract some stout-hearted tourists and to send others scurrying for the next boat out.

The practice of dynamite-throwing from the island's heights can be traced back to the Italian occupation of the Dodecanese in the early 20th century. Legend has it that one Easter, Kalymniots set off dynamite from one mountain and, while the Italian authorities were hurrying to investigate, then set off charges on the opposite mountain. As one man put it, it was a way of saying "We're alive" to the colonisers. Why has this "tradition" persisted, with the Italian occupation now a distant memory? Perhaps as a reminder, not only to neighbouring Turks but to Athenians and other Greeks, that Kálymnos is not to be trifled with.

Hospitality and honour

Local loyalties run high in Greece. One aspect of localism that tourists may find themselves on the receiving end of is local claims to being more "hospitable" (filóxeni) than their neighbours. "Neighbours" is a relative term: people will claim that Southern Europeans are more filóxeni than Northern Europeans, Greeks more than Italians, their town or village more than Athenians, and they themselves more than the person across the street. Greeks often buy in bulk – 2kg of cheese, a couple of watermelons – in order to always have food on hand to offer guests, invited and uninvited alike.

If you think you detect a competitive nature to hospitality in Greece, you are not far off the mark, as generosity is closely tied to Greek notions of honour. Acts of generosity are part of building one's reputation. They also, as noted by anthropologists, make claims to the higher status of the giver than the receiver.

This often has a faint feel of role reversal in cases where the receiver of hospitality comes from a Northern European country or the United States: Greeks are well aware that their country's voice is routinely ignored in international contexts, especially since the advent of the economic crisis, and so by being generous they are in a sense also subtly communicating the message: "You may be from a powerful country with the whip hand over us, but for the moment you are dependent on me".

All this is in no way to deny the genuineness of generous offers, nor the curiosity they may express about life in other countries over a proffered cup of coffee. A generous appreciation of your host's hospitality and, in some cases, a postcard, text message or email from abroad is all that is usually expected in return.

Women have a prominent role in Greek religious life.

A SONG OF THE MOUNTAINS

Throughout the centuries, the Greeks have used their landscape – rugged mountains, rolling plains – as a metaphor to describe the different natures of the people living there, a convention this old Cretan folk song (composed by hilldwellers, one presumes) cunningly exploits:

Fie on the young men down on the plains
Who taste the good things in life,
The choicest foods,
And are base to look at, like creeping lizards.
Joy to the young men up in the hills
Who eat the snow and the dew-fresh air
And are fine to look at, like the orange-tree.

Ýdra greengrocer.

LITERATURE

Greece was the cradle of European poetry and drama; modern writers keep the tradition alive with outstanding novels, drama and especially poetry.

When someone asked Greece's most famous composer, Mikis Theodorakis, where he got his inspiration for the hundreds of songs he had written in his lifetime, he said: "It's perfectly simple. I never thought of my music as anything but a way of clothing Greek poetry".

Perhaps only a Greek would have given such an answer. Relative to the size of its population, more poetry is published in Greece than in any other European country except Slovenia, and it is still common for Greeks to present their friends with slim volumes of verse they have written and self-published. Poetry is something people still revere and read for pleasure, and the marriage of poetry and music, familiar from the folk-song tradition, still endures.

Folk songs and the oral tradition

Both Greeks and non-Greeks have sought traces of continuity between ancient and modern Greece, and found it – if sometimes only in their imagination – in the folk songs and dances of rural Greece. In the 19th century, philhellenes and early Greek nationalists viewed the folk tradition as a way of establishing Greece's legitimate claim to liberation from the Turks. Certainly the country's folk songs are remarkable in their rich variety of imagery and metaphor, and it is not surprising that the first poets of modern Greece used them as a source of inspiration.

Although the tradition is dying out, it is still possible, in a village in the mountains of Epirus or the Peloponnese, to come upon a festival or a wedding where the night is filled with songs like this:

*Now the birds, now the swallows,
now, now the partridges,
now the partridges chatter and speak:*

Dionysios Solomos, writer of the lyrics to the Greek national anthem.

*Wake, my lord, wake my good lord
wake, embrace a body like a cypress,
a white throat, breasts like lemons…*

Some of the most memorable folk lyrics of Greece are the laments for the dead. In these powerful songs, usually performed by women, Death is addressed in the person of Charos (from the ancient Charon), a sinister figure on a black horse:

*Why are the mountains black, why so heavy with clouds
is the wind fighting them, is rain lashing them?
The wind doesn't fight, nor the rain lash.
Only Death crosses them, carrying off the dead.
He drags the young in front of him, the old behind*

and the tender children are lined up on his saddle. You will have to search hard for such songs in the tourist-laden landscape of the Aegean Islands, once the source of an astonishing variety of music, song and dance. Yet even on Skópelos you just might overhear men in a taverna conversing in mandinádes (rhyming couplets), ordinarily set to music on the island of Crete. Crete is in fact exceptional in preserving a lively, traditional music scene where song lyrics are still improvised by local performers, but do not expect to hear the old island songs of Mýkonos, Santoríni or Rhodes when you visit.

no clear answer. Most of Greece was untouched by the Renaissance, but a notable exception was the island of Crete, which had been under Venetian rule until its conquest by the Ottomans in the mid-17th century. Some argue that the plays and poems produced on that island from the 15th to the 17th centuries mark the beginning of modern Greek literature. The most famous of these works is the *Erotókritos*, a long romance in verse by Vitsentzos Kornaros. Remarkably, this written text became part of the oral tradition of the island, all 10,000 lines of it being sung as if it were a folk song until

The epitaph on Nikos Kazantzakis' grave: "I don't hope for anything, I don't fear anything, I'm free".

Fortunately, until recently, there existed an exceptionally active recording industry in Greece, and among the best sources of folk-song texts are the booklets accompanying CDs of same, some with translations supplied. Recording notes will also provide the serious Greek music fan with lyrics to the popular urban songs of Greece, the *rebétika*, though English versions are often merely summaries. Risqué and laced with slang referring to hashish smoking, they open an interesting window onto the shady life of Piraeus in the early to mid-20th century.

What is modern Greek literature?

The question of where Ancient Greek literature ends and modern Greek literature begins has

THE GREEK DOSTOYEVSKY

The Murderess, by Papadiamantis, may well be one of the most daring stories of its day. It tells the story of an old woman who, having witnessed the misery of local women's lives, begins to murder infant girls rather than let them grow up. At the end of the story, she drowns while being pursued by the police, her guilt punished by divine rather than human justice; but Papadiamantis's sympathetic treatment of her character brings many assumptions of traditional Greek behaviour into question. "Once married, she was her husband's slave... when she had children, she served them, and when they had children, she became their slave".

the 20th century. It is rare to hear more than a small section of the poem sung today, but it is an exhilarating experience to listen to even a handful of these verses performed in a Cretan nightclub, preserved since the Renaissance in popular memory.

Another contender for the source of modern Greek poetry is the Ionian island of Zákynthos. Like Corfu, the other Ionian Islands had been part of the Venetian Empire from the late 14th to early 15th century. The aristocracy were Italians, often married to local women, and the poet who is often referred to as Greece's

for the non-Greek reader to discover the prose of 19th-century Greece. Only lately have the works of two other remarkable prose writers begun to appear in English: Alexandros Papadiamantis and Georgios Vizyenos Papadiamantis (1851–1911) was the son of a village priest from Skiáthos and most of his fiction is set on that small Aegean island. The 200 stories he produced in his lifetime, including the novella *The Murderess*, offer a vivid, unsentimental portrait of Greek island life. They are written in a combination of formal Greek and village dialect reminiscent of Dickens or Hardy.

A statue of early writer Adamantios Korais.

"national" poet was the child of such a union. Born on Zákynthos in 1798, Dionysios Solomos was educated in Italian but, fired by the spirit of the Greek revolution, he began to write in Greek. His most famous poem is the *Hymn to Liberty*, which became the lyrics of the new nation's anthem. Solomos's co-islander Andreas Kalvos, who spent most of his life in Italy, also achieved national recognition as a poet. Between them, the two poets inspired the national school of Romantic poets.

The 19th century

Emmanuel Roïdis's wickedly satiric novel *Pope Joan* has achieved a deservedly wide readership in several languages, but it is otherwise difficult

Translations of the half-dozen stories of Georgios Vizyenos (1849–96) have only recently become available in English. Enigmatic and sophisticated, his short stories are, like Papadiamantis's, preoccupied with questions of guilt and traditional Greek mores.

The early 20th century

Poetry flourished during the 20th century in Greece, a period dominated by four tragedies: the Greco-Turkish War of 1919–22 that resulted in the loss of an ethnic Greek presence in Asia Minor; World War II, when Italian, Bulgarian and German troops occupied the country; the 1946–49 civil war; and the military dictatorship of 1967–74, which put a temporary end to the

Greeks' struggle for democracy and freedom of expression. Poetry, often sung poetry, gave a voice to people's suffering during these periods. The banning of poetry and song during these crises was a reflection of how powerful such expression was.

With the restoration of democracy in 1974, Greece's entrance into the European Community and the galloping urbanisation of the post-dictatorship era, tastes in literature changed. Songs and poems no longer talked about the heroism of the people or the beauty of Greek nature, but about the disillusionment of urban

the new urban reality of a country whose population had increased by over 25 percent as a result of the Asia Minor war. More daring than their rural contemporaries, they experimented with Modernist techniques. The most original of these writers were Nikos Pentzikis, Giannis Skaribas and Giannis Beratis.

Prize-winning poets

Those poets who matured in the early to mid-20th century are best known outside of Greece. In 1963 and 1979 respectively, two Greek poets, George Seferis (pseudonym of Georgios

Odysseus Elytis, Nobel Prize winner in 1979.

life or private concerns. Prose, which had occupied a secondary position to poetry, proliferated in the last half of the 20th century. With few exceptions, the better early-modern Greek prose writers had favoured the short story over the novel; but in the aftermath of the Asia Minor defeat, a group of novelists emerged who chronicled the events of the period and became known as the Aeolian School. Two were refugees from Asia Minor (Stratos Doukas and Ilias Venezis, and the third from the island of Lésvos, a few miles off the Turkish coast. All three began their literary careers on Lésvos; their prose was realistic and the Greece they depicted was rural.

Meanwhile, in Athens and Thessaloníki, a number of young writers began writing about

A NON-CONFORMIST LIFE

Thanks to his unorthodox views and writings, Nikos Kazantzakis was to court controversy not only throughout his life, but even after his death in 1957. When his book *The Last Temptation of Christ* was first published, the Orthodox Church sought to prosecute him, then excommunicated him. When it was made into a film in 1988, Athenian priests together with Orthodox parishioners marched on the cinemas, and projection screens were slashed in anger. Today, admirers can make for the Kazantzakis Museum in the village of Myrtiá, 24km (15 miles) due south of Iráklio, where well-arranged displays illustrate an extraordinary literary and political life.

Seferiadis) and Odysseus Elytis (born Odysseas Alepoudelis), won the Nobel Prize for Literature, drawing attention to the extraordinary flourishing of poetry in a country that was considered a cultural backwater by many western Europeans. A third poet, Constantine Cavafy (Konstantinos Kavafis; 1863–1933), was admired by E.M. Forster and W.H. Auden and became one of the most influential poets of the 20th century.

Living and writing his whole life outside modern Greece, in Alexandria, Cavafy removed himself still further from his contemporaries by setting most of his poems in the past. Like

as Homer's original. These figures tower over modern Greek literature like a formidable Dead Poets' Society, their works overshadowing those of their contemporaries and followers. Kazantzakis, of course, was also a novelist, and if English-speakers have read any modern Greek novels, they are probably his *Alexis Zorba, Christ Recrucified* or *Freedom and Death.*

Poetry out of conflict

Scarcely known outside Greece are the Greek poets who were Cavafy's near-contemporaries – Kostas Karyotakis, Kostis Palamas, Angelos

George Seferis, Nobel Prize winner in 1963.

Cavafy, the characters that inhabit his elegant, ironic poems are Greeks of the eastern Mediterranean whose Hellenism is based on language and a common respect for Greek culture. His poem, Ithaka, may be the most often quoted modern Greek poem of all:

Ithaka has given you your lovely voyage
Without Ithaka you would not have set out.
Ithaka has no more to give you now.

Two other poets who benefitted from international attention and foreign translations were Nikos Kazantzakis and Giannis Ritsos. Kazantzakis's modern sequel to *The Odyssey* (1938), in Kimon Friar's fine translation, was probably read by more English-speakers than Greeks, despite the fact that it is twice as long

Sikelianos and Kostas Varnalis. It was left to the somewhat younger poets who came of age in the 1930s to bring modern Greek poetry into the mainstream of European writing. Despite their political differences, these poets drew on what they saw as the enduring virtues of the Greek spirit as a way to confront the evils and privations of the war years. For Seferis, Ritsos, Kazantzakis, Andreas Embirikos, Elytis, Nikos Kavadias and many others, the war was a devastating experience that initially united Greeks against a common enemy and then tore them into two bitterly opposed camps who fought one another in a civil war lasting until 1949. During this period, many writers and intellectuals were persecuted by right-wing forces and imprisoned on Aegean Islands. Giannis Ritsos was among those who spent years in prison and exile. Others, like Seferis, spent the war years outside Greece. But no Greek writer was left unscathed, and these dark years inspired some of the greatest works of modern Greek poetry.

Elytis, whose long poem *To Áxion Estí* (*Worthy it is*), memorably set to music by Mikis Theodorakis, drew on all the traditional resources of the Greek language – ancient, Byzantine, folk song – to create a modern secular liturgy. Beginning with the poet's childhood on Crete, *To*

outside the country, you have to be translated; and even then the chances of being recognised are small unless you are discovered, like Cavafy, by an E.M. Forster, or recognised by a Nobel Prize. Since the 1960s, tourism has helped create a market for Greek literature, especially if it fits the traveller's ideas of what Greece is all about. Writers who instead concentrate on the less attractive themes of modern urban life are less likely to appeal to non-Greek readers. One brilliant exception is the Istanbul-born writer Petros Markaris (1937–), who has made a name for himself with his ingenious crime nov-

A Karagiózis shadow puppet show.

Áxion Estí spares the reader none of the horrors of the war – including a long passage from a soldier's diary on the Albanian front – but ends in a redeeming "Gloria", praising the beauty of the Greek island and its lovely women:
Sífnos, Amorgós, Alónisos
Thásos, Itháki, Santoríni
Kós, Íos, Síkinos.
Praised be Myrto standing
on the stone wall facing the sea
like a beautiful eight or a jug
with a straw hat in her hand.

The post-war writers

The central challenge to Greek literature is that so few people read Greek. To become known

els set in Istanbul or Athens, featuring Detective Costas Haritos.

Greek writers, many of them women who began publishing in the 1950s and 1960s, were mostly born in Athens or Thessaloníki. They matured in a period of tentative democracy that was rudely interrupted by seven years of stultifying dictatorship (1967–74). Reluctant to adopt the themes of earlier generations, they wrote about personal relationships, disillusionment and Athenian life. Among the contemporary women Greek poets whose works exist in English translation are Katerina Angelaki-Rooke, Kiki Dimoula, Jenny Mastoraki, Maria Laina and Rhea Galanaki (now better known as a novelist). This is necessarily a brief list, not intended to diminish the brilliance of their male contemporaries, among whom Manolis Anagnostakis (died 2005), Titos Patrikios, Nasos Vagenas, Tassos Denegris (died 2009), Yannis Kondos and Mihalis Ganas stand out.

Of this generation, Katerina Anghelaki-Rooke (born 1939) is probably the poet who has been most widely translated and therefore the most instrumental for the reception of Greek poetry abroad. Anghelaki-Rooke is brilliantly articulate in French, English and Russian and has translated the works of many of the most "untranslatable" writers from those languages into Greek – including Dylan Thomas and Pushkin. Her old red house on Égina has long been a mecca for foreign writers and scholars of Greek literature, many of whom have relied on Anghelaki's sharp insights into her country's literature as their guide to reading and translation. Her own poems are characterised by a combination of frank, lyrical sexuality and ironic self-criticism. As she writes in *Penelope Says*:

The body keeps remaking itself
getting up and falling into bed
as if it had been chopped down,
sometimes sick and sometimes in love hoping
that what it loses in touch it gains in essence.

In prose as in poetry, women writers have emerged since 1950, to rival their male counterparts. Novels about Greek society may be the traveller's best guide to the changing mores and manners of Greek life. And since many Greek writers have chosen their own recent history as a subject for their fiction, novels and short stories may also be a good introduction to the vicissitudes of the period. Alki Zei's *Achilles' Fiancée*, for example, is a gripping *roman-à-clef* about the period of the civil war and its aftermath, when Leftist guerrilla fighters took refuge in the Soviet Union. Among the other outstanding contemporary Greek novelists whose works have been translated into English are Costas Taktsis, Thanasis Valtinos, Margarita Liberaki, Maro Douka, Eugenia Fakinou, Menis Koumandareas, Apostolos Doxiadis and Vangelis Hatziyannidis.

Drama

Modern Greek dramatists have not, as yet, achieved the international recognition of their poetry- and fiction-writing colleagues. Despite a lively national theatrical scene that

began promisingly in the 19th century and continues to satisfy the tastes of a large local audience, only a handful of Greek plays have been translated. Surprisingly, women dramatists were among the first to compose original plays, notably Evanthia Kairi, whose *Nikiratos* was produced in 1826.

Many writers better known in other fields turned their hand to writing plays, among them Kazantzakis, Palamas and Sikelianos; but in the post-war period, the theatre has been dominated by a group of writers whose primary concern is the theatre. The most outstanding

Poet Katerina Anghelaki-Rooke.

of these was the prolific Iakovos Kambanelis (1922–2011).

Another delight for those who have some knowledge of Greek is the shadow puppet theatre. The hero of these charming, ribald, satiric performances, Karagiózis, is an anti-hero with whom Greeks have always identified. Set in the Ottoman period, the comic puppet plays, once watched by open-mouthed children and their guffawing parents in the village square, have always been tailored to fit each new political crisis and allowed Greeks to laugh at themselves, even in the harshest periods of their history. As the song-writer, Dionysios Savvopoulos, put it:

What consumes me, what saves me
Is that I dream like Karagiózis…

A bouzoúki maker in Rhodes.

MUSIC AND DANCE

Music in Greece goes far beyond Zorba's Dance played on a bouzouki and reflects the country's complex political and cultural history.

The sounds of Greece: the whine of motor-scooters; the thrumming of ferry-boat engines; passengers and taxi-drivers shouting at one another; the clang of church bells; sheep and goats bleating, their bells tinkling, donkeys braying, and music – loud music blaring from nightclubs, cars, cafés. The Greeks do not seem to need or desire quiet; they fill any silence with noise. They also love music, and even if it has to compete with ambient noise, they listen to it constantly.

What may surprise the visitor is that nearly all of the music they play is distinctively Greek. It may be influenced by American, Spanish or Brazilian music, but more often than not it is Greek in instrumentation or rhythm. Anyone who came to Greece 40 years ago must lament the steady erosion of Greece's traditional folk music; however, despite globalisation and modernisation, Greek music is still flourishing and full of surprises.

A continuous tradition?

Anyone who has attended the famous Dora Stratou folk-dance performances in Athens, or any other presentation of Greek music for tourists, will have been told that modern Greek music and dance preserve some of the features of their ancient Greek origin. These claims are hard to substantiate, since we have almost no idea what ancient Greek music sounded like. We know its instruments and its famous system of modes (such as Dorian, Lydian, Aeolian), but only a few tantalising fragments of notation have survived. Greek vases show dancing figures, accompanied by lyre, flute and tambourine, who could as well be dancing at a modern Greek wedding, but neither these line-dances nor their instrumentation are unique to Greece.

These ceramic figurines show that the Minoan people also enjoyed dancing.

What was unique about Greece was the desire of 19th-century western philhellenes and early Greek nationalists to see, in modern Greece, traces of continuity with the mythical world of antiquity. The claims that early folklorists made for a continuous tradition were not only slim, but they were based almost entirely on the poetry of Greek songs, ignoring both the astonishing variety and richness of the music, and also the ritual context in which it was performed. Like all folk music, Greek songs and dances were not originally performed for entertainment but were associated with religious festivals, weddings, funerals or seasonal work.

Music of the mainland

While there is some overlap between these categories, Greeks usually make a distinction between regional folk music (*dimotikí mousikí*) and popular or city music (*laïkí*). In the case of regional folk music, they also distinguish between music from the mainland (*steriani*) and music from the islands and coastline (*nisiótika, paraliakí*). Mainland Greece is further divided into regions that have their own musical traditions: Epirus, in the northwest, Macedonia, Roúmeli, Thrace and the Peloponnese.

The most common rhythms of the main-land are the threes of the *tsamikós* (taking its name from the Albanian Cham tribe), the sev-ens of the *kalamatianós* (named after the town of Kalamáta in the Peloponnese but common throughout central and southern Greece) and the slow double and triple time of the *syrtós* and *sta tría*. Once, it was common to hear music per-formed outdoors by classic pairs of instruments, either a large drum (*daoúli*) and folk oboe (*zourná*), or a bagpipe (*gáida*) and tambourine (*daïrés, défi*); nowadays it is more common to hear an ensemble that includes clarinet, violin, drum and perhaps an accordion or a hammered dulcimer (*sandoúri*).

In addition to Epirus, other areas of main-land Greece where the traveller may still be lucky enough to find live music at a summer *panigýri* (religious festival) are Thrace and Mac-edonia, both of which have a wide variety of local songs and dances. In central Greece and the Peloponnese, you are these days more likely to find recorded music at such events.

The islands and Asia Minor

The islands once boasted an amazing variety of musical traditions. West of the Greek mainland in the Ionian Islands, which had for centuries been under Venetian control, people sang songs in four-part harmony. Called *kantádes*, these

Street parade musicians.

Improvised rhymed couplets in 15-syllable metre (mandinádes) are a common feature of Aegean island music and persist to this day, especially on the islands of Crete, Kárpathos and Kálymnos.

songs, usually accompanied by a guitar, were clearly influenced by Neapolitan folk song. Partly because of their western European character and partly because they were songs that could be sung in a restaurant or tavern, *kantádes* became very popular in Athens where they were still sung by groups of men and women until the 1960s. The island of Zákynthos remains famous for its *arékia*, the local variant of *kantádes* and, although the genre is slowly dying out, it is not uncommon to hear the islanders perform these light and charming songs. The Ionian Islands were also, in the 19th and early 20th centuries, a regional centre for Italian opera, which was performed in opera houses on both Corfu and Kefaloniá.

In the Aegean, music is usually somewhat arbitrarily divided into groups conforming to the grouping of islands. Here, the dance rhythms are mostly double, with the most common dance being some variety of *syrtós*. The exceptions are the nine-beat rhythms of the *zeibekikó* and *karsilámas*, plus the four-beat couples' dance, the *bállos*, found in the Aegean islands and off the coast of Asia Minor, particularly Lésvos, and the Dodecanese. The traditional local instruments were the *lýra* (not to be confused with the ancient Greek lyre) or bowed viol, and the *tsamboúna*, or island bagpipe. As with the mainland instruments, there has been a shift in instrumentation, with the violin replacing the *lýra* on most islands, accompanied by the *laoúto*, akin to a mandolin, often with the addition of accordion, hand-drum or clarinet.

Whereas live music has all but disappeared from many Aegean islands, Crete is something of an exception. Any traveller wanting to discover more about Greek folk music might well begin his or her journey in Crete. Still performed on the classic combination of the Cretan *lýra* and *laoúto*, Cretan music continues to flourish and is being performed by young as well as older players. Not only is the tradition of improvised poetic couplets still preserved, but sections of the long poem *Erotókritos*, a 17th-century verse play, are still performed as part

of many singers' repertoires. Cretan dancing is spectacular, and the combination of music and dance, whether it is performed in a noisy nightclub or at a village wedding (sometimes lasting for three days), is still awe-inspiring.

The islands of the central Aegean, especially the Cyclades, have become so overwhelmed by tourists that these days it is difficult, on most of them, to hear live music. Those lucky enough to encounter it at some special occasion like a wedding will discover the vanishing beauty of the *nisiótika*, songs and dances performed by a violin-led ensemble. The islands near the Turk-

A traditional wedding on Ýdra.

ish mainland, especially Lésvos, once had a very different musical tradition, one strongly influenced by the cosmopolitan cities of Smyrna (modern Izmir) and Aïvali (Ayvalık), both of which had large Greek populations until the 1920s. On Lésvos, there were many local varieties of the Asia Minor songs and dances, some only found in a particular village, and it was through its principal town, Mytilíni, that many of the features of Asia Minor music found their way into the popular music of Greece.

One type of music that the tourist is unlikely to encounter – in part because it is considered bad luck to perform them outside their proper context – but which is rich in its lyrics and striking in its emotional style of performance, is the *mirolói* (funeral lament). It is rare for women to perform such songs at funerals in urban centres, but in the remote countryside, no funeral is complete without its chorus of women lament-singers. In most regions of Greece, laments are distinguished from songs. They are a genre apart, and yet they have melodies that may be performed as separate instrumental pieces in other contexts – even at weddings, strangely enough. It is through these songs that women communicate with the other world, addressing the dead directly and often berating them for leaving the living behind.

Byzantine music was influenced by the chant of Syria and Palestine rather than Greece or Rome, and was probably based on melodies already familiar to the congregation from the local folk tradition. The *okotíhos*, which forms the basis of all Byzantine chant, was not a system of modes like those of ancient Greece, but based on such a collection of songs. What was important was the association of a set of melodic formulas with their liturgical function: certain tunes came to have a symbolic function in the Church and were incorporated into the hymns.

By far the greatest composer of Byzantine

A tsamboúna, the island bagpipe.

While these laments are performed in the context of a Christian ritual, they are remarkable in their lack of Christian references and in their striking pagan imagery. Despite repeated clashes with the Orthodox Church, village women have been permitted to continue improvising these laments as part of the funeral service, with priest and female chorus taking turns to articulate conflicting messages about the afterlife.

Religious music

Greeks often refer to the music of the Orthodox Church simply as Byzantine music. This is only partly true. While some of the music heard in the Orthodox services dates to the Byzantine period, much of it was composed later. Early

hymns was Romanos O Melodos (Romanos the Melodist), born in Syria in the late 5th century and probably active at the height of the Emperor Justinian's reign. His combination of dramatic poetry with melody has never been surpassed in the Eastern Christian tradition and his hymns still form part of the Orthodox liturgy.

There is now a considerable variety of music performed in Greek churches, some of it accompanied by an organ, and some including polyphonic arrangements, although many churches still retain the earlier style of monophonic singing (without harmonies) by a chorus, with a drone supplied. The richest music of the Church calendar can be heard at Easter week, particularly the Thursday evening Crucifixion service, and at the Epitáfios, or Good Friday evening liturgy. Don't miss a chance to hear young Nektaria Karantzi, the only student of the great Thracian singer Khronis Aïdonidis, performing Byzantine music in either a secular or church setting.

The sound of the city

For many visitors to Greece, one of the attractions is the "Zorba factor". That dance of Anthony Quinn and Alan Bates on a Greek beach in the 1964 movie *Zorba the Greek*, accompanied by the rapid twanging of the *bouzoúki*, spells a particular exuberance and excitement regarded as

Asia Minor music brought into Greece through the islands and by the flood of refugees who arrived in the mainland following the Greco-Turkish War of 1919–22.

The Asia Minor style was generally performed in cafés known as *cafés-aman* in the towns of the Anatolian coast, where the ensembles were made up of a violin, guitar, *oud, sandoúri or kanun* (zither) and perhaps an accordion. Non-Muslim women and men both performed in these venues and their repertoire of songs often included rather daring and humorous underworld songs about hash-

Musicians on guitar and mandolin, Skiáthos Town

quintessentially Greek. Granted, the two men are dancing on a Cretan beach, but they are not dancing a Cretan dance. They are dancing urban music composed by Greece's most famous modern composer, Mikis Theodorakis. It is music and dancing derived from a particular style of Greek music called *rebétika*, a style that still forms the basis of much of modern Greece's popular music and is played by revival groups all over Greece.

Rebétika is a music associated with certain ports of Asia Minor and Greece from the beginning of the 20th century onwards, though it probably existed around the east Aegean coast and the Black Sea for decades before that.

Rebétika is often, but not always, divided into two types: the Piraeus-style *rebétika*, and the

ish, drinking, prison and prostitutes. Leading female performers in this genre were Rita Abatzi and Roza Eskenazi.

With the arrival of the refugees, cafés-aman sprang up in Piraeus and Athens, and the taste for this music in the Greek communities of the US led to a burgeoning recording industry. Refugees, many of them poor and unemployed, also joined local musicians in the back streets of Piraeus, where a new sort of music began to grow in popularity. This was performed not by the traditional café instruments, but on the *bouzoúki*, a long-necked, lute-like instrument that had already been observed in the Cyclades being used for folk music by the great traveller James Theodore Bent early in the 1880s.

By the 1930s, the *bouzoúki* and the songs it accompanied were all the rage in Greece. Rather like the urban blues of the US, or the tango of Argentina, the songs of the prewar *rebétika* were daring in their lyrics and appealed to an audience that revelled in hearing about the shady milieu they depicted.

Markos Vamvakaris, the central member of the "Piraeus Quartet", is often regarded as the "father" of *rebétika*. Other outstanding figures were Stratos Pagioumtzis, Giannis Papaïoannou, the prolific songwriter Vassilis Tsitsanis and his singers Sotiria Bellou, Ioanna Georgakopoulou

extraordinary experiment in Greek popular music. After the terrible years of World War II and the civil war, Greeks were demoralised and emotionally exhausted. The two composers deliberately set out to provide the public with a new sort of popular music that would elevate and inspire. They both recognised *rebétika* as the only musical form that could reach a broad public, but as classically trained musicians, they wanted to extend the boundaries of popular song and combine it with the poetry of the country's leading poets.

Beginning in the late 1950s, the two compos-

Mikis Theodorakis, who won international fame.

and Stella Haskil, whose recordings are as fine an introduction as one could wish to *rebétika*.

The heyday of the *rebétika* lasted from the 1930s to the 1950s, but the songs were revived in the 1970s, beginning in the years of the dictatorship (1967–74) when the music of Theodorakis was banned by the colonels and other composers either refused to compose or found their lyrics censored. References to smoking hashish also appealed to a generation of young Greeks who identified with the streetwise, social outcasts of *rebétika*.

Popular music of the 1960s–1970s

Mikis Theodorakis and his fellow-composer Manos Hatzidakis were the leaders of an

ers transformed Greek music and produced some of the most exciting popular music in Europe by joining the rhythms of the *rebétika* (particularly the dramatic 9/8 of the solo male dance, the *zeïbekikó*) with the poetry of Seferis, Ritsos, Nikos Gatsos and Elytis. In the case of Mikis Theodorakis, this music acquired a strong political dimension because of his commitment to the freedom of the persecuted Greek Left. During the dictatorship, his music was banned and he was imprisoned for years, making his music still more popular among the population at large. Gatsos was just one of a group of lyricists such as Manos Eleftheriou and Kostas Virvos, who were not "straight" poets but nonetheless of critical importance for Greek song.

Theodorakis and Hatzidakis's music has had a lasting effect on Greek music. Not only are their songs still popular (Theodorakis's music is still likely to be played at the latest Athens street demonstration), but they inspired a younger group of composers to follow in their footsteps, writing music for the theatre and cinema as well as song cycles. Among the best known of these composers, who belong to what is loosely termed the New Wave or more specifically *éntkhno* (folk-influenced orchestral music), are Dionysios Savvopoulos, Giannis Markopoulos, Manos Loïzos and Stavros Xarhakos.

like Stamatis Kraounakis the late Nikos Papazoglou and Nikos Xydakis, are less widely known. The same decade saw the emergence of a movement called Ta Paradosiaká (The Traditional), concentrating on the rediscovery of Ottoman and Asia Minor traditions in Greek music, with Turkish musicians joining performances. Leading figures were Irishman Ross Daly, a virtuoso musician resident on Crete, and Sokratis Sinopoulos, a master of the *polítiki* (Constantinople) *lýra* and *laoúto*.

As a direct outgrowth of this, the hottest contemporary music is apt to feature collaborations between Greeks and Turks, for example the long-

Island wedding in full swing.

The contemporary music scene

Some of the best-known figures of the Greek musical scene are singers rather than composers, though some do write their own material. Maria Farandouri, George Dalaras (Giorgos Dalaras), Mariza Koch, Alkinoös Ioannides, Dimitris Mystakidis, Sokratis Malamas, Haris Alexiou, Nena Venetsanou, Glykeria, Eleftheria Arvanitaki, Dimitra Galani, and most recently Savina Giannatou plus Martha Frintzila, have all become internationally popular. The phenomenon of World Music has created a demand for certain types of Greek sounds, both folk and urban, and these singers have represented Greek music to a broad audience.

Composers who came of age during the 1980s,

running shared appearances of Glykeria and Thessaloníki-resident Dilek Koç, or the concert tour of multinational musicians which accompanied the release of *My Sweet Canary*, an Israeli-produced documentary on the life and career of Roza Eskenazi. Top musical venues are widely dispersed around central Athens and the outer suburbs, from Votanikós, Gázi or Psyrrí to Exárhia and Neápoli. Athens by night is still full of music that lifts the spirits and lasts till morning. And for those fortunate enough to catch a concert by a star performer, discover a good if little-known *rebétika* group performing in a small club, or stumble on a wedding in the mountains of Crete, the splendid, haunting music that once filled the air of Greece may still set the night on fire.

RELIGIOUS FESTIVALS

Greek religious festivals – and there are many – celebrate saints' days and other events in the religious calendar with devotion and high spirits.

Greek island life is punctuated throughout the year by saints' days and religious festivals or *panigýria*. As there are around 300 saints in the Orthodox calendar, there is an excuse for a party most days of the year.

Easter is the most important festival of the year. It's a great time to visit, with traditional services marking the Resurrection everywhere from humble chapels to mighty monasteries. Colourful, noisy and potentially dangerous – on Kálymnos they throw dynamite to ensure Christ has truly risen – it's like Firework Night and Christmas rolled into one.

During Holy Week, or *Megáli Evdomáda*, churches are festooned in purple ribbons and velvet. On Maundy Thursday, monks on Pátmos re-enact the washing of Christ's feet at the Last Supper, while that evening sees the moving Crucifixion liturgy. On Good Friday, the *Epitáfios*, or bier of Christ, is decorated by the women and paraded through the streets as sombre hymns are chanted.

On Easter Saturday evening, the church livery changes from purple to red-and-white. At midnight, everything is plunged in darkness as the priest lights the first candle from the holy flame, to represent the light of the world, and intones: *"Hristós anésti"* (Christ has risen). This is the signal for the congregation to light their candles. Families then break the Lenten fast with Easter soup made from the lamb's viscera and later play conkers with red-dyed eggs.

On Easter Sunday, there is great rejoicing as a lamb or kid is barbecued outdoors over charcoal, with the usual music and dancing. There are often parties on Easter Monday, and on some islands (especially Crete) an effigy of Judas is filled with fireworks and burned.

Saints' days are celebrated by panigýria (festivals) at hundreds of small chapels throughout the islands.

"Clean Monday" is the end of the pre-Lenten carnival, with exuberant celebrations on some islands, including kite-flying and flour fights.

Bishops lead the procession of Saint Gerasimos's silver casket to the monastery, Kefaloniá. The parade is accompanied by the singing of religious songs.

Priest blessing the bread, Síkinos.

CELEBRATING ALL YEAR ROUND

Greeks mix piety and pleasure with gusto for all their festivals, from the most important to the smallest fair. The biggest religious festival after Easter, the Dormition of the Virgin *(Kímisis tis Panagías)* on 15 August, draws Greeks home from all over the world.

Following a liturgy on the evening of the 14th, the icon of the deceased Virgin is solemnly processed through the streets, possibly while accompanying brass bands play dirges. There are communal celebrations afterwards, particularly spectacular in Kárpathos, with dazzling costumes, special dances and traditional songs.

Every month, there are festivals on the islands for everything from sponges to snakes, and national holidays like *Óhi* or "No Day" (28 October), with patriotic parades to mark the Greeks' emphatic refusal of Mussolini's surrender ultimatum.

Celebrations begin the night before feast days and everyone in the community takes part, from babies to grannies. Patron saints are honoured with services followed by barbecues, music and dance.

n Orthodox believer venerates the Holy icons at Skopje Cathedral during the Good Friday processions. On Good Friday the Orthodox church remembers the passions and the crucifixion of Jesus Christ. The following evening, believers gather in front of the churches around the country waiting for midnight, when the priests proclaim that "Christ is risen". The Macedonian Orthodox Church celebrates Easter according to the Julian calendar.

In Ólympos, the remote mountain village on Kárpathos, the eldest daughter, or kanakára, wears her traditional costume and dowry of gold coins for major festivals.

Ítar boys escort the procession of the Epitáfios in Thessaloníki.

FOOD AND DRINK

Simple recipes using seasonal, local ingredients is the key to Greek cuisine – but food for the Greeks is about more than just cooking and eating.

Starters of féta cheese and fava, which is made from puréed yellow peas and similar to pease pudding.

T*he cook sets before you a large tray on which are five small plates. One of these holds garlic, another a pair of sea-urchins, another a sweet wine soup, another ten cockles, the last a small piece of sturgeon. While I'm eating this, another is eating that; and while he is eating that, I have made away with this. What I want, good sir, is both the one and the other, but my wish is impossible. For I have neither five mouths nor five hands… – Athenaeus: The Deipnosophists*

The scene conjured up by Athenaeus in the quote describes the frustration Greeks, as well as tourists, often feel when they fail to taste all the dishes that are part of a *mezédes* spread. It is obviously an age-old problem, as the passage comes from a semi-fictitious Greek work of the 3rd century BC. Although pizza, hamburgers, *gýros* and the ubiquitous Greek salad can render modern Greek food banal, the age-old tradition of sharing many small dishes – as prelude to a meal or the meal itself – lives on.

Greeks were essentially vegetarian until about the mid-20th century, not by choice but because it was not possible to pasture large herds and provide meat for everybody. The traditional Greek diet, frugal yet delicious, was based on the agricultural produce of each region: vegetables, weeds and leafy greens – foraged from the hills or cultivated – and grains, mainly in the form of home-made bread. Olive oil was the principal fat used, while olives, beans and other legumes, local cheeses and yogurt were everyday staples.

Only occasionally was the diet enriched with some fresh or cured fish, or with meat. Meat was a rare, festive dish, consumed on Sundays, at the major festivals of Easter and Christmas, as well as on important family feasts. But after the mid-1960s, as the country became more affluent, meat gradually took on a significant role at the Greek table. Around that time, the Greek demographic structure also changed.

Some four out of 10 middle-aged Greeks now living in big cities originally came from agricultural areas. They relocated in the last 50 years or so, bringing with them the cooking and culinary habits of their mothers and grandmothers. Although well settled in the urban environment, most of them have kept their ancestors' village homes and visit them on long weekends, during the summer holidays, as well as at Christmas and Easter. Many have also kept much of their land, so it is still common for Greek families to produce the olive oil they consume; about 18kg (40lbs) per person each year. People who do not produce it themselves buy it from friends who have a surplus.

Along with olive oil, *psomí* (bread) was the basic staple food up until the mid-1960s, as it used to be in ancient and Byzantine times. Although Greeks can now afford a great variety of foods, they still consume enormous quantities of bread. Traditional breads are often made with a combination of wheat, barley and sometimes maize flour, using sour old-dough starter. Barley grows easily with

well for many months, they are easy to carry in the field and are the ideal food for sailors. Moreover, baked every two or three months, they made efficient use of oven heat, as wood is scarce on most islands.

Outside influences

In its long history, Greece has been subjected to many culinary influences. The Venetians and Genoese, who ruled much of the country during the Middle Ages, and later the Ottoman Turks, who ruled northern Greece and Crete up until the early 1900s, have all left their marks on

For a taste of real Greek cooking, follow the locals to backstreet tavernas.

An indication that Greeks still take their religious fasts seriously can be found in the branches of McDonald's in Greece, where special Lenten menus are offered during these periods.

only spring rainfall in mountainous southern Greece and on the islands, so it has been a staple for centuries. Today, in Crete and other islands *paximádia* (rusks) – slices of twice-baked and completely dry barley bread which only need to be briefly soaked in water to soften – are still very popular. *Paximádia* are perfectly suited to traditional lifestyles: they keep

Greek cooking; since then, the cuisine brought by Asia Minor refugees has been of paramount importance. But the most important factor in shaping people's eating habits was the rules of the Greek Orthodox Church. Even non-religious Greeks sometimes abstain from foods deriving from animals – meat, dairy products and eggs – during the fasting periods that precede Easter, Christmas and 15 August. This is the reason why many traditional dishes such as *gemistá* (stuffed vegetables), *yaprákia* or *dolmádes* (stuffed grape or cabbage leaves), *píttes* (filo-wrapped pies) come in two versions: one with meat and/or cheese, and one without, often called *gialantzí* ("liar's" *dolmádes*, ie fake, meatless) for fasting days.

Festival food

Numerous religious holidays are scattered throughout the year. Many have evolved from ancient celebrations and are often closely related to the seasons and the lunar calendar. Easter, Greece's most important feast, seems to have its roots in the agricultural spring festivals of antiquity. Celebrated in the open country, amid fragrant herbs and multicoloured flowers, the Easter table features succulent spit-roasted baby lamb or kid – at the right age for slaughter in spring – and salads of wild greens, tender raw artichokes

The informal tavern is the most common form of eatery.

and fresh fava beans. *Magirítsa*, a delicious soup made with chopped lamb's innards, spring onions and dill, with a tart egg-and-lemon sauce, is eaten during the small hours of Easter Sunday, after the midnight Resurrection Mass. Traditional Easter sweets are stuffed with *myzíthra*, a generic name for the various regional creamy fresh cheeses of the season, usually made with a combination of goat's and sheep's milk.

Pork is associated with Christmas and New Year, as pig slaughtering and curing is done from October onwards. Fish is consumed on 25 March, and always at meals that follow funerals. Despite its many islands, fish and seafood has never been plentiful enough to become

an everyday food in Greece, not even for those who live by the sea. The fish and seafood of the Aegean is delicious but scarce, and the best fish islanders manage to catch is sold to the big cities for much-needed cash.

Dining out

Despite its rich culinary heritage, Greece has a very recent restaurant tradition and the finest *magirevtá* (cooked dishes) are still best savoured in the home. People eat lunch at around 3pm and dinner at around 9pm – in the summer at around 10pm or even later. Breakfast is usually just a cup of coffee and a biscuit. Wine accompanies the meals, especially dinner, and a salad of fresh, raw or blanched seasonal vegetables or greens is always part of the everyday menu. Seasonal fruits are the most common dessert. Sweets were originally part of the festive table but now tend to be eaten daily, while meat (until the recent economic crisis) had also become an almost everyday staple.

Traditionally, two kinds of restaurants attract the Greeks when they want to entertain their families and friends. A *psistariá* (grill house) offers charcoal-grilled meat (baby lamb, kid, pork, veal and chicken), often by weight. *Psarotavérnes* (fish taverns) are scattered all over the shoreline, on the islands and the mainland. Fresh fish and seafood, the catch of the day, is grilled or fried according to the customer's choice. Both meat and fish taverns offer a few appetisers and seasonal salads.

Frugal, ingenious Greek cooks have learned to complement a few simple ingredients with rice, potatoes, some cheese and a few pieces of meat to create dishes that dieticians now hold up as models of the famously healthy Mediterranean diet. The irony is that modern Greeks, in their quest to distance themselves from their poverty-stricken past, have enthusiastically forsaken this traditional fare and adopted the unhealthy eating habits of northern Europeans and Americans.

Local foods

Many traditional foods had nearly disappeared when, in the mid-1990s, a trend towards updated homestyle cooking began to emerge in Athens and gradually all over the country. Visitors should ask for regional specialities – for example, *píttes* (cheese- or herb-stuffed turnovers) in Epirus; *trahanás* soup (pasta made with yogurt and sourdough) all over the mainland; *lahano dolmádes* (stuffed cabbage leaves) or local *loukánika* (sausages) almost everywhere; and *loúza* or *lóza* (pork loin macerated in wine and air-dried or smoked) in the Cyclades. Look out, too, for thyme honey on small, unforested islands, and *pastéli* (a sesame seed and honey sweet), home-cured caper greens, and wonderful local shepherd's cheeses, often just called *tyráki* (small cheese).

In the Cyclades and the Dodecanese, goat's and sheep's milk cheeses are a real treat, but

> Greek food traditionally follows the seasons. Cooks do not make gemistá (stuffed tomatoes and peppers) or melitzanosaláta (aubergine dip) in the winter, even though these vegetables are now available all year round.

they seldom travel further than their island of origin. Greece is finally beginning to capitalise on its delicious artisan foods, with fancy delis in the largest cities and speciality boutiques on many tourist islands. There are now even a few truffle *(troúfa)* reserves scattered across the mainland – Greek beech and oak forests are perfect for their culture.

Greek wines

Some of the most admired wines in antiquity were produced in Greece. Oar-powered cargo ships carried clay amphoras filled with the precious liquid to ports and markets all over the Mediterranean. Yet if we were to try these wines today, we would probably find them undrinkable. They were mainly sweet, and contained flavourings and herbs such as thyme, mint and even cinnamon. Seawater and pieces of pine bark were also added as preservatives, to keep the wine from turning sour.

The Byzantines continued to add resin to some wines. A more refined legacy of this is modern *retsína*, a white wine laced with Aleppo pine resin. *Retsína* was widely consumed until the mid-1970s. But as the new generation of quality Greek wines gradually spread, its consumption declined sharply. Today, many medium-sized and small wineries, employing modern techniques and talented oenologists,

combine indigenous and imported grape varieties to produce quality wines.

Greek vineyards are diverse, following the contours of the country's morphology. Omnipresent hills and mountains divide the land into small regions, each with its own microclimate. Many indigenous grape varieties – many of which existed also in antiquity – are grown, which acquire different characteristics in each region. According to EU regulations and Greek law, the system of controlled appellations of origin (AOC) matches the Greek varieties to the areas where the best of their kind is tra-

Grilled octopus makes for an affordable seafood meal.

ditionally produced. But you will also find exceptional regional wines outside of these AOC classifications.

Northern Greece

Macedonia, perhaps the most rewarding mainland wine region, is the home of the *xinómavro* grape, which produces well-loved, robust red wines. Naoussa is the best-known example, while Amyndeon, made from the same grape, is a lighter red and can also be a pleasant still or sparkling rosé. *Xinómavro* combined with the **n**egóska variety – another Macedonian native – makes Goumenissa, a meaty red. By itself, *negóska* yields a soft red. Extensive vineyards on the central peninsula of Halkidikí produce the Côtes de Meliton wines, both white and red, from a combination of French (Cabernet Sauvignon and Cabernet Franc) and Greek varieties. The Dráma region is not yet an AOC, but the two Lazaridi wineries make upmarket wines based on Sauvignon Blanc and Sémillon for whites, and Cabernet Sauvignon plus Merlot for reds.

In Epirus, the most isolated, mountainous region of northwestern Greece, Zitsa, a fresh, fruity, often sparkling white is produced from the *débina* variety. In the valley below Métsovo, Katöï, a fine, rich red, is made from imported

retsína. Matsa in Kántza is one of the best Attic vineyards, known for fine white wines based on *malagouziá* grapes, native to western Greece.

In the northeastern Peloponnese, Nemea, made from *aïgiorgítiko* grapes, is one of the most versatile Greek reds. Mantineia, a delicate aromatic white wine, is produced at vineyards north of Trípoli, mostly from *moskhofílero* grapes. The Pátra area yields dry and sweet white and red wines. Muscat of Patras and Muscat of Rio as well as the dark Mavrodáfni (Mavrodaphne) are three well-loved sweet dessert wines.

Greek wine producers use both indigenous and imported grape varieties.

Cabernet Sauvignon vines. For maps and details of all northern-Greek Wine Roads, visit www.wineroads.gr.

Thessaly produces two distinguished wines. Rapsani vintners make a red with a fine bouquet, from *xinómavro*, *stavrotó* and *krasáto* grapes grown on the southeastern slopes of Mount Olympos. Anhíalos, on the shores of Pagasitikos, has a fresh white wine, made from a blend of *savatianó* and *rodítis* grapes.

Central Greece and Peloponnese

Attica, the region around Athens (not an AOC region), nonetheless produces very interesting wines. The main variety here is *savatianó*, traditionally used for the production of

Some scholars believe that medieval Monemvasiá used to be where malmsey wine (called also malvasia or malvoisie) was made. Others claim that this wine, mentioned by Shakespeare, was actually produced in Crete, with the boats transporting it merely stopping at Monemvasiá on their way north. This magnificent sweet white is no longer made in Greece, but apparently resembled madeira.

The islands

On the island of Límnos, a quaffable white wine is produced from Alexandrian Muscat grapes, while the *limnió* variety, mentioned by Aristotle, produces light, fragrant red wines. Lésvos boasts the all-organic Methymeos winery in the remote village of Hídira, producing superior reds and whites from a local heirloom type of grape, grown in a volcanic caldera. In northeastern Híos, the Ariousos winery has recently revived the ancient red grape varieties *krasséro* and *agianítis* in a line of quality reds, as well as more conventional whites. Vineyards on Sámos, a mountainous island, are planted on terraced hills, rising to 800 metres (2,625ft); Ageri is the best-value label of dry white wine here, made from *moskháto* grapes, *fokianós* and *rítinos* grapes are the source of easy-drinking rosé, while the local fortified dessert wines, in

The ubiquitous oúzo.

four grades, are world famous. Rhodes produces dry whites mainly from *athíri* grapes, and dry reds made chiefly from *mandilariá* grapes, as well as sparkling wines of middling quality.

Crete produces 20 percent of Greek wines. Although far to the south, the cool etesian winds never let the temperature rise much, and lofty Mt Psilorítis keeps hot African winds from reaching the northern slopes where most vines are cultivated. Arhánes and Pezá are two appellations of dry red made from *kotsifáli* and *mandilariá* grapes. Another red, Dafnés, is made from the ancient grape liátiko. A dry red made from *liátiko* and *mandilariá*, and a very popular fruity white mostly from *vilána* grapes, comprise the AOC of Sitía.

Santoríni, the spectacular volcanic island, produces lovely white wines made from *asýrtiko* or aidáni grapes, as well as good reds from the *mandilariá* and *mavrotrágano* varieties. To guard their vines from the strong etesian winds, local growers shape their branches into intricate basket shapes, inside which the grapes grow. *Vi(n)sánto* is a marvellous fortified sweet wine made from partly sun-dried white grapes. Similar sweet wines, often called *liastó*, are produced throughout the Cyclades. On Páros, sprawling vines produce a red with dark colour and a characteristic bouquet, made from *mandilariá*, *savatianó* and *monemvasiá* grapes (the latter unrelated to the medieval malmsey-producing grape).

Corfu, Zákynthos and Levkáda produce interesting wines, but only Robóla from Kefalloniá, a dry white from the eponymous grapes, is an AOC.

FIRE WATER: OÚZO AND OTHER SPIRITS

The most popular Greek drink, traditionally served with *mezédes* is undoubtedly *oúzo*, produced across the country. Many people enjoy it so much on holiday they take a bottle home, only to find the pleasure doesn't travel well; it's not the same without the fierce Greek sunshine, a beautiful beach and a plate of Greek olives.

Only *oúzo* made in Greece can bear that name according to EU regulations. *Oúzo* is made from distilled grape-pressings left after the wine-making process, and takes its flavour from anise, fennel seeds and other spices.

Some people say the best *oúzo* is from Lésvos;

others will insist that the *oúzo* of Tyrnávos, Thessaly, or that of Híos, is superior. In Híos, there also exists *mastíha*, a sweeter version of *oúzo* that is flavoured exclusively with mastic, which is the aromatic sap of the mastic bushes that grow on the island.

Another popular strong alcoholic drink, akin to Italian *grappa*, is made from the distillation of grapeskins and stems. This is called *tsípouro* in central and northern Greece and *rakí* or *tsikoudiá* in Crete, where it is recommended as a universal panacea. On Rhodes and Sámos, a nearly identical distilled clear spirit is called *soúma*.

ART AND ARCHITECTURE

The Classical, Hellenistic, Roman and Byzantine
eras left Greece with an artistic heritage that
has inspired later artists and architects.

Few countries have influenced Western art
more than Ancient Greece. But because
of its geographical position, Greece itself
has been subjected to many influences. The origins of Greek art lay in Neolithic Anatolia, the
Middle East and Egypt. Greece, in turn, influenced Rome, and thus Western Europe and the
Byzantine world. Absorbed into the Turkish
Ottoman Empire for 500 years, on liberation
Greece was on the receiving end of Western
influences, often mixed with its Byzantine heritage. The region's fine marbles, good clays and
early exploitation of Cypriot copper ensured an
enduring artistic gift.

The Bronze Age

The earliest art is that of the Cyclades. Neolithic
and Bronze Age cultures developed complex
settlements, but the most characteristic artefacts
are the Cycladic idols, placed for unknown
purposes with early burials. Here, the Greek
love of idealised, perfect forms is already
apparent. Facial details, save for relief noses,
were probably painted on.

By 2300 BC, Minoan civilisation had
emerged fully in Crete and on neighbouring
Santoríni, characterised by palace complexes
such as Knossos and Phaistos, and the town at
Akrotíri. Architecture was labyrinthine, of stone
with plastered and frescoed walls, and looked
inwards onto courtyards which were venues for
elaborate games, including bull-leaping as represented in paint and ivory figures.

The sacred bull – suggested by the twin
horn symbol – was represented in terracotta,
and as rhytons (drinking vessels) of gold or
soapstone. The frescoed composite plants
and chariots pulled by winged beasts, and the
sculpted flounced dress of the snake goddess, a

The Lion Gate, Mycenae.

protective deity, demonstrated Mesopotamian
influence. Sea and land creatures – shells, octopuses, bees – inspired vase decoration and jewellery. The double-headed axe, used as a motif,
was a sacred symbol.

The peaceable, sophisticated Minoan culture
declined around 1450 BC as the Myceneans
of the mainland gained ascendancy. Warlike
and great sea traders, they adopted Minoan
motifs such as wasp-waisted costumes and
the downward tapering column seen on the
Lion Gate at Mycenae (*c.*1600 BC). This entry
to the citadel/palace is the first large-scale
European sculpture, relying on a corbelled
arch technique also used for the Cyclopean-
scale vaulted chambers at Tiryns, and more

adventurously for tholos ("beehive") tombs, the most impressive of which is the Treasury of Atreus (*c.*1375 BC) at Mycenae, a 15-metre (49-ft) span dome with side chamber. Earlier shaft graves have revealed elaborate niello-inlaid bronze daggers, lion and bull-head rhytons, and the remarkable, haunting and somewhat heraldic gold masks placed over the faces of the dead.

Geometric and Archaic art

Iron Age peoples entered Greece *c.*1120 BC: Mycenaean society finished and the so-called

standing figures were carved, perhaps as personifications of gods, as grave markers, or as worshipper figures. Early *kouroi* demonstrated Egyptian influence in their stance and braided hair. Over time, the males become less anatomically stylised and the girls' clothing become looser; smiles were depicted, and the feel was for naturalism. These statues represented ideal figures shown in the prime of life: in time, the depiction of the ideal came closer to reality, but the sense of idealisation was never lost.

Central to this concept was harmonic proportion. In the evolution of the temple, a

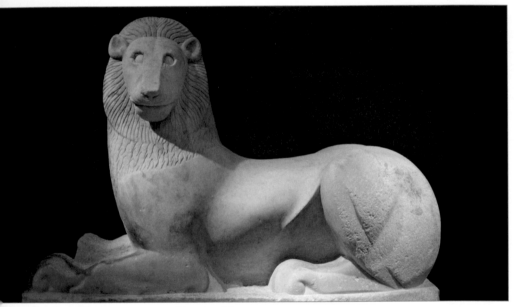

Sphinx, Kerameikos Cemetery museum, 6th century BC.

Dark Ages, preceding the Geometric period, ensued until about 900 BC. Few Geometric artefacts except pottery vessels survive. Decorated with geometric horizontal banding, including spirals akin to Minoan and Mycenaean work, and also the "Greek key" (properly known as the meander pattern), these were often associated with burials. Some depict funerary processions with geometrised figures; others assumed anthropomorphic shapes. From *c.*850 BC, small figurines of seated goddesses, charioteers, animals and warriors appeared in bronze, ivory and ceramic.

The Archaic period, *c.*750–490 BC, was one of rapid development. In sculpture, large *kouroi* (nude male) and *korai* (draped female)

perfectly balanced system of horizontals and verticals developed. Archaic temples followed the Doric form: it was sturdy (likened to a man), with sharply fluted columns that had simple capitals and no base. These carried an entablature featuring square metope panels between vertical triglyph mouldings. The form of a colonnaded, box-like structure as a "home" for the deity, often sited on a hilltop, created a perfect backdrop for the open-air ceremonies.

Classical art

The subsequent Classical period, 490–336 BC, saw further rapid developments. Although known by report, scarcely any early Greek paintings survive: ceramic decoration gives some clues to its qualities. Archaic vase-painting had been dominated initially by a Corinthian "orientalising" style of fabulous beasts, and then by a vigorous Athenian style of figurative ware in which black figures were placed against the red of the pot (black-figure ware). Around 500 BC, a reversal of the process yielded red-figure ware, in which a finer linearism captured greater detail and movement, enhanced by the development of foreshortening and eventually rudimentary perspective.

The greater structural strength of bronze when cast hollow led to more adventurous

> Early writers tell of panel paintings of exact mimicry of nature by the masters Zeuxis and Apelles. In sculpture, too, much has been lost, and many works are now known only through Roman marble copies of lost bronzes.

poses of movement, as with the *Poseidon* (or Zeus) recovered from the sea off Évia in 1928. The sculptor Polykleitos's *Doryphoros* (Javelin thrower) was originally in bronze. In this, he realised *controposto* – the establishment of convincing weight distribution in a figure.

Late Classical sculpture saw the emergence of a more private attitude to the figure, particularly in portraiture and the self-involved statues of Praxiteles; notably his *Knidian Aphrodite* and the *Hermes with the infant Dionysos*. The former introduced the nude female figure, previously rare. A feminine architectural theme was provided by the more slender and elegant Ionic style of temple, where the spiral volutes of the capitals were equated to a girl's curling hair. In these temples, the entablature rejects the Doric metopes and triglyphs, but might include a continuously sculpted frieze section. After 370 BC, a more forceful sculptural manner emerged with Skopas of Paros. His active military reliefs foreshadowed the dynamic work of Alexander the Great's favoured sculptor, Lykippos, whose *Apoxyomenos* (Sweat-scraper) was given a tight muscularity and the smaller proportioned head of an aggressive figure.

Hellenistic art

Alexander's accession in 336 BC, marking the beginning of the Hellenistic era, was followed by the rapid expansion of the Greek Empire:

his capital was established at Babylon, and the centres of artistic production tended to move eastwards, particularly to Anatolia. Pergamon was especially important sculpturally during the period 250–160 BC. In sculpture, emphasis was put on movement, as in the *Nike of Samothrace* (now in the Louvre in Paris), realism, the display of emotion and more complex poses. From this period survive many mass-produced ceramic figures of gods, dancing figures and satyrs, often known as Tanagra figures after the town in Boeotia. During this luxury-loving age, the continuance of refined goldwork for jewel-

Vase excavated at Elefsína.

lery, and filigree and leaf diadems was matched by the remarkable Derveni krater, a copper-alloy *repoussée* wine vase used as a cinerary urn despite its Dionysiac scenes.

In architecture, a new, complex quality was introduced with the foliate Corinthian column capital, first used at the Choragic monument to Lysikratos, Athens, in 336 BC. The Corinthian order was often used on a gigantic scale, as in the Temple of Olympian Zeus, Athens, c.170 BC. Houses appear to have been simple structures, judging from painted Thracian tomb chests preserved in the Thessaloníki Archaeological Museum.

The absorption of Greece by Rome after 146 BC reaffirmed Roman admiration and development of Greek forms of art and architecture. Indeed, apart from sculptures, a few larger episodes such as the mosaic *Battle of Isos* (Pompeii, *c.*50 BC) are known through their Roman copies. The practical bent of the Romans emphasised physically truthful portraiture and its use as propaganda (see the *Augustus* from Athens's Roman agora), and hero worship as with the bust of *Antinoös* from Pátra. Roman forms of arched architecture were adopted, as was a preference for sumptuous palaces. The surviving Galerius Gateway, AD 298–303, at Thessaloníki con-

an art of symbolism, and because of a fear of idolatry, sculpture in the round became rare, as did the nude; figures thus became defined by their drapery. Many artefacts of this mystic art were produced in Byzantium and exported to the Balkans. Levantine motifs, particularly from silks, were mixed with Roman ones in an art that emphasised richness and sophistication, religiosity and secularity, although little survives of the latter type.

Architecturally, two forms of church emerged alongside the Roman basilica form of nave, aisles and apse: one, the central

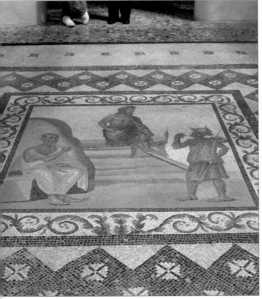

Mosaic depicting the arrival of Asklepios, god of healing, on Kós, with Hippocrates to the left; Kós Archaeological Museum.

Corinthian columns on the Temple of Olympian Zeus, Athens.

veys something of their splendour: its reliefs reflect the Roman-Hellenic interest in illusionism and narrative.

Christianity and Byzantium

That Christian communities were quickly established in Greece is demonstrated by St Paul's letters to the Corinthians and Thessalonians. Constantine the Great's decision to make Byzantium (modern İstanbul) his capital in 330, coupled with his advocacy of Christianity (though he himself did not convert until on his deathbed), determined the future direction of Greek religion and what is known as Byzantine art. Christianity led to

PHEIDIAS THE GREAT

From 447 to 432 BC, Pheidias mastered the depiction of narrative schemes and vigorous action in his reliefs and statues for the Temple of Zeus at Olympia and the Parthenon in Athens. The Parthenon reliefs were brightly painted. For both temples, Pheidias created gigantic divine statues of ivory and gold, now lost. A perfect blend of naturalism with idealism had been achieved, well seen in the *Nike adjusting her sandal* (Temple of Nike Apteros, Athens Acropolis). The narrative interest had a parallel in dramas and the creation of semicircular theatres moulded from the contours of the land.

domed space, sometimes over an octagon (as at Ósios Loukás), and the other a cruciform domed space (such as Ágii Apóstoli, Athens). In these, the dome was often emphasised by the image of almighty Christ giving his blessing (the Pandokrátor), a fitting symbol as one took communion below.

Many paintings were destroyed during the Iconoclastic crisis of 726–843, when the validity of figural imagery was challenged. However, Néa Móni on Híos has good mosaics from *c.* 1050, and Mystrás has fine 13th- and 14th-century paintings. Other devotional

> *Surviving decoration is often mosaics of pigmented glass tesserae, usually implanted with gold leaf, that were set at slight angles so that in the flickering candlelight the images shimmered.*

works were relief-carved ivory codex (book) covers, boxes and *pyxes*; but most characteristic were icons (tempera- or occasionally encaustic-painted panels of saints). These were initially domestic and often for women at home, but were later placed on pillars flanking the space to the altar. In turn, more icons were added to the *témblon* or barrier before the altar, and in time they multiplied to create an iconostasis or screen separating nave from chancel and congregation from clergy (as with the fine example found in Megálou Meteórou monastery). An arrangement of a central Christ flanked by Mary and St John the Baptist, Saints Peter and Paul and other apostles and saints in order of importance became known as the Great Deisis. Such screens greatly enhanced the mysticism of the Orthodox Church, which formally dates from the Great Schism of 1054.

Byzantine culture was increasingly under threat, first from Islam but also from the West, particularly its former allies, Venice and Genoa. However, it did experience an artistic revival in manuscripts and the paintings at Mystrás, which show a greater interest in plasticity, under the Palaeologos dynasty (1261–1453).

The capture of Byzantium by the Ottoman Turks in 1453 meant Greece became nominally part of the Islamic world, although from as early as 1204, the Ionian and some of the

Aegean Islands, the Dodecanese, Crete and several mainland cities were ruled by Venice, Genoa and other Western powers (see page 48). In consequence, Venetian and Frankish influence was felt in architecture, notably on the Peloponnese, the northeast Aegean islands, the Cyclades and on Crete, in both military and domestic architecture. After 1453, many refugee painters emigrated to the Venetian-held Ionian Islands, Crete or Venice itself, so Venetian influence is evident in the 16th- and 17th-century icon-painting of Mihaïl Damaskinos, Emmanuel Tzanes and Theodoros Poulakis.

Mosaic from the Monastery of the Panagía, Ýdra.

Art under the Ottomans

Ottoman rule in Greece allowed religious tolerance, but the Islamic scepticism of figurative imagery was nevertheless felt, particularly in larger public works. Although icon-painting persisted, more emphasis was put on the decorative arts in which Eastern and Western influences are found, especially in textiles – including kilims – jewellery and metalwork (lamps, platters and other domestic utensils). Often distinct, lively regional and island vernacular styles are apparent, particularly in embroidery.

Domestic architecture favoured timber-panelled rooms which stylistically linked traditions from İstanbul with European precedents. The emigration of many Greeks in all directions, known as the diaspora, helped fuse many influences into Greek art. One notable example is that of Greek craftsmen working at İznik on ceramic ware with Grecian subject matter. Many domed Ottoman civic buildings have been destroyed, but numerous others survive, especially in regions united with Greece after 1881. These include the *bezesténi* (covered bazaar), two baths and several mosques in Thessaloníki, a hammam and three mosques in Rhodes, plus scattered mosques, baths and ornate fountains in Ioánnina, Tríkala, Lárissa, Návplio, Halkída, Véria,

> Crete's most famous painter is Domenikos Theotokopoulos, whose Adoration of the Magi (Benáki Museum, Athens) shows his work as an icon painter before his move to Venice and later to Spain – where he was known as El Greco.

independence in 1830. A Bavarian prince was appointed king and it is therefore Germanic influence, particularly from Karl Friedrich Schinkel, that dominates neoclassical archi-

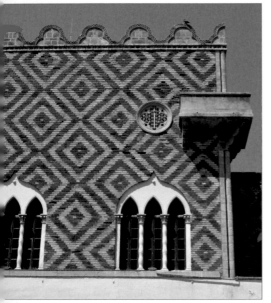

The Italian-style Governor's House in Rhodes New Town.

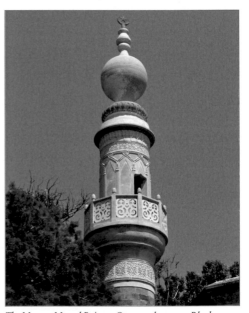

The Mosque Murad Reis, an Ottoman legacy on Rhodes.

Kós, Crete, Lésvos and Híos. In the last three locales, hammams and mosques have been restored for use as event venues.

Neoclassicism

Roman Pompeii, discovered in 1763, provoked a renewed interest in antiquity, and the German scholar Johann Joachim Winckelmann suggested that Greek art was superior to Roman. Consequently, a pro-Hellenic movement arose in Western Europe which, allied to growing nationalist aspirations, led to a resurgence of interest in Classical Greece (often known as neoclassicism) which dominated the arts during and after the War of Independence of 1821–28 and full

tecture – especially in Athens, the capital from 1834.

Monumental, largely Ionic structures that reflect mainstream European neoclassicism are Friedrich Von Gärtner's Royal Palace (1835–43), and the work of two Danish architects, Christian Hansen's National Capodistrian University (1837) and Theophilus Hansen's National Library (1888–91) and Academy (1856–85), the Observatory (1842) and the Záppio (1874–88). Ernst Ziller, though belonging to the next wave of immigrant architects, contributed the Numismatic Museum (originally the Schliemann residence: 1878–80), the Presidential Mansion (1891–97) and many other landmark buildings across Greece.

Native architects adopted the style, notably Lysandros Kaftantzoglou (Athens Technical University) and Stamatis Kleanthis, Schinkel's student. The latter built the neoclassical Wortheim house (Athens, 1843) and also the Renaissance-revival-style mansion of the Duchess of Plaisance, now part of the Byzantine Museum (Athens, 1840–48). This eclectic attitude gained pace and, unsurprisingly, Byzantine adaptations found favour, as with Kaftantzoglou's Athens Eye Clinic, and as late as 1933 with the church of Ágios Konstandínos, by Aristotelis Zahos, at Vólos.

(1873, both in the National Gallery in Athens). Given the dominance of German tutors at the Royal School of Fine Arts, Teutonic concepts affected students like the Tiniot Lazaros Fytalis, whose *Shepherd* (1856, National Gallery) owes something to Schadow. Ioannis Vitsaris's Pavlopoulos Tomb (1890, Athens Próto Nekrotafío) demonstrated interest in western Baroque, while Kostas Demetriades's *Male Figure* (1910, National Gallery) picked up contemporary naturalist tendencies.

In painting, portraiture – at first somewhat naïve – and subject painting took off follow-

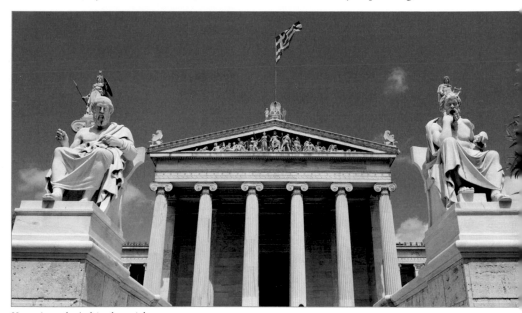

Hansen's neoclassical Academy, Athens.

Scores of houses composed as assemblages of geometric forms with classical detailing and an overall symmetry show the popularity of the neoclassical style.

Just as architecture paralleled the mainstream European patterns, so too did painting and sculpture. Sculpture, marginalised during the Byzantine and Ottoman years, was revived, initially in the Classical taste, especially at Tínos where a school of decorative carving flourished. The greatest exponent of this school was Yannoulis Chalepas, celebrated for his *Oréa Kimoméni (Sleeping Beauty)* Grave Monument (1877) in Athens' Próto Nekrotafío (First Cemetery). Other examples are the Corfiot Pavlos Prosalentis's *Plato* (1815), or Leonidas Drosis's *Penelope*

ing independence, thus supplementing the Venetian-influenced religious works that had been popular in the Ionian Islands in the 18th century, such as Panagiotis Doxaras' *Birth of the Virgin* (Zákynthos Museum), as well as his painted ceiling for the Ágios Spyrídon church in Corfu.

Events of the 1821–28 battles provided many dramatic paintings with a romantic flavour and occasional religious overtones, such as Theodoros Vryzakis's *Exodus from Mesolóngi* (1853, National Gallery). Greek life was also celebrated, as in the Munich-trained Nikolaos Gyzis's *Children's Betrothal* (1877, National Gallery) or Nikiforos Lytras's *The Dirge on the Isle of Psará* (pre-1888). Both artists were also attracted to Orientalist subjects, while Gyzis (1842–1901) had a marked predilection in later years for symbolism and mysticism. By the late 19th century, other artists were picking up on new subjects, landscape and portraiture (Polychronis Lembesis) and still life (Périclès Pantazis), while others fell under the spell of Impressionism and its offshoots – for example, Symeon Savvides's Boats on the Bosphorus (1903, National Gallery).

The 20th century

Greek artists of the 20th century broadly followed major European trends and readily accepted modernism, not least because many studied in Paris or Germany. (An important exception was the neo-Byzantinist Photis Kontoglou, who, although well-travelled in Europe and Africa, remained rooted in Orthodox tradition.) However, where most progressive Western developments occurred before 1930, Greek modernist artists were latecomers; consequently, in international terms much appears derivative.

Elements of Cubism appear in the paintings of Kostantinos Parthenis, and of Nikos Hadjikyriakos-Gikas, for example *Athenian*

> A key figure in post-war architecture was Emmanouel Vourekas, responsible for the landmark Hilton Hotel on Vassilís Sofías, which Conrad Hilton considered the most beautiful of the 53 in his chain.

Houses (1927–28); in *Sky* of 1966, Gikas touches on futurism (both pictures are in the National Gallery). Surrealist imagery akin to Giorgio de Chirico surfaced with Nikos Engonopoulos (*Poet and Muse*, 1938, National Gallery), and persisted in later artists such as Christos Karas (*Three Graces*, 1974, National Gallery). Perhaps more successful was Ioannis Tsarouhis's interpretation of Matisse's linearism, as in Youth in an Overcoat (1937, National Gallery), also seen in Yiannis Moralis's figurative work of the 1940s and 1950s (as in *Figure*, 1951, National Gallery). Moralis's classicist realism was typical of much painting produced during the dictatorship; sometimes painterly as with Panagiotis Tetsis, or linear with Giorgos Mavroïdis. Such work can feel

more truly Greek than the experiments with abstraction and recent conceptual and postmodernist art.

Sculptors of the early 20th century were likewise often trained in Paris. Consequently, the impact of Maillol is felt in Michael Tombros's *Fat Woman* (1926, National Gallery), and Despiau in Bella Raftopoulou's *Sculpture* (1932, National Gallery). These matched an interwar concern for the figure while embracing some abstraction, a trend that lingered into the 1950s and 1960s with Georgios Kastriotis's enchanting *Dance* (1953, National

Farewell at Sounio, Theodoros Vryzakis.

Gallery), and Yannis Pappas's *Male Figure* (1965, artist's collection). But generally, from 1949, abstraction and the international style tended to prevail. Kostas Koulentianos's *Tree* (1988, Athens, Portalakes collection) reflected the spirit of Chadwick; Takis's *Light Signals* (1985, Paris, private collection) revealed a dull post-modernist wit; and Hrysa Vardea's *New York Landscape* (1971–74, Athens, Mihalarias collection) used light intriguingly but in a formally predictable presentation.

In architecture the eclecticism that persisted into the 1930s extended to vernacular forms. Not just with Zahos, who drew inspiration from Macedonian and Aegean traditional building, but also Dimitris Pikionis who, with a greater eye for functionalism, came closer to modernism in his Pefkákia School (1933, Athens), and as a landscape architect designed the approach zone to the Acropolis during the 1950s. Zahos was also in part responsible for the rebuilding of Thessaloníki following the fire of 1917. True modernism was introduced with buildings on Híos by the Bauhaus-trained Ioannis Despotopoulos, aka Jan Despo; P Mihaïlidis, who worked with Le Corbusier; and Patroklos Karantinos who studied under French pioneer Auguste Perret, and then worked on the

Athens School of Music (1976); the Museum of Cycladic Art by Yiannis Vikelas (1986) with its serene interior; the solar-powered Mytaras house by Mihalis Souvatzidis (1985); the round Ágios Dimítrios School by Takis Zenetos (1976); and the sculptural Emmanouíl Benáki Street apartments by Atelier 66 (1972). These and others parallel the best architecture in any modern city.

Across the country, Aris Konstantinidis designed most of the Bauhaus-y late-1950s hotels of the government-owned Xenia chain, though surviving specimens are looking

Icon painter in his studio showroom.

ambitious ministry-led programme of new school buildings in the 1930s. Many Athenian blocks of flats were in the modernist manner, examples being those by Kyriakos Panagiotakos on Themistokléous (on the corner with Arahóvis), or those by Mihaïlidis and his colleague Thoukidydis Valentis on nearby Zaïmi (on the corner with Stournára).

The 1950s and 1960s rebuilding of the rapidly expanding cities saw, as in most countries, much shoddy and uninspired concrete building, both public and private. Nevertheless, certain structures, essentially to internationalist patterns, are particularly distinguished, especially around Athens: the Mégaro Mousikís (completed 1991); the

rather dated (if not derelict) unless privatised and revamped.

Into the 21st century

Nothing of comparable merit has emerged indigenously since the millennium; "facadism" – whereby buildings from the 1920s or 1930s are gutted and rebuilt inside, preserving only their original street profile – is big on Athens' main boulevards. The most iconic structures of the 2004 Olympic Games – the new roof of the OAKA stadium in Maroúsi, suspended by cables from giant swooping arches, and a couple of pedestrian suspension bridges relying on his trademark leaning single pylon – were the work of Spanish architect Santiago Calatrava.

Loggerhead turtles have lost their
nesting beaches to mass tourism.

FLORA AND FAUNA

As befits its wide variety of habitats, Greece
contains a great diversity of wildlife – including
some of Europe's last bears, wolves and jackals.

Greece is a land of tremendous ecological diversity, second in Europe, in this respect, only to the Iberian Peninsula. Biomes range from the temperate forests of the Píndos and Rodópi mountains in the north to the arid semi-desert of eastern Crete, or from the alpine vegetation on the bald, rocky upper slopes of mountains like Smólikas and Ólympos to the delta marshlands of Évros or even the dunes of islands such as Rhodes and Límnos. The current mosaic of landscapes and habitats is due to a combination of geography and the hand of man. Sited in the region where Europe butts up against Asia Minor, and only a short hop from Africa, Greece lies at an ecological crossroads.

Since Neolithic times (12,000 to 3,000 BC), man has wrought enormous changes on the landscape, clearing the primeval forests that once covered much of the country for fuel, shipbuilding, pasture and agriculture.

Habitats

Somewhat less than a quarter of Greece is now forested, with the largest tracts being in the north of the country, in the Rodópi Mountains and the Píndos ranges. Here you have a variety of oak, chestnut, beech and other broadleaf woodlands, with tracts of fir and pine forest more related to the Scandinavian north than to the Mediterranean south of Europe. Drive inland, north from Amfípolis on the coast of Central Macedonia, and you will pass through three of Europe's major vegetation zones in the space of 150km (90 miles): Mediterranean, Central European and Northern conifer, typified by trees like birch, Scots pine and Norway spruce.

Pastureland covers some 40 percent of the country, while around 30 percent is cultivated land. Areas where traditional agriculture is

Olive groves on Lésvos.

still practised are often rich in wildlife but, as elsewhere in Europe, labour-intensive traditional practices are declining. Terrain unsuited to modern agriculture is being abandoned to scrub, which means a decline in the diversity of habitat; where intensive modern agriculture has taken over, the use of herbicides, insecticides and fertilisers degrades the land from a wildlife perspective. There are, however, still plenty of mature olive groves which provide a good habitat for birds and insects.

One of Greece's most emblematic habitats is Mediterranean *maquis* – scrubby, drought-resistant vegetation that covers much of the mainland and islands. This consists of low trees like the glossy-leaved kermes oak (*Quercus coccifera*) and the holm oak (*Quercus suber*), with its thinner, tapering leaves; hardy shrubs like myrtle, arbutus, strawberry tree and bay; and the fragrant under layer of phrygana – plants like wild rosemary, oregano, lavender and thyme.

On river banks, you will notice trees like willows, oleanders, plane trees and poplars; species such as Australian eucalyptus have also been widely introduced. Eucalyptus thrives in the dry climate, but ecologists view the species with circumspection or downright hostility due to the amount of water these trees suck out from the soil and the damaging effects that has on the soil's pH value. Seaside tamarisks, which tolerate saline soil, are nearly as disdained by purists.

Wetlands are one of the most threatened habitats in Greece – three-quarters of the country's original wetlands have been lost, and many others are under extreme pressure, what with the heavy demands for water for agriculture and tourist usage as well as targeted drainage for construction. Nevertheless, Greece still possesses various wetlands of great importance, including many protected under the international Ramsar Convention: Pórto Lágos and lakes ranges Vistonís and Ismáris; the Néstos Delta; Lake Mikrí Préspa; the Misolóngi lagoons; Amvrakikós Gulf; lakes Vólvi and Korónia; Lake Kerkíni; the contiguous deltas of the Aliákmon, Axiós and Loudías rivers; Évros Delta; and the Kotýhi lagoons. These encompass a variety of habitats from river deltas, shallow lagoons, salt-marsh, swamps, reed beds and lakes.

Elusive mammals

Man's impact on the wildlife of Greece has been as significant as his impact on the land's habitats. The Barbary lions and Anatolian leopards known to the Ancient Greeks are long gone, hunted to extinction. And many of the most famous species that have survived are scarce and elusive – only the luckiest or most patient visitors will glimpse them in the wild.

In the mountains of northern Greece, you can still find areas of real wilderness, where some of the country's rarest land mammals are to be found. First among these are the continent's most southerly population of European brown bears (*Ursos arctos*), found in the North Píndos range along the border with Albania and FYROM, and also in the Rodópi Mountains of Eastern Macedonia and Thrace, close to the border with Bulgaria.

The conservation body ARCTUROS (www. arcturos.gr) – which has an information centre in Aktós, near Flórina – sets out to protect both the 150-odd animals that survive and the habitat they live in. Bears have been protected by law since 1969, but still suffer from illegal hunting and habitat destruction.

Wolves

The wolf is officially listed as "vulnerable": population estimates range from a few hundred to low thousands, mainly in the Rodópi Mountains along the border with Bulgaria, but also

The profusion of flowers and plants provides food for an equal profusion of insects.

along the borders with FYROM and Turkey, the Píndos mountains of west-central Greece, Kerkíni, Falakró and the Évros region. Wolves died out in the Peloponnese sometime between 1940 and 1970, and their survival elsewhere is precarious: they are threatened principally by habitat loss through logging, illegal hunting, road kills, hybridisation with dogs, and habitat disturbance through recreational tourism.

ARCTUROS works to protect Greece's population of wolves (*Canis lupus*) who have a sanctuary at Agrapídia. It is only fairly recently that wolves have enjoyed protected status – official bounties were paid until 1980 and, until 1991, they were still considered "vermin", which meant they could be hunted to protect livestock. Although wolves do take sheep from time to time, other ungulates – mainly red deer (*Cervus elaphus*), fallow deer (*Dama dama*) and roe deer (*Capreolus capreolus*) – form the preferred diet.

Wild sheep, otters, lynx

Other notable mountain mammals include three species of wild sheep: the nimble chamois (*Rupicapra rupicapra*), the European mouflon (*Ovis musimon*) and the Cretan wild goat/ibex (also known as the *agrími* or *krí-krí*; *Capra aegagrus cretica*), with its bearded chin and curved horns,

> A type of very small wild horse has lived on the island of Skýros since ancient times. There are fewer than 150 surviving pure-bred members of this unique breed.

most dramatic on the large males. This latter species, worshipped in antiquity, is now endangered, largely due to hunting. It is mainly found in the Gorge of Samariá national park in western Crete, but during the 1960s, breeding colonies were established on nearby islands like Día and Ágii Pándes in an effort to save it from extinction.

Otters (*Lutra lutra*) can still be found but are scarce, and your best chance of seeing them is in river-rich areas like Thessaly, Préspa or Víkos-Aóös in Epirus. Similarly elusive are members of the cat family – the endangered lynx (*Lynx lynx*), with its characteristic ear tufts, which survives in the Víkos-Aóös National Park; and the much smaller wild cat (*Felix sylvestris*) – resembling a large grey domestic cat, with black stripes and a bushy tail – which are found in a variety of habitats on the mainland and as part of a small, threatened population on Crete, only confirmed to exist in the late 1990s.

Common mammals

Other woodland mammals include the wild boar (*Sus scrofa*) and the common Eurasian badger (*Meles meles*); the former is found on larger wooded islands as well as the mainland. In northern conifer forests, look out for the red squirrel (*Sciurus vulgaris*) with its bushy tail, white underbelly and ear tufts (a subspecies is also endemic to Lésvos). The pine marten (*Martes martes*) is distinguished from its more widespread cousin, the beech or stone marten (*Martes*

foina), by its creamy, yellowish throat patch, as compared with the latter's which is pure white. In addition to these two types of martens, you might see other members of the mustelid family, including the weasel (*Mustela nivalis*) and the European polecat (*Mustela putorius*). The most common nocturnal mammals you are likely to see are the country's numerous species of bat.

The red fox (*Vulpes vulpes*) is common and widespread, unlike a similar-looking animal more commonly associated with Africa and western Asia: the golden jackal (*Canis aureus*). Greece is the northwesternmost limit of the jackal's

Brown bears in the Rodópi Mountains.

range, but populations have collapsed since the 1980s. Now under a thousand remain, mainly in wetlands and *maquis* regions of Fokída, the Peloponnese, Halkidikí and the island of Sámos, as confirmed by a 2008–09 WWF survey (www.wwf.gr). Hunting jackals was forbidden in 1990, but they are still persecuted for stealing sheep and chickens, frequently taking the blame for kills by stray dogs. In fact, 50 percent of their diet is vegetarian, and the rest comes from carrion and hunting live reptiles, frogs, insects, small rodents and the ubiquitous rabbits.

Reptiles and amphibians

Not all of Greece's wildlife is elusive, and nor does tracking it down always demand time and effort. Basking in the sun or making a dash for it, geckos can often be seen in rocks and along paths.

Other curious lizards of Greece include the Mediterranean chameleon (*Chamaeleo chamaeleo*), growing up to 30cm (1ft) long, and unmistakable with its prehensile tail, wedge-shaped head and bulbous eyes, now found only on Sámos, plus its cousin the African chameleon (Chamaeleo africanus), confined to Pýlos in the Peloponnese. The large, rough-scaled agama lizard (*Laudakia stellio*) lives in parts of northern Greece, and on Corfu, Paxí, the

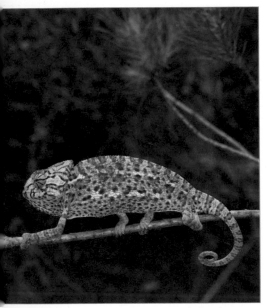

The Mediterranean chameleon is now only found on Sámos island.

Cyclades, Dodecanese and the eastern Aegean islands. The Aegean Islands in fact have numerous reptilian endemics: six species of lizards and three types of snake are not found anywhere else in Europe.

Greece's snake species include Europe's most venomous, the nose-horned viper (*Vipera ammodytes*), with distinctive zigzags on its back; but most – like the grass snake (*Natrix natrix*) or the fast-moving Dahl's whip snake (*Columber najadum*) – are harmless.

One of Greece's most famous reptiles is the yellowish Hermann's tortoise (*Testudo hermanni*), once heavily exploited for the pet trade, but now protected. It lives in scrubby land in

coastal regions throughout the country; keep an eye out for it when looking around ruins. A related species found nearly as widely is the spur-thighed tortoise (*Testudo graeca*); its cousin, *Testudo marginata*, is mostly restricted to the north of the country, and the Sporades.

Greece is home to two species of toads and 11 kinds of frogs, including tiny tree frogs and the highly endangered *Pelophylax cerigensis*, restricted to just a few hundred individuals on Kárpathos and Rhodes.

Marine life

Greece has more coastline than any other Mediterranean country – some 15,000km (9,300 miles) of it. The benign temperature of the Aegean and its relatively small tides make it good snorkelling territory. Look out for two types of octopuses – the common (*Octopus vulgaris*), with double rows of suckers, and the curled (*Eledone cirrhosa*), with single rows of suckers – plus cuttlefish, sea urchins, starfish, sea cucumbers, gorgonian and anemones. You may also spot pipefish (*Sygnathus acus*) and seahorses (*Hippocampus*).

At local harbours, you will primarily see various species of breams, parrotfish, hake, swordfish, mackerel and dogfish-type shark among the fishermen's catch. The Mediterranean is heavily overfished, with industrial fleets being particularly to blame; one prestige species that bears the brunt of this is the bluefin tuna (*Thunnus thynnus*).

Loggerhead and hawksbill turtles

Among the most vulnerable marine species is the loggerhead turtle (*Caretta caretta*). Many

FAVOURITE LIZARDS

While the majority of wild animals are eager to keep away from people, some species actually visit you, in what might be called the wildlife equivalent of room service. Perhaps the most enchanting of these are the country's three species of geckos (commonest the orangey-tan *Hemidactylus turcicus*) – the most keen-sighted of all lizards, whose large eyes are perfect for hunting insects at night or in darkened rooms. Not only do they look cute, but their ability to run along vertical and even upside-down surfaces thanks to the adhesive pads on their feet inspired the development of Velcro fasteners.

die each year, entangled and drowned by fishing nets, but the real threat to their continued survival is the status of their ancestral nesting sites. Many of the beaches turtles once chose to nest on have lost out over the years to tourism developments; the only significant remaining nesting sites are on Zákynthos, the Peloponnese and Crete. Natural hazards have always meant that only a tiny proportion of eggs laid make it to adulthood: animals like foxes predate on the eggs (laid between the end of May and August), and birds eat hatchlings (which emerge from July to the end of October) as they

overcoming past mismanagement and hostility from tourist concerns at Laganás.

Dolphins and whales

On boat trips, keep your eyes peeled for one of the cetaceans that can be found in Greek waters: the common dolphin (*Delphinus delphis*), frequently seen playing in schools in the bow wave of boats; its larger, darker cousin, the bottlenose dolphin (*Tursiops truncatus*), the dolphin most commonly seen in aquariums; the striped dolphin (*Stenella coeruleoalba*); a long-finned pilot whale (*Globicephala caretta*);

Mediterranean monk seals are a protected species.

make their way to the sea. But human disturbance has even more devastating effects. Noise and curious tourists can cause adult turtles to abandon nests, and light pollution disorientates hatchlings, causing them to head inland, where they die, rather than out to sea. Similar problems afflict the hawksbill turtle (*Eretomochelys imbricata*), which occasionally is found around the Ionian islands.

If you are keen on turtle protection, stay away from nesting beaches at night and think of joining ARCHELON, the Sea Turtle Protection Society of Greece (www.archelon.gr). They have set up protected zones and rescue stations on Crete, the Peloponnese and Zákynthos, where the National Marine Park established for the turtles is finally

a sperm whale (*Physeter catadon*); or a fin whale (*Balaenoptera physalus*).

The monk seal

Perhaps Greece's most important marine mammal, however, is the predominantly brown or grey Mediterranean monk seal (*Monachus monachus*), unusual among seals because it lives in warm waters. It eats mainly fish, squid and octopus, and can grow to over two metres (6ft) in length and weigh more than 300kg (660lbs). In ancient times, monk seals were common – they figured on Greek coins from as far back as 500 BC and featured in the writings of Homer, Plutarch and Aristotle. Now, however, they are one of the most endangered mammals in the

> Greater flamingos (Phoenicopterus ruber) used to overwinter from Africa at salt marshes on Kós, Sámos, Lésvos and Límnos, but for unknown reasons they ceased arriving in about 2007.

world. Between 300 and 500 individuals survive, with Greece, Dalmatia and Morocco having the only significant populations, and it is a battle to save them.

Whereas in ancient Greek times they were trusting, they are now shy of man and confined to the most isolated coasts. During Roman times and the Middle Ages, they were hunted assiduously for their pelts, meat and oil, but they have also been hard hit in the last hundred years by pollution, disease and a steep decline in fish stocks. Until very recently, they were persecuted by fishermen who viewed them as competition for fish stocks and who resented them for damaging fishing nets. Now one of the reasons for their continued vulnerability is disturbance through tourism – often unwittingly, as when yachts seek out the type of deserted coves where the caves in which the seals live and breed are located.

Among their last remaining strongholds are Sámos and northern Kárpathos, where perhaps 30 individuals live, and the National Marine Park of the Northern Sporades, created in 1992, which has a population of about 55 seals. The main society fighting for their protection is the Hellenic Society for the Study and Protection of the Monk Seal (www.mom.gr). It is based on Alónisos, where it runs an exhibition centre in Patitíri and the Seal Treatment and Rehabilitation Centre for sick and orphaned seal pups at Stení Vála; there is also an information centre in Diafáni, Kárpathos. MOM's work has helped bring about some small encouraging signs: local attitudes towards the animals have shifted, so that they are rarely intentionally killed; and scientists believe that local seal birth rates – about eight annually – have stabilised. More information on this fascinating creature can be found at www.monachus-guardian.org.

Birds

Sited on important avian migration routes, Greece is an excellent destination for birdwatchers, especially in spring and autumn, but also in winter, when many northern European birds come to avoid the cold. Enthusiasts should contact the Hellenic Ornithological Society (www.ornithologiki.gr).

One of the best wetland sites in the country is the Préspa National Park, on a mountainous plateau in western Macedonia, comprising the almost all-Greek Lake Mikrí (Little) Préspa, and Lake Megáli (Great) Préspa, its waters and shoreline shared with Albania and FYROM. Here you can find breeding colonies of both great white pelican (*Pelecanus onocrotalus*) and Dalmatian pelicans (*Pelecanus crispus*), as well as the threat-

Both black and white storks migrate through Greece, nesting on the way.

ened pygmy cormorant (*Phalacrocorax pygmaeus*), which also breeds on lakes Kerkíni and Petrón.

Another critical site is the Évros Delta, where you can see wetland and pastureland birds like the lesser white-fronted goose (*Anser erythropus*), the crane (*Grus grus*), the Eurasian spoonbill (*Platalea leucorodia*), the glossy ibis (*Plegadis falcinellus*), the purple heron (*Ardea purpurea*) and the white stork (*Ciconia ciconia*), which is also highly visible across central mainland Greece in summer, nesting on church belfries and utility poles.

As for seabirds, one of the most important is the Audouin's gull (*Larus audouinii*), which is endangered but still found across the Aegean, while great cormorants (*Phalacrocorax carbo*) and smaller shags are widespread in the Sporades, Cyclades and east Aegean.

Short-toed larks (*Calandrella brachydactyla*) and calandra larks (*Melanocorypha calandra*) are common on open agricultural land. Your eye might also be caught by the vivid hues of the turquoise-coloured European roller (*Coracias garrulus*), not to mention the smaller bee-eater (*Merops apiaster*), both of which you may see perched on fence or telegraph wires.

Other glamorously coloured birds include the golden oriole (*Oriolus oriolus*), which is country, but, like most birds of prey, they are vulnerable to hunting and poisoned bait, often put down to kill foxes or – illegally – wolves. The lammergeier (*Gypaetus barbatus*), a type of vulture famous for its habit of dropping bones from a great height to smash them so that it can extract the marrow, has vanished from Crete but may just still hang on in the mainland mountains. Three other vultures are more commonly seen in Greece – the griffon vulture (*Gyps fulvus*), the black vulture (*Aegypius monachus*) and the white-and-black Egyptian vulture (*Neophron percnopterus*). Other major birds of

The endangered imperial eagle.

frequently found in woodland and orchards; and the kingfisher (*Alcedo atthis*), found near streams and waterways, as well as hiding in sea-level rock formations. In olive groves and open country, watch out for the ground-feeding hoopoe (*Upupa epops*), with its unmistakable pinkish head and crest and a long curved bill.

Birds of prey

The Dadiá Forest in Thrace is one of the best places in Europe to see birds of prey, including three highly endangered birds: the imperial eagle (*Aquila heliaca*), the white-tailed or sea eagle (*Haliaetus albicilla*) and the golden eagle (*Aquila chrysaetos*). The latter still exists elsewhere in remote mountainous regions of the prey include the fish-eating osprey (*Pandion haliaetus*) and numerous types of kites, harriers, hawks, buzzards and falcons.

Perhaps the most famous of Greece's falcons is the Eleonora's falcon (*Falco eleonorae*). Similar to a peregrine but with a longer tail and more slender wings, it is often seen in groups hunting off coastal cliffs in the Aegean. Over two-thirds of the entire world population of this threatened bird species spend their summer months in Greece, hunting insects during spring and early summer, and delaying their breeding season so that they can raise their fledglings on migrant birds heading to Africa in the autumn, before they too head off on their long annual migration to overwinter on Madagascar.

La Grotta Bay, Corfu Island.

Líndos acropolis, Rhodes.

White-washed buildings in Parikia
Town, Paros.

INTRODUCTION

A detailed guide to the entire country, with principal
sites clearly cross-referenced by number to the maps.

Mandráki church.

As Henry Miller wrote in *The Colossus of Maroussi*, "marvellous things happen to one in Greece – marvellous
good things which can happen to one nowhere else on
earth. Somehow, almost as if He were nodding, Greece still
remains under the protection of the Creator. Men may go
about their puny, ineffectual bedevilment, even in Greece,
but God's magic is still at work and, no matter what the race
of men may do or try to do, Greece is still a sacred precinct – and my belief
is it will remain so until the end of time".

Another quotation, this time from a dictionary, defines
the Greek word "chaos" as "disordered, formless matter said
to have existed before the ordered universe". Chaotic is certainly one way of describing the physical geography of a
country characterised by heaps of rocks, furrowed mountain
ranges and a jagged coastline. Flat, fertile areas such as the
Thessalian plain are the exception.

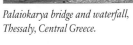

The extensive Pindos mountain range in the west forms
the country's backbone, while in the east, the peaks of
Mount Olympos, at nearly 3,000 metres (10,000ft), are the
highest in Greece. The coast is a series of so many coves and
inlets that it runs to a length of 15,000km (9,300 miles).

*Palaiokarya bridge and waterfall,
Thessaly, Central Greece.*

The 60-odd inhabited islands that spill out into the seas surrounding Greece are divided into distinct groups: the Ionian islands to the
west, the Sporádes to the east, and the Cyclades and Dodecanese trailing
out southeast from Athens. The three largest islands are Crete, Lésvos and
Évia, the latter little known outside of Greece.

In this section, our expert writers will take you on 15 individual journeys.
Starting with the capital, Athens, we take a clockwise loop through the
mainland and then set sail for the many islands, finishing in the westerly
Ionian archipelago. En route, you will find the history, geography and local
culture of each area covered in detail. The opening hours given for sites and
museums are for summer only (May–September), unless otherwise stated;
different hours usually apply from October to April. Tourist facilities on
the islands in particular tend to close abruptly once the summer season has
finished – which varies from early September when school starts, to late
October for Rhodes, and the southerly "Great Island" of Crete.

The chapters have been loosely designed as two-week itineraries, but of
course the longer you stay, the better. Perhaps, like Lord Byron, you will
one day be able to declare: "It is the only place I ever was contented in".

ULGARIA   Kárdžali   **Edirne**   *BLACK SEA*

răma   **Xánthi**   **Komotiní**   **T U R K E Y**   **İstanbul**

avála

Liménas   **Alexandroúpoli**   Keşan   *Marmara Denizi*

onikós   Thásos   Kavakköy

lpos

sos   **Samothráki**   **Çanakkale**   **Bandırma**   Bursa

Áthos   Fengári   Thermá

Athos   1611   (Loutrá)

2033

Thrakikón Pélagos   Gökçeada   Abíde

thonía

Mýrina   Ayvacık   Edremit   Balıkesir

Límnos

Ágios Evstrátios   Mólyvos   **T U R K E Y**

Giourá

Pipéri   **Mytilíni**   Akhisar

Sporádes   **Lésvos**

os   Plomári

Skýros   Psará

a   Skyros

ea)   **Híos**   Urla   **İzmir**

Paralía Kymis   Híos   Çeşme

Pyrgí

Karystos   **Sámos**   Vathý   Aydın

Ándros   Karlóvassi   (Sámos)   Denizli

Ándros   **Ikaría**

Kéa   **Tínos**   Foúrni

Giáros   Ág.   Agathonísi

ýthnos   Tínos   Kírykos   Arkí

Ermoúpoli   **Mýkonos**   Lipsí

Sýros   Pátmos   Milâs   Muğla

Sérifos   **Cycládes**   Léros

Páros   **Náxos**   Kálymnos

Sífnos   Andíparos   **Náxos**   **Bodrum**

Kímolos   Íos   Amorgós   **Kós**   Kós

Síkinos   Kéfalos   Fethiye

Mílos   Folégandros   Astypálea   Nísyros   Sými

Dodecanese   Tílos   Ródos   Kaş

Anáfi   Sýrna

Santoríni   Hálki

(Thíra)   Mt Atávyros   **Megísti**

1215   Líndos   (Kastellórizo)

Kritikó Pélagos   **Ródos**

(Rhodes)

Kárpathos

à

Réthymno   **Iráklio**   **Kríti (Crete)**

(Rethimno)   Ida   (Heraklion)   Kásos

Arkádi   (Psiloritis)

lora   Plakiás   2456   **Ágios**   Sitía

Sfakion   **Nikólaos**

Ag.   Knossos   Zákros

Galíni

ávdos   Ierápetra

Greece

0   50 km

0   50 miles

THE MAINLAND

The mainland of Greece contains a wealth
of historical monuments, in landscapes
that are often breathtaking.

*Woodland surrounding
Mýtikas peak.*

Many visitors to Greece head straight for the islands – of which there are of course dozens to choose from, offering everything from sybaritic nightlife to serene tranquillity, from historical marvels to stunning natural beauty. Naturally, this book explores Greece's offshore assets in great detail later on (see page 227). But to bypass the Greek mainland is to overlook the heart of the country, to miss its range of dramatic scenery, and to neglect some spectacular ruins recalling the grandeur of ancient civilisations.

The six chapters that follow explore this rich and varied land, starting in Athens, birthplace of democracy and home to the most impressive remains from the Classical period to be found in Greece. However, relics of ancient civilisations can be seen throughout the mainland – the ancient strongholds of Mycenae and Tiryns, predating the Trojan War; the holy site of Delphi, regarded by the ancients as the centre of the world; the stadium and temples of Olympia, where the Olympic Games began; and wonderfully preserved theatres at Epidauros, Argos, Dodona and elsewhere.

Monuments from the Byzantine period include elegant churches and monasteries decorated with glorious mosaics or frescoes. Thessaloníki, the second city of the Byzantine Empire, has a rich heritage of these stylish churches, and the monasteries of Dafní and Ósios Loukás are world famous for their art treasures. Venetian and Frankish occupation enriched Greece's coastline with picturesque castles and walled cities such as Monemvasía, Návplio and Koróni. Throughout the country, archaeological museums are treasure-houses of beautiful and intriguing relics of Greece's complex past.

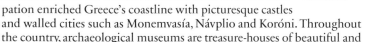

*The Temple of Poseidon
at Sounion.*

But the Greek mainland is not just about history: its timeless landscapes are often captivating. The rugged mountain ranges of central and southern Greece, snowcapped for four months of the year, descend through craggy ridges to sea-girt peninsulas and promontories. Deep gulfs and inlets penetrate the land, bounded by mountains cradling tiny harbours and fishing villages, or bordered by pine slopes. Elsewhere, a narrow coastal plain meets the sea in a fretwork of bays, some of them inaccessible overland.

Metaxourghiou Ⓜ
PL. KARAÏSKAKI
Pátras, Lamia ↗
National Theatre
National Archaeological Museum ⑬

LENORMAN
ODYSSEOS
VERANZEROU
KAROLOU
IEROTHEOU
NIKIFOROU
KOUMOUNDOUROU
MENANDROU
SATOVRIANDOU
VERANZEROU
XOUTHOU
KOTZIOU
3 SEPTEMVRIOU
DOROU
KANINGOS
KLISSOVS
THEMISTOKLEOUS

PL. METAXOURGIOU
AG. KONSTANDINOU
PLATIA OMÓNIAS
Omonia Ⓜ
PATISIOU EOLOU
PANEPISTIMIOU
EXAR
GRAVIAS
EMM. BENAKI
ZALO
KIAFAS

ALEXANDROU
KALLERGI
DELIGIORGI
NIKIFOROU
VILARA
GERANIOU
SOKRATOUS
ATHINAS
GLADSTONOS
NIKITARA
THEMISTOKLEOUS

MEG.
ZINONOS
VOLLIGARI
KOLONOU
ZINONOS
LYKOURGOU
STADIOU
SANTAROZA
FIDIOU

MARATHONOS
GIATRAKOU
LEONIDOU
JASONOS
KERAMIKOU
DELIGIORGI
P. TSALDARI (PIREOS)
ANAXAGORA
EVPOLIDOS
EMM. BENAKI
ARSAKI
State Opera House

THERMOPYLON
KERAMIKOU
AGISILAOU
ACADIMOU
KOLOKYNTHOUS
PL. ODIOU
SAPFOUS
PL. KOTZIA
G. STAVROU
IPPOKRAT

GRANIKOU
AGISILAOU
MYLLEROU
EPIKOUROU
KRATINOU
PESMAZOGLOU
National Library

SALAMINOS
SALAMINOS
ALOG. SAMOUIL
SOFOKLEOUS
SOFOKLEOUS
Univ

KERAMEIKOS
PLATIA ELEFTHERIAS
KORINIS
Varvákios Agorá (Covered Market) ⑫
EOLOU
Pánepis
KORAI Ⓜ

Benáki Museum Annexe
PSARMILIGOU
Benáki Museum (Islamic Collection) ⑤
Ag. Dimitrios
PSYRRÍ
PL. IEROU LOHOU
Ág. Theodóri ㉓
DRAGATSANIOU
KLAVTHMONOS
STADIOU
PLATIA KOLOKOT

⑲ Ag. Triada
Kerameikos Cemetery
Ág. Geórgios ㉕
Athens City Museum
PL. KOLOKOTRONI
Nat Hist Mus ⑭

ERMOU
MONASTIRAKI ⑪
ERMOU
Ag. Irini
LEKKA
KARA. SER

EPTAHALKOU
PL. THISIOU
Thisio Ⓜ
ADRIANOU
Kimisis Theotokou
Kapnikaréa
ERMOU
PERIKLEOUS
ERM

POULOPOULOU
VASSILIS
IRAKLIDON
Herakleidon Museum
Hephaisteion
Monastiraki Ⓜ
PLATÍA MONASTIRÁKI
MITROPOLEOS
Mitrópolis
PETRAKI
MITROPO

NILEOS
AKAMANTOS
Ancient Greek Agora
Stoa of Attalos ③
PANDROSOU
Kyriazopoulos Collection of Pottery
Hadrian's Library
Museum of Greek Folk Music Instruments ⑧
Mikri Mitrópolis
YPITOU

AG. MARINAS
Observatory
Church of the Holy Apostles
ROMAN AGORA
Aerides (Tower of the Winds)
Abdi Efendi Haman
Jewi Muse of Gre

Hill of the Pnyx
APOST. PAVLOU
Ardittós
Kanellópoulou (Canellopoulos Museum) ⑨
Frissíras Museum
Muse Greel Art
PLÁKA

Pnyx
see Acropolis map
Acropolis ①
St Catherine's Chapel
Choregic Monument to Lysikrátos
Hadrian's

Prison of Socrates
Herodeio (Theatre of Herodes Atticus) ⑦
Theatre of Dionysos ④
DION. AREOPAGITOU
⑥
Temp Olympia

Filopáppos
Monument of Filopáppos
Atelier-Museum Spyrou Vassiliou
MAKRYGIÁNNI
Akropoli Ⓜ
Acropolis Museum ②
VEÍKOU
Sounion
ATH. DIAK

Goulandris Natural History Museum

NEÁPOLI

LYKAVITÓS

Athens

0   200 m
0   200 yds

Theatre of
Lykavitós

Lykavitós
20

Ág. Geórgios
(St George's
Church)

HOIDA

Ág. Nikólaos

DÓRAS DISTRIA

Gennadios
Library

Cultural Centre-
Hellenic Theatre
Museum

KOLONÁKI

PLATIA
DEXAMENIS GLYKONOS

Hymettus (Ymettós),
Moni Kesariani
Mégaro Mousikis
24

Numismatic
Museum

Hadjikyriakos-
Ghikas
Gallery

PLATIA
KOLONÁKI

PL. MEGALISTOU
GENOUS SCHOLIS

Theoharakis
Foundation

Benáki
Museum
18

Goulandris
Museum of
Cycladic Art
17

PL. PAVLOU
MELA

Ágios
Geórgios

National Art Gallery -
Alexandros Soutzos
Museum

VASILISIS SOFIAS

VASILISIS SOFIAS

Evangelismos

PL.
MADRITIS

Syntagma
15

Parliament
(Old Palace)

PL. P. MELA
(RIGILLIS)

Byzantine
& Christian
Museum
21

War
Museum

22

NATIONAL GARDENS
16

Presidential
Palace

VASIL. GEORGIOU II.

VASIL. GEORGIOU II.

PANGRÁTI

Záppeio
(Exhibition Hall)

PL.
SKOUZE

PL.
MESOLOGHIOU

Ethnikós
(Athletics Field)

1896
Olympic
Stadium

ARDITTÓS

Sounion ↓

The Acropolis at dusk.

ATHENS

Both East and West converge in this vibrant metropolis, lively and brimming over, just like its inhabitants. The city is also home to some of the country's finest, cutting-edge museums.

I f there is one quality for which Athens (Athína in Greek) should be credited, it is elasticity. Throughout its long history, the city has by turns been obscure, triumphant and, now, the capital of the modern Greek state. Athens is barely mentioned in Homer, but emerged as a growing power in the 6th century BC. During the Periclean "golden age", Athens became a great centre of art and literature, commerce and industry. With Macedonian expansion came the first shrinkage, though Athens remained a prestigious intellectual centre with particular emphasis on philosophy and oratory.

During the Hellenistic period, Athens was overshadowed by the great kingdoms founded by Alexander's successors – but not obliterated. The rulers of Egypt, Syria and Pergamum courted the old city with gifts of buildings and works of art. Yet it was already beginning to rest on its laurels, to turn into a museum-city, a "cultural commodity" rather than an active, living organism. Besieged and sacked by Lucius Cornelius Sulla in 86 BC, restored and pampered under two phil-Athenian Roman emperors, Augustus and Hadrian, sacked again by the Herulians in AD 267 and Alaric the Goth in AD 395, Athens entered the Byzantine era as a small provincial backwater, shorn of all its glory.

Évzone guards outside the Parliament.

The edict of the Byzantine emperor Justinian forbidding the study of philosophy there (AD 529) rang down the curtain on the ancient city.

From broken city to capital

Under Latin rule (1204–1456), invaded, occupied and fought over by the French, Catalans, Florentines and Venetians, Athens shrank even more. It was only after the Ottoman conquest in the 15th century that it began to expand again, but still falling far short of its ancient limits. There were more

Main Attractions

The Acropolis
New Acropolis Museum
Strolling in Pláka
Varvákios Agorá
Sunday/Easter services at
  Agías Irinis
National Archaeological
  Museum
Benáki Museum
Hadjikyriakos-Ghikas Gallery
Dáfni mosaics
Poseidon Temple, Soúnio

setbacks, including a devastating Venetian incursion in 1687. Athens finally rose from its ruins after the War of Independence, an "exhausted city", as Christopher Wordsworth noted in 1832, that was suddenly raised, unprepared, to the status of capital of the new Greek state.

Athens is thus a town that has grown haphazardly since then, and too fast. It never had a chance to mellow into venerable old age. Old and new have not blended too well; you can still sense the small, pre-1940s city pushing through the huge sprawl of today's modern capital, like the proverbial thin man struggling to get out of every fat man. Occasionally, you come across what must have once been a suburban villa, ensconced between tall office buildings, its owner still fighting with hermetically closed windows against building-site dust and the roar of the traffic.

Congestion in Athens can be unbelievable, particularly when there is some work stoppage or demonstration underway and traffic is forced off the main streets, or it increases because the metro or buses are on strike. When it works, however, public transport makes journeys to, and through, the heart of the city, in a matter of minutes. Fairly thorough pedestrianisation of central Athens has made it more liveable and inviting, palpably less polluted.

In addition, branching off from the manic central arteries are the minor veins of the city, relatively traffic-free. Most apartment blocks have balconies and verandas, and there you can see the Athenians in summer emerging from their afternoon siesta in underpants and nighties, reading the paper, watching the neighbours, watering their plants, eating their evening meal.

Later on after dark, younger Athenians head out for nightlife, still fairly lively and long despite the economic pinch. The original district for this was Psyrrí, just beyond Monastiráki (with which it shares a metro station). Accounts of hip Psyrrí's demise in popular lore are greatly exaggerated, but it is true that the margin of trendiness and gentrification spreads steadily outward and further northwest, encompassing the formerly dismal neighbourhoods of Gázi, Rouf, Keramikós, Metaxourgío and Votanikós. Hot venues, for cutting-edge arts events as well, change regularly – consult a listings website or ask a friendly local.

The Acropolis

Seen from the right angle driving east on the **Ierá Odós** (the Sacred Way), especially at night, or looking up at its rocky bulk from the Pláka, the **Acropolis ①** (daily 8am–8pm; various ticket combinations available) still has a presence that makes the grimy concrete of modern Athens fade into insignificance. Climb up in early morning in summer or early afternoon in winter, when the crowds are thinnest, and a strip of blue sea edged with grey hills marks the horizon. On a wet or windy day, walking across its uneven limestone surface feels like being on a ship's deck in a gale.

The Acropolis nowadays looks like a stonemason's workshop, much as it must have done in the 440s BC when the **Parthenon ④** was under

construction as the crowning glory of Pericles' giant public works programme. Some of his contemporaries thought it extravagant: Pericles was accused of dressing his city up like a harlot. In fact, the Parthenon celebrates Athena as a virgin goddess and the city's protector. Her statue, 11 metres (37ft) tall and constructed of ivory and gold plate to Pheidias's design, once gleamed in its dim interior; in late antiquity, it was taken to Constantinople, where it disappeared.

Conservators have taken down hundreds of blocks of marble masonry from the Parthenon to replace the rusting iron clamps inserted in the 1920s with non-corrosive titanium (rust made the clamps expand, cracking the stone, while acid rain turned carved marble surfaces into soft plaster). The restorers also succeeded in identifying and collecting about 1,600 chunks of Parthenon marble scattered over the hilltop, many blown off in the 1687 explosion caused by a Venetian mortar igniting Ottoman munitions stored inside the temple. When

The previously traffic-clogged road of Dionysíou Areopagítou around the base of the Acropolis has been pedestrianised, part of a plan to link the ancient sites with a car-free promenade. This, and its continuation Apostólou Pávlou, are now popular places for evening strolling.

Acropolis Museum exhibits.

THE PARTHENON FRIEZE

The Parthenon Marbles are a 76-sq-m (500-sq-ft) stretch of sculpted figures – mostly from the frieze – carved under the direction of the master-sculptor and architect Pheidias. By 1799, when Lord Elgin was appointed British ambassador to the Ottoman Empire, the Parthenon was in a sorry state, having been practically destroyed and then plundered by the invading Venetians in 1687. Elgin negotiated a permit from the sultan to remove "some blocks of stone with inscriptions and figures", which he did between 1801 and 1812. He then shipped the marbles back to Britain, and in 1816 sold them to the British Museum, where they remain today.

The marbles are an integral part of one of the most beautiful buildings that still survives from antiquity, say the Greeks, and can be better appreciated in the city that made them. A key aim in building the **Acropolis Museum** was to reunite the surviving sculptures that once adorned the Parthenon: with its controlled environment, there were hopes that the museum would overcome what had ostensibly been the main objection to the return of the marbles, namely Athens' lack of a suitable location in which to display them. So far, however, the world's major museums claim that to return the marbles would set a disastrous precedent.

In Ottoman times, the Turkish military commander housed his harem in the Erechtheion.

The impressive Acropolis Museum.

they are replaced, about 15 percent more building will be on view. New blocks cut from near the ancient quarries on Mount Pendéli (14km/9 miles north of Athens), which supplied the 5th-century BC constructors, will fill the gaps.

The **Erechtheion** **B**, an elegant architecturally complex repository of ancient cults going back to the Bronze Age, is already restored. The Caryatids now supporting a porch over the tomb of King Kekrops, a mythical founder of the ancient Athenian royal family, are modern copies. The surviving originals were moved to the Acropolis Museum to prevent further damage from the *néfos*, the ochre summer blanket of pollution, now thankfully less frequent, that hangs over Athens.

Completed in 395 BC, a generation later than the Parthenon, the Erechtheion also housed an early wooden statue of Athena, along with the legendary olive tree that she conjured out of the rock to defeat Poseidon the sea-god in their contest for sovereignty over Attica.

The **Propylaia** **C**, the battered official entrance to the Acropolis built by Mnesikles in the 430s BC, was cleverly designed with imposing outside columns to awe people coming up the hill. Parts of its coffered stone ceiling, once painted and gilded, are still visible as you walk through. Only reassembled recently, the exquisite square temple of **Athena Nike** **D** (finished in 421 BC) stands on what was once the citadel's southern bastion. It supposedly occupies one of the spots – the other is Cape Sounion – where Theseus's father, King Aegeus, is said to have thrown himself to his death on seeing a black-sailed ship approaching the harbour. Theseus had promised to hoist a white sail for the return voyage if he had succeeded in killing the Minotaur on Crete, but carelessly forgot.

Acropolis Museum

The sculptures that Lord Elgin left behind are in the **Acropolis Museum** **2**, below the Parthenon by Akrópoli metro station (www.theacropolismuseum. gr; Apr–Oct Mon 8am–4pm, Tue–Thu and Sat–Sun until 8pm, Fri until 10pm, Nov–Mar Mon–Thu 9am–5pm, Fri until 10pm, Sat–Sun until 8pm). Opened in 2009, the Acropolis Museum is the result of a competition won by New York-based Swiss architect Bernard Tschumi. From outside, the concrete-and-glass building, with its retro, mid-20th-century feel, is starkly antipathetic, in contrast to two neighbouring, listed apartment blocks on Dionysíou Areopagítou, threatened with demolition but ultimately saved by public outcry; no. 17, of 1930s vintage, ranks as Athens' best surviving example of Art Deco.

Once inside, however, the building works much better, effectively harnessing natural light for the optimum presentation of sculptural objects (a different proposition from the kind of light called into play when displaying paintings or drawings). From the entry on Dionysíou Areopagítou, a glass walkway leads over excavated sections of ancient Athens, including dwellings, wells, water and sewage works, an olive press, and even a Classical symposium hall with mosaic flooring. The excavations extend well under the museum which hovers above, supported by 100 massive anti-seismic columns, and muted natural light filters through the glass panels that make up much of the flooring.

From the ground floor, the upper levels are reached by a ramp, simulating the approach to the Acropolis and watched over by the six scarred but still impressively female Caryatids (one of them a copy, as the sixth original resides in the British Museum in London). On the first floor, the Archaic exhibition features the famous "Calf-bearer" or Moschophoros, and various coquettish *korai* (sculptures of women) revealing the Archaic ideal of beauty – look closely and you can make out their make-up, earrings and the patterns of their crinkled, close-fitting dresses.

Then up past the second-floor restaurant and shop to the top floor and the pièce de résistance: a glass gallery holding a reconstruction of the Parthenon pediments, of the same size and compass orientation as the real Parthenon looming just outside the wrap-around windows. The friezes, including the triangular western aetoma, are mounted at eye level – unlike the originals, which sat overshadowed by the eaves so that the ancient Athenians couldn't really appreciate them. The authentic fragments which Greece retains have been mounted; everything else is a plaster cast, pointedly awaiting the return of their prototypes, the so-called Elgin Marbles, from the British Museum.

The Agora and Theatre of Dionysos

Just to the north of the Acropolis lies the **Ancient Greek Agora** (daily 8am–8pm). The main entrance to this site is on Adrianoú Street, but there is an alternative way in behind the church of the Holy Apostles. While the Acropolis was mainly a religious site, the Agora was used for all public

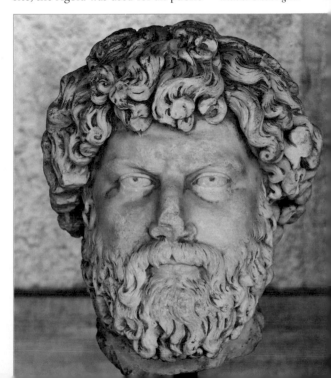

Sculpture in the Stoa of Attalos, in the ancient Greek Agora.

The Tower of the Winds.

The well-preserved Hephaesteion temple.

the form of a kneeling *kouros* (a statue of a nude youth). The *Hephaisteion* (also known as the Theseion), the temple opposite, is the most complete surviving Doric order temple and gives some idea of what the intact Parthenon looked like – though the vaulted ceiling dates from its time as a church.

On the south side of the Acropolis lies the **Theatre of Dionysos ❹**. The marble seating tiers date from around 320 BC and later, but scholars generally agree that plays by playwrights such as Aeschylos, Sophokles, Euripides and Aristophanes were first staged here at religious festivals during the 5th century BC. A state subsidy for theatre-goers meant that every Athenian citizen could take time off to attend (entrance on Dionysíou Areopagítou; daily 8am–8pm).

Just east of the theatre, in Pláka's Platía Lysikrátous, stands the **Choregic Monument to Lysikratos**, the earliest example of the use of external Corinthian columns (the last and most ornate order of ancient Greek architecture). The inscription commemorates the victory of Lysikratos in 334 BC in a drama contest; the elegant monument was originally crowned by a tripod. During medieval times, a Capuchin monastery, which hosted Lord Byron during his second stay in Athens, incorporated the monument.

purposes: commercial, religious, political, civic, educational, theatrical, athletic. Today, it looks like a cluttered field of ruins.

The reconstructed **Stoa of Attalos ❸**, a 2nd-century BC line of shops, contains a wonderful, small archaeological museum (8am–8pm); top marks go to a small perfume vial in

Cemetery and Islamic art

Beyond modern Thisío district, the **Kerameikos Cemetery ❺** (daily 8am–8pm) in the potters' district of the city was a burial place for prominent ancient Athenians. An extraordinary variety of sculptured monuments – tall stone urns, a prancing bull, winged sphinxes and melancholy scenes of farewell – overlooked the Sacred Gate, from which the paved Sacred Way led to Eleusis, where the mysteries were held. In the site museum (daily 8am–8pm) is a collection of grave goods, an excellent guide to Greek vase-painting, from a squat geometric urn with a rusting iron sword twisted around its neck to the white *lekythoi* (oil or perfume flask) of Classical Athens, and self-consciously sophisticated Hellenistic pottery.

Nearby, on the corner of Agíon Asomáton and Dipýlou Streets, an annexe of the Benáki Museum houses an **Islamic Art Collection** (www.benaki.gr; Thu–Sun 9am–5pm), which ranks among the best in the world. More than 8,000 artefacts chart the evolution of Islamic art and civilisation up to the 19th century. The superb displays include a 16th-century velvet saddle from Bursa and the marble-faced interior of a 17th-century Cairo reception room.

Roman Athens

A few Roman monuments recall a time when Athens was revered, but stripped of its movable artworks. The 2nd-century Emperor Hadrian, a fervent admirer of Classical Greek culture, erected an ornate arch, known as **Hadrian's Arch** ❻, marking the spot where the Classical city ended and the provincial Roman university

town began. On the side facing the Acropolis is the inscription "This is Athens, the ancient city of Theseus", on the side facing the Olympieion it reads "This is the city of Hadrian and not of Theseus".

Little of this Roman city can be seen beneath the green of the **Záppio Park** and the archaeological area behind the towering columns of the **Temple of Olympian Zeus** (Stilés Olympíou Diós; daily 8am–8pm). Work on the temple had been abandoned in around 520 BC when funds ran out, but Hadrian finished the construction and dedicated the temple to himself.

Later in the century, Herodes Atticus, a wealthy Greek landowner who served in the Roman senate, built the steeply raked theatre on the south slope of the Acropolis (the **Herodeio** or **Iródio Theatre** ❼, now used for Athens Festival performances) as a memorial to his wife Regilla. A 1st-century BC Syrian, Andronikos of Kyrrhos, was responsible for the picturesque **Tower of the Winds** ❽ (Aérides; daily 8am–3pm), in the **Roman Agora**, a well-preserved

The towering columns of the Temple of Olympian Zeus.

marble octagon that is a highlight. It is decorated with eight relief figures, each depicting a different wind direction, and once contained a water-clock. Later, it served as a *tekke* (ceremonial hall) for Ottoman dervishes. The other standout of the forum is **Hadrian's Library** (daily 8am–3pm), an enormous colonnaded-courtyard building subsequently adapted to accommodate a four-apsed Byzantine basilica, from which mosaic flooring survives.

Pláka

Pláka, the old quarter clustering at the foot of the Acropolis, has been restored to its former condition (or rather to a fairly good reproduction of it), cars prohibited (for the most part), derelict houses rescued and streets tidied up. It has become a delightful, sheltered place to meander in; you might almost imagine yourself in a village, particularly in the winding narrow streets of the Anafiótika district that nestles below the Acropolis.

Pláka is also the best place to track down Athens' Ottoman past. The

Pláka is full of tourist souvenirs.

15th-century **Fethiye Mosque** beside the Roman Agora is one of the finest, and oldest, examples of Muslim architecture in the city; it is unfortunately closed to visitors. However, nearby on Platía Monastiráki the Tsizdarákis Mosque (1759) now houses the **Kyriazopoulos Collection of Pottery** (temporarily closed for relocation; visit www.melt.gr for more details). The mosque's interior has been sensitively conserved and is well worth a look, especially the brightly painted *mihrab*. Perhaps the most fascinating remnant of Turkish life, however, is the 16th-century **Abdi Efendi Hamam** (www. melt.gr Wed–Mon 8am–3pm) on Kyrrístou. This *hammam* (Turkish bath) with its warren of atmospheric rooms has been beautifully restored; a well-produced guide gives background on the building and the place of bathing in Greek and Turkish culture.

Just uphill from the hammam at the eclectic **Canellopoulos (Kanellopoulou) Museum** ❾ (Tue–Sun 8am–3pm), a new wing shelters exquisite ancient objects like Archaic ceramic birds in flight and relief sphinxes on a *pithos*; the original 19th-century mansion is now devoted to early Christian and Byzantine displays, like several Fayyum portraits, Coptic textiles and rare icons. Nearby, at Pános 22, the well-labelled Man and Tools annexe of the **Museum of Greek Folk Art** (www. melt.gr; Wed–Mon 8am–3pm), showcases extinct or vanishing craft-trades and their implements – some truly bizarre, like a *kataïfi* dough-extruder.

A few steps from Aérides, also housed in a neoclassical mansion, is the excellent **Museum of Greek Folk Music Instruments** (www.instruments-museum.gr; Tue–Sun 8am–3pm; free), showcasing the collection of Fivos Anoyanakis. On two floors are documented and displayed every instrument ever played in Greece, their sounds to be heard at the adjacent listening posts. The shop, a branch of the premier record store Xylouris, stocks (of course) plenty of Greek traditional music CDs, while the lovely garden often hosts summer-evening concerts by top contemporary Greek musicians – check the posters out front.

At the eastern edge of Pláka is another pair of worthwhile museums. Highlight of the **Museum of Greek Folk Art** at Kydathinéon 17 (temporarily closed for relocation; visit www.melt.gr for more details) is a completely reconstructed room of murals by the naïve artist Theophilos of Lésvos (1868–1934). At the end of Kydathinéon, at Níkis 39, the **Jewish Museum of Greece** ❿ (www.jewish museum.gr; Mon–Fri 9am–2.30pm, Sun 10am–2pm) records the long presence of Jews in the territory of modern Greece through documents, costumes and liturgical items, with frequent special exhibits and events.

Monastiráki

This entire area, essentially Athens' central bazaar, is a vast sprawl of shops, which get more upmarket towards Platía Syndágmatos. **Monastiráki** ⓫ brings to mind the market described in a 4th-century BC comedy by

Euboulos: "Everything will be for sale together in the same place at Athens, figs, summoners, bunches of grapes, turnips, pears, apples, witnesses, roses, medlars, honeycombs, chickpeas, lawsuits, beestings-puddings, myrtle-berries, allotment machines, irises, lambs, waterclocks, laws, indictments". Kitsch-collectors will find much to interest them: Greek kitsch is arguably the most orgiastically hideous in

The kombológi – a small chain of stone or wooden "worry-beads" – is good for relieving tension.

Busy Monastiráki.

Relief in the National Archaeological Museum.

A slice of Athenian nightlife.

the world. Monastiráki Square, by the eponymous metro station, emerged from the throes of an overhaul completely pedestrianised and more inviting; the little central monastery-church of the name, originally 11th-century, is usually open.

Retaining a traditional pattern, similar shops still tend to cluster together, as can be seen from those around the **Mitrópolis** (Athens' cathedral), specialising in ecclesiastical articles. The cathedral itself dates from the mid-19th century and is as large as it is undistinguished. However, next door the small **"old cathedral"** (formally known as Panagía Gorgoepikóös or Ágios Eleftheríos) dates from the 12th century, although its masonry is a hotchpotch of materials reused from earlier churches. Above the door arch is a 2nd-century relief showing the calendar of Attic festivals.

Robustly vulgar **Pandrósou Street** bills itself as the **Flea Market**, though the genuine article(s) – liveliest at weekends – is/are at **Platía Avyssinías**, crammed with old furniture dealers. In the lanes all around are daily shops

selling everything from old engravings to superannuated light fixtures. Head north up Athinás or its side-streets from Monastiráki square and you find the shops get more practical: wood stoves, hand-tools, screws, chainsaws, irrigation systems, hats, camping gear, knobs and knockers – truly a serendipitous accumulation.

Equally so are the goods in the **Varvákios Agorá** ⓬, a 19th-century gem roughly halfway between Monastiráki and Omónia squares on the east side of Athinás Street, originally endowed by Ioannis Varvakis, hero of Yiannis Smaragdis' 2012 film *God Loves Caviar*. This is the city's main covered meat-and-fish market, where shoppers mill between open stands displaying fish, seafood and any type and part of animal you can imagine. Near the base of Eólou is the flower market on **Platía Agías Irínis**, flanked by the eponymous church which features the finest Sunday-morning and Easter chanting in the city, courtesy of the Lykourgos Angelopoulos choir.

Omónia to Sýndagma

The city's heart, now largely pedestrianised, lies within an almost equilateral triangle defined by **Platía Omónias** in the north, Monastiráki in the south and **Platía Syndágmatos** to the southeast.

North of Omónia (also close to Viktória metro station) and crammed with treasures from every period of antiquity is the **National Archaeological Museum** ⓭ (www.namuseum.gr; daily 8am–8pm;) see page 146. It emerged from a five-year refit in 2008 and retains its rank as one of the world's great galleries.

Omónia itself went in for a facelift at the millennium. However, it remains traffic-plagued and the rather bleak concrete piazza that now covers the centre of the square is drearily unimaginative. The parallel streets of Stadíou and Panepistimíou run southeast from Omónia to Platía Syndágmatos. Halfway down Panepistimíou is Christian and Theophilus Hansen's neoclassical trilogy of the **National Library, University and Academy**. Erected between 1837 and 1891, they are built of Pentelic marble and draw heavily on ancient Greek architectural forms. Startlingly bright painting and gilding gives some idea of how the now-stark marble of ancient monuments may have first appeared.

Further along is the house of Heinrich Schliemann, designed by Ernst Ziller (1878), now home to the **Numismatic Museum** (www.enma.gr; Mon 1–8pm, Tue–Sun 9am–4pm). Of greater interest is the **National Historical Museum ⑭** (www.nhmuseum. gr; Tue–Sun 8.30am–2.20pm), which occupies the prominent Old Parliament Building on Stadíou. Arranged thematically as much as chronologically, the museum covers episodes like the War of Independence to the Balkan Wars by way of a folklore collection and foreign philhellenes.

Sýndagma Square (Platía Syndágmatos, or Constitution Square) is the de facto centre of the city, dominated by the **Parliament Building ⑮**, which was originally the Royal Palace, built in 1836–42 for King Otto. The changing of the *Évzone* Guard, a favourite tourist spectacle, takes place hourly in front of the Parliament.

Ermoú, running west from the square, is now a long pedestrian walkway with fashion outlets, enlivened by pavement buskers. Improved lighting makes this an attractive area to wander in the evening in search of a taverna or café – of which there are many in the perpendicular lanes. Also on Ermoú is the attractive Byzantine church of **Kapnikaréa**, thought to date from the 11th century; inside are frescoes executed by the neo-Byzantinist Photis Kontoglou.

The **National Gardens ⑯** (sunrise to sunset; free), much the coolest spot downtown during summer, are just behind the parliament building. Full of tangled bowers and ponds alive with terrapins, ducks or fish, there are also constant rivulets of water running along recessed troughs and numbers of escaped parrots or budgies in the trees. It was laid out by Queen Amalia as the palace gardens during the 19th

The Benáki Museum contains treasures from all periods of Athens' history.

The National Archaeological Museum.

Athens is a treasury of Byzantine art.

The Parliament.

century. She used the new Greek navy to bring back botanical specimens from their voyages around the world. Sadly, the single café is grossly overpriced – you'll have better luck at the popular Aigli, just outside the gardens proper, next to the 1888-vintage **Zappeio hall**, another Theophilus Hansen work, which hosts regular conferences and is often surrounded by nocturnal book fairs.

Kolonáki

Chic Kolonáki is the city's upmarket shopping district – though half its shops have closed down thanks to the crisis – as well as being the location of many diplomatic missions and some highly desirable apartments. It is not, however, devoid of culture; Kolonáki – or rather its southerly margins – has some of the finest museums in the city.

Going back to 3000 BC, the two-wing **Museum of Cycladic Art** ⑰ (www.cycladic.gr; Mon, Wed, Fri–Sat 10am–5pm, Thu 10am–8pm, Sun 11am–5pm) features a unique collection of slim, stylised Cycladic statuettes in white marble, beautifully mounted. These figures, mostly of the third millennium BC, were scorned by 19th-century art critics as hopelessly primitive, but their smooth, simple lines attracted Picasso, Brancusi and Modigliani. Mostly female, the figures hail from graves scattered throughout the Cyclades islands; to this day, scholars are still uncertain of their true purpose. The museum is also renowned for frequent special exhibits with un-Cycladic themes.

The **Benáki Museum** ⑱ (www.benaki.gr; Wed, Fri 9am–5pm, Thu, Sat 9am–midnight, Sun 9am–3pm), together with its two annexes and fantastic temporary exhibits, easily counts as the best all-round museum in Athens. Its wonderfully eclectic permanent collection of treasures from all periods of Greek history includes jewellery, costumes, and two icons attributed to El Greco. Among the most impressive exhibits are the collection of traditional costume, mostly bridal and festival dresses, and the reconstructed reception rooms of a mid-18th-century Kozáni mansion. Also compelling are the displays of gold on the ground floor, and the collections relating to the Greek struggle for independence. The museum has a gift shop selling covetable stock and a pleasant if pricey terrace restaurant. For information on the **Benáki Museum annexe** ⑲, see feature on page 152.

Mount Lykavitós ⑳ (Lycabettus; 215 metres/704ft) rises above Kolonáki, crowned by the tiny chapel of Ágios Geórgios. The easiest way to get to the summit is by the funicular railway that starts from the top of Ploutárhou Street (every 30 minutes, in summer 9am–1.30am). From the top, the views over the city are spectacular.

While not strictly speaking in Kolonáki (being on the far side of Vassilísis Sofías), three other nearby museums merit a visit. The **Byzantine and Christian Museum** ㉑ (www. byzantinemuseum.gr; daily 8am–8pm) was originally housed in a mock-Tuscan villa, commissioned by the 19th-century philhellene Duchesse de Plaisance (who has a suburban metro station named for her). Most exhibits, dating from the early Christian period

to 13th-century Attica, now reside in an impressive modern underground wing. Despite being subterranean, the galleries are light and spacious, and the artefacts (including the 7th-century Hoard of Mytilene) well-displayed and informatively labelled; what was once a specialist collection has been transformed into one of Athens' major museums.

Right next door is the **War Museum** (www.warmuseum.gr; summer Mon–Sat 9am–7pm, Sun until 5pm, winter Mon–Sat 9am–5pm, Sun until 3pm), established during the 1967–74 dictatorship and thus usually disdained or overlooked. Outside stand assorted 20th-century artillery and aeroplanes, while the interior offers a surprisingly absorbing collection of uniforms, weaponry and documents, particularly good on Greece's tribulations during World War II.

Near the Hilton hotel hulks the modern **National Art Gallery** ㉒ (temporarily closed for renovation; visit www.nationalgallery.gr for more details). The core collection of Greek art from just before independence to

Icons and church relics on display at the Byzantine Museum.

recent years does a good job of placing it in social context and as part of international trends. Few artists here except Nikos-Hadjikyriakos Ghikas – who gets a room to himself – are household names overseas, but that's no reflection on their merit. Best modern piece has to be Photis Kontoglou's mural, which adorned his own house. Again, there are frequent, popular temporary shows which often rope in Greek and foreign masterpieces.

Byzantine Athens

Of the city's Byzantine past little remains, but a dozen or so churches, many dating from the 11th century and most in Pláka, can be tracked down. One of the best – and one of the few normally open – is **Ágii Theodóri** 23 just off Platía Klavthmónos, built in the 11th century in characteristic cruciform shape with a tiled dome. The masonry is picked out with slabs of brick and decorated with a terracotta frieze of animals and plants.

On Athens's eastern and western limits lie two famous monasteries: Kesarianí and Dafní. **Kesarianí** 24

(Tue–Sun 8.30am–3pm) on Mount Hymettus, surrounded by high stone walls, is named after a spring which fed an aqueduct constructed on Hadrian's orders. Its waters, once sacred to love goddess Aphrodite, were long credited with healing powers (and encouraging child-bearing), though sadly are no longer potable. The monastery church dates to the 11th century but the frescoed figures who gaze out of a blue-black ground were painted mostly in 1682. Highlights include, in the conch, the Virgin Enthroned flanked by the Communion of the Apostles; the vaulting contains scenes from the life of Christ, while the narthex displays assorted miracles.

Dafní 25 is 11km (7 miles) out of town on the road to Eleusis (bus from Platía Eleftherías, near Psyrrí; Tue, Fri 8am–3pm; free). This small monastery is a curious architectural combination of Gothic and Byzantine, occupying the site of an ancient sanctuary of Apollo. The church is decorated with magnificent 11th-century mosaics, most famously a fierce-looking Christ Pandokrátor, staring

Inside the National Gallery.

down from the vault of the dome, surrounded by Old Testament prophets. The building dates from 1080 but the Gothic porch was added in the 13th century when Dafní belonged to Burgundian Cistercian monks and served as the burial place of the Frankish Dukes of Athens.

Piraeus

Athens' port is a city in its own right but most people merely pass through on their way to the islands. From central Athens it is most easily reached by metro (line 1; 40 minutes journey time); alternatively, express bus X96 runs to Piraeus (Pireás) from Athens airport via the coastal suburbs, with stops near the hydrofoil quay, Platía Karaïskáki, the metro station and the northeast quay.

Piraeus Archaeological Museum (Tue–Sun 8am–3pm) has various wonderful bronzes. On the first floor is a graceful, Archaic Apollo *kouros*, pulled from the sea in 1959; made in 530–20 BC, this is the earliest known life-sized bronze statue. Two other bronze statues, of Athena and Artemis and both

dating to the 5th century BC, were found shortly after in Piraeus when new sewers were being dug.

The hills of Athens

Central Athens is said to have eight hills (*lófi*). As well as Lykavitós and the equally conspicuous rock of the Acropolis, flanked by the **Pnyx** on one side, and **Philopappou** (Filopáppou) on the other, where Athenians fly kites on the first day of Lent, there are: the hill of **Ardittós**, next to the marble horseshoe **stadium**, built by Herodes Atticus in AD 143 and totally reconstructed in 1896 (the first modern Olympic Games were held there – it is now a popular concert venue); the **Hill of the Nymphs**, capped by the grey 19th-century, Hansen-designed **Observatory**; the barren, windblown **Tourkovoúnia**; and **Lófos Stréfi**, something of a "needle park" for local down-and-outs.

For a real escape, you have to go further afield, up one of the three mountains that encircle Athens. The road-accessible summit of **Mount Hymettus** (Ymittós), 5km (3 miles)

A Byzantine moscaic, Dafni Monastery.

Taking in the fabulous view from the top of the hill of Philoppappus.

GETTING TO THE ISLANDS

If you want to catch a ferry to one of the islands, your ticket agent should tell you which quay/gate (numbered E1–E10 going clockwise around the port) your boat departs from. Gates E1 to E3 are too far to walk to in the heat; a free shuttle bus (every 10min), from gate E5, takes you there. As a general guide, boats to the Cyclades depart from E5–E7 opposite the metro station, or E10; slow boats to the Argo-Saronic from E8 on the far side of Platía Karaïskáki, southwest of the metro; direct boats to Crete leave from E3–E4, on the north side of the port; hydrofoils and catamarans to Argo-Saronic islands leave from E9 on Aktí Miaoúli; Dodecanese-bound boats leave from all the way around the port at E1; while those for the northeast Aegean go from E2.

Athens' New Museums and Galleries

Beginning before the millennium and continuing through challenging economic circumstances, Athens has added an impressive roster of mostly private art museums to its portfolio of galleries.

The best known is the **Benáki Museum annexe** (www.benaki.gr; Thu, Sun 10am–6pm, Fri–Sat 10am–10pm), housed in Greece's former main Lada showroom in Pireos 138 (nearest metro is Keramikós), now renovated and expanded. As many as five separate exhibits may be going on at any one time, showcasing 20th-century art or architecture; recent highlights have included retrospectives of Greek photographers Voula Papaioannou and Kostas Balafas, the Czech Josef Koudelka, the Greek architect Emmanouel Vourekas and the Belgian expressionist-surrealist James Ensor. There's also a tempting shop and popular café-restaurant.

Just about walking distance away is the **Herakleidon** (Iraklidón 16 in Thisío; www.herakleidon-art.

Modern European Art at the Frissiras Museum.

gr; June–Oct Sun 10am–6pm; new annexe in Apostolou Pavlou 37 in Thisío; June–Oct daily 10am–6pm), with large permanent collections of M.C. Escher and Victor Vasarely prints plus always-stellar temporary exhibits (eg Toulouse Lautrec); again, the well-stocked shop is hazardous to your wallet.

A slightly longer walk south, along pedestrianised Apostólou Pávlou, leads to the **Atelier-Museum Spyros Vassiliou** at Webster 5a (the museum will be transferred to a new site in 2016; www.spyrosvassiliou.org), exhibiting some 40 works of this versatile artist (1902–1985) in his former studio and family dwelling. Vassiliou's long career encompassed stage design, posters and a later preponderance of acrylics on canvas.

From here, you can continue easily on foot, across Dionysíou Areopagítou, to the Frissiras Museum (Monís Asteríou 3 and 7; www.frissiras museum.com; Wed–Fri 10am–5pm, Sat–Sun 11am–5pm), the largest collection in town devoted to modern European art, mostly portraiture, of the last 50 years; the permanent holdings at no. 7 (may close owing to staff shortages) feature familiar names like Paula Rego, R.B. Kitaj and David Hockney, while the no. 3 premises have nonstop temporary shows.

Across Sýndagma, next to the French embassy at Vasillís Sofiás 9, the galleries of the elegant **Theoharakis Foundation** (www.thf.gr; Mon, Tue, Wed, Fri, Sat, Sun 10am–6pm, Thu 10am–8pm) are another reliable bet for blockbuster temporary exhibits – recent ones have featured modern Russian painters and the seminal late 1800s Greek painter Nikolaos Gyzis.

Just a block or so behind, at Kriezótou 3, is perhaps the best small Athens art museum for the uninitiated: the **Hadjikyriakos-Ghikas Gallery** (www.benaki.gr; Wed–Sat 10am–6pm), technically yet another annexe of the Benáki. It's somewhat misnamed – while indeed installed in the former home of the great painter, with his top-floor residence and atelier preserved as at his death in 1994, most of the many galleries honour (with intelligent labelling) just about everybody who was anybody in 20th-century Greek cultural life. To name just a few: the archaeologist (and neo-Byzantine architect) Athanasios Orlandos, architects Dimitris Pikionis and Aris Konstantinidis, the photographers Nelly's (sic), Takis Tloupas and Spyros Meletzis, the caricaturist Bost, painters Yiannis Moralis and Yorgos Manousakis – a painless if not so quick (allow 2 hours to visit) introduction to intellectual currents in the modern nation.

east of Athens, beloved of honey-bees, glowing violet at sunset, makes a tranquil vantage point from which to contemplate the whole of Attica. **Mount Párnitha**, just over an hour northwest, was sadly burnt to a crisp in August 2007, losing all of its thick fir forest.

Below Mount Pendéli on the northeast is Athens' most exclusive suburb, **Kifisiá**, populated, like Kolonáki, with the city's great and sometimes not so good, who reside in often whimsical early 20th-century villas. Kifisiá's only specific attraction is the **Goulandris Natural History Museum** (www.gnhm.gr; Tue–Fri 9am–2.30pm, Sat–Sun 10am–3pm), devoted to the flora, fauna and geology of Greece.

Excursion to Attica

Outside Athens, a 69km (43-mile) drive to **Cape Sounion** on the windy tip of the Attica peninsula takes you to the Doric **Temple of Poseidon** (daily summer 9am–sunset, winter from 9.30am). Completed in 440 BC, its slender, salt-white columns, fetchingly illuminated by night, are still a landmark for ships sailing to/from Piraeus. Lord Byron set a bad, much imitated example by carving his name on a column on the north side. Today, the grounds swarm with introduced guinea fowl (*frangókotes*), effectively mascots of the site. Down the hillside, you can see the remains of ancient ship sheds in the bay below; a sandy beach northwest of the temple, with its pricey tavernas, is more likely to appeal.

Just 10km (5 miles) north of Soúnio on the Attic east-coast road is **Lávrio**, the industrial hub of Attica before the rise of Piraeus, with an explosives plant and metalworks. Mining was still practised locally from the 19th century until 1989 by French and Greek companies, extracting arsenic, silver, lead, iron, and ferromanganese; the ancient silver-mine tunnels, between Soúnio and Lávrio in Keramíza district, can be toured (follow signs to Keramíza, and take old clothes). The town itself, mostly passed through en route for its ferry boats to Kéa and the north Aegean, deserves a halt. The partly neoclassical centre has been gentrified

Zéa Marina.

*Stunning Ágios
Spyrídon cove at
Pórto Ráfti.*

*View of Athens from
Mount Hymettus.*

Excursion to Brauron

From Lávrio, it's easy to continue to the **Sanctuary of Artemis** at **Brauron** (modern Vravróna) on the east coast of Attica, 35km (22 miles) directly from Athens. A 5th-century BC colonnade visited by owls at twilight is flanked by a 16th-century chapel, built on the site of an altar to Artemis. Nearby is the still-flowing sacred spring, an arm of the Erásinos River running past the site. In Classical times, well-born female children aged from seven to twelve ("little bears") performed a ritual dance at the quadrennial Arkteia festival honouring Artemis as the goddess of childbirth and virgins. Their plump statues – dressed like miniature adults, often clutching birds as offerings – are now in Room 3 of the much-improved site museum (Tue–Sun 8am–3pm), while in Room 2 are several fine stelae of the goddess, flanked by some of her totemic animals (stags, lions, dogs), facing groups of worshippers approaching with bulls to sacrifice in her honour. Room 1 helps you make sense of the sanctuary before visiting it.

and pedestrianised, the harbour front has charm, though conventional attractions are limited to a good, central archaeological museum and – at the north entrance of Lávrio – the rehabilitated French mining company buildings which you can visit (ask at the nearby café-restaurant).

Excursion to Marathon

The battle of **Marathon** in 490 BC was fought on a seaside plain 42km (26 miles) northeast of Athens, between the modern villages of Néa Mákri and Marathónas. What can be seen today are the presumed burial mounds of the Athenians and of the Plataeans, and the Archaeological Museum (Tue–Sun 8am–3pm).

The burial mound of the Athenians, a circular tumulus 9 metres (30ft) high, 50 metres (164ft) in diameter, and 185 metres (600ft) in circumference, has a modern copy of the ancient stele on the top (the original is in the National Archaeological Museum). The mound is impressive, but nothing compared to the victory it symbolises. The mighty Persian Empire, the largest on earth, had sent its army against Athens, and approximately 9,000 Athenian soldiers were joined before the battle by 1,000 soldiers from Plataea in Boeotia. A runner was sent to ask the Spartans for help, but the Spartans did not arrive until after the battle. The Athenians won despite being outnumbered by a factor of three, with the Persians losing 6,400 men and the Athenians 192. The Athenians were cremated and buried together in the mound. The mound of the Plataeans is near the archaeological museum, about 3km (2 miles) to the west. Nothing marks the Persian graves, but they seem to have been buried to the northeast, around the small church of the Panagía Mesosporítissa.

Excursion to Rhamnous

Rhamnous (Tue–Sun 8am–3pm; the temple of Nemesis, the fortress is closed), the site of an ancient fortress town on the northern borders of Attica with a sanctuary of Nemesis, lies 53km (33 miles) from Athens and 13km (8 miles) from Marathon. The sanctuary contains two temples, today merely foundations. The older, built after Xerxes' defeat in 480 BC, was dedicated to Nemesis and also to Themis, the god of justice. The slightly larger Doric temple of Nemesis, built in 436–32 BC, almost touches the older temple. The fortified garrison, its walls roughly 800 metres down from the sanctuary towards the shore, flourished in the 5th and 4th centuries BC.

Excursion to the Sanctuary of Amphiareion

The city-state that built the **Sanctuary of Amphiareion** (daily 8am–3pm) late in the 5th century BC was ancient Oropos, now buried beneath modern Skála Oropós, known for its Évia-bound ferries. The sanctuary, 37km (23 miles) north of Athens, had its acme during the Hellenistic period, much patronised by those in search of advice or medical help. The supplicant sacrificed a ram to Argive hero Amphiaraos, after which a dream would either cure the illness or answer a question. The surviving remains, in a lovely valley overlooked by pines, comprise a temple of the cult hero, a Roman theatre with many seats and a stage building, a long stoa, plus a small museum.

The Temple of Poseidon.

A NATIONAL TREASURE TROVE

The National Archaeological Museum in Athens houses a fabulous collection of ancient art and artefacts.

The museum (www.namuseum.gr/wellcome-en.html) provides an unrivalled survey of ancient Greek art. Don't be intimidated by the collection's size, but plan carefully, using the ground plan available from the ticket booth. During tourist season, avoid midday, when coach tours march through the galleries.

The first gallery in from the foyer is the confusingly named Prehistoric Collection, devoted to artefacts from the Mycenaean period (1600–1100 BC). The so-called Mask of Agamemnon is just one of three hammered-gold death masks on display, along with bronze items and octopus-motif pottery. In flanking rooms which completely circle the ground-floor perimeter, you'll find numerous examples of ancient Greek sculpture, from the Archaic era (750–490 BC) to the Classical (490–336 BC), Hellenistic (336–146 BC) and Roman (146 BC–AD 330) periods. Note the fine Eleusinian cult relief of the goddess Demeter offering grain to Triptolemos, watched by Persephone. In the far south gallery is the famous Roman group of Aphrodite, watched by Eros, about to whack a dirty old Pan with her sandal.

Two outstanding bronze statues are the 2nd-century BC Little Jockey from the Artemísion wreck, beyond the Myceneaean room, and the Ephebe of Antikythera. The small bronze objects collection, towards the rear left of the building, has exquisite statuettes, helmets and griffon heads. Just behind is the well-selected Egyptian exhibit, a fast gallop through that civilisation, with the eclectic Stathatos collection around the corner.

The upper floor is principally ancient Greek pottery, including finely detailed Tanagra figurines, near rooms of glass, precious metalwork and jewellery. The famous Thera frescoes are just a small portion of the displays in the Minoan Akrotíri room.

Herakles defeating king Vousiris and his servants in Egypt, c.470 BC.

The northeasterly galleries by the ticket booth house splendid Archaic kouroi and kourai (standing statues of men and women respectively), most of them from atop graves. The exceptional kore of Merenda is featured in the orientation leaflet, while this 7th century kouros was found in the Sanctuary of Poseidon at Sounion.

Minoan fresco depicting blue cavorting monkeys on the island of Santoríni.

FABULOUS FRESCOES

In the middle of the 2nd millennium BC the Cycladic island of Thera (today Santoríni), was much influenced – probably even ruled – by the Minoan civilisation of Crete. A Minoan settlement at Akrotíri on Santoríni, dating to approximately 1630 BC, was excavated by Spyridon Marinatos between 1967 and 1974. The most beautiful finds from Akrotíri are its frescoes. Just two, of boxers and antelopes, are kept in the National Archaeological Museum, while the rest remain on Santoríni.

Late in the 17th century BC, Thera's volcano erupted in a tremendous explosion. The entire settlement of Akrotíri, including buildings up to three storeys high, was beautifully preserved beneath volcanic ash. The frescoes decorated the interior walls of houses in the ancient town. Most of them show everyday scenes, such as a naked fisherman carrying home a bountiful catch, elegant ladies, blue cavorting monkeys, graceful antelopes, but there is also a 5.5-metre- (18.5-ft-) long detailed fresco of a naval campaign.

ronze Horse and Jockey of Artemesium (2nd century BC).

he range of exhibits in the useum is huge; it has one f the world's largest llections of carved reliefs.

Also from the Artemision wreck is a mid-5th-century BC bronze Zeus (or possibly Poseidon), in the act of hurling a now-vanished thunderbolt or trident.

This gold death mask found by Heinrich Schliemann at Mycenae and dating to the 16th century BC has become famous as the "Mask of Agamemnon". In fact, the Trojan Wars occurred much later.

THE PELOPONNESE

Steeped in ancient history – from Agamemnon's Mycenae to the first Olympic stadium – this giant peninsula also offers fine beaches, turquoise-coloured bays, and the wild and unspoilt Máni.

The Peloponnese (Pelopónnisos) takes its name from the legendary hero Pelops, plus the Greek for island, *nísos*, although it is seldom considered an island. Driving over from Attica (Attikí), it's easy to miss the little isthmus – riven by the Corinth Canal, lending some credence to the "island" tag – that joins the Peloponnese to the mainland. The area's medieval name was the Moreás, now rarely used; it derives either from an abundance of mulberry trees (*mouriés*) or more probably from the mulberry-leaf shape of the peninsula.

Korinthía province

By an administrative quirk, Korinthía province in the northeast includes a bit of the central mainland northeast of the canal; 13km (8 miles) beyond the spa resort of Loutráki lies the **Perahora Heraion ❶**, with an Archaic **Hera temple** and a *stoa*. Another important ancient sanctuary, the venue for the quadrennial Isthmian games, can be found at **Isthmia** on the southwest side of the canal; the Roman baths here retain extensive floor mosaics of sea creatures real and imaginary, while the well-arranged if one-room site **museum** (Tue–Sun 8.30am–3pm) features vivid *opus sectile* panels from AD 375 portraying harbour scenes, sea creatures, Nile bird

life and revered ancient personalities, as well as finds from the local shrines to Poseidon and Palaimon.

The canal itself, dug between 1882 and 1893, is obsolete in our era of mega-container ships, but a few freighters and yachts still squeeze through its 23-metre-wide (75-ft) channel, to the delight of spectators up on the pedestrian bridge – who can also watch the antics of the bungy-jumpers who practise here. At the Saronic Gulf end of the canal, two flanking cafés provide vantage points to watch the

Main Attractions
Nemea Zeus Temple
Ancient Mycenae
Návplio
Epidauros Theatre
Loúsios Gorge Region
Mystrás
Monemvasiá
Ancient Messene
Ancient Olympia Museum
Vouraïkós Rack-And-Pinion Train

Aphrodite and pastoral mosaic at the Ancient Corinth Museum.

Amfilohía · Houni · Karpenísi · Gardíki · Óros Íti 2152 · Lamía · Mólos · Loutrá (Éduipsou) · Evvia (Euboea) · Prokópi · Óros Kandílio · Mandoúdi

Katoúna · Potamoúla · Megálo Horió · Moshohóri · Thermopýlae · Ág. Geórgios · Ág. Konstandínos · Roviés · Límni · Moní Galatáki

Dytiki · Strátos · Prousós · Domnísta · Pávliani · Káto Graviá · Regínio · Livanátes · Arkítsa · Skála · Alaí · Óros Parnassós · Malesína

Agrínio · Astópetra · Thérmo · Thermón · Pendagií · Trikorfá · Amfíklia · Tithoréa · Orchomenós · Atalándi · Martíno · Akréfnio

Ellada · Angelókastro · Matarága · Káto Makrinoú · Lidoríki · Pendeóri · Itéa · Desfína · Dístomo · Livadiá · Palovoúna · Petra · Vágia · Thíva (Thebes)

Astakós · Etolikó · Pleuron · Mórnos · Kábos · Galaxídi · Delphi · Aráhova · Orhomenós · Moní Ósios Loúkas · Kavírion · Melissohóri · Erythres

Mesolóngi · Návpaktos · Psathópyrgos · Ágios Nikólaos · Eráni · Andíkyra · Paralía · Thísvi · Elopía · Mégara

Kalógria · Pátra · Égio · Diakoftó · Akráta · Lykoporiá · Xilókastro · Kiáto · Heraion · Perahóra · Loutráki · Salamína

Metóhi · Káto Aháia · Petrotó Ahea · Katarráktis · Flámboura · Kalávryta · Steno · Trikala · Soúli · Sikyón · Kórinthos · Archéa Kórinthos (Ancient Corinth) · Ístmia

Várda · Hióna · Káto Vlasía · Agía Lávra · Spílio Limnón (Cave of the Lakes) · Dóxa · Agíou Geórgiou Feneoú · Stymfalía · Neméa · Dervenákia · Mycenae · Mykínes · Ireón · Árgos · Tiryns · Lygourió · Agnoúndos · Epídavros · Paleá Epídavros

Amaliáda · Pýrgos · Olympía · Levkohóri · Magoúliana · Vytína · Levídi · Mantíneia · Nestáni · Lerna · Navplio · Epídavros (Epidauros)

Katákolo · Olympía · Dimitsána · Karkaloú · Stemnítsa · Trípoli · Anadokámbos · Myli · Joló · Astros · Parálio Ástros

Zahário · Andrítsena · Bassae · Karýtena · Megalópoli · Tegea · Ág. Andréas · Paralía Tyroú · Krankri · Ermióni

Kyparissía · Meligalás · Parádhisia · Peloponnisos · Trýpi · Kosmás · Tyrós · Leonídio · Pláka · Ýdra (Hydra)

Filiatrá · Messene · Mavromáti · Ithómi · Messíni · Kalamáta · Mystrás · Spárti · Amýkles · Elonís · Poúlithra

Marathópolis · Nestor's Palace · Hóra · Boúka · Petalídi · Avía · Tsérnia · Kastaniá · Skála · Geráki · Kyparíssi

Romanós · Giálova · Kámbos · Kardamýli · Stoúpa · Selenítsa · Plátsa · Élos · Ríhéa · Monemvasiá

Methóni · Koróni · Finikoúnda · Nomitsís · Langáda · Ítylo · Gýthio · Mólai · Géfyra · Néapoli

Pýlos · Sapiéndza · Shíza · Ákra Akrítas · Aréopoli · Mavrovoúni · Flomohóri · Poúnda · Elafónisos

Máni · Pýrgos Dírou · Lakonikós Kólpos · Lágia · Vátheia · Pórto Kágio · Ákra Ténaro (Matapán) · Ág. Pelagía

Gerolíménas · Kýthira · Kýthira · Kapsáli · Diakófti

Peloponnese

0   20 km

0   20 miles

Andikýthira, Kastéli-Kíssamou, Kríti

workings of the submersible bridge on the old highway to Athens – taking a dive whenever ships pass.

If you're intent on reaching ancient Epidauros directly, especially for a performance, carry on south of Isthmía along the fast, partly coastal road via confusingly named Paleá Epídavros, once the harbour for the ancient sanctuary. On the way, pause at the 11th-century monastery of Agnoúndos, where the tall, narrow katholokón (the church of the monastery) has fine frescoes from the 11th to the 18th centuries (the highest being the oldest).

Ancient **Corinth ❷**, 4km (2½ miles) southwest of modern **Kórinthos**, could not help but prosper through domination of trans-Isthmian haulage in pre-canal days. The Hellenistic city was razed by the Romans in 146 BC in reprisal for resistance, but refounded a century later as capital of Greece. What remains (daily May–Sept 8am–8pm, Oct 8am–6.30pm, Nov–Apr 8am–3pm), despite devastating earthquakes in AD 375 and 521, is the most complete imperial Roman town plan in Greece. Corinth's well-deserved reputation for

vice and luxury predictably exercised Saint Paul when he arrived in AD 52 for an 18-month sojourn.

A typically Roman obsession with plumbing is evident: there are the graphically obvious latrines off the marble-paved **Lehaion Way**, the still-functioning **Lower Peirene Fountain** at its end, and the ingenious **Glauke Fountain**, its four cisterns hewn from a monolith and filled by an aqueduct. Of the earlier Greek city, only seven columns of a Doric **Apollo Temple** still stand, though the site **museum** (same hours as site) retains a generous collection of late Archaic pottery and some intricate Roman-villa mosaics from Corinth's glory years.

Rather more evocative, however, is the nearly impregnable hilltop fortress of **Acrocorinth** (Akrokórinthos; daily 8am–3pm), long the military key to the peninsula and necessarily held by every occupying power. Enter via the gentler west slope through a set of triple fortifications to find yourself amid weedy desolation; little is left of the Ottoman town here, evacuated after Greek rebels took it in 1822.

FACT

The word "currant" derives from the word "Corinth" – a reference to the city's long-established trade in dried grapes, still one of Greece's most successful exports.

The Corinth Canal was completed in 1893.

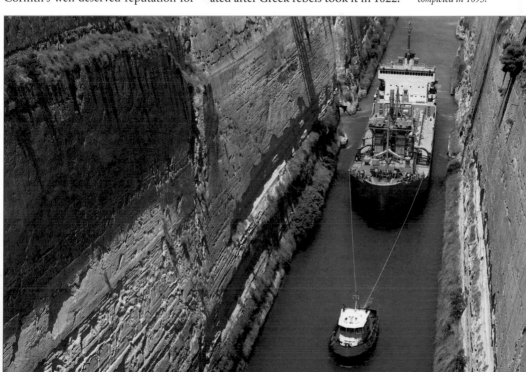

Most sieges, however, were successfully resisted thanks to the **Upper Peirene Fountain**, a subterranean structure near the southeast corner of the ramparts. At the very summit stand foundations of an **Aphrodite Temple**, reputedly once attended by 1,000 sacred prostitutes; the view all around is quite marvellous, stretching up to 60km (40 miles) in every direction.

Nemea and Stymfalía

The toll motorway to Kalamáta forges southwest from modern Kórinthos. Near **Dervenákia**, an exit leads west 8km (5 miles) to ancient **Nemea**, yet another shrine with its own biennial games. You can see the **stadium** where these events – supposedly inaugurated by Herakles, slayer of the Nemean lion – were held, but the most striking landmarks are nine Doric columns and two architraves of a 4th-century BC **Zeus Temple**, mostly re-erected since 1995; its fellows, toppled by Byzantine vandals, lie all about like many sausage slices. The dispersed site (summer daily 8am–3pm), including a well preserved baths and worthwhile

museum, occupies the floor of a bucolic valley; surrounding vineyards produce the grapes for the full-bodied Nemea red wines, some of Greece's best, with several roadside vintners in Arhéa Neméa village open for tasting and purchase.

From Neméa, it's easy to continue west to the valley and shallow, reedy lake of **Stymfalía**, site of yet another of Herakles' labours (dispatching the Stymphalian birds), closed to the northwest by often snowcapped Mount Zíria (2375m). Highlight of the area is the excellent roadside Environment Museum of Stymfalia (www.piop.gr; Wed–Mon Mar–mid-Oct 10am–6pm, mid-Oct–Feb 10am–5pm), which ably documents all rural local activities, from lake-fishing to bee-keeping, and provides a viewing platform for the ducks, grebes and coots who gather on the water. The way continues west via Kastaniá village to the eerie upland of Feneós; at its north edge there's a namesake village, the scenic Dóxa lake and Agíou Georgíou Feneoú **monastery**, offering exceptionally vivid 18th-century

Návplio waterfront and the fortress-island of Boúrtzi.

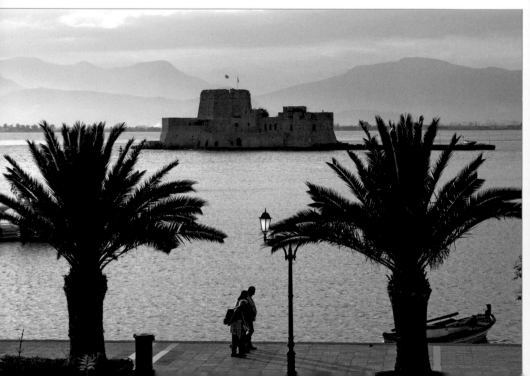

frescoes and friendly monks. Return to the Corinth gulf coast via **Tríkala** village on the north flank of Zíria, divided into three districts; this was the first mountain resort in Greece, owing to easy access from Athens since the 1920s.

Argolída province

The twisty old highway enters the Argolid plain at modern **Mykínes**, a village devoted to citrus and tourism; nearby stands ancient **Mycenae** ❸, a fortified palace complex covering an easily defendable, ravine-flanked ridge. Mycenae gave its name to an entire late Bronze-Age era – and made the reputation of a German self-taught Classical scholar (and self-made millionaire), Heinrich Schliemann. From 1874 to 1876, he excavated here, relying on little other than intuition and a belief in the literal accuracy of Homer's epics. Greek archaeologists had already revealed the imposing **Lion Gate** of the citadel, but the rich tomb finds Schliemann made, now in the National Museum of Athens, amply corroborate Mycenae's Homeric epithet "rich in gold". Later revisionists point to Schliemann's sloppy excavating techniques and economy with the truth – the gold death mask which prompted his boast "I have gazed upon the face of Agamemnon" is now dated to 300 years before Troy – but the dedicated amateur did beat the experts to the greatest archaeological trove of that century.

At the site itself (daily Apr 8am– 7pm, May–Oct 8am–8pm, Nov–Mar 8am–3pm), little remains above waist height inside the perimeter walls of the palace, though a rather alarming secret stairway descends to a siege-proof cistern in the northeast corner. Outside, however, are two burial chambers of unsurpassed ingenuity: the tholos tombs dubbed, very speculatively, the **Treasury of Atreus** and the **Tomb of Clytemnestra**, also known as "beehive" tombs after the manner of their construction.

Ancient Argos

The onward road divides at **Árgos** ❹, capital of Argolída province and a major agricultural centre. Tomatoes and citrus – the latter introduced by American advisers after World War II – are grown extensively; the modern town itself is of little interest apart from its **Archaeological Museum** (currently closed for refurbishment). But just south, beside the Trípoli-bound road, sprawl the ruins of **ancient Árgos**; most notable is the huge, steeply raked theatre. From the opposite end of town, drivers can reach the Frankish castle atop Lárissa hill, site of the ancient **acropolis**, for a view nearly on a par with that of Acrocorinth, extending from Mt Zíria to Návplio (Nauplion), by way of the low hillock of ancient Tiryns.

Just over halfway to Návplio from Árgos loom the 13th-century BC ruins of Homer's "wall-girt" **Tiryns** (May–Oct Mon–Fri 89am–8pm, Sat–Sun 8am–3pm, Nov–Apr 8.30am–3pm), another royal palace complex. The site, an 18-metre (60-ft) bluff rising from an ancient marsh, was not as

Mycenae's treasures were uncovered by the archaeologist Heinrich Schliemann.

Inside the Treasury of Atreus at Mycenae.

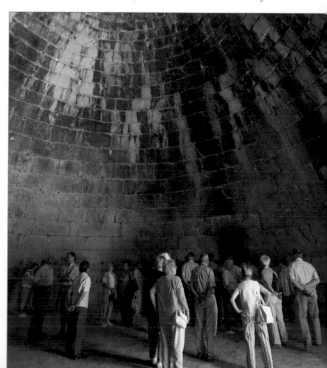

naturally defensible as Mycenae, so the man-made fortifications – originally twice their present height – were necessarily more involved. Massive masonry blocks reaching 3 cubic metres (100 cu. ft) each were joined in mortar-less walls termed "Cyclopean", after the only beings thought capable of manoeuvring them. No heraldic lions over the entry-gate here, and no beehive tombs; but Tiryns intrigues with a **secret stairway** (off-limits) to the westerly postern gate and, near the southeast corner, a corbel-ceilinged **gallery** (viewable past a barrier), its walls polished smooth by the millennial rubbings of sheltering sheep.

Návplio and Epidauros

Návplio ❺, rising in tiers at the southeast corner of the plain, is more than a little mirage-like, for the well-preserved old town retains an elegance a world away from utilitarian Árgos just 12km (7 miles) to the northwest. The neoclassical architecture, pedestrian-friendly marble streets and interlocking fortresses date mostly from the second Venetian occupation of 1686–1715,

and subsequent Ottoman reconquest; the fortified rock here had been a pivotal point in their struggles for control of the Aegean from the 15th century onward. Between 1829 and 1834 Návplio served as the country's first capital, but today it's a laid-back place, despite playing a role as an upmarket resort; it stays busy year round, thanks to Athenian weekenders.

Návplio is overawed by **Akronavpliá**, four separate fortresses of various ages just overhead, plus, on an easterly hill, the sprawling, early 18th-century castle of **Palamídi** (daily Apr 8am–7pm, May–Oct 8am–8pm, Nov–Mar 8am–3pm), whose meandering curtain wall encloses seven self-contained bastions designed to withstand the strongest artillery of the era. Yet its Venetian garrison capitulated with barely a fight in 1715 to the Ottomans, who in turn surrendered to the Greek rebels after a more protracted siege in 1822. Just under 900 steps (or a road) lead up from the Old Town to the summit – and to more eyefuls of the Argolid.

Down in town, excellent museums include the Archaeological Museum

High-perched Karýtena.

(Tue–Sun 8.30am–3pm), in a restored Venetian barracks, where pride of place goes to a complete set of Mycenean armour; the Peloponnesian Folklore Foundation Museum (www.pli.gr; Mon–Sat 9am–2.30pm, Sun 9.30am–3pm); and, in the new quarter, an annexe of Athens' National Gallery (www.nationalgallery.gr; Mon, Thu, Sat 10am–3pm, Wed, Fri also 5–8pm, Sun 10am–2pm), always with stellar temporary exhibits.

Some 27km (17 miles) east of Návplio, **Epidauros** (**Epídavros**) ❻ is visited mainly for the sake of its magnificent 4th-century BC **theatre**, whose perfect acoustics tour guides perpetually demonstrate with coins dropped on the orchestra floor. Because it lay buried until the late 19th century, the theatre masonry survived the ages relatively unscathed, and restoration has been minimal. It is now the venue for sell-out performances of ancient drama during July, as part of the Hellenic Festival; special buses from Athens are laid on, as are boats from Aegina to nearby Paleá Epídavros port.

The theatre is just one part of a vast sanctuary (daily Jan–Mar 8am–5pm, Apr 8am–7pm, May–Oct 8am–8pm, Nov–Dec 8am–3pm) to the healing demi-god Asklepios, extending northwest, and steadily being excavated and re-erected. Standing tall already are the propylon of the Hestiatoria, the Enkimitirion colonnade, and the Tholos of Polykleitos, a circular, once-domed structure with a concentric maze in the foundations thought to originally contain serpents (sacred to Asklepios), and centre of the god's cult. The site museum is, by contrast, of specialist interest.

Arkadía province

Heading west from Návplio along the Argolid gulf coast road, past Lerna (modern Mýli), where Hercules slew the many-headed Hydra, you enter Arkadía – specifically, its easterly sub-region of Kynouría – just before **Parálio Ástros** ❼ an established

beach resort whose older houses back against a headland crowned with a medieval fortress built atop a Mycenean acropolis. Ástros, 5km (3 miles) inland, has a worthwhile archaeological museum and 5km further west, adjacent to medieval Loukoú monastery with fine 16th-century frescoes being steadily cleaned and rather worldly nuns, the fascinating remains of an arcaded Roman aqueduct so encrusted with lime stalactites as to form a Dalí-esque sculpture.

The road south from Ástros passes fine beaches like Kryonéri and Poulíthra before turning inland at sizeable Leonídio, homeland of Tsakonian – a relict Dorian dialect being revived in writing on local signage. Now your way creeps up through a spectacular, Wild-West type gorge, past the convent of Elonís, to the "hill station" of **Kosmás**, high amidst fir trees on the flank of Mt Párnom and the best base to explore this range, blessed with good walking and one of the starriest night skies in Greece. From Kosmás, it's easy to cross the mountain (in your own car) to either Mystrás or Monemvasiá.

Sheep on the road near Trípoli.

Loánnou Prodrómou is one of Greece's most spectacular monasteries.

Chapel overlooking the Loúsios Gorge.

temple, and Mantineia, now amidst a major wine-growing district.

Exiting the motorway at Nestáni, passing close by the freakish neo-Byzantine wedding-cake church of Agía Fotiní at Mandínia, the main westbound road skirts the base of fir-cloaked, blade-like **Mount Ménalo** with its ski resort (the closest to Athens), via the handsome villages of **Levídi** and **Vytína** ❾, the latter a popular weekend base for Greeks. Beyond Vytína, towards Ilía province, the most logical and compelling halt is **Langádia**, its famous masons responsible for sturdy stone houses teetering on a slope above the local gorge.

But the main attraction of montane Arkadía resides along the Loúsios valley, reached by a turning south between Vytína and Langádia. Near the head of the Loúsios valley, **Dimitsána** ❿ sprawls engagingly over a saddle demarcated by the river, its skyline graced by four belfries. The imposing mansions here date from its mercantile golden age, the 1700s. Specific local sights include the **Open Air Water Power Museum** (www.piop.gr; Wed–Mon

Both the old highway from Mýli and the inland expressway converge on the pear- and apple-planted uplands around dull **Trípoli** ❽, capital of Arkadía province. This has little to offer aside from a good **archaeological museum** (www.tegeamuseum.gr; Tue–Sun 8.30am–3pm) with finds from Trípoli's ancient nearby predecessors: Tegea, with a tumbled Athena

Mar–mid-Oct 10am–6pm, mid-Oct–Feb 10am–5pm), with mill workings in situ, and further down the same side road, cliffside **Emyalón Monastery** (closed 1–5pm), with four resident monks, and frescoes from 1608.

Stemnítsa ⓫ 11km (6.5 miles) south of Dimitsána along the east flank of the Loúsios, has been officially renamed Ypsoúnda, but the Slavic toponym remains more popular; it's an atmospheric, introverted place in a hidden cirque, with imposing mansions looking only at each other. A single jewellery shop recalls the former silver-smithing industry, while a Folklore Museum (daily 8.30am–3pm, closed Feb) highlights pan-Hellenic items, local dress and (best of all) fascinating publicity posters for a local karagiózis (shadow-puppet) player.

Hyperbolically dubbed the "Toledo of Greece", thanks to its evocative castle and houses overlooking a kink in the **Alfiós River**, the sleepy demeanour of **Karýtena** ⓬, 16km (10 miles) beyond Stemnítsa, belies a tumultuous history. Established as the seat of a Frankish barony during the 13th century, it was later retaken by the Byzantines, who endowed Karýtena with three churches (Ágios Nikólaos has fine 18th-century frescoes) and an arched bridge over the Alfiós. Both bridge and town figured on one side of the old 5,000-drachma note; the beturbanned Independence War chieftain Kolokotrónis glared out from the other, for he successfully resisted a long Ottoman siege here in 1826.

All of these hill towns serve as gateways to different parts of the **Loúsios Gorge**, which in its relatively short extent has a lot to offer. Canoeing and kayaking on the two local rivers are offered locally by several outfitters, while a marked hiking trail threads the canyon from just below Dimitsána to the Atsíholos bridge. The first significant stop, also reached by road from Dimitsána, is the restored Néa Filosófou monastery on the west bank, home to two monks, with late 17th-century frescoes including Jesus walking on the Sea of Galilee; a little beyond, the 10th-century Paleá Filosófou monastery is largely ruined

FACT

In March 1821,
Germanos, the local
Archbishop of Pátra, gave
his blessing to an uprising
against the Ottomans,
which led to the liberation
of all Arkadía.

and almost indistinguishable from its cliff-side surroundings.

Further downstream, also accessible by narrow roads from Stemnítsa or **Ellinikó** village, awaits the spectacular 11th-century monastery of Agíou Ioánnou Prodrómou (St John the Baptist; closed 1–5pm), one of those swallow's-nest-type monasteries which the Orthodox Church loves to tuck into cliff faces. It has just three monks, frescoes and a well-stocked ossuary. The west-bank trail (and a branch of the road) continues to the medieval Kokkorás bridge, the Byzantine chapel of **Ágios Andréas** and excavated ancient **Gortys**, an *asklipeion* or therapeutic centre; the architectural highlight here is a peculiar round structure, thought to be a bathhouse. Finally, a minor road from Karýtena descends to the two-arched Atsíholos bridge and then the eponymous village, beyond which awaits Kalamioú monastery, new and old. A caretaker monk at the newer foundation will unlock the 1713-vintage church, covered with superb, rare frescoes such as two Christs Emmanuel in the vaults,

and a visualisation of the Byzantine hymn Epi Soi Haire. A short stair-path leads to cliff-clinging old Kalamioú, mostly ruined except for a rock-cut church sheltering slightly older, moderately well preserved frescoes of the Life of Christ.

From Karýtena, the main road west follows the Alfiós, past its co-mingling with the Loúsios, to **Andrítsena** ⓭, actually over the border in Ilía province. Sadly, shuttered traditional shops along the main street recall the village's past as a major entrepôt with 3,000 souls; today's permanent population is a tenth of that. A steady trickle of summer tourist traffic passes through to the 5th-century temple of **Apollo Epikourios** at **Bassae** (Vásses), 14km (9 miles) south. Although the most intact ancient shrine in Greece and a Unesco World Heritage site, it's unlikely to enchant, concealed as it is by a colossal, guy-wired permanent tent to protect it from winter frosts.

More rewarding for many is the **gorge of the River Néda** 18km (11 miles) south, just below modern Figália village and ruins of ancient Phigaleia,

Mount Taÿgetos on a fine spring day.

whose citizens originally built the temple in gratitude for Apollo having lifted a plague. A marked, 90-minute trail loop (or a steep road, just passable to ordinary cars) descends past the ruins – best of these a temple of Athena, whose altar glimpses the sea – to the lushly vegetated north bank of the river, where a spur path goes briefly west to the *stómio* or tunnel-cave, through which the Néda runs underground for 10km (6 miles). Photogenic waterfalls on the Marathónios tributary stream feed the main river just before it disappears from view.

Lakonía

As you descend the 64-km (40-mile) road from Trípoli to modern Spárti, the long ridge of **Mount Taýgetos** with its striated limestone bands looms into sight on the right. Ahead stretches the olive-and-citrus-rich floodplain of the Evrótas River, belying the stereotypical image of ancient Sparta as a harsh, "spartan" place (the province's name, Lakonía, also lives on abroad as "laconic" – supposedly the distinguishing characteristic of the Classical natives).

Spárti ⓮, the modern successor to ancient Sparta, is an unexciting place redeemed only by some attractive squares and neoclassical facades, vestiges of Bavarian town planning in 1834. The archaeological museum (daily 8am–3pm) is particularly rich in late Roman floor-mosaics from local villas, and eerie votive offerings from the **sanctuaries of Apollo** at Amýkles and **Artemis Orthia** on the acropolis – where youths were flogged until bloody to honour the goddess. At the acropolis itself, however, 700 metres northwest of town, not much remains aside from a badly eroded theatre and the sparse remains of the Byzantine church of **Ágios Níkon**.

What little the Spartans built was appropriated for the construction of Byzantine **Mystrás** ⓯ 6km (4 miles) west (daily Apr–Aug 8am–8pm, Sept–Oct until 6.30pm, Nov–Mar 8am–3pm). A romantically ruined walled town, clinging to a conical crag and topped by a castle, Mystrás is a corruption of mezythrás, the Greek for "cream-cheese maker" – thought to be a reference to this cheese's traditional conical shape.

Originally founded by the Franks in 1249, Mystrás grew to a city of 20,000 souls under the Byzantines, becoming the capital of the Morean despots after 1348.

The church of **Perívleptos monastery** contains a complete cycle of frescoes depicting the *Dodekaeorton* or 12 major church feasts, with such light touches as children up a tree in the Entry to Jerusalem. Nearby **Pandánassa** convent, the newest church built in 1428 and now home to nuns, has a typically Gothic exterior as well as vivid frescoes within, the best of these neck-craningly high. By contrast, the oldest church, the **Mitrópolis** or cathedral of Ágios Dimítrios, is resolutely conservative in structure, notwithstanding awkward domes added later; here frescoes include a complete cycle of Christ's Miracles.

Mystrás's Perívleptos church has some superb frescoes.

A horse walks through narrow alleys at Monemvasiá.

Monemvasiá's fortifications cling to a crag by the sea.

The **Vrondóhion** monastic complex harbours yet another 14th-century church, the more daring **Afendikó**, the weight of its six domes borne by a system of piers below and colonnaded gallery above. Sea monsters bob in the Baptism fresco, while above the altar, apostles marvel at Christ ascending in a mandorla.

Monemvasiá and Gýthio

Originally the port of Mystrás, **Monemvasiá ⑯**, lies 94km (58 miles) southeast of Spárti. Like Mystrás, it's a fortified double town, clinging to a limestone plug rising 350 metres (1,150ft) from the sea and inevitably nicknamed the "Gibraltar of Greece" – although the "Dubrovnik of Greece" would be an equally apt term for the tile-roofed, wall-encased lower town on the south slope. Supporting a population of 50,000 in its heyday as a semi-autonomous city-state, Monemvasiá prospered by virtue of its fleets and handy location, halfway between Italy and the Black Sea. Never taken by force, it did surrender on occasion through prolonged siege – no food

could grow on the rock, though enormous cisterns provided water.

The lower town, within its 900-metre three-sided circuit of Venetian walls, is invisible as you cross the causeway until the massive west gate (closed to vehicles) suddenly appears. Immediately above the gate perches the house in which prominent poet Giannis Ritsos was born in 1909; one wonders what the conservative locals made of his forthright Marxism and bisexuality. On his death in 1990, he was buried in the nearby cemetery, with one of his poems chiselled on the gravestone in lieu of religious sentiment.

Linked by a maze of tunnels, arcades and cul-de-sacs at the end of steep, cobbled lanes, many of the lower-town houses have been bought up and restored by wealthy Athenians and foreigners. Masoned steps zigzag up the cliff face overhead to the older, upper town, first settled and fortified in the 6th century AD but abandoned since the early 1900s and now utterly ruined. The sole exception to the desolation is the 14th-century **Agía Sofía** church with its 16-sided dome, poised

THE BYZANTINE GEM

Until the Ottomans took over in 1460, Mystrás flourished as a major cultural centre, attracting scholars and artists from Serbia, Constantinople and Italy. The latter's influence is evident in the brilliantly coloured (and remarkably well-preserved) frescoes which adorn Mystrás's churches – these are as crammed with extraneous figures, buildings and landscapes as any Italian painting of the time. The churches are a composite of three-aisled-basilica ground plan and domed cross-in-square gallery, making them airily well lit by Byzantine standards. Proto-Renaissance sensibilities (and the Frankish wives of most of the despots) inspired belfries and colonnaded porticoes. It is easy to see why Mystrás is regarded as the last great Byzantine architectural flowering before the onset of the Ottoman era.

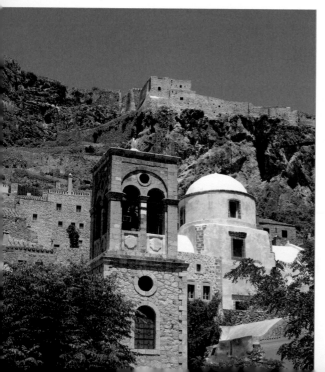

at the edge of the northerly cliff and the first point in Monemvasiá to catch the sunrise.

Overnighting at Monemvasiá is expensive, and beaches are remote; if you have transport but not the wallet, there are wonderful alternatives to either side. **Kyparíssi**, 56km (34 miles) north with the final approach along a one-lane corniche, is an idyllic Shangri-La grouped in three neighbourhoods, with a good pebble beach and fish tavernas. Elafónisos, the Peloponnese's only inhabited island, 39km (24 miles) to the south towards Neápoli via Poúnda jetty, has a single town with all amenities but some of the best beaches around at Símos (south of town) and Panagítsa (west).

Gýthio ⓱, 65km (40 miles) west of Monemvasiá, is a port town on the ferry routes to Kýthira and Crete, a holiday resort in its own right, and a deceptively congenial gateway to the austere Máni. The quay is lined by tiled vernacular houses and pricey seafood tavernas; across the Lakonian Gulf the sun rises over **Cape Maléa**, and Mount Taýgetos is glimpsed one last time on

the north. In ancient times, Gýthio served as Sparta's port, and more recently exported acorns for use in tanning. There are few sights, apart from a Roman theatre and the Museum of the Mani (Tue–Sun 8am–2.30pm) on **Marathonísi** islet (ancient Kranae), tied to the mainland by a causeway.

The best nearby sandy beach – and weirdest sight – is 5km north at Selinítsa, where an enormous, derelict smugglers' freighter, the Dimitrios, has been grounded in a few feet of water since 1981.

The Máni

An arid, isolated region protected by Taýgetos' southerly outriders, the **Máni** was the last part of Greece to espouse Christianity (in the 9th century), but made up for lost time by erecting dozens of small country chapels. Little grows except stunted olive trees, though in late summer an extra dash of colour is lent by hedges of fruiting prickly pears. "Outer" or **Éxo Máni** (Ítylo northwest to Kalamáta) is more tourist-friendly, fertile and better watered; "Inner" or **Mésa Máni**, south

A view towards Monemvasiá.

FACT

Nearby vineyards produced Malvasia sweet wine – similar to Madeira, and known as Malmsey or Malvoisie in the west – but local production ceased by the 15th century. Following the opening of the Corinth Canal, Monemvasiá lost all commercial and military significance.

of a line connecting Ítylo with Gýthio, has the more noteworthy churches on the west shore, and tower-studded villages sprouting from the east-coast settlements. But extreme conditions have prompted wholesale depopulation, and the villages here only fill during the autumn hunting season.

From Gýthio, the main road into the Máni passes the castles of **Passavá** and **Kelefá**, the only Ottoman attempts at imposing order locally, before reaching **Areópol** ⓲, main market town and tourist base of the Inner Máni. Formerly Tsímova, stronghold of the Mavromihális clan, it was renamed after independence for Ares the god of war, in recognition of its contribution to the independence struggle. Two churches, both 18th-century, distinguish it: **Taxiárhis** with its campanile and zodiacal apse reliefs, and frescoed **Ágios Ioánnis**, near which is a worthwhile museum of Christianity in the Máni, located inside the Pikoulakis Towerhouse (Tue–Sun 8.30am–2.40pm).

Some 8km (5 miles) south, just off the west-coast road towards **Cape** **Mátapan** (Ténaro), the caverns at **Pýrgos Diroú** are the sole organised tourist attraction in the Máni (daily summer 8.30am–4pm, winter 8.30am–3pm); visits are partly by boat along a subterranean river, and queues can be long.

Between here and Geroliménas stand various frescoed Byzantine churches; sadly, most are permanently locked, and hunting for the warden can be futile. Two of the best, at Áno Boularí, are also the easiest to access. Apply in the Geroliménas post office for the keys to **Ágios Stratigós**, with extensive frescoes from the 12th to the 18th centuries; and to nearby **Ágios Pandelímon** which has the earliest (10th-century) frescoes around, depicting saints Pandelímon and Nikitas in the apse. **Geroliménas** ⓳ itself, 20km (12 miles) from Areópoli, can offer tavernas and accommodation, but not much else – it dates only from 1870. The 35 ridgetop tower-houses of dramatic, deserted **Váthia** ⓴, 10km (6 miles) further east, have become photogenic synonyms for the Máni.

Gýthio waterfront.

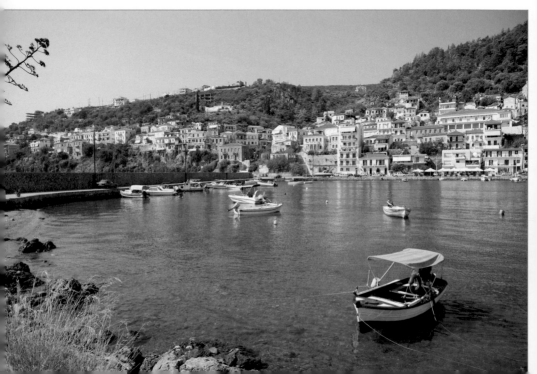

The main tarred road out of Gero-liménas loops along the eastern shore via **Lágia** (famed for its broad-based, tapering towers and purple-marble quarries) and **Flomohóri** (with the highest towers and pebbly **Kótronas** beach below) before re-emerging at Areópoli. Just across the ravine dividing Inner Máni and Areópoli from Outer is bluff-top **Ítylo ㉑** lushly set and – unlike so many of its neighbours – relatively prosperous; below the village lie the frescoed monastery of **Dekoúlou** and the beach resort of **Néo Ítylo**.

The pride of **Langáda ㉒** village 14km (9 miles) north, is the central 11th-century church of **Metamórfosi tou Sotíra**, whose frescoes still await uncovering and restoration; contiguous **Plátsa** and **Nomitsís** have four more Byzantine chapels. Mass tourism takes over at the picturesque fishing port of **Ágios Nikólaos** (Selenítsa); nearby **Stoúpa ㉓** has two sandy bays and plenty of facilities as well. **Kardamýli ㉔** ranks as the premier resort before Kalamáta, offering a long pebble beach, a late-medieval citadel and some good walking just inland.

Messinía province

Kalamáta can also be approached directly from Spárti via the spectacular 60-km (37-mile) road which crosses Mount Taýgetos. **Kalamáta ㉕** itself suffered a devastating 1986 earthquake which left half the population homeless; despite subsequent emigration, it's still the biggest town hereabouts (40,000 people), with an attractive seafront and some lively untouristy tavernas to recommend it.

The worthiest nearby target is ancient **Messene ㉖**, 27km (16 miles) north, the Peloponnese's most up-and-coming archaeological site (www.ancientmessene.gr; daily 9am–4pm), at modern Mavromáti village. Already excavated and commendably labelled are the enormous stadium, the biggest in Greece, an intact tomb at its far end, extensive colonnades, an *ekklesiastirion* (type of theatre), and the hulking Arcadia Gate in the walls (raised against the Spartans, Messene's deadly enemy) of the ancient city, which flourished into Roman times, and was supplied with water from the still-gushing spring in the centre of the modern village.

WHERE

It was on Marathonísi that Paris and Helen legendarily spent their first night together, and so launched a thousand ships.

Váthia in the Máni.

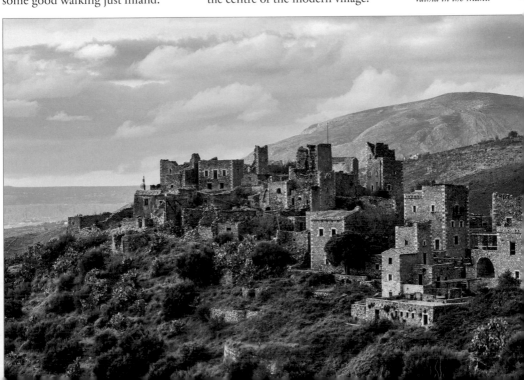

Most visitors to Messinía province, however, have their sights set on the low southwesterly promontory ending in **Cape Akrítas**, with its fine beaches and balmy climate. Prime destination is **Koróni** ㉗, founded by Venice in 1206 to guard the sea lanes between the Adriatic and Crete. The castle here still shelters a few houses, orchards and pine groves, but a convent occupies most of it. The town outside the walls (built since 1830) has weathered tourism well, its vernacular houses with their wooden balconies still lining the steep stair-streets. **Zánga beach**, one of the best in the Peloponnese, extends for 3km (2 miles) west.

Methóni ㉘, another "eye of Venice" lying 35km (22 miles) west, grew wealthy after 1209 from the pilgrim trade to Palestine. Its sprawling castle (daily 8am–3pm; free), washed on three sides by the sea, combines military architecture of various eras: beyond the Venetian sea-gate, a Turkish octagonal tower – the Boúrtzi – overlooks two islets, while a French arched bridge of 1828 spans the Venetian moat. Little remains of the medieval town inside, however, and the modern village outside the walls is not nearly as attractive as Koróni's, and nor is the beach.

Pýlos ㉙, 13km (8 miles) north, is another rather sleepy town; despite its pleasant setting on huge, landlocked **Navaríno Bay**, what life there is seems confined to the immediate environs of **Platía Tríon Navárhon**, the main square. The bay has seen two momentous naval battles: in 425 BC, when the Athenians bested the Spartans off **Sfaktiría island**, and in October 1827, when a combined French, Russian and English armada sank Ibrahim Pasha's Ottoman fleet, thus guaranteeing Greek independence. The three allied admirals are honoured by an obelisk in their namesake square. The huge Venetian-Ottoman fortress of Niókastro (Tue–Sun 8am–3pm) dominating Pýlos contains a huge mosque-church, being restored, and a collection of fine historical or ethnographic engravings installed inside the French barracks of 1828.

For beaches, you'll have to head for the north end of the bay beyond Giálova, where perfectly half-circular

Methoní's Baírtzi, a fine example of Ottoman military architecture.

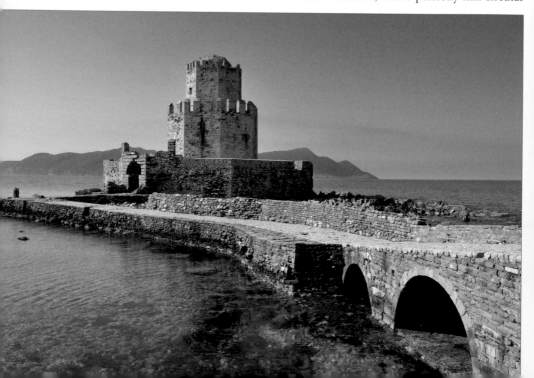

Voïdokiliá bay is both beach and wildlife refuge, featuring on every poster and postcard of Messinía. About 11km (6 miles) north of Giálova lies the Bronze Age Palace of **Nestor** (closed for restoration until further notice), discovered in 1939, excavated more recently and now protected by a synthetic roof. The elderly museum at Hóra Trifylías (Tue–Sun 8.30am–3pm) desperately needs a refit, but a huge trove of gold tomb finds from Peristéria manages to shine through.

On your way out of Messinía, stop – halfway between Filiatrá and pretty Kyparissía – at Agrílis for Fournier's **Castle** (always viewable), the brainchild of a returned Greek-American. This four-storey, crenellated, turretted folly with pseudo-heraldry is flanked by outsized figures of the Trojan horse, Helen and Hector – a monster of kitsch unequalled (given stiff competition) in Greece, but hugely enjoyable.

Olympia and the Cape of Kyllíni

From **Kyparissía** it's a pleasant coastal drive to ancient **Olympia** ㉚, where the Kládeos River meets the Alfiós. The sanctuary here served for two millennia as a religious and athletic centre; of all the Hellenic competitions associated with shrines, the Olympic Games, held every four years at the late-summer full moon, were the most prestigious, and the pan-Hellenic truce declared for their duration was honoured by the various city-states on pain of stiff fines. Although the first verified games were held in 776 BC, the Altis, a sacred forest at the base of the hill of Kronos, was consecrated to pre-Olympian deities as early as the second millennium BC. Recent fires have stripped the hill's pines, but the site is still liberally planted with Zeus' oaks, and in early spring, judas trees provide vivid flashes of colour.

The most salient monuments at the Olympia site (daily 8am–8pm) are the **Palaestra** training centre, whose courtyard colonnade has been re-erected; the **workshop of Pheidias**, the celebrated sculptor (identified by a cup found with his name inscribed); the Leonidaion guesthouse, with its lobular central pool; the Archaic **Hera temple**

Sturdy tower-house typical of the Máni region.

FEUDS IN THE MÁNI

While there may be some truth to Maniot claims that they are descended from the ancient Spartans, more crucial to the region's history was the arrival, during the 13th to the 15th centuries, of refugee Byzantine nobility. These established a local aristocracy, the Nyklians, which formed competing clans; only they had the right to erect tower-mansions.

Poor farmland and a fast-growing population spurred not just piracy and banditry, but complex vendettas between clans. Blood feuds could last for years, with sporadic truces to tend crops; women, who delivered supplies, were inviolate, as were doctors, who treated the wounded impartially. Combatants fired at each other from neighbouring towers, raising them as high as five storeys so as to lob rocks onto their opponents' flat roofs. The vendettas generally ended either with the annihilation or utter submission of the losing clan. Rather than rule the Máni directly, the Ottomans encouraged the feuding in the hopes of weakening any concerted rebellions, appointing a Nyklian chieftain as bey to represent the sultan.

The office passed between rival clans, but under the last bey, Petros Mavromihalis, the clans united, participating in the Greek independence uprising as of 17 March 1821. Rather less illustriously, the brother and son of "Petrobey" assassinated first president Ioannis Kapdistrias on 9 October 1831, for perceived insults to the Mavromihalis clan.

TIP

To see the best
examples of the
distinctive Maniot tower-
houses, head for the
villages of Váthia, Kítta,
Nómia and Flomohóri.

with its dissimilar columns; the enormous **Zeus temple**, now reduced to column sections; and the **stadium** with its 192-metre (630-ft) running course and surviving vaulted entrance.

In the newer **Olympia Museum** (daily 8am–8pm), among the best half-dozen in Greece, pride of place goes to the pediment reliefs recovered from the Zeus temple debris, now on display in the central hall, depicting the battle between the Lapiths and the Centaurs, with the god Apollo at the centre of the composition. Other unmissable items include the Hermes and baby Dionysos of Praxiteles, showcased in Room 8 at the right rear; the Geometric and Archaic bronze gallery (Room 2), offering a gorgon shield ornament, a hammered relief of a mother griffon, various helmets, griffon heads as cauldron ornaments; and the painted terracotta of Zeus with Ganymede in Room 4, near the heavily damaged Nike of Paionios. If time permits, the old museum nearby (Mon–Fri 9am–4pm) offers a fine late Roman mosaic, a statue of Hadrian's lover Antinoös, a stele of Herakles wrestling with the

Voïdokiliá beach, near Pýlos.

Nemean lion, and a bronze miniature of two human wrestlers.

The closest beaches to Olympia (modern Olymbía) are southeast of the picturesque cruise-ship port of Katákolo, full of converted old warehouses. More edifying targets lie northwest along the main highway, in **Gastoúni** ㉛ where the 12th-century church of Panagía Katholikó at the southwest edge of town offers narthex frescoes, recently cleaned, nearly on a par with those at Mystrás, including a wonderful bestiary amongst apocalyptic scenes.

Further into the cape ending at Kyllíni, **Hlemoutsi** ㉜ (Tue–Sun 9am–4pm) – visible from a great distance away, the name a corruption of Clermont – was the strongest purpose-built Frankish castle in the western Peloponnese, erected in 1220–23 by Geoffrey de Villehardouin to survey the straits with Zákynthos. Restoration of the hexagonal citadel inside the huge, fan-shaped bailey is ongoing, which means the rooftop viewpoint and some of the vaulted halls may be closed, but it's still well worth the trip. The adjacent modern village of Kástro is functional enough for an overnight or a meal, and the beaches just downhill, opposite Zákynthos, are excellent.

Aháïa province

Continuing deeper into Aháïa province along the coast north of **Kyllíni**, sample the enormous, 7-km (4-mile) beach of **Kalogriá** ③ and the swamps (plus umbrella-pine dune forest) just behind. This, one of the largest wetlands in the Balkans, has finally gained protected status as a national park; get the full story from the information office in Lápa, the village where you leave the main highway for the beach.

Pátra ④, 38km (24 miles) further, is Greece's third-largest city, and the principal port for ferries to Italy and some of the Ionian Islands. With its fearsome traffic, anonymous post-war architecture and lack of beaches, it's hardly the ideal spot for a quiet holiday retreat; only the ancient **acropolis** (with an originally Byzantine castle) seems peaceful. But linger at Carnival time to witness Greece's best observance, with parades, floats and conspicuous attendance by students and the gay community.

Some 44km (27 miles) east along the motorway toward Athens, **Diakoftó** ⑤ is the start/end point of the famous rack-and-pinion (odontotós) railway up the precipitous **Vouraïkós Gorge**. Long one of the most popular train-rides in Greece, its future – like the entire railway system – is threatened by troïka demands for closure, but while it lasts, take advantage (current news on www.odontotos.com). Because of the grade, it takes well over an hour to cover the mere 22km (14 miles) to Kalávryta, terminus of the line and victim of a fierce Nazi reprisal in December 1943 when the town was burned and all the men shot. Today it is busiest in winter, thanks to the Mt Helmós ski resort overhead, but you can also use it as a base to visit the **Spílio Limnón/Cave of the Lakes** ⑥ (www.kastriacave.gr; daily 9.30am–4.30pm, may open longer at holidays), 17km (11 miles) south near Kastriá village, where tours take in the first 500m of a series of small lakes formed by natural dams.

Kalamáta is best known for its prosperous export trade in large, shiny purplish-grey olives. They are excellent eaten with oúzo.

Pátra is awash with colour at Carnival.

The meandering road to Metéora.

CENTRAL GREECE

A region rich in temples and monasteries, from Delphi – mythical centre of the ancient world – to the Monastery of Ósios Loukás and the dramatic Metéora peaks.

Roúmeli, the poetic medieval term for south-central Greece, encompasses the present-day provinces of Étolo-Akarnanía, Evrytanía, Fokída, Viotía and Fthiótida – even more ancient place-names revived by the modern Greek state. Few contemporary visitors concern themselves much with these tongue-twisting toponyms as they rush headlong towards the main attraction of the region, the Classical site at Delphi. Their single-mindedness is forgiveable, since Delphi uniquely combines a wealth of monuments with a breathtaking setting.

The drive from Athens takes anywhere from 2.5 to 3.5 hours depending on your route; the most historic, scenic one follows a steep but well-paved road over the pine-covered mountains from near dreary **Elefsína** – perhaps detouring for a pebble-beach swim and a fish lunch or – with a late start out of Athens – even an overnight at **Pórto Germenó ❶** on the Gulf of Corinth – to **Thíva (Thebes) ❷**. The modern town has been built on top of the ancient one, so little is visible of the ancient Thebes so prominent in Greek myth and history. A small ancient palace has, however, been excavated and the excellent archaeological museum (closed for renovation until further notice) contains tomb and sanctuary finds from Bronze Age to Classical

Boeotia, especially the painted sarcophagi from Tanagra.

Livadiá and Aráhova

The next main town, **Livadiá ❸**, was a major power base for the Frankish Crusader fiefdoms during the 13th and 14th centuries. In the gorge of the River Érkyna yawns the entrance to the ancient Oracle of Trophonios, near a graceful Ottoman bridge and below the Catalan-built castle. Springs nurture a dense colony of plane trees, a pleasing backdrop to

Main Attractions

Pórto Germenó
Ósios Loukás
Ancient Delphi Site
Delphi Museum
Galaxídi
Návpaktos
Karpenisiótis Valley
Makrynítsa, On Pílio
Tsangaráda & Its Beaches, Pílio
Agíou Nikoláou Anápavsa, Metéora

Ósios Loukás monastery.

Central Greece

0   20 km
0   20 miles

the handful of tavernas on the pedestrianised banks.

Beyond **Livadiá,** the road west begins to climb into the foothills of **Mt Parnassós.** The left turn for Dístomo village and the **Monastery of Ósios Loukás ❹** (Tue–Sun 9am–5pm), dedicated to a local 10th-century ascetic named Luke, is clearly marked. The monastery commands a wonderful view over a secluded valley in the shadow of Mt Elikónas. The smaller chapel of the Virgin (on the left) dates from the 10th century; the 11th-century *katholikón,* or main church, contains superb mosaics, survivors of a 1659 earthquake. The best and easiest to view, including a *Resurrection* and *Washing of the Apostles' Feet,* are in the narthex.

The village of **Aráhova ❺** clings to the toes of Parnassós; formerly a bastion of pastoral culture, it has now adopted a new role as a ski resort, with Athenian-weekender chalets sprouting rapidly on the outskirts. Tourist souvenirs, including various types of pasta and the almost-purple local wine, are pitched more at Greeks than foreigners.

Delphi

The ancient site of **Delphi ❻** is 11km (7 miles) further along, built on terraces at the base of sheer cliffs, the whole poised to topple over into the Plístos Gorge. One of the major religious centres – indeed, reckoned the geographical centre – of the ancient world, a much-consulted oracle functioned here for over a millennium until the proscription of paganism in AD 391. Since its excavation by the French towards the end of the 19th century, Delphi has ranked as the most popular, memorable ruin on the mainland, attended as well by gliding birds of prey launching themselves from the palisades. A visit involves steep climbs rewarded by ever-changing viewpoints and new monumental treasures.

The first locale, on the south side of the road, is the so-called **Marmaria** (daily same hours as main site below; free), comprising a gymnasium (complete with a straight track and a round bath) and the sanctuary of Athena Pronaia. Pronaia means "guardian of the temple" and ancient visitors passed first through this shrine. The original 7th-century BC temple was destroyed by the Persians, and replaced by the present complex; the most interesting structure here is the 4th-century *tholos* (a circular building with a vaulted or conical roof), whose purpose remains unknown.

On the north side of the road gushes the Castalian Spring (fenced off). Parts of the older, rectangular fountain right next to the road date to the 6th-century BC, although thin marble slabs on the floor are Hellenistic or early Roman. All pilgrims had to perform ritual ablutions here.

The main sacred precinct at Delphi is the **Sanctuary of Apollo** (daily 8am–8pm), above the road past the Castalian Spring. Many of the ruins exposed today date from Roman times, but just as many monuments, including the stadium and main

The Sanctuary of Athena Pronaia, Delphi.

Plays were performed at Delphi's theatre during the Pythian Festival, held every four years.

temple, are earlier. For the casual visitor, highlights include the Athenian Treasury, the Athenian stoa and the Temple of Apollo.

The top sights at Delphi

The Doric-order **Athenian Treasury** (late 6th- or early 5th-century) was pieced together by French archaeologists in 1904–06, using the inscriptions covering its surface as a guide. The late-6th-century **Athenian stoa,** today retaining three complete Ionic columns before a polygonal wall, was a roofed area protecting trophies from various Athenian naval victories, including the defeat of the Persians at Salamis in 480 BC. An inscription reads: "The Athenians have dedicated this portico with the arms and bow ornaments taken from their enemies at sea".

The **Temple of Apollo** just above the Athenian stoa is the third confirmed temple to have stood here, and there are literary rumours of three even earlier ones; two 7th- and 6th-century predecessors were done for by fire and earthquake respectively. What

you see dates from 369–329 BC, and is impressive enough, measuring 66 by 26 metres (215 by 85 ft): six columns were re-erected by the French. The god Apollo was associated, among other things, with prophecy, his main function here. His oracle resided under the temple flooring in the *adyton* chamber, where a chasm in the earth belched forth noxious and possibly mind-altering vapours. Consulting the oracle of Delphi consisted of several stages. The petitioner's question would be relayed to the god Apollo by a priestess known as the Pythia, who could hear the answer only when she was in a trance – induced, conveniently enough, by residing in the vapour-filled adyton. Her ravings, in turn, could be understood only by the sanctuary's priests, who interpreted them for the supplicant – often ambiguously – for a suitable fee. One of the oracle's more memorable pronouncements was that Oedipus would kill his father and marry his mother – thereby giving the world its most tragic hero and Freud his Oedipus complex.

The small **theatre** above the temple, originally 4th-century but thoroughly restored during the Roman era, seats 5,000 people and has marvellous acoustics. The **stadium**, a long narrow oval, is well worth the somewhat steep walk beyond the theatre. It retains 12 rows of seats on the north side and six rows of seats, now mostly tumbled, on the south (sadly, off-limits). You will easily find the starting and finishing lines, the limestone blocks complete with grooves for the runners' toes.

The **Delphi Museum** (Mon–Tue 10am–5pm, Wed–Sun 8am–8pm; entrance included in site ticket) underwent a comprehensive refit in the run-up to the 2004 Athens Olympics, further highlighting its magnificent collection. The bronze charioteer of 470 BC with his onyx eyes is the most famous denizen, but look out also for two huge 6th-century *kouroi* (standing statues of men), the votive, life-sized bull made from hammered silver sheets, the Ionic Sphinx of the Naxians, dating from 565 BC, and the Siphian frieze with scenes from the Trojan War and a battle between the gods and the titans.

The coast of Fokída

Below Delphi and its namesake modern, touristic village, a vast plain of olive trees stretches south towards the Gulf of Corinth. Literally gritty **Itéa** was once the ancient port of Delphi and still ships out the odd cargo of purple-red bauxite, strip-mined from the flanks of Mt Gióna to the west. But the real star of this often bleak coast is little **Galaxídi ❼**. With its Venetian-influenced mansions, the place seems closer in style to Koróni or Návpaktos than the rough-hewn village houses of Fokída.

Local shipowners prospered during the 18th and 19th centuries when Galaxídi was, amazingly, the fourth-busiest harbour in Greece – thus the elaborate housing. But captains refused to convert to steam after the 1890s, and the place sank into obscurity until being redis-covered by wealthy Athenians looking for a pleasant weekend bolt-hole. Foreign tourists are thus few, but there are plenty of comfortable lodgings and expensive restaurants along the south harbour quay, where yachts congregate.

The coastal road of Fokída heads west, passing **Ágios Nikólaos** (regular

The Naxian sphinx, now at the Delphi Museum, stood on a tall Ionic column below the Apollo Temple terrace.

Galaxídi, a popular weekend retreat for wealthy Athenians.

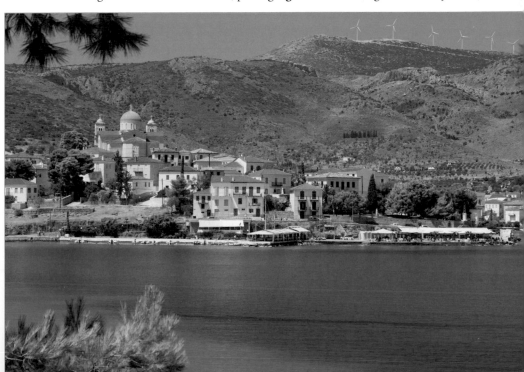

ferries to Égio on the Peloponnese) and **Trizónia,** the only inhabited island in the Gulf of Corinth, before arriving at **Návpaktos** ❽, just inside Étolo-Akarnanía.

Walk or drive up from the little egg-shaped Venetian harbour to the sprawling, pine-tufted castle above. Much the largest place on the gulf's north shore, today Návpaktos gracefully combines the functions of low-key resort and market town. The better hotels and most restaurants stand behind plane-tree-shaded Grímbovo beach, although bathing there is dubious; retire instead to westerly Psáni beach.

Étolo-Akarnanía

Continuing further west into Étolo-Akarnanía from Návpaktos, the landscape becomes flatter and less dramatic; the main sight en route is the earthquake-proof **suspension bridge** at the **Río-Andírrio straits,** the longest in the world (2,880m/9,449ft) and clearly visible from jets 10,500 metres (35,000ft) up. The road veers inland briefly before arriving at **Mesolóngi** ❾, where Lord Byron died on 19 April

1824. The Ottomans had been trying to take the town since 1822; in April 1825, the final attack was mounted by 30,000 troops against 5,000 active insurgents. After a year of close siege, about half the population of 20,000 – combatants and civilians alike – broke out but were ambushed, with only about 1,600 surviving. Those remaining in town fired their own powder magazines, killing themselves, several thousand children and the elderly, plus many Turkish attackers.

The northeast entrance to the town through the Venetian wall is known as the **Gate of the Sortie**, built by King Otto where the inhabitants defied the siege. To the west lies the **Garden of Heroes** (signposted "Heroes' Tombs"), with a tumulus covering the bodies of the anonymous defenders; the tomb of the Greek commander, Markos Botsaris; and a statue of Byron. Today, Mesolóngi is, more on sentimental than practical grounds, the capital of Étolo-Akarnanía, and lives mostly from the products of the vast and sometimes whiffy lagoons which surround the town on three sides: salt, *avgotáraho*

The Rio Andirrio bridge in the Gulf of Corinth.

(compressed grey-mullet roe), and smoked eels. The latter two items can be sampled at several tavernas on and around Athanasíou Razikótsika, at the heart of the old quarter, or at Tourlída, out on the lagoon.

Beyond Mesolóngi, and the enormous walls of ancient **Pleuron** on the mountain side, the road splits near **Etolikó** ⓾, a strange place built as a medieval refuge on an island in a lagoon. The more popular highway goes through the **Klisoúra Gorge** past unsightly **Agrínio**, commercial capital of the province, and on through tobacco fields to **Amfilohía** at the southernmost tip of the Amvrakikós Gulf.

A more interesting route to western Epirus veers off at Etolikó and mostly follows the coast all the way. Once across the mighty Ahelóös River and over the hills of the **Lesíni ash forest,** you emerge at **Ástakos,** a minor ferry port with services to Itháki but also a major yacht anchorage. The onward road offers spectacular views over small and large members of the Ionian archipelago before cruising through **Mýtikas** and **Páleros,** two little resorts

in the lee of Lefkáda which make excellent meal stops or overnight halts. At the end of the journey is **Vónitsa**, with its little castle, gulf-front tavernas and, as usual hereabouts, a merely functional beach; from here you are poised to head either southwest to Lefkáda or northwest through a tunnel under the mouth of the Amvrakikós Gulf to Préveza.

North into Evrytanía

From Návpaktos, a little-used but highly scenic road goes northeast into the valley of the Évinos River, beloved

The Venetian castle at Návpaktos extends down to ramparts guarding the harbour.

Welcoming Lord Byron at Mesolóngi by Theodoros Vryzakis, 1861.

THE BATTLE OF LEPANTO

The Ottomans used Návpaktos as a base before sailing out to their defeat in the naval battle of Lepanto (the Venetian name for Návpaktos), crushed by an allied Christian armada commanded by John of Austria in 1571. An Ottoman chronicler lamented, "The Imperial fleet encountered the fleet of the wretched infidels and the will of Allah turned another way".

For all its resonance in the West, however, the battle – gleefully celebrated as the first major bloodying of the "Terrible Turk" – had little local effect, since the Ottomans had already taken Cyprus that summer, and they quickly rebuilt their navies and went on to conquer Crete within a century.

Willows, planes and laurels border the Piniós River which cuts through the Vale of Témbi, making it a delightful place to hike. You can also take a canoe or kayak trip through the gorge.

Karpenisiótis valley, nicknamed the "Greek Switzerland".

of rafters, and then climbs again to the basin of Lake Trihonída, the largest natural body of fresh water in Greece. On a plateau out of sight to the northeast lies the lively town of **Thérmo** and its predecessor, ancient **Thermon** ⑪ (Tue–Sun 8am–3pm), the main religious centre of the ancient Aetolians.

Beyond Thérmo, the gradient steepens as you head north through the forest to Evrytanía province. First up are **Prousós** ⑫ village and monastery, poised on the precipitous,

landslide-prone north slopes of Mt Panetolikó; its isolation made the area a haunt of revolutionary hero Karaïskakis. Some spectacular gorges bring you to the main **Karpenisiótis valley,** heart of Evrytanía and nicknamed the "Greek Switzerland". Helvetic indeed are the green slopes and fir trees, matched by Swiss-style stratospheric accommodation prices. The ski centre on Mt Veloúhi, north of the provincial capital of **Karpenísi** ⑬ is a popular target, as are day-walks up Mounts Kaliakoúda and Helidóna, the valley's 2,000-metre (6,200-ft) flanking peaks. The main villages just outside Karpenísi (which was ravaged by World War II and the civil war), more appealing for a stay or a meal, are Megálo Horió, Mikró Horió, Voutýro, Gávros and Koryskhádes.

North from Fokída to Thessaly

From the Delphi area, it is also possible to head straight north between mounts Parnassus and Gióna towards **Lamía** ⑭, capital of its own province and a pleasant lunch stop. On the way, you pass near to a hallowed site of Ancient Greek heroism. In antiquity, **Thermopylae ⑮** was a narrow passage between the cliffs and the sea, although today silt from a nearby river has displaced the coastline by almost 5km (3 miles). In 480 BC, the Spartan general Leonidas held the pass for three days against a vastly larger Persian army, until the Persians, tipped off by the traitor Ephialtes, outflanked the defenders by using a higher pass. Leonidas ordered most of the Greek army to retreat, but covered their flight by fighting to the end with his hand-picked guard of 2,300 men. A monumental statue of Leonidas now marks the spot, across the road from the grave mound for the Greek dead. Just beyond are the still-popular hot sulphur springs (Thermopylae means "hot gates") after which the pass is named.

Less than one hour's drive along the motorway from Lamía, **Vólos ⑯**, capital of the Thessalian province of Magnisía – is certainly not the most photogenic of towns. Destroyed by several earthquakes between 1947 and 1957, it is a busy, modern port, a sort of compressed version of Thessaloníki and Piraeus. That said, it is also a spirited town, with (like most of Thessaly) a tradition of leftist politics, a university, and arguably the densest Greek concentration of *ouzerís* along its waterfront. This gets leafier and more Aegean as you head east towards the excellent **archaeological museum** (Tue–Sun Jan–Mar 8am–3pm, May–Oct 8am–5pm), which houses finds dating back to Neolithic times and Vólos' early days as ancient Iolkos.

Mount Pílio

The great Thessalian plain, once the bed of an inland sea, is ringed by mountains; the only natural outlet is where the Piniós River exits through the fabled **Vale of Témbi,** a 10-km (6-mile) gorge between **Mount Olympos** (Ólymbos) and **Mount Óssa.** Looming above Vólos is **Mount Pílio** (Pelion), legendary home of the centaurs. These fantastic beings had the legs and bodies of horses, the arms and heads of men, and – well-versed in magic and herbology – served as the wise tutors of several ancient heroes, including

Picturesque Damoúhari port.

FACT

Ambelákia, to the north of Lárisa, is where the world's first cooperative was founded in 1778 around the weaving and natural dying of textiles.

Achilles. Probably the centaurs were a mythologisation of an aboriginal tribe who, hiding in the dense Pílio forests, preserved the lore of pre-Hellenic ages.

Intriguingly, the entire region was a prominent centre of learning in Greece during the 17th and 18th centuries. Many important officials of the Austro-Hungarian Empire, of the sultan's inner circle and even of the Russian court, were educated on Mount Pílio. The peninsula probably became such a nursery of Greek erudition owing to its timber-based wealth and distance from grasping Ottoman officials.

The Pílio Peninsula (www.pelionet. co.uk) has two faces: the damp, shaggy northeast flank dropping to the Aegean, with excellent sand beaches of near-Caribbean hue; and the balmy, olive-covered slopes fringed with pebble shores lapped by the Pagasitic Gulf. Even if you fly to Vólos' airport at Néa Anhíalos and pick up a hire car, a week is realistically needed to tour it. The obvious, over-subscribed target is **Makrynítsa** ⑰, 17km (11 miles) north of Vólos, with its large concentration of 18th-century mansions and a fountain-and-church-flanked square. But **Vyzítsa** ⑱ to the east is quieter, with nearly as many grand houses.

Zagorá ⑲ and **Tsangaráda** in the northeast each comprise four villages in one, their several parishes strung out along kilometres of road: because of abundant water, few Pílio communities form dense clusters as on the islands. Tsangaráda is also a major hiking trailhead, for example down to the beach at Damoúhari or inland along an old trail once used by the locals to reach the rail station at Miliés.

The main developed coastal resorts are **Ágios Ioánnis** ⑳, near Zagorá, **Plataniá** in the far south and **Áfyssos** closer to Vólos. For contrast, try to stop at relatively unfrequented villages like **Láfkos, Sykí** and **Promýri** in the south. **Tríkeri** ㉑ and its port Agía Kyriakí, at the crab-claw southwest tip, lead a largely separate existence, with a strong maritime tradition. Beaches are too numerous to list, although the postcard stars tend to be of **Mylopótamos** with its natural arch, and **Damoúhari** port with its tiny Venetian castle, both below Tsangaráda.

The Metéora

Heading up to the Metéora, you may want to detour to **Ambelákia** ㉒, some 30km (20 miles) north of Lárisa.

The village's outstanding architectural heritage includes the mansion of George Schwartz (Tue–Sun 8am–3pm), whose painted rooms evoke domestic interiors of the Ottoman bourgeoisie.

As you approach **Kalambáka** from Tríkala, towering rock formations – the **Metéora** ㉓ – rise before you in one of the great spectacles of mainland Greece. Some of the most extraordinary monasteries in the world cling to these massive pinnacles, whose name derives from the verb *meteorízo*, "to suspend in the air". These cones, cylinders and rounded buttresses, flecked with vegetation and caves like so many unbrushed, carious molars, are remnants of river sediment deposited at the margins of the prehistoric sea covering the plain

Postcard-perfect Mylopótamos beach.

of Thessaly some 25 million years ago. Tectonic-plate pressure and erosion by the young Piniós River are jointly responsible for their present shape.

Heading north out of Kalambáka through the village of **Kastráki**, set unimprovably in the shadow of the rocks, you encounter monasteries in the following order. **Agíou Nikoláou Anápavsa** (Sat–Thu 9am–3.30pm, Nov–Mar until 2pm), built around 1388, has well-cleaned frescoes by the monk Theofanes of the Cretan School (*c.*1527), including a stylite (column-dwelling) hermit being supplied by winch-hoist, as would have been done locally. **Megálou Meteórou** (summer Wed–Mon 9am–5pm, winter Thu–Mon 9am–4pm) is the largest and highest monastery, although its church is overshadowed by a collection of rare icons and manuscripts in the refectory. **Varlaám** (summer Sat–Thu 9am–4pm, winter Sat–Wed 9am–4pm), founded in 1517, offers 16th-century frescoes by Franco Catellano (partly retouched in 1870), including an Ascension and a *Pandokrátor* in the two domes respectively. It is also the last monastery

to preserve in situ its old windlass mechanism, formerly used for elevating monks and supplies; a new electric pulley lifts the latter now.

Beautiful little **Roussánou** (Tue–Thu summer 9am–5.45pm, winter 9am–2pm), completely occupying a knife-edge summit, was built in 1545 for monks, later abandoned, and re-occupied by nuns in the 1970s. It too has vividly gory 17th-century frescoes dwelling on martyrdom by various unpleasant means. **Agías Triádos** (Apr–Oct Wed–Fri 9am–5pm, Nov–Mar Tue–Fri 10am–4pm), with a final approach of 130 steps tunnelled through a rock, has frescoes in its *katholikón* (main church) which were thoroughly cleaned during the 1990s. Like other monastic churches here, this was built in two phases, resulting in two domes, two *Pandokrátors* and two complete sets of Evangelists. **Agíou Stefánou** (Tue–Sun summer 9am–1.30pm, 3.30–5pm, winter 9am–1pm, 3–5pm), like Roussánou, is run as a convent but, heavily damaged by bombs during World War II, is the obvious one to skip if time is running short.

A painting of Jesus at the Monastery of the Transfiguration of Christ.

The Varlaám monastery as seen from Megálou Meteórou.

ROCK-TOP MONASTERIES

Religious hermits were already colonising the caves in this region by the 10th century, but legend attributes the first rock-top monastery (Megálou Meteórou) to the Athonite monk Athanasios, midway through the 14th century. Progress was slow as materials were transported first by rope ladder, then by winches and baskets, and it took nearly three centuries to finish Megálou Meteórou, by which time it was just one of 24 religious communities that were flourishing on the summits. After the 17th century, the monastic impetus slowed, and the more flimsily erected structures began to crumble on their exposed perches; the vicissitudes of modern Greek history since independence further hastened decline, and today only eight of these extraordinary buildings survive, of which just six are inhabited and open to pilgrims.

Sunset over the Víkos Gorge.

EPIRUS

A spectacular mountain region of limestone peaks, wooded valleys and traditional stone villages, the northwest also offers a pristine national park where bears and wolves still roam.

nland Epirus (Ípiros in Greek) is a world apart from the azure, sun-bleached Greece of the coasts. Its character is determined by the limestone peaks and deep river gorges of the Píndos range, which attains its greatest height just before the Albanian border in mounts Smólikas (2,637 metres/8,645ft) and Grámmos (2,520 metres/8,270ft). The winter precipitation, the highest in mainland Greece, ensures that forests are shaggy and rivers foaming.

An isolation enforced by both mountains and climate fostered the growth of medieval semi-autonomous villages built by traders and craftsmen returning from abroad. Local stone and wood has been transformed into imposing houses, with street cobbles, walls and roof slates blending in a uniform grey which, far from being depressing, is a classic example of harmonious adaptation to environment.

In antiquity, this was considered the limit of the civilised world; few ruins have been unearthed besides shadowy oracles at Dodona (Dodóni) and Acheron, and the planned Roman town of Nikopolis. The Byzantines had scarcely more time for this rugged terrain south of the Vía Egnatía, even though during the 13th and 14th centuries, the Despotate of Epirus extended from the Ionian

Sea to Thessaloníki. This mini-state sheltered members of the Byzantine nobility who had fled the imperial capital when it was sacked by the Fourth Crusade in 1204. They left behind intriguing churches around Árta, joining earlier masterpieces at Kastoriá in western Macedonia.

Like the rest of northern Greece, Epirus was not incorporated into the modern state until March 1913, during the First Balkan War and some 80 years after the end of the initial Greek War of Independence.

Main Attractions
Karavostasi Beach
Parga
Nikopolis Mosaics
Árta Byantine Chuches
Ionnina Lakefront
Ancient Dodona Theatre
Western Zagorohoria
Old Bridges near Kipi, Zagorl
Hiking the Zagorian Pindos

The coast at Párga.

Low impact tourism in Zagóri

The area suffered from neglect and mass emigration, but archaeological initiatives and financial incentives have boosted the economy, and many buildings have been restored. This is most notable in the Zagóri district of Epirus, where entire villages are now preserved as homogeneous traditional settlements. Simultaneously, old roads have been widened and paved, and new ones bulldozed, giving access to the tiniest hamlets. Because of the nature of tourism here, Zagóri is one of the few places in Greece where more than lip service is paid to the idea of quality trekking routes – although trails off the most popular itineraries can be haphazardly marked and maintained at best, and facilities in the villages where you finish a day's hike can be rudimentary.

As in the whole of Greece, a touristic plum as lucrative as Zagóri has inevitably become the focus of ongoing battles between conservationists, developers and entrepreneurs. Dirt roads serving timber tracts and the high pastures scar the landscape, as does the national power corporation's reservoir at the sources of the Aöös River. Cuttings and tunnellings for the Vía Egnatía have a significant visual impact, especially near Métsovo. Yet during the late 1980s and early 1990s, not a few shepherds and villagers allied themselves with urban mountaineers, local tourism personnel, international ecologists and even the European

Kayaking Federation to halt a scheme promoted by Ioánnina-based interests for a second dam on the lower Aóös, plus various ski lifts and roads which would have ruined the national park at the heart of Zagóri.

From Igoumenítsa to Párga

The modern port of **Igoumenítsa ❶**, at the very northwestern corner of mainland Greece, is the third busiest in the country after Pátra and Piraeus (Pireás), a turnstile sort of a place where an enforced halt should be avoided at all costs. Far more rewarding is the coastal road south, which after 33km (20 miles) reaches the side road for **Karavostási ❷**, indisputably the finest beach in Thesprotía province. Two rivers at each end of the long strand are responsible for the ample sand, and since it is an archaeologically protected area, development is still limited. Just up the hill from the side-turning sits the village of **Pérdika**, whose pedestrianised centre offers a range of tavernas and a surprisingly lively night scene, courtesy of Athenians and Greeks returned from overseas.

From the Karavostási-Pérdika junction, a few more kilometres – via the well-preserved castle of **Agiá** (daily all day; free) – bring you to **Párga ❸**, Epirus's main coastal resort and deservedly so for its fine beaches, tiered houses and dominant Norman-Venetian castle. From the 14th to the late 18th centuries, this was the Serene Republic's lone stronghold in Epirus, peopled by Souliot Orthodox Christians in constant conflict with their Muslim neighbours, as well as a small community

The Víkos Gorge.

Boats moored in the bay of Párga.

EMIGRATION AND REVIVAL

During the 20th century, the remoteness that once protected this region undermined its continued vigour. The ravages of World War II and the subsequent civil war, along with poor communications, the non-sustainability of traditional livelihoods and apparently punitive government neglect, spurred massive emigration, particularly to North America, Germany and Australia. By the 1970s, many Epirot villages were in an advanced state of physical and social decline. Numerous houses were left to decay (or shoddily repaired), while others sheltered an ever-dwindling population of the economically inactive elderly.

But matters have slowly changed. The government has acted to integrate the region into the national economy, most obviously with frequent flights to Ioánnina and good roads, including the Vía Egnatía expressway and its ambitious tunnels through the Píndos, plus the pending Ionian Highway up from Mesolóngi. Emigration has slowed down and just occasionally – thanks to tourism, subsidies for logging or grazing, and better infrastructure – even halted. Attitudes towards village life have softened, with traditional architecture and methods now viewed less as stumbling blocks to economic prosperity and more as cultural heritage to be preserved.

of Jews who lived from the export of citrons to Europe for Jewish liturgical use. The British acquired it in 1814 and soon ceded it to the rapacious Ali Pasha of Ioánnina; the townspeople collected their holy relics and moved to Corfu and Paxí. Párga now enjoys 100 percent hotel occupancy (mostly from package tours) from early July through to early September, although out of season it still makes an atmospheric stop.

Oracle of the dead

Some 22km (14 miles) southeast, beside **Mesopótamos** village, lies the **Necromanteion ❹** (Nekromán-dio; daily summer 8am–8pm, winter 8.30am–3pm) of Acheron, the venerable oracle of the dead described by Circe in *The Odyssey*. Today, the Ahérondas River (one of the legendary rivers swirling around Hades) has silted up the surrounding agricultural plain, but in Homeric times the oracle was a suitably mysterious, tree-fringed island in a lagoon. Suppliants entered the sanctuary via a maze of corridors and were then lowered by a pulley into a vaulted underground chamber to

Church of Panagía Parigorítissa.

experience whatever spectral hoax the resident priests had concocted.

The Ahérondas enters the sea at **Ammoudiá** just 5km (3 miles) to the west. The river makes bathing at the beach here cold, and should you choose to stay the night, the mosquitoes are out in force after dark. But lunching at the row of tavernas on the pedestrianised quay, where tour boats for hire to the Necromanteion bob at anchor, is exceedingly pleasant; and a small but excellent visitor information centre (Mon–Sat erratic hours; free) at the town entrance covers the natural history and ethnology of the area.

Inland from the Necromanteion, closer to its source, the Ahérondas squeezes through a spectacular gorge. From the village of **Glykí ❺**, a side track signposted for the "Skála Dza-vélenas" dead-ends at the start of the *skála*: a spectacular 90-minute path down to the river bed and up into the realm of the Souliots, a Christian tribe never completely subdued by the Ottomans. From Glykí, continue south another 30km (19 miles) to the combined side turning for **Zálongo**

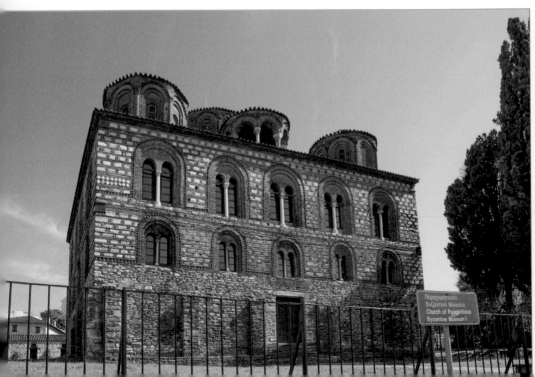

Church of Parigorítissa / Byzantine Museum

and ancient Kassope. The former, a mountain top monastery of little intrinsic interest, was witness to a dramatic incident in 1803 which has since become a staple of Greek nationalist legend known by every schoolchild: trapped by Ali Pasha's forces, several dozen Souliot women fled to a nearby pinnacle, where – rather than submit to the enemy – they danced off the edge into thin air clutching their children. A hideous 1961 sculpture by aptly named Georgios Zongolopoulos celebrates their defiance.

Kassope, Nikopolis and Préveza

Nearby, **Kassope** ❻ (temporarily closed) is less visited and eminently rewarding: a minor Hellenistic city whose jumbled ruins are matched by a fine view over the Ionian Sea and Lefkáda island. No views are to be had from the artificial Roman city of **Nikopolis** ❼, some 15km (9 miles) south and 600 metres (2,000ft) below, but in recent years the site has been tidied up and made more comprehensible, especially the theatre, and three superb floor mosaics in the Dometios basilica. A site museum (summer daily 8am–8pm, winter Sun–Fri 8.30am–3pm), 2km south towards Préveza, ably documents Roman and early Christian life here with statuary, coins, household implements and grave goods.

Préveza ❽, once a sleepy, shabby provincial capital, has also been spruced up, partly to cater for package tourists in transit between Áktio airport and the fine beaches to the north or Lefkáda. In its old bazaar, with rather more character than Párga's, a clutch of restaurants still offer the gulf's famous sardines, and summer nightlife is loud and varied. A few years ago, a tunnel under the gulf finally replaced the old RO-RO ferry ride across to Áktio.

Artá and Byzantine churches

Some 50km (31 miles) over on the far side of the gulf lies **Artá** ❾, the ancient Ambracia and capital of King Pyrrhus (he of the original pyrrhic victory). It later became the seat of the Despotate of Epirus, and retains a legacy of churches from that era. Most notable is the enormous, cubic **Panagía Parigorítissa** (Tue–Sun 8.30am–3pm), which dates from the late 13th century and betrays Italian influences in its palazzo-like exterior. High in the dome, supported by a gravity-defying cantilever system, floats a magnificent mosaic of the Pandokrátor (Christ in Majesty); it's the finest on the mainland after Dafní near Athens, despite damage from World War II bombing by the Italians.

In the citrus groves around the town lie other late Byzantine churches and monasteries, the most beautiful of which is **Panagía Vlahernón** in the village of **Vlahérna**, 6km (4 miles) to the north. Despot Michael II added the domes in the 13th century, and is thought to be entombed inside. A magnificent floor mosaic is on view under glass near the altar.

Ioánnina

Lining the shores of **Lake Pamvótis** (Pamvótida), spread below the stark

Nikopolis, "City of Victory", was founded by the emperor Augustus.

Fethiye Tzami, Kastro.

Ioánnina's lake and Aslan Pasha Mosque.

face of Mount Mitsikéli, **Ioánnina** ❿ has been one of Greece's great cities for nearly 1,000 years: a beacon of Hellenic culture, a traders' *entrepôt* and, in the 19th century (its last glorious epoch), the capital of the infamous Ali Pasha. Today the town remains one of Greece's liveliest provincial centres.

Ioánnina's layout is testimony to Ali's dubious legacy. While he left behind the city's most distinctive monuments (its mosques, and the redoubtable Kástro in its present form), he also had much of the city burned to deny it to a besieging Ottoman army, sent by the sultan to put down his unruly vassal in 1820. This, along with a 1960s penchant for large apartment blocks, has resulted in the relentlessly modern Ioánnina which lies outside the old town.

The wide expanse of central **Platía Pýrrou**, joined to the plazas of Akadimías and Dimokratías and lined by various public buildings, makes an obvious starting-point for a city tour. Just east of Dimokratías stands the archaeological museum (Tue–Sun 9am–4pm), home to a fine collection of bronzes and tablets inscribed with questions for the Dodona oracle.

Except for a couple of cinemas with good first-run fare, this area is no longer the main nocturnal hub of Ioánnina. That has shifted downhill along Avérof towards the Kástro to take better advantage of the town's setting, past two shop fronts selling the famous local bougátsa (custard or cheese pie) at Dimokratías 2 and Avérof 3 respectively. State-of-the-art late-night bars cluster at the far end of Ethnikís Andístasis, in a former tradesmen's bazaar by the lake, and around Platía Mavíli, on the opposite side of the citadel. On summer nights, the latter – better known as Mólos – throbs with townspeople taking an evening stroll along the waterfront, which is lined with vendors selling roast corn, halvás and bootleg CDs of local clarinet music from gas-lit pushcarts.

Kástro, the five-gated, walled precinct of various Epirot rulers including Ali Pasha himself, best conjures up Ioánnina's colourful past. A tangle of alleyways rises to a fortified promontory jutting out into the lake; at the lower corner looms the **Aslan Pasha Mosque,** now home to the Municipal Ethnographic Museum (daily summer 8am–8pm, winter 9am–4pm), with its diverse collection of Epirot costumes, jewellery and donations from the city's once-large Jewish community.

One of Ali Pasha's most infamous exploits – involving Kyra Frosini, the beautiful Greek mistress of Ali's eldest son – is supposed to have taken place near the mosque-museum. In the most common variant of the tale, Ali punished the girl for resisting his advances by having her and 17 female companions tied up in weighted sacks and drowned in the lake. Islamophobic-kitsch postcards of the incident are still sold, depicting wild-eyed "barbarians" and swooning Greek maidens in the clutches of their tormentors.

At the summit of the citadel looms the **Fethiye Tzami** (Victory Mosque) and one of Ali's heavily restored palaces – today an indifferent Byzantine Museum (Tue–Sun 8am–3pm). The former treasury nearby makes an appropriate showcase for displays on the city's traditional silver industry.

After defying the sultan for three decades, Ali finally met his end on the islet of **Nisí,** on the far side of the visibly polluted lake (bus-boats make the trip from Mólos all day until 11pm). A small house in the grounds of Ágios Pandelímon monastery was his last hide-out; here, trapped on the upper storey by a Turkish assassin, Ali was shot through the floorboards then decapitated.

Monasteries with more peaceful histories, and a fine island loop walk, lie in the opposite direction. The nearest to Nisí village, **Agíou Nikoláou Filanthropinón,** contains vivid late-Byzantine frescoes; some depict unusually gruesome martyrdoms, while others, by the entrance, depict ancient sages such as Plutarch, Aristotle and Thucydides.

Diversions around Ioánnina

Some 20km (12 miles) south of Ioánnina lies **Dodona** ⑪ (Dodóni), Epirus's main archaeological site (Tue–Sun 8am–3pm), nestling in a valley at the foot of Mount Tómaros. According to Herodotus, its oracle (the oldest in

EAT

Alas, Nisí's tavernas are touristy and poor in quality; if Ioanninans want a lakeside meal, they patronise the half-dozen restaurants which line Pamvotídas, the shoreline street heading northwest from Mólos.

Across Lake Pamvótis to the city of Ioánnina.

ALI PASHA IN IOÁNNINA

Unlike most large Greek centres, Ioánnina's history does not predate early Christian times, when an earthquake blocked the natural drainages of the surrounding plain and thus created the lake. Its name derives from an early church of St John the Baptist, long since vanished. After the Latin conquest of Constantinople in 1204 and the establishment of the Despotate of Epirus, Ioánnina grew in size and importance as refugees from "The City" swelled its population. It surrendered to the Ottomans in the 15th century; in 1788, Ali Pasha designated this town of 35,000 inhabitants (large for that time) his headquarters. Nicknamed "the Lion of Ioánnina", this maverick Albanian Muslim tyrant paid only minimal allegiance to the Ottoman sultan while establishing an autonomous fiefdom.

The monastery of Agíou Nikoláou Filanthropinón, near the island-village of Nissí, is worth a visit for its vivid frescoes.

Inside the caves at Pérama.

Greece and, until the 4th century BC, the most important) was established by a priestess abducted from a similar one in Egyptian Thebes. Zeus – considered resident in the trunk of a holy oak tree – was worshipped here, priests and priestesses deciphering the rustlings of the leaves which were the god's sacred pronouncements. The carefully restored **theatre,** dating from the 3rd-century reign of King Pyrrhus, has a capacity of 17,000 spectators – always far too large for the needs of the little

town that existed here from 1000 BC until early Byzantine times. It is now, sadly, roped off; foundations of the Zeus sanctuary lie beyond it.

Though now superseded by the Vía Egnatía expressway south of town, the old highway east into Thessaly curls clockwise around the lake. This road passes **Pérama** (daily 9am–5pm), one of Greece's most spectacular cave systems, on the outskirts of Ioánnina. Then, after a long, twisting ascent, the village of **Métsovo** 58km (36 miles) from Ioánnina, appears in a ravine below. It ranks as the "capital" of the Vlach, famous for its imposing houses, handicrafts, cheeses and the traditional costumes still worn by some of the older inhabitants.

Apart from the wonderful frescoes covering the interior of the medieval monastery of Ágios Nikólaos, a short walk below town, the only other recognised sight is the **Arhondikó Tosítsa Museum** (Metsovo Folk Art Museum; www.metsovomuseum.gr; Fri–Wed summer 9am–1.30pm, 4–6pm, winter 9am–1.30pm, 3–5pm; guided tours only), its reconstructed interior displaying fine woodwork and textiles.

Unlike so many Greek mountain villages, Métsovo is thriving: local worthies who made their fortunes abroad have set up endowments to encourage local industry, such as the nearby ski resort whose clients periodically fill the dozen or so hotels – of a better standard than most in Ioánnina.

East of Métsovo towards the Metéora in Thessalía (Thessaly), the Katára Pass ("Curse Pass", 1,694m/5,557ft) for decades accommodated the highest paved road in the country, but this is now abandoned and absolutely impassable since the Vía Egnatía opened.

The Zagorohória

The road northwest out of Ioánnina leads to the region of **Zagóri** which forms a culturally and geographically distinct region of Epirus. Its 46 villages – called the Zagorohória – lie in an area bounded by the

Métsovo–Ioánnina–Kónitsa highway and the Aóös River. Because of the region's infertile soil, local men emigrated to major commercial centres in Eastern Europe during the Ottoman era, subsequently returning to their homeland with considerable wealth. This allowed locals to hire a representative to send taxes to the sultan directly rather than suffer from tax-farmers, securing a large measure of autonomy.

Central Zagóri is best reached by the side road some 14km (9 miles) out of Ioánnina, prominently marked for the **Víkos Gorge**. **Vítsa** village has fine traditional houses, a shaded central square, one of the oldest churches in the region (Ágios Nikólaos), and the easiest trail access to the floor of the gorge, the intricately engineered Skála Vítsas. Just up the road, more frequented **Monodéndri** ⓭ supports a taverna offering local cuisine on its lower plaza, near the photogenic basilica of Ágios Athanásios flanking the classic path descending to the gorge. For the less committed, either the 1990s-vintage, rather tasteless *kalderími* (cobbled path) to the eyrie of

Agía Paraskeví monastery, or the 7-km (4-mile) drive up to the Oxiá overlook, will afford breathtaking views.

From the junction below Vítsa, the easterly main road passes the turning for exquisite **Dílofo** on its way to the major villages of Kípi, Kapésovo and Tsepélovo. **Kípi** ⓮ stands nearest to a much-photographed cluster of 18th- and 19th-century packhorse bridges, the most famous of which is the three-arched Plakída span. East of Kípi, **Negádes** has a frescoed basilica, one of the best examples of the Zagorian style, while above and to the north perches Kapésovo, with a rural museum in its enormous old school.

Exhibits in the Arhondikó Tosítsa Museum, Métsovo.

Vradéto

Kapésovo also marks the start of a one-hour path incorporating the most amazingly sinuous of all Zagorian *kalderímia* (paths) ending at **Vradéto**, the highest (1,340 metres/4,400ft) – and formerly most desolate – village in the area, now enjoying a mild renaissance (although the winter population is still only seven). Continue on foot for about 40 minutes and you

Métsovo elders.

ZAGORIAN PEOPLE AND LANDSCAPE

Zagóri's villages differ markedly: the east is populated largely by Vlachs (more properly, Arouman), a people rooted in Greece since antiquity, speaking a Romance language and living as caravan-drovers and shepherds driving their flocks from summer to winter pastures. Early in 1944, the occupying Germans retaliated against local resistance by burning most of the eastern villages, which were later rebuilt haphazardly. The western and central Zagorohória show more of a Slav/Albanian influence in place names and architecture; happily, most survived the war unscathed and today constitute one of Greece's showpieces.

The Zagorian landscape embraces sheer rock faces, limestone dells, dense forests, upland pasture and deep canyons. The national park at its core, comprising the Víkos Gorge plus the Voïdomátis and Aóös rivers, was established partly to protect a threatened population of bears, lynx, wolves and birds of prey. Yet even in the remotest corners there are signs of man: a post-Byzantine monastery with belfry, or a graceful, slender-arched bridge from the Ottoman period. Unfortunately, the pastoral culture that used to feature prominently is in sharp decline; EU subsidy policy means that few shepherds now occupy the high pastures, and unattended cattle herds have mostly replaced the tenanted sheepfolds of the past.

Pápingo Trail

The four-to-five-day hiking loop outlined below begins and ends in the Pápingo villages where there is plentiful accommodation, as well as reliable tavernas.

Be prepared to hike into and out of Pápingo, along the trail linking it to Klidoniá village on the Ioánnina–Kónitsa highway, if you happen not to coincide with the bus service. The alpine refuge on Astráka col, just visible from Megálo Pápingo, is open from May to October (visit www.astrakaref-uge.com or tel: 6973 223100 to reserve bunks). It is a 900-metre (2,950-ft) ascent of at least three hours, with water available at regular intervals. If the refuge is full, camp near the spring at the north end of the seasonal **Xiróloutsa pond** (15-minute path descent east from the col). Spend the balance of the day with a short walk (1 hr each way) up to **Drakólimni,** an alpine tarn at 2,050 metres (6,725ft) altitude, ideal for views and picnics, just northwest of the 2,500-metre (8,200-ft) Gamíla peak.

Pápingo peaks.

A five-to-seven-hour hike the next day takes you between mounts Astráka and Gamíla, through alpine meadows grazed by cattle, and past the head of the Mégas Lákkos Gorge to Tsepélovo (steep final descent; net altitude loss of 850 metres/2,800ft). Water is scarce, so plan accordingly. You should have a comfortable overnight stay in one of Tsepélovo's dozen hotels and smaller inns, although reservations are advisable during July and August.

From the ravine flanking Tsepélovo to the west, a crumbled but discernible *kalderími* climbs the cliff to the uplands towards Vradéto; after about 90 minutes you are forced onto a paved road for the final 45 minutes. From Vradéto (café serving drinks only), descend the amazing *skála* to Kapésovo (45 minutes), then use the old dirt track (not the asphalt highway) to arrive in **Koukoúli** within the next 45 minutes and in time for lunch. You can stay overnight here at the single inn, or carry on eastwards to Kípi (another 45 minutes), which has another taverna as well as several inns.

From either Koukoúli or Kípi, there are marked routes into the upper end of the Víkos Gorge, crossing it by the Misíou bridge and ascending the stair-*kalderími* to Vítsa (2 hrs), with abundant accommodation and a taverna or two. A three-hour track partly shortcuts the road up to Monodéndri, 300 metres (985ft) above Kípi, with several more inns and tavernas.

A signposted, well-renovated *kalderími* takes you down to the usually dry bed of the Víkos Gorge (45 minutes). A fairly strenuous path marked as the O3 route negotiates the length of the canyon, on its true left bank after the first few minutes. At the intersection of the gorge and the Mégas Lákkos side canyon (2.5 hrs), a potable spring flows (unreliable after July). Continue through thick forest, then open pasture, before reaching the movable sources of the Voïdomátis River (4.5 hrs from Monodéndri), which well out of the base of the Pýrgi formations.

Bearing left on an obvious cobbled path leads to **Vitsikó** (Víkos) village, 45 minutes away, where you will find two inns; the O3 route crosses the river, heading up and right, reaching either of the Pápingos within two hours, for a day's total of 6.5 hours. About 90 minutes along, there is a divide in the path where you cross a stream on the left to head up to Megálo Pápingo, rather than continue straight to Mikró Pápingo.

will reach Belói viewpoint, more or less opposite Oxiá. Twelve kilometres (7 miles) further, the paved road arrives at **Tsepélovo ⑮**, flanked by rural monasteries and crammed with more mansions. Frescoed Rangóvou monastery stands just below.

Back on the Ioánnina-Kónitsa highway, you pass through **Kalpáki,** where, in the early winter of 1940–41, the Greeks halted the Italian invasion, rolling Fascist troops back into the snowy Albanian Mountains for a season of hell; a small roadside museum (daily May–Sept 9.30am–1pm, 5–8pm, Oct–Apr 9.30am–3pm) tells the tale in full. Just beyond, a 19-km (12-mile) side road heads east to the focus of most Zagorian tourism, the paired villages of **Pápingo ⑯**, **Megálo** and **Mikró.** They have become quite fashionable, especially during peak holiday seasons, but there is no denying their superlative setting at the foot of the 600-metre (1,970-ft) Pýrgi, the sheer outriders of Mount Gamíla. This massif (the heart of the national park) offers fine hiking, most notably to newt-filled **Drakólimni** (Dragon Lake).

The icy **Voïdomátis River,** popular with kayakers, drains out of the lower Víkos canyon at Klidoniá, where a lovely old bridge marks the edge of the national park a few hundred metres in from the busy highway. An even bigger one spans the Aóös River some 10km (6 miles) north, where it exits some narrows to a vast floodplain. A 90-minute walk along the southern bank of the Aóös Gorge leads below steep, forested slopes to the **Stomíou monastery,** magnificently perched on a cliff.

Kónitsa ⑰ itself offers a fine view of the floodplain, but an earthquake in 1996 and massive shelling during the civil war put paid to any real architectural distinction here. For that, head 23km (14 miles) west to the monastery and namesake village of **Molyvdosképastos,** just where the Aóös enters Albania. The monastery's early 14th-century church betrays a Serbian influence with its high, stovepipe dome. Early in the 1990s, it was reinhabited by rather zealous monks, who encourage your conversion on the spot.

Dodona's theatre.

Due east of Kónitsa looms 2,637-metre (8,650-ft) **Mount Smólikas,** roof of the Píndos and second summit of Greece after Mount Olympos. From several of the Vlach villages along the Aóös north bank, trails lead up towards the peak and yet another "Dragon Lake", and then onward to either Kerásovo village on the northern toes of the mountain, or to Samarína at the eastern end of the range.

The 105-km (65-mile) road from Kónitsa to **Neápolis** is the main paved connection between Epirus and western Macedonia. It follows the valley of the Sarandáporos River upstream, between Smólikas and Mount Grámmos, site of the final battles of the civil war, passing faded blue-painted graffiti "Elefthería Gia Vória Ípiros!" ("Freedom for Northern Epirus!") – an expression of lingering irredentist sentiment for the Albanian portion of Epirus, home to perhaps 70,000 remaining Greek Orthodox.

Hiking in the Píndos

Kónitsa bridge over the Aóös river.

The North Píndos offer many rewarding hiking routes, from strenuous, multiday, high-level treks to various interconnected day hikes. Landscapes vary from the limestone dells of the Gamíla uplands to the forested Víkos Gorge floor. In these days of global warming, the best seasons are no longer high summer but from mid-May to mid-June, and September to early October. Although the local trail system is extensive on paper, it is unevenly maintained and often badly waymarked; the usual method is multicoloured paint splodges or, for the long-distance O3 route, metal diamond-shaped symbols nailed to trees.

The 1:50,000 *Pindus Zagori* topographic map issued by Anavasi cartographers (available in Greece and the UK) is essential if not infallible, as is a keen sense of direction, an ability to double-check trail information from villagers, and a good sense of humour. In any month, the Píndos weather can change rapidly with little warning, so rain gear and a light tent are essential – the latter also because indoor accommodation can fill up suddenly.

THESSALONÍKI

Greece's second city does not live in the shadow of Athens. It has its own distinctive character, with more Balkan influences and a host of splendid Byzantine churches.

To a visitor approaching by sea, contemporary **Thessaloníki** ❶ presents the uniform facade of modern apartment blocks characteristic of so many Mediterranean seaside cities. At the beginning of this century, the same view was marked by minarets rising elegantly from a tile-roofed town picturesquely climbing between medieval ramparts to an upper quarter, with vast cemeteries outside the walls. When more than half the town was destroyed by the Great Fire of August 1917, British and French architects (who were accompanying Allied expeditionary forces at the time) were promptly commissioned to produce a new town plan.

Surviving Art Deco buildings enhance the wide, sea-facing boulevards they designed, although their advice to ban high-rises was disregarded. But the fire spared much, including the old hillside quarter of **Kástra**. Roman ruins, Byzantine churches, Ottoman public and domestic buildings, and displaced Jewish tombstones lie encircled by Roman and Byzantine walls, or scattered alongside asphalt boulevards and pedestrian lanes. And after years of neglect, this great architectural heritage has been signposted and selectively renovated.

One of Greece's liveliest and most interesting cities, Thessaloníki was founded in 316–315 BC by the Macedonian king, Kassander, who named it

after his wife, and it rose into prominence under the Romans, boosted by their **Via Egnatia** "trunk road", which stretched from the Adriatic to the Hellespont (Dardanelles). Saint Paul visited twice, and wrote two Epistles to the Thessalonians; Christianity (and the city) got further boosts from the Byzantine emperors, especially Theodosius (who issued his edict here, banning paganism) and Justinian, who began new churches to supplement those adapted from Roman structures. Despite Slavic and Arab raids, frequent

Main Attractions

Platia Aristotélous
Museum of Byzantine Culture
Rotunda of Ágios Geórgios
Ágios Dimítrios
Kástra
Lefkós Pýrgos (White Tower)
Eptapyrgío
Modiáno market

The Arch of Galerius.

They say you can always tell a Thessalonian in the rest of the mainland; with a spring in their step, they seem a head taller than the characteristically hunched-over, down-trodden Athenians. They are also said to be the best dressed, which explains the variety of shops and department stores.

earthquakes, fires, adjacent malarial swamps and a spotty water supply, resilient Thessaloníki prospered. Even in temporary decline, it made a rich prize for the Ottomans in 1430.

Sephardic settlers

After 1500, large numbers of Sephardic Jewish refugees from Spain and Portugal settled here, giving Salonica – as they called it – it's most distinctive trait for the next four centuries. On the eve of the Balkan Wars, they accounted for just over half the population of 140,000, making it the largest Jewish city of that era. In 1943, 70,000 remained to be deported to the Nazi death camps, and fewer than 1,000 remain today.

Following the three wars leading up to 1923, the city came to epitomise a Greek refugee town: in absolute numbers, Athens may have had more, but by proportion of population, Thessaloníki contains more citizens with Anatolian ancestry than anywhere else in Greece. There are abundant Turkish surnames (such as Dereli and Mumtzis) and spicy cuisine rarely found elsewhere in Greece; indeed, the city has some of

the best places to eat in the country. Its own self-deprecating nicknames have long been I *Protévousa tón Prosfigón* (The Refugee Capital), after the ring of 1920s settlements, all prefixed "Néa" (New), across eastern Macedonia, and *Ftohomána* (Mother of the Poor).

But 21st-century Thessaloníki is not all changing demographics. After years in Athens' shadow, it has come into its own. The International Fair held every October in permanent grounds by the university promotes the city as a Balkan trade centre and the natural gateway to the upper Balkans. Thessaloníki is confidently on the move, with innovative restaurants and clubs occupying historic buildings, its native musicians (such as Sokratis Malamas) frequently at the forefront of Greek song.

A tour of the city

Platía Aristotélous Ⓐ is the hub of the downtown city, stretching up from the waterfront towards the Roman Agora and the dominant church of Ágios Dimítrios. The sunny cafés and bars are popular here, especially in the early evening, while morning shoppers

Thessaloníki

0   500 m
0   500 yds

enjoy the daily market to the west, and lunchtime and evening diners fill the pavement tables of market restaurants to the east. Leofóros Níkis follows the seafront and is a good place for a stroll or a fashionable bar-hop from the port to the White Tower, with views across the wide blue bay to Mount Ólympos.

The city has, unsurprisingly, been as hard hit by the financial crisis and austerity measures as anywhere in Greece, so plans for an underground metro system, following the line of Egnatía, and for the seafront road to be sunk below ground to leave the zone free for pedestrians and the bar clientele to enjoy, have both suffered delays and are not expected to be completed for some years.

At the eastern end of the seafront, behind the White Tower (more on this later), is the **archaeological museum B** (www.amth.gr; Apr–Oct Mon 8.30am–8pm, Tue–Sun 8am–8pm, Nov–Mar Mon 10.30am–5pm, Tue–Sun 8.30am–3pm), which displays Macedonian, Hellenistic and Roman finds from the entire region, including the notable **Síndos** collections.

Sumptuous jewellery and household effects in gold, silver and bronze vie for your attention. Just beyond the Archaeological Museum is the **Museum of Byzantine Culture C** (www.mbp.gr; daily Apr–Oct 8am–8pm, Nov–Mar 9am–4pm; combined tickets recommended), with artefacts from the Early Christian period (4th–7th century) through to the Middle Byzantine period (8th–12th century). The exhibits in this modern building are beautifully displayed and clearly explained; among the most impressive pieces are a 5th-century mosaic floor, wall paintings from a local house, and some extraordinary early textiles.

Roman Thessaloníki can be seen in **Platía Navarínou D** in the shape of the excavated remains of the Hippodrome and the **Palace of Galerius Caesar,** the Christian-hating Emperor who martyred the city's patron saint, Demetrius, in AD 305. And on the inland side of Via Egnatia survives the western part of **Galerius's** triumphal **arch**, erected over this highway in AD 297 to celebrate a victory over the Persians. The reliefs on the arch repay close

On the waterfront.

During Ottoman rule, most Byzantine churches were converted into mosques, and their interiors coated in whitewash. This fresco, from Ágios Dimítrios in Thessaloníki, is one that survived.

Great people-watching on the waterfront.

inspection, showing, as well as Galerius himself, Diocletian and Julius Caesar.

The other remaining building in this Roman complex is the **Rotunda of Ágios Geórgios** Ⓔ (daily summer 8am–7pm, winter 8am–5pm; free), just northwest of the arch. Perhaps intended as Galerius's mausoleum, this is one of the few remaining examples of circular Roman architecture, enduring largely through conversion into a church, then a mosque. Glorious 4th-century wall mosaics partially survive, high up inside the dome and recesses; the truncated minaret is the city's last surviving one.

The largest Greco-Roman site is the **Agora** Ⓕ or forum (AD 32–138) on Platía Dikastiríon, uncovered in 1966, which was the social and religious centre of ancient Thessaloníki. Its theatre provides a summer concert space.

Byzantine Thessaloníki

More fine and important Byzantine churches survive in Thessaloníki than in any other Greek city. The earliest examples are clear adaptations of the colonnaded Roman basilica, in turn descended from Greek temples, with the outermost columns replaced by walls. The most significant are near the Agora: 5th-century **Ahiropíitos** Ⓖ (hunt for fine mosaic patches under the arches, between ornate columns) and its heavily restored contemporary, **Ágios Dimítrios** Ⓗ (daily 8am–10pm; free), the largest church in Greece. Both are double-aisled basilicas with a central nave.

Ágios Dimítrios is the city's main church. It was founded shortly after the saint's demise, on the site of his martyrdom and was almost entirely rebuilt after the 1917 fire, which spared only the apse and the colonnades. Six small mosaics of the 5th to 7th century, featuring the saint, survive mostly above the columns standing on either side of the altar. The fire was responsible for the rediscovery of the crypt (Tue–Thu 8am–3pm, Fri 8am–1.30pm, 7–10pm, Sat–Sun 7.30am–2.30pm; free), which is thought to be partly constructed from the Roman baths where the saint was imprisoned; a reliquary found on the site supports this. Also here are the attractive remains of a fountain that previously fed a fishpond.

Below the Agora to the west of Ahiropíetos is **Panagía Halkéon** (daily 7.30am–noon; free), founded in 1028. The brick-built church is in the shape of a cross and contains a cycle of frescoes dating back to the 11th century. During the Ottoman occupation, it served as the mosque of the local coppersmiths.

South of Ahiropíetos is the 8th-century **Agía Sofía** Ⓘ (Holy Wisdom; daily 8am–1pm, 5–9pm; free), built in conscious imitation of its namesake in Constantinople. This one, 10 metres (33ft) wide, has a vivid Ascension, with the Apostles watching Christ borne heavenward by angels, rather than the *Pandokrátor* (Christ Enthroned) that became the rule later. In the apse and the *ikonostásis*, you can detect traces of an earlier mosaic of the Cross behind the Virgin Enthroned. It was one of a pair, and the other figural cross survives in the adjacent vault.

The steep alleys of **Kástra** ❶ are about a 20-minute walk from the seafront. Since the late 1980s, this neighbourhood of dilapidated half-timbered houses below the acropolis (citadel) has been transformed from poor and despised to renovated and trendy, with scattered tavernas and cafés.

Tiny 5th- or 6th-century **Ósios Davíd** ❸ (Tue–Sat 9am–5pm, Sun 10am–2pm; free), all that's left of the **Látomos Monastery**, is tucked away in this district. The west end of this church has vanished, but visit for the sake of an outstanding early mosaic in the apse, revealed in 1921 when Ottoman whitewash was removed. It depicts the vision of the Prophet Ezekiel of Christ Emmanuel, shown as a beardless youth seated on the arc of heaven, surrounded by the symbols of the Evangelists. Together, the mosaics of Ósios Davíd and Ágios Dimítrios rank as the best pre-Iconoclastic sacred art in Greece, and predate the more famous work in Ravenna in Italy.

Another batch of churches all well uphill from the Via Egnatia date from the 13th and 14th centuries – examples of a cultural "golden age" at odds with the Byzantine Empire's political decline and the numerous disasters visited on Thessaloníki from the 10th to the 12th century. Financial constraints meant that frescoes, rather than mosaics, were the preferred ornamentation in these churches, most of them attached to now-extinct monasteries. By far the best of these is **Ágios Nikólaos Orfanós** ❹ (Tue–Sun 8.30am–2.45pm; free), at the northeast edge of Kástra. Among the better-preserved and more unusual frescoes are *Christ Mounting the Cross* and *Pilate Sitting in Judgment*, the very image of a Byzantine scribe; in *Washing of the Feet*, it seems the talented painter inserted an image of himself on horseback, wearing a turban.

At the nearby monastery of **Vlatadon**, the only one among the city's 20-odd to still be occupied by monks, you may hear peacocks cry. The monastery was founded in around 1360 by the Empress Anna Paleologina, but 11th-century wall paintings survive in the small church, which is open during services.

FACT

Churches often fly flags showing a two-headed eagle on a yellow background. This is the symbol of Byzantium. The Patriarch of the Greek Orthodox Church still resides in the ancient Byzantine capital of Constantinople, today's Istanbul.

The Roman Rotunda, built in the 4th century AD, is now the church of Ágios Geórgios.

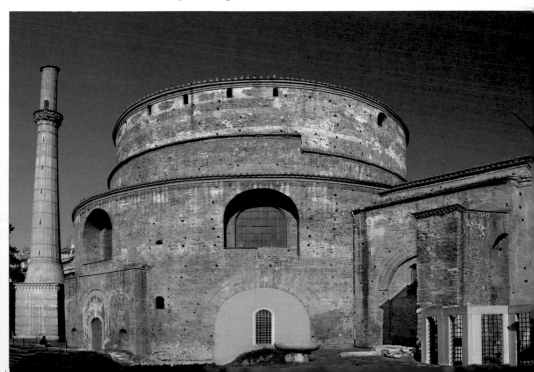

The city walls

Thessaloníki's seafront **Lefkós Pýrgos** (**Thessaloníki**) (White Tower; www. site.lpth.gr; Tue–Sun 8.30am–3pm), effectively the city's logo, was built during the brief Venetian occupation as an addition to the Roman-Byzantine walls. The Ottomans used it as a prison; that, and the massacre of unruly Janissaries here in 1826, earned it the epithet "Bloody Tower". The Greeks whitewashed it post-1912 – thus the new alias – and then removed the pigment in 1985. A spiral staircase, with small windows, emerges at a lovely café and then the crenellated roof terrace, affording fine views over the seafront and bay, and up to Kástra.

The vanished curtain wall leading inland from here past the university linked the White Tower with the **Chain Tower**, the northeastern corner of the fortifications; beyond it lies the **Eptapýrgio** (Yedi Küle in Turkish), the Seven Towers Fortress, on the northeastern corner of the old walled **acropolis**. The seven towers on the northern side of the Eptapýrgio incorporate part of the Early Christian acropolis walls,

The view from the city walls.

and the six towers on the southern side were built during the Middle Byzantine period. The Ottomans made considerable additions to the fortress, transforming it into a jail in the late 19th century, and it continued to function as a jail until the 1980s. It is now sometimes used as an exhibition space.

Ottoman and Jewish Thessaloníki

Thessaloníki was taken by the Ottomans in 1430, 23 years before the fall of Constantinople. The new overlords converted most churches into mosques during the first century of their rule, tacking on minarets and whitewashing over mosaics and frescoes. As a result, there are few purpose-built Ottoman mosques, though there are other interesting civic buildings. Worthy 15th-century specimens include the graceful Ishak Pasha or **Alatza Imaret Mosque** at the base of Kástra – around the corner from the **Yeni Hamam**, or bathhouse, engagingly restored as a bistro, concert hall and summer outdoor cinema – and the dilapidated **Hamza Bey Mosque** on the Via Egnatia, last used as the Alcazar cinema. It has yet to get the same treatment as the nearby **Bezestén**, a refurbished six-domed covered market now tenanted by luxury shops. The nearby **Bey Hamam** **O** (visit by request only), dating from 1444, has intact stalactite vaulting over the entrance and inside.

At the rear of the Turkish consulate, at 7 Apostolou Pavlou, stands the wooden house where Mustafa Kemal (Atatürk), founder of the Turkish republic, was born in 1881 (daily 10am–5pm; free). And a few hundred metres east of the archaeological museum, at the edge of the 19th-century "New Town", is the **Yeni Cami** or "New Mosque" – an Art Nouveau folly erected by the influential Ma'min (Dönme). This so-called crypto-Jewish sect followed the 17th-century self-proclaimed Messiah, Shabbetai Zvi, into Islam. In the mass exchange of populations between Greece and Turkey in 1923, most of the Ma'min were among the 100,000 Muslims who left the city.

By contrast, there are few tangible traces of Thessaloníki's Jewish past, owing to the 1917 fire and the Nazi desecration of cemeteries and synagogues in 1943. Only the Art Deco **Monastirótou synagogue** **P**, near the Ministry of Northern Greece, survived the war. Centrepiece of the vast central market – which extends to either side of Aristotélous, selling everything from wooden furniture to live poultry – is the covered **Modiáno** **Q**, a fish, meat and produce-hall named after the Jewish family that established it. Their former mansion, out beyond the Yeni Cami, now houses the Folk and Ethnological Museum of Macedonia (www.lemmth.gr; Fri–Tue 9am–3.30pm, Wed until 9.30pm), which has informative displays on housing, costumes and handicrafts. Though only half-occupied today, the Modiáno still supports several authentic, atmospheric *ouzerí* in the west arcade.

Close by, the Louloudádika Hamam or Flower-Market Bath was also known as the **Yahouda Hamam** or Jewish Bath **R**; the Jewish clientele is gone, but the flowers are still outside. In the same area, on Agíou Miná, is the **Jewish Museum of Thessaloníki** **S** (www.jmth.gr; Tue, Fri, Sun 11am–2pm, Wed, Thu 11am–2pm, 5pm–8pm; free). This two-storey museum presents the history of the Jewish community in Thessaloníki and contains interesting material from the ancient, destroyed, Jewish cemetery.

Outside the city

For an escape from the city, try a half-day excursion to **Panórama**, an affluent village 11km (7 miles) to the east whose views justify its name; several *zaharoplastía* sell such Anatolian specialities as *salépi* (orchid-root drink), *dódurma* (Turkish ice cream) and *trígona*, triangular cream pastries. **Hortiátis**, 10km (6 miles) north of here, has since ancient times supplied Thessaloníki with water. It also retains some pines spared by arsonists, plus good tavernas. From either point, you can on a clear day look southwest across the Thermaïc Gulf to glimpse the bulk of **Mount Olympos** (Ólymbos) to the southwest, the traditional separation point between Macedonia and Thessaly.

EAT

For atmospheric bars, restaurants and clubs, head for Ladádika, the former red-light district and port quarter behind the passenger ferry terminal.

Panagía Halkéon, one of the city's many Byzantine churches.

MACEDONIA AND THRACE

Along with a landscape of fertile plains and forbidding mountains, you'll find a wondrous mix of peoples here – as well as the major holiday playground of Halkidikí.

Main Attractions

Kastoriá
Préspa Lakes
Dion
Vergína
Mount Áthos
Kavála
Philippi
Xánthi
Dadiá Forest Reserve

Kastoriá City.

Thessaloníki ❶ (see page 205), first city of northern Greece and "capital" of Macedonia and Thrace, stands halfway between Albania to the west and Turkey to the east, and scarcely 100km (60 miles) south of FYROM (the Former Yugoslav Republic of Macedonia) and Bulgaria – a boundary settled after World War I. Bordering so many Balkan states, into which ancient Macedonia (Makedonía) and ancient Thrace (Thráki) spread, has given the region great ethnic variety and cultural richness.

Northern Greece does not possess the magnificent archaeology and stunning temples of the centre and the south and its latitude spells a short summer season. But it does have some key sites, a large number of Byzantine churches and some handsome Ottoman-era domestic architecture; as well as varied and dramatic landscapes and exceptional areas of wildlife, from snow-capped mountains to broad, fertile plains. Dominating the southern part of this region is Mount Olympos, the highest mountain in Greece, which you can climb from Litóhoro (see page 216).

Northwest Macedonia

Coming from Epirus, you officially enter Macedonia just before **Pendálofos** ❷, the only place of any importance or appeal en route. Its fine stone houses – still in the Epirot style – straggle across the ravines which give the town its name ("Five-hills"). At **Neápolis** ❸, the road divides: north to Kastoriá, southeast to **Siátista** ❹. Perched on a bleak ridge some 20km (12 miles) from the fork, this small town is noted for its fine 18th-century mansions or *arhondiká* – the residences of the *árhons*, or leading citizens – offering a glimpse into the self-contained society that flourished here during late Ottoman times. Then a wealthy centre for fur-trading, tanning, wine-making and a stopping point for caravans on the trade route to Vienna, Siátista declined when commercial networks changed after Greek independence.

Start with the **Nerandzópoulos mansion** on Platía Horí, whose warden has the keys to other interesting structures such as the **Manoúsi**, **Kanatsoúli** and **Poulikídou residences**. Visiting these will give you a good background for nearby Kastoriá, another town which prospered from the fur trade.

Returning north, the road follows the upper valley of the **Aliákmonas River**, the longest in Greece, whose 300-km (185-mile) course arcs from the Albanian border to the Thermaic Gulf. Soon you reach the **lake of Orestiáda**, or Kastoriá, almost divided in half by the eponymous town built on a peninsula. On the town's southern outskirts lies a significant military cemetery, the last resting place of government troops who were killed during the battle for Grámmos-Vítsi, which brought an end to the civil war. In the town itself, a lakeside plaza named after General James Van Fleet serves as a reminder that American equipment and advisers guaranteed a royalist victory over communist insurgency.

Kastoriá

Kastoriá ❺ is one of northern Greece's more appealing spots, a peaceful mountain town on a peninsula jutting into a large tranquil lake, with a popular promenade of restaurants and bars. Its 54 surviving medieval churches indicate its importance in Byzantine times. Many were erected as private chapels by rich furrier families, and shops still sell myriad furry items, mostly made from mink. (*Kastóri* is the Greek for beaver, now extinct.)

The Byzantine art and architecture here is among Greece's finest, showing strong folk and Slav influences. You can see the best in a single morning, starting with the fine icon collection at the **Byzantine Museum** (closed for restoration), and working your way south to the **Karyádis quarter**, with its fine old mansions.

Triple-aisled **Ágii Anárgyri** – built in 1018 by Emperor Basil II – sits at the northeast edge of town, overlooking the lake. Nearby **Ágios Stéfanos** is the second-oldest church in town (10th-century), again with intricately geometric masonry and an unusual women's gallery inside. South of the museum, tiny **Panagía Koumbelidíki** is unmistakable with its disproportionately tall, drum-shaped dome, the only one in town, painstakingly rebuilt after Italian bombing in 1940. There are some fine frescoes inside and a highly unusual Holy Trinity, complete with bearded God, in the barrel vault.

Continuing south and downhill, the extensive frescoes of the single-aisled basilica **Ágios Nikólaos Kasnítsi** are the best-preserved in Kastoriá; female saints predominate in the narthex, which long served as the women's section, while the image of the Virgin in the Assumption on the west wall is curiously reversed right-to-left. Finally, the **Taxiárhis tis Mitropóleos** is the oldest surviving church (9th-century), with a later (14th-century) fresco of the

Panagíaki Koumpelidíki is one of 54 medieval churches in Kastoriá.

Waterfall at Édessa.

The village of Ágios Germanós and the Préspa Lakes.

Virgin Platýtera adored by archangels in the apse.

In the low-lying Karyádis (Dóltso) district, inland from the southern lake-front, stand the restored **Natzís** and **Immanouíl arhondiká** (residences of the *árhons*, or leading citizens) of the same style and era (18th century) as those in Siátista. The **Folklore Museum** (daily 10am–noon, 4–6pm) is lodged in the Mansion of Nerantziz Aïvazís on nearby Kapetán Lázou. The refurbished mansion dates from the late 17th century when it stood on the lake shore, and it shows how the wealthy Christian and merchant Aïvazís family lived. From here, a narrow lake-shore lane heads 2.5km (1.5 miles) east to **Panagía Mavriótissa** monastery, now in ruins apart from two Siamese-twin churches – one 11th-century, the other 14th, both with fine frescoes. Peacocks strut, providing a fine view for the diners who patronise the adjacent lake-view restaurant.

To the Préspa Lakes

Some 36km (22 miles) north of Kastoriá, following a branch of the Aliákmonas, is the side road to the **Préspa Lakes ❻** basin. This atmospheric backwater, where the northwestern borders of Greece meet those of FYROM and Albania, was designated a Balkan Park by the governments of the three countries in 2000. There are two lakes: **Mikrí Préspa**, shallow and reedy, lying mostly in Greece, and deeper, reed-free **Megáli Préspa**, shared by Albania, FYROM and Greece.

MikríPréspa is the nesting ground for some extraordinary bird life, notably two endangered species of pelicans and pygmy cormorants, but also for a unique trout and a hardy breed of small cattle. The bird life is most active in the spring. The cattle are in the surrounding hills, also a haven for bears and wolves, although you will be lucky to spot any of them.

The best single target in the region is **Ágios Germanós ❼**, which has a visitor centre, good lodging and two frescoed Byzantine churches. **Psarádes**, the only Greek village on **Megáli Préspa**, also has an information centre and more tourist facilities, and offers the opportunity to take a highly worthwhile boat excursion to the painted cave-church of **Panagía Eleoússa**. Mikrí's islet of **Ágios Ahíllios** has an evocatively ruined 10th-century basilica and is connected to the mainland by a 1-km (0.5-mile) long pontoon. The main road leading east passes through nondescript **Flórina**, worth a stop only for its wonderful Museum of Modern Art (daily summer 6–9pm, winter 5–8pm; free), then on towards Thessaloníki.

On the northern horizon, you will notice snowy **Mount Vóras** (Kaïmaktsalán). This area saw little peace during the first half of the 20th century, with the Macedonian Struggles (1903–08), the Balkan Wars (1912–13), and a two-year battle in World War I between Serbs and Greeks on one side, Germans and Bulgarians on the other. World War II and subsequent civil war strife add to a narrative equalled in few parts of the globe.

Vergína, Véria and Pella

Traces of Phillip II of Macedonia (382–336 BC) who united the Greek people, and of his son Alexander the Great

(356–323 BC), whose empire stretched as far as India, are scattered in a broad arc west to southwest of Thessaloníki, at the edges of the current flood plains of the Axiós and Aliákmonas rivers. In ancient times, the Thermaïc Gulf covered this plain, but the silt-bearing rivers have pushed the shoreline east. All of these sites can be toured with your own transport in a full day out of Thessaloníki.

Dion ❽, northeast of Mount Olympus (Ólympos), was founded by Macedonian kings both as a military mobilisation ground and a precinct holy to the Olympian gods; its ruins, dating largely from the Roman and Byzantine eras, were buried by an earthquake-triggered mudslide in the 5th century AD (www.ancientdion. org; daily Apr–Oct 8am–7pm, Nov–Mar 8am–3pm). Since 1990, well-preserved mosaics have been found here, the best – of Medusa – transferred to safekeeping in the completely modernised village museum (Tue–Sun Apr–Oct 8am–3pm, Nov–Mar 8.30am–3pm). However, pride of place in the museum goes to a 1st-century

Macedonia and Thrace

Pella's Lion Hunt mosaic.

subterranean chamber tombs of Philip II and three others lay undiscovered until Manolis Andronikos of the Aristotle University of Thessaloníki broke through to the tombs on 8 November 1977. It was one of the most important archaeological discoveries of the 20th century. The dazzling treasures of the chamber tombs (www.aigai.gr; Mon noon–8pm, Tue–Sun 8am–8pm), including gold artefacts, ivory carvings and vivid paintings, are impressively displayed as Andronikos found them. Lesser tombs (same hours) and a summer palace, the **Palatítsa** (closed for renovations), lie just up the hill.

Some 18km (11 miles) northwest, **Véria** sits at one end of an escarpment running north to Édessa. Extensive Ottoman neighbourhoods of vernacular houses have been preserved, and more than 35 Byzantine churches are open to the public. Begin at the Véria Byzantine Museum (Tue–Sun 8.30am–3pm), wonderfully housed in a restored 19th-century flour mill at Thomedoú 1, but don't miss the 14th-century wall paintings in the Hristós Monastery (Tue–Sun 8.30am–3pm).

BC hydraulis or water organ, a type of pipe organ and the oldest to be found in the world.

Vergína ❾, on the south bank of the Aliákmonas, was formerly **Aigai**, the first Macedonian capital, and remained the royal necropolis. It got its modern name after the exchange of populations in 1923, when incoming Greeks called it after a fairytale queen. Now a Unesco World Heritage Site, the

North of Véria, in the Mieza suburb of **Náoussa** (about 2km/under a mile from the centre), there are substantial and attractive grass-covered remains of the school of Aristotle (open access), and imposing Macedonian tombs can be visited at **Lefkádia** (daily summer 9am–4pm winter 7am–3pm).

Some 43km (27 miles) from Véria, **Édessa** ❿ is unlike any other Greek town because of the numerous rivulets that wind through it heading for its waterfalls. A path leads down the ravine, through cascade mist, past a cave in the cliffside; upstream, on top of the bluff, is a medieval bridge serving the Via Egnatia. Offering further reasons to linger, the attractive 19th-century Városi quarter at the precipitous edge of town has a Folklore Museum (Tue–Sun 10am–6pm), with a nice collection of household items and traditional objects, and an Open-Air Water Museum (daily 10am–10pm), in

MOUNT OLYMPOS

The imposing bulk of Mt Olympos (Ólympos) – Greece's highest mountain at 2,917 metres (9,568ft) – dominates the horizon southwest of Thessaloníki. The ancient Greeks believed the mountain was the home of the gods, presided over by Zeus. Its summit defied climbers for years, not least because of the numerous bandits who lurked in the surrounding region. Sultan Mehmet IV is supposed to have attempted the mountain in 1669, but it was not until 1913 that two Swiss mountaineers with their Greek guide managed to scale the highest peak, Mýtikas ("the needle").

The climb is usually tackled from the village of Litóhoro, south of Kateríni, with an overnight stay in either the Giósos Apostolídis or Spílios Agápitos mountain refuge (book in advance during the summer through the SEO or EOS mountaineering clubs respectively, both of which have an office in Litóhoro). The climb itself is not technically difficult: the initial part is just a walk in, but the last section is steep and very exposed. You will need a good sense of balance and a head for heights, particularly when taking what is known as the Kakí Skála ("evil stairway") for the final few hundred metres. This overlooks the Kazánia chasm, a sheer drop of 500 metres (1,650ft).

a complex that includes the mills and the old hemp factory, now a café and occasional performance space.

Pella ⓫, a third of the way back to Thessaloníki, was the Macedonian capital after the mid-4th century BC. From here, Philip II ruled a united Greece after 338 BC, and here also his son Alexander studied under Aristotle – and trained for his fabled campaigns in the Orient. Most of the imperial capital is yet to be unearthed, but the superb mosaics of a lion hunt, Dionysos riding a panther, and other mythological scenes, more than justify a visit to the site and the museum (both summer Mon 1–8pm, Tue–Sun 8am–8pm).

East to Halkidikí

Many roads lead east out of Thessaloníki. One heads initially north to the town of **Kilkís** and the Greek shore of **Lake Doïránis**, then into the Strimónas river valley towards the road crossing into Bulgaria at **Promahónas**. On the way you can dip slightly south to the Límni Kerkinis wetlands, home to 300 species of birds at various times of year and a developing eco-tourism centre.

A more direct, northeasterly road leads to **Sérres** ⓬, important since Byzantine times and still a prosperous town. It was burned down by the retreating Bulgarians in 1913 and has been largely rebuilt, but two Byzantine churches remain, much altered by war and restoration: 11th-century **Ágii Theodóri** and 14th-century **Ágios Nikólaos**. A domed Ottoman building, called Bezesten, in the central square serves as a museum (Tue–Sun 8am–2.30pm).

In a wooded mountain valley 19km (12 miles) north is another, more venerable foundation: the monastery of **Tímiou Prodrómou**, where Gennadius Scholarios, first patriarch of Constantinople after the city was captured by the Ottomans in 1453, elected to retire and is entombed.

The busiest road east of Thessaloníki skirts the lakes of **Korónia** and **Vólvi** en route to Thrace, but a slightly less travelled one veers southeast towards **Halkidikí**, a hand-like peninsula dangling three fingers out into the Aegean. Long a favoured weekend playground of Thessalonians, since the 1980s it has also seen ever-increasing

FACT

The convoluted route of the Central Macedonian railway has led cynics to assert that European contractors who built the railways for the Ottomans were paid by the kilometre. In truth, the sultan, having been at the wrong end of some Russian gunboat diplomacy in Constantinople, decreed that the track was to be shielded from bombardment from the sea.

Mount Ólympos.

FACT

Porto Karrás is a gated community created by Greek ship-owner Yiannis Karrás in 1973. The Grand Resort has two massive 5-star hotels and the biggest private marina in northern Greece.

foreign patronage, especially Hungarians, Czechs, and Bulgarians in search of sun, sand and sea on a cheap sunny package or on a few tanks of fuel. Little is left to suggest the area's important role in classical times, when local colonies of various southern Greek cities served as battlefields during the first decade of the Peloponnesian War between Athens and Sparta. However, fossils and a half-million-year-old skull have been discovered in the **Petrálona Cave** (daily 9am–7pm in summer; closes 5pm in winter), 50km (31 miles) southeast of Thessaloníki, revealing the existence of prehistoric settlement.

The tips of Halkidikí

At **Stágira** on the way to Áthos, a modern statue of Aristotle overlooks the Ierissós Gulf and the philosopher's birthplace, ancient Stageira. **Xerxes's Canal**, now silted up, was built around 482 BC across the neck of Áthos peninsula to help the Persians avoid the fate suffered in their previous campaign, when their fleet was wrecked sailing round Áthos cape. This and Xerxes's floating bridge over

Ouranoúpoli on Halkidikí.

the Hellespont were considered by the Greeks to be products of Persian megalomania – "marching over the sea and sailing ships through the land". The medieval **Potídea Canal** still separates the **Kassándra** peninsula from the rest of the mainland and serves as a mooring ground for fishing boats. The nearby site of ancient Olynthos (Tue–Sun 8am–2.30pm) is surprisingly rewarding, with extensive remains.

The beautifully forested slopes of Mount Holomóndas cover the centre of rolling hills (the palm of **Halkidikí's three-fingered hand**); **Polýgyros**, with a dull archaeological museum, is the provincial capital, but **Arnéa** ⓭ sees more tourists for the sake of its woven goods and well-preserved old houses. Kassándra, the westernmost "finger", had little life before tourism – most inhabitants were slaughtered in 1821 for participating in the independence rebellion, and the land lay deserted until resettlement by post-1923 refugees from the Sea of Marmara. **Néa Potídea** ⓮, by the canal, and **Haniótis,** near the tip, are probably your best bets for human-scale development on a generally oversubscribed bit of real estate.

Sithonía, the middle finger, is greener, less flat and less developed; the **Mount Áthos** monasteries owned much of it before 1923, so again there are few old villages, apart from rustic **Parthenónas**, just under Mount Ítamos. The adjacent clutter of **Néos Marmarás** ⓯ and the mega-resort of **Pórto Karrás** are exceptions to the rule of ex-fishing villages converted slowly for tourism, with ample campsites, low-rise accommodation and beautiful sandy beaches. **Toróni** on the west coast is still relatively unspoiled, while nearby **Pórto Koufós**, landlocked inside bare promontories, is a yachter's haven. **Kalamítsi beach** on the east coast has an idyllic double bay, although **Sárti** further north is the main package venue.

Following the coast north past **Pyrgadíkia** fishing hamlet brings you to the base of Áthos, the easterly finger, whose pyramidal summit rises in solitary magnificence across the gulf to the east. Several resorts, including the beach-fringed islet of **Ammouliani** and cosmopolitan **Ouranoúpoli** ⓰, grace Áthos, but most people come here for the Holy Mountain because Ouranópoli is the entrance to Mount Áthos. For people not entering Mount Áthos, tour boats from Ouranópoli go around the peninsula, making it possible for these impressive monasteries to be seen from a respectful distance.

Mount Áthos

The fame of **Áthos** ⓱ (www.inathos.gr) derives from its large monastic community, today nearly 2,000 strong. In past ages, these monks earned it the epithet "holy", now an intrinsic part of the Greek name: **Ágion Óros**, the Holy Mountain. Its Christian history begins with the arrival of hermits in the mid-9th century, roughly 100 years before the foundation of the first monastery. Peter the Athonite, the most famous of the early saints, is said to have lived in a cave here for 50 years.

The first monastery, **Megístis Lávras**, was founded in AD 963 by St Athanasios, a friend of the Byzantine emperor, Nikiforos Fokas. Thereafter, foundations multiplied under the patronage of Byzantine emperors who supported them with money, land and treasures; in return, these donors are prayed for, and imperial charters zealously guarded in the monastery libraries.

The 20 surviving monasteries are all coenobitic, a rule in which monks keep to strict regulations under the direction of an abbot, or *igoúmenos*. Property is communal; meals are eaten together in the *trapezaría* or refectory. All monasteries observe a Greek liturgy except for the Russian **Pandelímonos**, the Serbian **Hilandaríou** and the Bulgarian **Zográfou**; all adhere to the Julian calendar, 13 days behind the Gregorian, and all (except for **Vatopedíou**) keep Byzantine time, reckoned from the hour of sunrise or sunset. Many monks prefer to live in smaller, less regimented monastic communities, the *skítes* and *kelliá* which are dotted around the peninsula but still dependent on the main

TIP

The northeast has hotter summers and cooler winters than the rest of Greece. The best time to visit Halkidikí is in June or early July, when the land is still green and the hills still covered in flowers.

Dionysíou monastery, built on a rock high above the sea.

THE MONASTERY TRAIL

Megístis Lávras is still the most important and imposing of the twenty surviving monasteries, which are spread throughout the peninsula and vary greatly in size, opulence and cultural interest. An increasing number of roads are being bulldozed, but the network of paths that link the monasteries is still the best way to get between them. Roads (and boats) extend down the Athonite northeast coast as far as Megístis Lávras, beyond which an often spectacular trail system rounds the end of the peninsula, taking in all monasteries and skítes (dependencies) as far as Osíou Grigoríou, keeping clear of the road system for the most part. As the length of stay is restricted by the requisite permit (see www.mountathosinfos.gr), it is best to choose a cluster of monasteries in one area and reserve accommodation months in advance.

monasteries. A few choose to live like hermits in an *isyhastírion*, a rough, unadorned hut or a cave, perched precipitously on a cliff edge.

In the 1970s, Áthos was perhaps at its nadir, with barely a thousand monks – many of limited educational and moral attainment – dwelling in dilapidated monasteries. Since then, a renaissance has been effected. The Holy Mountain's claims to be a commonwealth pursuing the highest form of spiritual life known in the Orthodox Christian tradition appear to have struck a chord, and the quality and quantity of novices from every corner of the globe (especially Russia, following the collapse of Communism) is on the rise.

The number of pilgrims to Áthos has grown, too, even though the appropriately Byzantine process of obtaining an entry permit is expressly designed to discourage the frivolous and the gawkers (and women are not allowed entry). Only genuine religious pilgrims need apply; or at least that is the ideal. Political if not doctrinal strife is never far from the Holy Mountain. Most monks are born Greek, and

prefer Greek predominance. Slavic novices and pilgrims have complained, since 1990, that they are discriminated against vis-à-vis Greeks. But divisions among Greek monks are well known, involving entire bodies of monks moving from one monastery to another in stormy disputes with abbots or civil authorities.

If you are a man and you want to visit Áthos (no women allowed), you must phone or fax (no email) most monasteries to reserve space in guest quarters often bursting with as many as 100 men a night in full season and, once there, put up with the squealing of other guests' mobile phones. Accommodation and food are free, but taxi rides from one monastery to another can be costly. Walking is the best way to visit the monasteries, but the distances can be great and you will only get to visit a handful of monasteries anyway in your limited allotted time. Only time will tell if the Mountain can defend itself against the world.

Kavála

North of Áthos, the coast road threads through several resorts on the Strymonic Gulf, popular with Thessalonians and Serrans, before crossing the Strimónas itself at ancient **Amphipolis**. Scant ruins remain of this city, a Thracian settlement colonised by Athens in 438 BC, atop a bluff protected on three sides by the river. Most passers-by content themselves with a glimpse from the river bridge of the **Lion of Amphipolis**, a colossal statue reassembled from fragments from the 4th and 3rd century BC. On the east bank, the road forks: a faster but less scenic coastal highway, or the inland road along the base of Mount Pangéo via **Elevtheroúpoli**, threading through picturesque, slate-roofed villages.

Both routes converge on the port of **Kavála** ⑱, Macedonia's second city; as Neápolis, it was an important stop on the Via Egnatia, and a port for ancient Philippi. Well into the 1920s, Kavála was a major tobacco-curing

Xánthi New Town.

and export centre, though today the harbour sees more passenger ferries en route to Thásos and the north Aegean than it does commercial traffic. A mansion from the tobacco boom days houses the Folk and Modern Art Museum (Mon–Fri 8am–2pm, Sat 9am–2.30pm), featuring the Thásos-born sculptor, Polygnotos Vagis. The treasures in the modern archaeological museum (summer Tue–Fri 8am–7pm, Sat–Sun 8am–2.30pm, winter Tue–Sun 8am–2.30pm) include tomb finds from both Avdira and Amphipolis.

The medieval walled **Panagía** quarter, southeast of the harbour, merits a leisurely stroll up to the hilltop citadel, tethered to the modern town by a 16th-century aqueduct. Start along **Poulídou**, passing a clutch of restaurants favoured by locals, arriving soon at the gate of the **Imaret** – a sprawling domed compound, allegedly the largest Islamic public building in the Balkans. Originally an almshouse and hostel, it is now an atmospheric hotel.

Philippi

Some 14km (8.5 miles) northwest, ancient **Philippi** ❶ – although named after Philip II – contains little that is Macedonian. From the acropolis, where three medieval towers rise on the ruins of Macedonian walls, you have extensive views of the battlefield which made Philippi famous. Here, in 42 BC, the fate of the Romans hung in the balance as the republican forces of Brutus and Cassius, participants in the assassination of Julius Caesar in 44 BC, confronted the armies of Caesar's avengers, Antony and Octavius. Upon their defeat, both Cassius and Brutus committed suicide; the Battle of Actium in 32 BC ended the struggle between the two victors.

The **Roman ruins** (daily summer 8am–8pm, winter 8am–3pm), mainly to the south of the highway, include foundations of both the forum and palaestra, plus a well-preserved public latrine in the southwest corner of the grounds. Philippi is reputedly the first place in Europe where St Paul preached the gospel. He arrived in AD 49, but offended the local pagans and was thrown into prison (a frescoed Roman crypt now marks the site). In AD 55, however, he got a better reception from the congregation later addressed in his **Epistle to the Philippians**. By the 6th century, Christianity was thriving here, as the remains of several early basilica-churches testify.

Driving east from Kavála, you soon cross the Néstos River, the boundary between Macedonia and Thrace, at the apex of its alluvial plain, a vast expanse of corn and tobacco fields. Some beautiful scenery along the Néstos Gorge can best be seen by train, or from the old highway, between Dráma and Xánthi.

Thrace

Ancient Thrace covered much of present-day Bulgaria and European Turkey, as well as the Greek coastal strip between the Néstos and Évros rivers. Greek colonisation of the coast from

ÁTHOS – NO WOMEN ALLOWED

Áthos is probably most famous for the ávaton edict, promulgated in 1060 by Emperor Constantine Monomahos, which forbids access to the Holy Mountain to all females more evolved than a chicken (although an exception seems to have been made for female cats, which are kept to control the rodent population).

How did this come about? Revisionists point to prior chronic hanky-panky between monks and shepherdesses, while the religious claim that the Virgin, in numerous visions, has consecrated lush Áthos as Her private garden – and women would simply be an unnecessary temptation. Over the years, many women have tried to gatecrash in disguise, only to be ignominiously ejected; a variety of women's groups in Greece and abroad have now taken up the issue.

A more serious challenge was posed in 1998 when the (female) foreign ministers of Sweden and Finland threatened to refuse to sign a decree upholding the Mount's "special status", since it contravenes one of the European Union's most cherished laws: freedom of movement (Greece is one of 11 EU states that signed the Schengen Accord abolishing border controls among member states in 2000). The Athonite authorities have, nonetheless, vowed to resist all attempts to change the Holy Mountain's single-gender character.

DRINK

In Xánthi, the numerous, modern bars and cafés along Vasilisís Sofías do a roaring trade, thanks to students from the University of Thrace, which has a campus here.

800 BC onwards often led to conflict with the native Thracian tribes. The Via Egnatia spanned the area, leaving scattered Roman and, later, Byzantine fortifications. Later, Thrace was overrun and settled by both Slavs and Ottomans. It was eventually and messily divided between Bulgaria, Turkey and Greece, between 1913 and 1923, following various wars. Although a traumatic population exchange between Turkey and Greece occurred in 1923, the Muslim inhabitants of the Greek part of Thrace were allowed to remain in return for protection granted to 125,000 Greek Orthodox living in Istanbul. (Today, the Greeks in Istanbul have been reduced to barely 2,000, whereas the population of Muslims of Thrace has increased slightly to about 130,000.)

An ethnic Turkish minority dwells principally in Xánthi, Komotiní and the plains southeast of the two cities; gypsies who adopted Islam and the Turkish language are also settled here. Another Muslim minority, the Pomaks, live in the Rodópi range above Xánthi and Komotiní; descended from medieval Bogomil heretics, they speak a Slavic language and traditionally cultivate tobacco on mountain terraces. The best base for exploration of this area and trekking is Stavroúpoli.

The open-air Saturday market at **Xánthi** ⓴, just 53km (33 miles) from Kavála, makes a good introduction to the region's Muslim demographics. The call to prayer rings out over the town five times a day. Turkish and Pomak women favour long, dark overcoats and plain-coloured yashmaks (head-scarves), now gradually being replaced by more stylish grey or brown coats and printed scarves. The gypsy women stand out in their colourful shalvar bloomers, their scarves tied behind the ears. Many men still wear burgundy-coloured velvet or felt fezzes, or white skullcaps.

Xánthi became a prosperous commercial and administrative centre in the 19th century, thanks to tobacco. Renowned masons were brought from Epirus to build merchants' mansions, tobacco warehouses and *hans* (inns). The *hans*, large square buildings around a central courtyard, were resting spots and trade centres near the marketplace. One of the handsome 19th-century mansions at the base of the old town has become a Folk Museum (Tue–Sun 8.30am–3pm). Further uphill lie the minarets and houses of the Turkish quarter, with numerous satellite dishes for tuning into Turkish-language TV.

At **Komotiní** ㉑, 56km (35 miles) east of Xánthi via the bird-stalked lagoon of **Vistonída** and the water-girt monastery of **Ágios Nikólaos**, Muslims constitute nearly half the population. The Democritus University of Thrace is based here and though it is less immediately attractive than Xánthi, there is an old bazaar of cobbled lanes (Tuesday is the busiest day), with tiny shops, 14 functioning mosques and many old-fashioned coffee houses. A **Folklore**

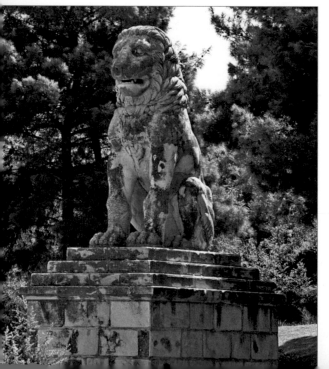

The Lion of Amphipolis.

Museum (daily 10am–1pm) just off the central park displays local embroidery, costumes and metalwork); the **archaeological museum** (daily 8am–3pm) keeps finds from such Thracian sites as **Avdira**, south of Xánthi, and **Maroneia**, south of Komotiní.

Avdira itself does not repay a visit in its bedraggled state, although it is famed for nurturing two major philosophers: Democritus (*c*.460–370 BC), who first expounded atomic theory, and the sophist Protagoras (c.490–420 BC). Odysseus legendarily called at Maroneia after leaving Troy on his return to Ithaca, procuring a sweet red wine which later saved him and his companions from the cyclops Polyphemus. A cave north of the sparse cliff-top site retains the name of **Polyphemus's Cave**.

Alexandroúpoli

The old road from Komotiní zigzags 65km (40 miles) through barren hills before coming down to the rather drab port of **Alexandroúpoli ㉒**, gateway to Samothráki island.

It's wisest to press on into the valley of the Évros River, especially if you're a birdwatcher. The delta, east of the Roman spa of Traianopolis, is excellent for waterfowl, while the **Dadiá Forest Reserve**, a successful World Wide Fund for Nature (WWF) venture, shelters black and griffin vultures. In between, you can pause at **Féres** for the sake of its 12th-century church, **Panagía Kosmosótira**, whose lofty, five-domed interior is generally open to visitors.

North of the turning for Dadiá, the first town of any size is **Souflí ㉓**, once famous for silk production. Corn fields have now replaced the mulberry trees whose leaves once nourished the silkworms, and only a small museum commemorates the vanished industry. **Didymótiho**, 30km (18.5 miles) further upstream, has a Byzantine fortress at the old town's summit and an abandoned mosque on the square, whose features speak of Seljuk (and earlier) prototypes.

From here, most traffic is bound for Turkish **Edirne**, whose graceful minarets are just visible from the Greek border town of Kastaniés.

FACT

During work on the 680-km (423-mile) Egnatia highway, Roman road-building techniques were revealed at a site near Komotiní. Much of the road has lasted 2,000 years, but it was here that archaeologists fully discovered the genius of Roman technology.

Xánthi at carnival time.

Skiáthos Town bathers.

THE ISLANDS

Greece has more inhabited islands than any
other European country – but it's anyone's
guess how many there actually are.

Island windmill.

The poet Odysseus Elytis once said: "Greece rests on the sea". It's an observation that few countries could claim with such confidence. Some 25,000 sq km (10,000 sq miles) of the Aegean and Ionian seas are covered by islands. And, in characteristic Greek fashion, the exact number of them has been the topic of discussion and dispute. There may be 3,000 islands and islets, of which 167 are inhabited. Or, according to someone else's calculations, there may be only 1,000, of which fewer than 70 are populated.

The criterion that defines a populated place is open to interpretation. Does a tiny outcrop, bare save for one goatherd and six goats, constitute an inhabited island? Can an island that is totally deserted except for annual pilgrimages to a small chapel at its summit claim to be inhabited?

The arithmetic matters far more to foreigners than to the Greeks, who are interested in sea and sky, in food and festivals, rather than in facts and figures. What is indisputable, however, is the sheer variety of landscape and experience to be found lurking behind the familiar images.

This is what we attempt to show in this section – islands with an ancient past and a modern outlook, an array of choices juxtaposed against pure, simple pleasures. In order to accommodate everything that is encompassed in the phrase "a Greek island", we have devoted space to tiny islands such as Kímolos and Lipsí, as well as the well-known giants like Crete and Rhodes and the holiday favourites such as Mýkonos and Corfu. We do not ignore the familiar, popular islands, of course, but we explore them to seek out the true heart of the place behind the tourist clichés.

The perfect horseshoe harbour of Ásos.

The best way to enjoy the islands is to arrive with a certain attitude of mind. By all means, begin by uncritically enjoying the cluster of blazing white buildings against a shimmering sea, donkeys set against a backdrop of olive groves, and so on – the images seared into the senses by holiday brochures. But, when the novelty wears off, or perhaps earlier, examine each island as if it were an onion and start stripping off the skins. How to strip the onion is a large part of what this book is about.

So, welcome aboard the ferry and prepare for a cruise around Europe's most fascinating and welcoming islands – however many of them there might be.

ISLANDS OF THE SARONIC GULF

Salamína, Aegina, Angístri, Póros, Ýdra and Spétses are all within easy reach of the mainland and popular with day-trippers. But they are distinctive, rich in history and remarkably attractive.

Athens and the islands of the Saronic Gulf are often lumped together in guidebooks. There is some sense in this, since many Athenians frequent these islands at weekends, while during the summer they become veritable extensions of the more fashionable Athenian neighbourhoods. Yet this view of the Argo-Saronic islands doesn't take into account their separate identities. They are islands, not suburbs, each with their own character.

Salamína (Salamis)

Salamína is best known for an ancient naval battle (480 BC) in which out-numbered Athenian ships routed the enormous Persian fleet – the ships being the "wooden walls" that the Delphic oracle had predicted would save the Greeks. Pride of the island is **Faneroméni Monastery** ❶ (typical midday closure) on the Voudóro peninsula, just 6km (4 miles) from the capital, **Salamína Town**; it's now a tenanted nunnery, with brilliant 17th-century frescoes, while its boathouse served as a retreat of the great poet Angelos Sikelianos.

The island is decidedly not posh but it is relatively undeveloped and can be reached quickly, just a few minutes' ride across from Pérama, through the waters which saw the battle, to the port of **Paloúkia** ❷. Most

Heading for Paloúkia.

of the inhabitants live in **Salamína** (also called **Kouloúri**), which has an archaeological museum (Tue–Sun 8am–3pm) and a Folk Museum (Mon–Fri 9am–4pm), plus decent tavernas. Cyclists will find Salamína's back roads uncrowded and untaxing on the stamina. The best beaches are on the south coast at Peráni and Peristéria.

Aegina (Egina)

Aegina (www.aeginagreece.com-com.gr) is close enough to be within easy reach of the mainland and far enough away

Main Attractions

Main Attractions
Faneroméni monastery, Salamína
Temple of Aphaea, Égina
Paleohóra, Égina
Halikiáda beach, Angístri
Volcano walk, Méthana
Póros Town, seen from Galatás
Ýdra Town
Walking to Kamíni & Vlyhós, Ýdra
Paleó Limáni, Spétses
Agía Paraskeví beach, Spétses

Aegina beach.

The 5th-century temple of Aphaea on Aegina.

to retain its island identity. About an hour and a half by ferry from Piraeus – or 45 minutes by hydrofoil or catamaran – it has little trouble attracting visitors. The island remains more popular with Athenians seeking a retreat from the city than with foreign tourists or other Greeks. The main local produce is pistachio nuts, sold all along the harbour street.

Shaped on the map like an upside-down triangle, the island's southern point is marked by the magnificent cone of **Mount Óros,** the highest peak in the Argo-Saronic islands, visible on a clear day from Athens's Acropolis. The island's centre and eastern side is mountainous; a gently sloping fertile plain runs down to the northwestern corner where **Aegina (Egina) Town** ❸ overlays in part the ancient capital of the island.

The town has numerous 19th-century mansions constructed when the first Greek president, Ioannis Kapodistrias (1776–1831), lived and worked here, as well as an enormous disused jail (being restored) that began life as a Kapodistrias-funded orphanage. Some

3km (2 miles) north of town is the **Christos Kapralos Museum** (June–Oct Tue–Sun 10am–2pm, 6–8pm, Nov–May Fri–Sun 10am–2pm), dedicated to this prominent Greek sculptor and painter, occupying his former studios.

The modern harbour, crowded with yachts and fishing boats, adjoins the ancient harbour, which is now the shallow town beach north of the main quay. The little beach ends at the ancient site of *Kolóna,* meaning "column", after the single conspicuously standing column of the **Temple of Apollo**. This Doric temple, built in 520–500 BC, was superseded by a late Roman fortress, fragments of which survive on the seaward side. Although from the sea the temple looks unimpressive, the view from its promontory is very fine. A small **museum** (Tue–Sun 8.30am–3pm) on the site features finds from 2,500 years of local settlement.

The island's most famous ancient monument is the **Temple of Aphaea** ❹ (Tue–Sun 9.30am–4.30pm), in the northeast, above the summer resort of **Agía Marína.** The temple crowns a hilltop in a pine grove commanding

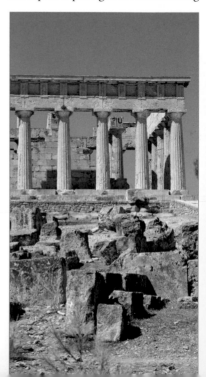

a splendid view of the Aegean. Built in about 490 BC, it is the only surviving Greek temple with a second row of small superimposed columns in the interior of the sanctuary.

On the way to the temple, you will pass the modern **Monastery of Ágios Nektários** (daily except for midday break), the newest (and very popular) Orthodox saint, canonised in 1961. Across the ravine from the monastery is ghostly **Paleohóra** ("old town"), established inland during the 9th century as protection against piracy. Abandoned after Greek independence, most of the surviving 38 churches are in utter disrepair, but you can still see the fragments of brilliant post-Byzantine frescoes in several unlocked chapels.

The west coast of the island is quite gentle, with passable sandy beaches at **Marathónas** and **Eginítissa,** but better reasons to head out here are to enjoy a meal in one of the many fish tavernas along the harbour at **Pérdika** ❺, or to take a boat from there to swim at the clean and sheltered bay on the uninhabited islet of **Moní.**

Angístri and Méthana

Angístri (Agístri) ❻, the small island facing Aegina Town, has become very much a destination in its own right, especially with trendy Athenians who guarantee a surprisingly lively nightlife. It is lapped by the cleanest, most aquamarine waters in this part of the gulf, and has considerable appeal inland with its dense pine forests. **Skála,** where conventional ferries call, is the main resort with the only sandy beach, though **Mýlos,** 1,500m west where hydrofoils stop, has more character, with a church, old houses, shops and again plenty of places to stay and eat. A bus links the two, and also plies to the two southerly hamlets of **Metóhi** and **Limenária,** both with tavernas. The most attractive, and famous, beach is pebbly **Halikiáda** south of Skála, supposedly Greece's oldest naturist cove; its 125-metre extent is colonised by a semi-permanent tent colony. Dragonéra cove on the west coast, looking west to the Peloponnese, is the runner-up.

Although linked to the Peloponnese via a road along a slender isthmus, **Méthana** ❼ is far easier reached

Póros Town harbour.

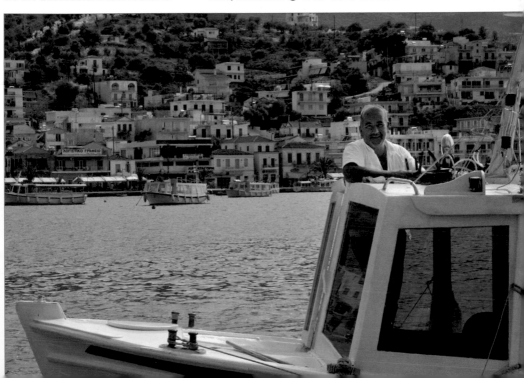

by sea as a regular stop on the line to Póros, and so ranks as an honorary Argo-Saronic island. It is in fact a dormant volcano, with lush vegetation and basalt-built cottages. Low-key Méthana port is distinguished only by its hot springs; a better destination, in the far northwest, is **Kaméni Hóra** hamlet; from here, a marked path leads 15 minutes through a chaos of solidified lava to a volcanic cavern, with fine views en route towards Angístri and Aegina.

Póros

The island of Póros is separated from the Argolid mainland by a narrow passage of water – *póros* in Greek means "passage" or "ford". As your boat turns into the ford from its northern entrance, the channel opens out and the white houses, tiled rooftops and hilltop clocktower of lovely **Póros Town** ❽ appear. Almost landlocked, it provides one of the most protected anchorages in the Aegean. Póros can also be reached (with considerably more effort) by driving via the **Isthmus of Corinth** to **Paleá Epídavros** and then further down

View from the Póros rooftops across to Galatás.

the coast to little **Galatás,** just across the channel.

Although Póros has numerous hotels, and Athenians have owned vacation houses here for decades, the island has never been as fashionable as Ýdra or Spétses, but during summer it gets every bit as crowded. Póros Town itself almost completely covers the sub-island of Sferiá, southwest of the small channel separating it from the larger part of the island, Kalávria.

North of the channel, you can still see the ruins of a Russian naval station established in the 1780s, but the most venerable building on Kalávria is the **Monastery of Zoödóhou Pigís** (Virgin of the Life-Giving Spring; daily 11am–1pm, 4–6pm), beautifully situated on a wooded hillside east of town and still home to a few monks. Below extends Monastiríou beach, perhaps the best on an island not known for stellar ones.

Above the monastery, a road climbs through pines to the ruins of the **Sanctuary of Poseidon** ❾, in a saddle between the highest hills of the island. The temple was excavated by

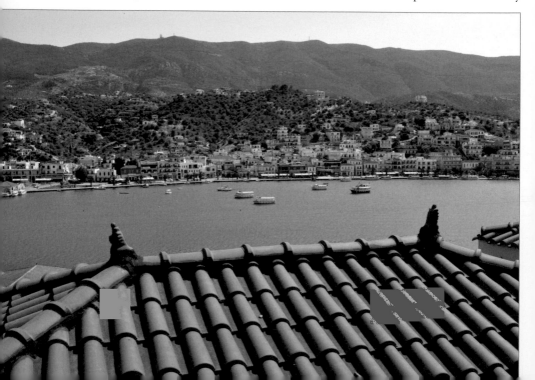

the Swedish Archaeological School during the 19th century, and they are digging again, so much is roped off, but its setting is rewarding.

Ancient **Troezen** ⑩ is about 8km (5 miles) from Galatás on the Peloponnese. The mythological hero Theseus is said to have grown up here before he went off to become king of Athens. Theseus also supposedly returned later to Troezen, providing Euripides and Racine with the plots for their famous plays about the young queen Phaedra who unjustly accused Theseus's son Hippolytos of having violated her. The most obvious ruins of Troezen are of a shrine to Hippolytos (only foundations remain) and a Byzantine basilica in a perilous state. Nearby, the **Diavologéfyro** (Devil's Bridge) may disappoint, being a small natural rock span once used as an aqueduct.

Ýdra (Hydra)

The island of **Ýdra** ⑪ – in antiquity Ydrea, "the well watered" – now appears as a long, barren rock. But the harbour, with its fine old stone buildings, is still lovely; the town has attracted the

artistic and the fashionable since the 1950s and the masses ever since.

The heart of the island is its harbour-town, also called **Ýdra**. All around the picturesque bay, white, tile-roofed vernacular houses climb the slope, interspersed with massive grey *arhondiká* (mansions of the shipping families who made fortunes in the 18th and 19th centuries), many of them designed by architects from Venice and Genoa. Along the quay are tourist shops and cafés, with the clock tower of the 18th-century **Monastery of the Panagía** in the centre; much of the masonry used to build it was taken from the ancient Sanctuary of Poseidon on Póros. The U-shaped harbour itself is girded by a little thread of a breakwater, and flanked by 19th-century cannons.

The town has many good backstreet tavernas, as well as extremely popular bars and clubs. Yet the higher reaches and the hills beyond remain surprisingly untouched; narrow alleys and steep staircases lead from one quarter to the next. The uniformity of white walls is broken again and again by a century-old doorway, a bright blue

FACT

Ýdra is one of the few places in Greece that has banned almost all concrete construction, as well as cars, and has therefore managed to retain its beauty.

Fisherman's catch, Ýdra harbour.

Donkeys carrying marble slabs, Ýdra.

Kamíni port, southwest Ýdra

window frame, a flight of striking scarlet steps, or a green garden fence. One stair-path ultimately climbs to **Agía Evpraxía,** the only inhabited (by nuns) and visitable (except at midday rest) rural monastery on the island.

Mandráki, northeast of town, has the only sandy beach, but heading southwest is more rewarding. A wide coastal path goes to **Kamíni** and **Vlyhós,** with its early 19th-century arched stone bridge. There are good tavernas in both places. Water taxis are the only way to reach **Ágios Nikólaos** and **Bísti** ⑫ beaches, the island's best, at the southwest tip, unless you undertake an arduous cross-country hike, equipped with a good map. An easier path-walk leads southeast and within 80 minutes to the equally good, pine-shaded pebble beach at **Limnióniza.**

Spétses

Spétses ⑬ is the southwesternmost of the Argo-Saronic Gulf islands, though just off the Argolid coast with which it has short-hop seagoing links. In antiquity, it was called Pityousa, "pine tree" island, and, despite huge fires in 1990

and 2001, it is still the most wooded of the group after Angístri. Tourist development here is more extensive than on Ýdra but less than on either Póros or Aegina, and in recent years, responsible planning has helped preserve the island's charm.

Although **Spétses Town** has its share of bars and fast-food places, the **Paleó Limáni** (Old Harbour) area still radiates a gentle grace. The 18th-century *arhondiká* (merchants' houses) you see in this part of the town now belong to wealthy Athenian families who return every summer.

Like Ýdra, Spétses' heyday was the late 18th century, when seagoing trade made it prosperous. Also like Ýdra, it became a hive of activity during the Greek War of Independence, offering its merchant fleet of over 50 ships for the Greek cause. The island is distinguished for being the first in the archipelago to revolt against Ottoman rule in April 1821, and the fortified main harbour of **Dápia,** still bristling with cannon, forms one of the town's focal points.

Laskarina Bouboulina, a great heroine of the Greek War of Independence, was from Spetses, and her great victory is celebrated every 8 September by a *panigýri* (religious festival, see page 96) focused on the church of the **Panagía Armáta** on the lighthouse headland close to the Old Harbour. A mock battle is staged and a model Turkish flagship is burned in the harbour amidst a fireworks display.

Although after the War of Independence Spétses' fleet declined, shipbuilding traditions continue unabated. The small **museum** (Tue–Sun 8.30am–2pm), in the imposing 18th-century *arhondikó* of shipowner Hatzigianni Mexi, contains polychrome prows of ships from the revolutionary fleet and an ossuary holding the bones of Bouboulína. Her own family mansion, also a museum (guided tours only; consult the sign outside for schedule) stands behind the Dápia.

Outside of town to the northwest is the **Anargýrios and Korgialénios College,** a Greek version of an English public school. John Fowles taught here and portrayed both school and island in his 1966 novel *The Magus*. The school has closed, though the

buildings are sporadically used as a conference centre.

The town beach of **Ágios Mámas,** busy **Agía Marína** a bit beyond, and amenitied **Ligonéri** east of town, can't compare to the beautiful beaches of **Zogeriá, Agía Paraskeví,** Agía Anárgyri and **Xylokériza** (going around the island's perimeter in an anticlockwise direction). **Ágii Anárgyriis** ⑭ is the most developed and sandiest, with proper tavernas and watersports.

Sandals for sale in Spétses.

Genteel Spétses Town.

Marble taken from the Temple of Apollo, Páros Old Town.

THE CYCLADES

From the hectic nightlife of Mýkonos and Íos to the rugged beauty of Mílos and Sérifos, and the unspoilt seclusion of Síkinos and Anáfi, there is something for all tastes among these islands.

For many people, the Cyclades are Greece; other island chains are mere distractions from this blue Aegean essence. They were inhabited by 5000 BC; by the third millennium, a fascinating island culture flourished here, with fine arts and crafts and lively commerce – as anyone who visits the excellent Museum of Cycladic Art in Athens will appreciate (see page 148).

Of the 56 islands, 24 are inhabited. There are three basic ferry routes from either Piraeus or Rafína ports: the easternmost takes in bucolic Ándros, religious Tínos, metropolitan Sýros, and cosmopolitan Mýkonos. The central line joins popular Páros, Náxos and Amorgós, concluding at spectacular Santoríni or remote Anáfi. The most western itinerary calls at Kýthnos, Sérifos, Sífnos and Mílos, usually extending to Folégandros and Síkinos. Especially in high season, links are possible between the basic routes. With scant links to other Cyclades, Kéa attracts Athenian weekenders.

Ándros

Ándros ❶ was settled centuries ago by Orthodox Albanians; their stone dwellings in the north contrast with the whitewash and red tile of the other villages. The port town, **Gávrio**, does have ample tourist infrastructure,

though more visitors bases themselves at **Batsí**, 6km (4 miles) south, a pleasant Cycladic fishing town with a long beach. On the east coast, **Ándros Town (Hóra) ❷** remains remarkably unspoiled. Because so many rich Athenians have weekend houses here, tourism has not been assiduously pursued. The prize exhibit in the **archaeological museum** (Tue–Sun 8.30am–3pm) is the famous Hermes of Ándros, a 4th-century AD copy of Praxiteles' 4th-century BC statue at ancient Olympia. Nearby, the **Goulandris Museum**

Main Attractions

Contemporary Art Museum, Ándros
Ermoúpolis Townscape, Sýros
Ancient Delos
The Cave, Andíparos
Náxos Old Town
Hozoviótissa Monastery, Amorgós
South Coast Beaches, Mílos
View over Caldera, Santoríni
Museum of Prehistoric Thera, Santoríni
Climb to Panagía Kalamiótissa, Anáfi

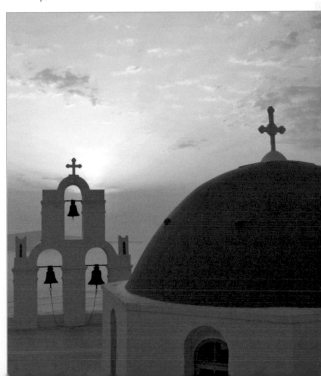

Santoríni, famous for its whitewashed villages and blue-domed churches.

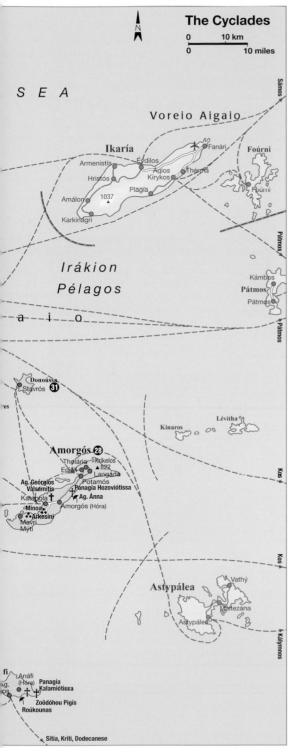

of **Contemporary Art** (www.moca-andros. gr; Apr–June and Sept Wed–Mon 10am– 2pm, July–Sept Mon 11am–3pm, Wed–Sun 11am–3pm, 6–9pm, Nov–Mar Sat–Mon 10am–2pm) has a fine permanent collection by both Greek and foreign artists, plus renowned temporary exhibits. South of the Batsí–Hóra road is the most spectacular of Ándros's 13 monasteries, **Panahrándou** ❸ (9am–1pm, 4.30pm–sunset); over 1,000 years old, but home to just one monk.

Ándros has many beaches – the best on the west coast, either side of Batsí, are **Hryssí Ámmos, Kyprí, Agía Marína** and **Dela-vóyas**. The east shore is more exposed to the meltémi, but try **Giália** north of Hóira, and **Kórthi** bay in the far south, popular with windsurfers.

Kéa (Tziá)

Kéa-bound boats leave from the mainland port of Lávrio, some 50km (30 miles) from Athens, and land at **Korissía** ❹. The main town, **Ioulída**, huddles below a rounded ridge overlooking the island's northern flank, a site chosen for its inaccessibility from pirates. The famous **Lion of Kéa**, a smiling, maneless beast almost 6 metres (20ft) long, is a 15-minute walk northeast of Ioulída. Carved from grey granite, it is probably early Archaic.

In the 19th century, there were a million oak trees on well-watered Kéa, and many still provide shade. Olive trees, however, are absent; since ancient times, the island has been noted for its almonds. The jagged west coast has many sandy coves, some accessible by boat only. **Písses**, with a square, Hellenistic watchtower at **Agía Marína** just inland, and **Koúndouros**, are two of the more developed beaches. Close to Korissía is Vourkári, with yachts at anchor and pricy tavernas, plus **Agía Iríni**, a Minoan excavation. Walkers are well served by a network of numbered trails, intelligently rehabilitated and marked thanks to EU funds.

Tínos

Tínos receives many thousands of tourists – but they are mostly Greek Orthodox here for the church, the **Panagía Evangelístria** or "Annunciated Virgin". In 1822, local nun Pelagía dreamt of an icon; it was duly unearthed and the church was built to house it. The icon's healing powers have made **Tínos Hóra ❺** the Lourdes of Greece. Women fall to their knees upon arrival, and crawl painfully to the church (less painfully since a carpeted lane for that purpose was installed on the main approach). Healing miracles often occur. Despite all the foregoing, Tínos is about half Catholic in population, with most of them out in the rural villages.

For a reminder of the Ottoman conquest, visit the peak of **Exóbourgo**, 643 metres (2,110ft), with its ruined fortress (Tínos was the last Cyclade to fall to the Turks, in 1715). A bus ride to Exóbourgo and beyond will also reveal some weird, mushroom-shaped, wind-sculpted rocks, especially above **Vólax** village, known for its basket-weaving.

Kolymbíthra ❻ in the north is Tínos's best beach. **Ágios Sóstis**, near Pórto on the south coast, is also a decent stretch of sand. Of the monasteries to see, the abandoned **Katapoliani**, near **Ystérnia**, is exceptional. **Kardianí**, the village southeast of

Ystérnia, is Tínos's most spectacularly set – though arcaded **Arnádos** and adjacent **Dýo Horiá** give it stiff competition. As on Kéa, a prepared network of trails appeals to walkers during the cooler months.

Kýthnos (Thermiá)

After iron-mining operations ceased, **Kýthnos ❼** lost its prime source of income. Foreign tourism has not supplemented it, but Athenian visitors have helped. **Mérihas** on the west coast has the biggest choice of accommodation. In summer, a "taxiboat" runs from Mérihas to **Episkopí**, **Apókroussi** and Kolóna beaches to the north, the best on the island. **Hóra**, 6km (4 miles) northeast of Mérihas, is exquisite: its streets are spanned by wood-beamed arches joining facing houses, while rock pavements are decorated with white-painted fish, stylised ships and flowers.

The island's alias of Thermiá derives from thermal baths at Loutrá, on the northeast coast, 5km (3 miles) north of Hóra. The recent advent of posh lodgings is helping to banish Loutrá's

Ermoúpoli harbour.

somewhat fusty reputation. Above Loutrá, at Maroúla, excavations have revealed the earliest known Cycladic settlement, dating from before 4500 BC. A ravine splits tile-roofed **Dryopída** ❽ (the medieval capital) into two; the chambered **Katafíki cave** here is linked in legend with the Nereids (sea nymphs in Greek mythology).

Sýros

Sýros ❾ remains the Cyclades' capital, but when Piraeus (Pireás) overtook it as a trade centre in the late 1800s, its port went into decline. However, it retains excellent inter-island ferry links and useful facilities. The capital, **Ermoúpoli**, has been "discovered", with the renovation of grand buildings, public and private, and multiplication of tourist facilities. The area called **Vapória** ("the ships"), uphill from the shopping streets, is where you'll find many 19th-century neoclassical mansions (a few doubling as hotels). The elegant, marble-paved main square, Platía Miaoúlis, is flanked by an imposing Town Hall, just behind which the restored Apollon Theatre

was originally modelled on La Scala in Milan. The entire Belle Epoque townscape is under Unesco protection. Like Tínos, Sýros is about half Catholic, with most of them residing in the hill village of **Áno Sýros** above Ermoúpoli.

Fínikas ❿, a beachside town in the southwest, is possibly named after the Phoenicians, probably Sýros's first inhabitants – or more likely after a palm tree (**fínikas** in Greek). The island's south is rounder and greener than the rugged, thinly populated north and has good beaches at **Possidonía** and **Vári** as well as Fínikas. Up the west coast, **Galissás** and **Kíni**, with the best beaches (and sunsets), are popular resorts. During Roman times, and again from 1948 until 1974, political prisoners were interned on **Gyáros**, the exceedingly bleak desert island to the northwest.

Mýkonos

Mýkonos ⓫ has become glamorous and prosperous by turning its rocky, treeless ruggedness into a tourist-pleasing package that works – making it more expensive than any other Greek

Most of the Cyclades islands that grew their own grain have windmills, but the majority have fallen into disuse.

Galissás beach resort.

Paraportianí (Our Lady of the Postern Gate; closed to the public) is probably Greece's most photographed church.

Little Venice, a row of buildings hanging over the sea on the west, is the least frenetic part of town, with atmospheric café-bars thronged at sunset. The **Folklore Museum** (Apr–Oct Mon–Sat 4.30–8.30pm; free) and the **archaeological museum** (Tue–Sun 8.30am–3pm), at different ends of Mýkonos's quay, are full of interesting objects. Caïques also depart from here for **Delos** ⑫, the sacred island that is the centre of the Cyclades (in myth, Mýkonos was Delian Apollo's grandson). Or you can strike inland to **Áno Merá,** 7km (4 miles) east, the only other village, and visit the red-domed Tourlianí monastery (9am–1pm, 2pm–sunset), which houses some fine 16th-century icons.

Freshly-caught octopus is served in most of the Cycladic islands.

island except Santoríni. Summer draws thousands of tourists to **Mýkonos Town** to sample its celebrated bars, August–September gay scene, cozy restaurants, and the clothes and jewellery shops. Despite the glitz, the portside Hóra is among the most solicitously preserved in the Cyclades, with its wooden balconies loaded with flowers, multicoloured domed chapels and whitewashed surfaces. The odd-shaped

Mýkonos nightlife.

Among Mýkonos beaches, **Paradise** is half straight nude, **Super Paradise** half gay nude, and both are stunning; below Áno Merá, **Kalafáti** is popular with windsurfers, and Eliá exclusively gay; **Platýs Gialós** and **Psaroú** in the west are popular with families.

Sérifos

A long easterly promontory encloses **Livádi** ⑬, Sérifos's harbour. With a half-dozen each of tavernas, hotels and café-bars, this is a pleasant place to stay, with good beaches on either side at **Livadákia** (where there's more prime accommodation) and **Ágios Sóstis. Sérifos Hóra** spills precipitously from a crag above; regular buses make the ascent, but the old stair-path (a 40-minute climb) makes for a more authentic approach.

Hóra has two parts, a somewhat neglected lower neighbourhood and the architecturally protected **Kástro**, with a scenic church at its east end. Kástro's central plaza with its trendy cafés, gaily coloured town hall and church of Ágios Athanásios provides a focus. The view from the edge of Hóra east over the gleaming bay and the other islands is spectacular.

From Hóra, numbered trails head north to either Kállitsos village, or Panagía plus Galaní villages, the latter two accessible also by road and very occasional seasonal bus. Between Kállitsos and Galaní stands the fortified medieval **Taxiárhon Monastery** ⑭, only open when the local parish priest is inside.

Sérifos abounds in little bays, many still unspoiled and very quiet outside of summer. Beyond Livadákia, Karávi is scenic and usually naturist; in the far southwest, **Megálo Livádi** and Gánema coves once hosted mines, whereas today there are handy tavernas.

Sífnos

Sífnos ⑮ was, and to a reduced extent still is, a potter's isle. In the narrow, pretty harbour, **Kamáres**, and at Platýs Gialós and isolated Hersónisos, potters still set out racks of earthenware to dry in the sun. Weaving and jewellery-making were the other crafts; there are fine examples of these in the **Folklore Museum** (Apr–Oct only daily 9.30am–2pm, 6–10pm) of the capital, **Apollonía**. Contiguous to Apollonía, **Artemónas** is Sífnos's wealthiest town, with mansions and old churches.

The oldest community, however, is **Kástro** ⑯, the medieval capital, perched 100 metres (330ft) above the sea and 3km (2 miles) to the east of

Lévkes countryside.

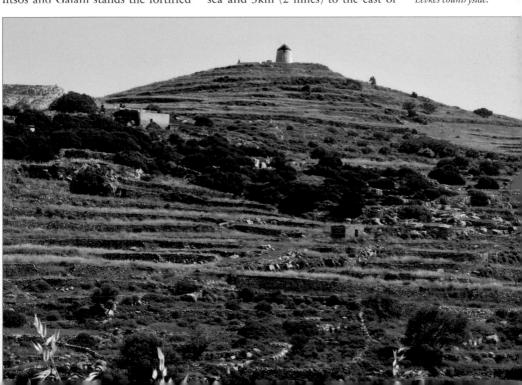

The Cycladic Bronze Age

Early Cycladic peoples left behind beautiful artefacts that arose out of thier organised and flourishing culture. The most famous and mysterious of these artefacts are without doubt the stylised marble sculptures which have been found in tombs.

Bronze Age settlements and cemeteries excavated on a number of Cycladic islands are generally considered to be the first complex, organised, settled communities in Europe. The Early Cycladic Bronze Age began about 3200 BC and is thought to have lasted until around 2500 BC. The later Bronze Age (2500–2000 BC) is divided by scholars into two periods: the Middle and Late Cycladic. These latter periods increasingly display the unmistakable influence of the Minoan culture of Crete, and show a move towards urban settlement. In general, the term Cycladic Culture refers to the Early Cycladic, and it is during this period

Cycladic bronze figurine.

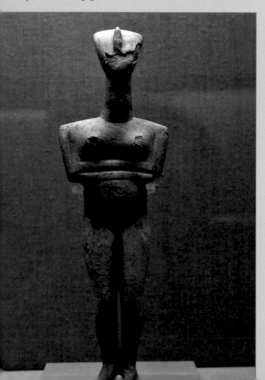

that the individuality of the culture of the Cycladic islands is most evident.

The settlements of the Early Cycladic were small, typically around 50 people, and comprised of densely packed stone-built housing, usually only of just one storey. Accompanying the settlements, outside the residential area, were cemeteries of small cist graves (rectangular graves lined with stone) and chamber tombs, which were clustered in family groups. The dead were inhumed in the contacted, or foetal, position along with everyday objects. Much of the phsyical evidence we have today about how Early Cycladic society functioned comes from these cemeteries.

The often stark difference in grave goods between tombs provides evidence of a heavily stratified society. While some graves contain a very rich variety of artefacts, including gold and silver jewellery, others have very little, often only a single marble figure. How these differences between rich and poor are played out is a matter of conjecture, but many artefacts that were found display a high degree of skill in their manufacture, which in turn suggests a class of skilled craft workers. Hunting, fishing, animal husbandry and agriculture provided food. The islanders were practised traders, pointing to the existence of a merchant class, presumably, among the wealthier members of society. Skilled sailors, they had contact with the Greek mainland, Crete, Turkey and even the distant Danube Basin.

White marble figurines

Of all the items left by these peoples, the marble figurines are perhaps both the most beautiful and enigmatic. Their different typologies are used by scholars to differentiate the various Cycladic eras. The predominately female figures are generally around 20cm (8ins) in length (a few near life-sized sculptures have been discovered) and are made of white marble. Almost two-dimensional in their execution, they have flattened oval heads, schematic breasts and folded arms; many features would have been painted on the marble (on the face, only the nose is rendered in relief). It is conjectured from the position of the feet that they were intended to lie horizontally, but there is no conclusive evidence for this, just as there is no evidence for their function. Explanations from scholars range from their being apotropaic (warding off evil), to divinities, symbolic after-death companions or ancestors.

Apollonía. Catalans and Venetians once ruled the island; the walls they built are still in evidence, as are some remains of an ancient acropolis. Most of the buildings are from the 14th century. The big Venetian building in the centre of Kástro is the **archaeological museum** (Tue–Sun 8.30am–3pm; free).

Sífnos's southerly coastal settlements make tranquil bases. A marked footpath leads from **Katavatí** just south of Apollonía to **Vathý**, a hamlet on a deep inlet also linked by road to Platýs Gialós. Vathý's most visually stunning feature is the **Taxiárhis** (Archangel) Monastery (open only for service on the feast day), poised as though ready to set sail onto the sands. But Sífnos's most famous postcard/poster subject is **Hryssopigís** (Golden Wellspring) **Monastery** (open only on the feast day), built in 1653 on an islet now reached by a small footbridge.

Andíparos

Until the end of the last glacial period 10,000 years ago, the small, pretty island of Andíparos (www.antiparos. info) was joined to Páros. A narrow channel now separates them, plied by short-hop ferries from Poúnda bringing visitors to its famous **Spílio** ⑰ (cavern; Apr–Oct daily 10am–6.30pm). Although only the topmost levels are accessible, and the impact is reduced somewhat by concrete steps down and a constant bilingual narration soundtrack, stalactite/stalagmite formations – 45 million years in the making – still impress. Arhilohos of ancient Páros was the first recorded visitor, the Marquis de Nointel the most flamboyant one, celebrating Christmas Mass here in 1673.

Andíparos Hóra itself is engaging, first put on people's radar by serving as location for the 1960 film Mantalena, which boosted Greek starlet Aliki Vougiouklaki's career – and subsequently made the little island an obligatory stop for alternative types transiting between Ibiza and India. The now barely inhabited **kástro** (medieval Venetian town plan where the houses are arranged in a defensive compound), complete with central cistern and chapel, is of a type seen only at Síkinos and Kímolos. The island

Páros church.

UNDERGROUND TOURISM

The **Cave of the Stalactites** (Apr–Oct daily 10am–6.30pm), the principal sight on Andíparos, was discovered during the reign of Alexander the Great, around 330 BC, and has been attracting visitors ever since. Despite the depredations of souvenir-hunters, who have broken and removed stalactites and stalagmites for centuries, it is still a fantastically spooky chamber, full of weird shapes and shadows.

Almost as impressive as the formations are the inscriptions left by past visitors, including King Otto of Greece and Lord Byron. The oldest piece of graffiti has sadly been lost – a note from several individuals stating that they were hiding in the cave from Alexander the Great, who suspected them of plotting his assassination. Another inscription (in Latin) records the Christmas Mass celebrated here by the French Marquis de Nointel in 1673, for an audience of 500.

In summer, buses and boats run to the cave from Andíparos Town, or else it's a two-hour walk. Then you descend more than 70 metres (230ft) from the cave entrance to the vaulted main chamber. There are concrete steps now, and electric lighting, making the descent easier, but the effect is still breathtaking. The entire cave is actually twice as deep as the part to which you are allowed access, but the rest has been closed because it would be too dangerous.

Páros is famous for the world's most translucent marble.

The snug little harbour of Náousa.

measures just 11km by 5km (7 miles by 3 miles), so there are no impossible distances, especially if you bring a scooter over from Páros. Lively nightlife and good sand have lured much trade to Andíparos from its larger neighbour. Tamarisk-shaded **Psaralíki**, within walking distance of town, is decent enough, but with your own transport (or the seasonal bus), **Sorós** 9km (5.5 miles) away on the southeast coast is Andíparos' best beach, with two tavernas.

Páros

The capital and main port of **Parikiá** (**Páros**) ⓲ resembles Mýkonos in appearance and in nightlife, but is gentler in spirit. The main sights here are the beautiful 4th-to-6th-century **Ekatondapylianí church** (Our Lady of a Hundred Doors; daily 7am–9pm), the **archaeological museum** (Tue–Sun 8am–3pm) just behind, and the Venetian **kástro** overlooking the southwest waterfront, built largely of ancient masonry. Páros is famous for the world's most translucent marble; you can still visit the ancient quarries at **Maráthi**

and pick up a chip, though the tunnels themselves are off-limits. Finally, Parikiá has one of the better town beaches in the Cyclades just northeast at **Livádia**, where tiny children confidently learn to sail at the Nautical Club.

Lévkes, the medieval capital, is the largest inland village. There are several 17th-century churches, and a lovely lower **platía** (square) flanked by cafés. Beyond Lévkes, best of the east coast beaches are Logarás and Hrysí Aktí, both with plenty of facilities and the latter a mecca for windsurfers. At the beautiful northerly port-resort of **Náousa**, the old harbour's colourful boats seem to nudge up right against the fishermen's houses, and the old quarter forms a quasi-**kástro**. With upmarket boutiques and restaurants, it proves more exclusive (and expensive) than Parikiá. Nearby beaches, some served by caïque, tend to be crowded; best head northeast to sandy **Lángeri** or **Sánta María**, or northwest to the lighthouse peninsula and **monastery of Ágios Ioánnis Détis** (always locked), giving its name to the **natural reserve** just behind, car-free and criss-crossed

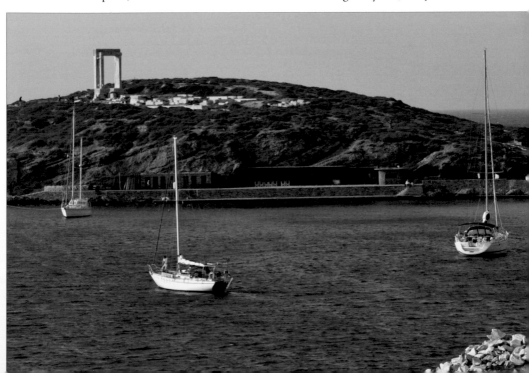

with marked hiking trails, the best ones converging on the lighthouse.

Southern Páros is comparatively little frequented; the standouts here are the workaday fishing port (with beaches and tavernas) of **Alykí**, and the so-called **Valley of the Butterflies** (Petaloúdes; daily June–Sept 9am–8pm), a walled oasis of huge trees. The black and yellow butterflies – actually Jersey Tiger moths – abound in early summer.

Náxos

Náxos ⑲ is the largest, loftiest and most magnificent of the Cyclades, replete with high, windswept ridges, long beaches, remote villages, ancient ruins, medieval monasteries or towers and a fascinating history. Central **Hóra (Náxos Town) ⑳** forms a labyrinth of Venetian-era mansions and fortifications, post-Byzantine churches, arcaded lanes and secluded restaurants. Hóra is divided into sections whose Latinate place names reflect the island's long Venetian occupation. The former French School, built into the ramparts, now houses

the **archaeological museum** (Tue–Sun 8am–3pm). On Palátia islet (accessible by causeway) north of Hóra's ferry dock, the colossal free-standing marble doorframe called **Portára** is all that remains vertical of a never-completed Apollo Temple dating 530 BC.

Near the northern tip of Náxos is the small resort of **Apóllonas ㉑**, with two beaches. A huge 6th-century BC *kouros* (statue of a man) lies on the hillside above the settlement, abandoned in the quarry when the marble cracked. There are two other small, but better defined **kouri** near Mélanes in the centre of the island.

Náxos, oddly, is famed for its baby potatoes, while vegetable gardens and fruit trees grow densely around the many inland settlements, next to Byzantine churches and crumbling Venetian manors. Three villages on the road from Hóra to Apóllonas are particularly worthy of attention: Koronída, Apíranthos and Halkí.

Koronída (alias **Komiakí**), the highest village on the island, is extremely attractive, has wonderful views over the surrounding vineyards,

FACT

When the original Venus de Milo was unearthed on the island in 1820, both arms were still intact. They were "amputated" during her clumsy removal from the island by the French. She's now in the Louvre.

The unfinished Temple of Delian Apollo on Náxos.

and is the original home of the local *kitrón* liqueur. **Apíranthos** ㉒ (aka Aperáthou) was originally settled by Cretan refugees in the 17th and 18th centuries. The town, whose streets are paved in marble, even looks Cretan. There are three small museums (Natural History, Geology, Archaeology; all Tue–Sun 8.30am–2pm) in the maze of lanes, plus cafés and tavernas from which to enjoy the view.

At the foot of Mount Zás – the highest (1001m/3097ft) mountain in the Cyclades – sprawls the Trageá, a vast plateau covered mostly in olive trees. **Halkí**, the Trageá's main town, has several fine churches, the best (on the road north to Moní) being **Panagía Drosianí** (The Dewy Virgin; daily 11am–5pm), built in stages between the 4th and 12th centuries and retaining some of the oldest, albeit battered, frescoes in Greece.

From Áno Sangrí just southwest of the Trageá, a paved road descends 5km (3 miles) through a beautiful valley to the well-reconstructed Temple of Demeter (grounds always unlocked; *c.*530 BC).

Laid-back sightseeing on the ferry to Náxos.

Some of the Cyclades' best beaches line the southwest coast, facing Páros. **Agíos Prokópios** and **Agía Ánna** are the most popular; **Pláka, Glyfáda** and **Alykó** are less developed and more scenic, with naturist areas.

Mílos and Kímolos

Lying to the southeast, volcanic **Mílos** ㉓ is a geologist's paradise. Snaking streams of lava formed much of the island's coastline, thrusting up weirdly shaped rock formations. The island has always been extensively quarried, once for obsidian, now for bentonite, perlite, pozzolana and kaolin.

Mílos has graciously adapted to its growing stream of tourism, concentrated in **Adámas**, the port, and Pollónia, a fishing village in the northeast. Inside **Agía Triáda** church (daily 9.15am–1.15pm, 6.15–10.15pm; free) in Adamás, Cretan-style icons dominate; Cretan refugees founded the town in 1853. The island's capital, **Pláka** (alias **Mílos**), has both an **archaeological museum** (Tue–Sun 8am–3pm) and a **Folklore Museum** (Tue–Sat 10am–2pm). A sunset hike

MINERALS AND MINING

Mílos is, in reality, a far older, cooled-down version of Santoríni – at some point in the distant past a volcano collapsed, leaving a caldera, which became today's huge central bay. Its volcanic mineral wealth has always been extensively mined: in prehistory for obsidian, nowadays for bentonite, perlite, barite, gypsum, sulphur, kaolin and china clay. Gaping quarries disfigure the landscape, especially in the east, and the local mining companies still provide employment for a quarter of the islanders. Kímolos has quarries from which Fuller's earth and, to a lesser extent, bentonite, are extracted. The latter has a number of uses (it even turns up as an ingredient in Nivea cream). Ironically, the chalk which gave the island its name (kimoliá in Greek) is no longer extracted locally.

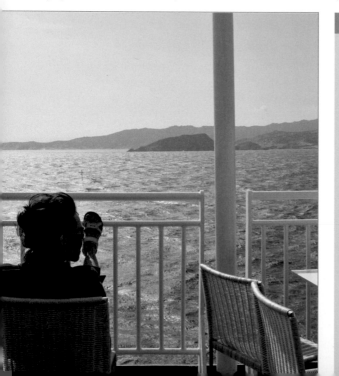

to the **Panagía Thalassítra** (Mariner Virgin), the chapel above Pláka, and the old **Kástro** walls gives splendid views of Mílos and, on a clear day, as far as Páros.

Southwest of Pláka lies the **Vale of Klíma**, on whose seaside slope the ancient Milians built their city. Excavations undertaken in the late 19th century uncovered a Dionysian altar, and remains of an ancient gymnasium. The theatre is very well preserved, probably because of its Roman renovation. Nearby, a marble plaque marks the spot where a farmer unearthed the Aphrodite of Mílos (Venus de Milo) in 1820. Below the theatre lies one of the island's prettiest villages, **Klíma**, with brightly painted boathouses lining the shore, as well as the only **Christian catacombs** (Tue–Sat 8am–6.30pm, Sun 8.30am–3pm; group tours only) in Greece. Carved into the hillside, they are the earliest evidence of Christian worship in the country. A 200-metre corridor is lined by tombs (all looted) which held around 5,000 bodies.

The island's best beaches lie along the southern limb of Mílos, at **Paleohóri** (with volcanic steam vents on the shore), **Agía Kyriakí, Firipláka** and **Provatás.** You'll need your own vehicle to reach them.

Ten km (6 miles) northeast from Adamás lies the rubble of the ancient city of **Phylakope** (daily 8.30am–3pm; free), whose script and art resemble the Minoan. It flourished for a thousand years after 2600 BC. **Pollónia** is a popular resort with a tamarisk-fringed if windy beach – making it a major windsurfing centre.

The tiny island of **Kímolos** ❷ – 36 sq km (14 sq miles), with a population of under 800 – is an irresistible presence for anyone who is staying in Pollónia. The small ferry takes just 20 minutes to cross the narrow channel to Kímolos's only landing, **Psathí**. Kímolos, once a pirates' hide-out, today provides refuge from the more crowded islands. Although it is seriously undeveloped, it has several reasonable south-coast beaches, like **Skála** and **Kalamítsi**, within feasible walking distance of the port. **Hóra**, the single town, is a 20-minute walk up from Psathí port. The core of Hóra is the

Náxos harbour and town.

gated, 16th-century Venetian **Kástro**, its perimeter houses still inhabited.

Folégandros and Síkinos

Despite its tiny size – 32 sq km (12 sq miles) populated by under 700 people – **Folégandros** ㉕ has played a not insignificant role in recent history: many Greeks were exiled here during both the 1930s' dictatorship and then the colonels' junta, following a precedent set by the Romans. Today, it is increasingly trendy for Greeks, French and Italians in particular, with a predictable effect on prices and retail-therapy opportunities.

Hóra is a magnificently sited medieval town with an inner **kástro** high above the sea. **Hryssospiliá** (Golden Cave) near Hóra, gapes in the cliff behind; a place of ancient worship and medieval refuge, it is closed for archaeological investigations. The island's "trunk road" continues beyond Hóra, threading the scattered ridge-line houses of **Áno Meriá**; paths and tracks lead southwest down to sheltered sandy beaches, the best of these being **Angáli**.

Although on the same ferry services as neighbouring Folégandros, rocky **Síkinos** ㉖ (population 240) so far seems to have shrugged off most tourism – unsurprisingly, as it's an austere island with few obvious diversions – and also escapes mention in the history books for long periods. The main rural monument, the **Iroön** at Episkopí, once identified as a temple to Apollo, is more likely to have been an elaborate Roman tomb, incorporated into a church during medieval times.

The three southeasterly beaches, **Aloprónia** (also the port and main resort), **Ágios Nikólaos** and **Ágios Geórgios**, face Íos. From Aloprónia harbour, it is an hour's hike (or regular bus ride) to Hóra, comprising the double village of Horió and **Kástro**, with its wonderful medieval defensive square. The abandoned convent of **Zoödóhou Pigí** looms above.

Íos

A tiny island with limited historic attractions, **Íos** ㉗ is not devoid of natural beauty or charm. The harbour of **Gialós** is one of the Aegean's

The brightly painted boathouses of Klíma.

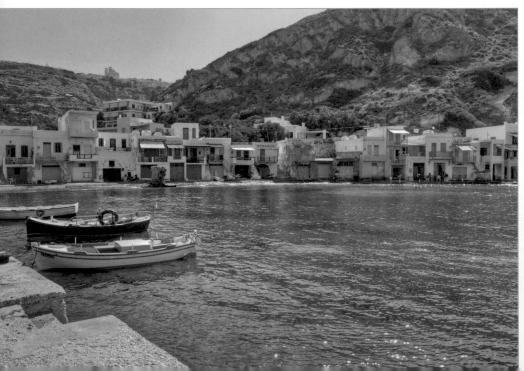

prettiest, while the hilltop Hóra (aka Íos), capped by a windmill, blazes with the blue domes of two medieval churches. Its layout and flanking palm trees look almost Levantine. But ever since the 1960s, Íos has drawn the young and footloose, and despite local efforts to diversify, in summer at least this remains its defining characteristic. Íos nightlife resembles a downmarket, younger Mýkonos, with the crowds returning by bus from the beach or Gialós and filling clubs of all sizes until the small hours. Once ensconced inside a bar, they could be anywhere in the Western world, with few older Greeks in sight.

However, Íos also has many good swimming beaches, especially on the southwest coast, where the main developed resort is **Mylopótas**. Occasional buses run to superior **Manganári bay** in the far south, or Agía Theodóti on the east coast. For (relative) seclusion, head under your own steam beyond the latter to **Psáthi** beach.

On the way to Psáthi are the remains of **Paleokástro**, a Venetian fortress containing the marble ruins

of what was the medieval capital. At a lonely spot toward the northern cape, behind the cove of **Plakotós**, is a series of **tombs**, probably Roman, yet one of these the islanders believe belongs to Homer, supposedly buried here while en route from Sámos to Athens.

Amorgós

A spine of mountains on **Amorgós** 🟤 – the tallest being Kríkellos in the northeast, at 822 metres (2,696ft) – precludes expansive views here unless you're on top of them. The southwesterly port-resort of **Katápola** occupies a small coastal plain, while the elevated **Hóra**, accessible by a regular bus service or a fine old trail, centres on a crumbled 13th-century Venetian castle. Hóra has no fewer than 40 churches and chapels – including one that holds only two people, the smallest church in Greece – as well as stepped plazas where cafés set out their tables.

The island's two most famous churches are outside Hóra. **Ágios Geórgios Valsamítis** (rarely open), 4km (2 miles) southwest, is built over a sacred spring; this church's pagan

Urn from Akrotiri on Santoríni. The largest Minoan city outside Crete, it was destroyed in a volcanic eruption in 1625 BC – at first, archaeologists thought they'd found Atlantis.

Tholária, traditional taverna, Amorgós.

oracle was only cemented over after World War II, but you can still hear it trickling below while fine frescoes stare at you from above. Half an hour east of Hóra, clinging limpet-like to tawny cliffs, the 11th-century Byzantine monastery of the **Hozoviótissa** (daily 8am–1pm, 5–7pm) – one of the most beautiful in Greece – is home to a revered icon of the Virgin from Palestine, three friendly monks, and a treasury-museum (same opening times as monastery).

Beaches in the northeast of Amorgós, around the second port-resort of **Egiáli**, are most alluring, especially the trio reached by the trail that runs northwest from the main beach. **Langáda** and **Tholária** are exquisite villages up the hillside, reached by well-marked paths, with tavernas and lodging. Indeed, hiking is the main reason to come to Amorgós – the premier trail (a 5-hour hike) goes from Potamós, above Egiáli, to Hozoviótissa.

Santoríni (Thíra)

Entering the bay of **Santoríni** ㉙ on a boat is one of Greece's great experiences. Broken pieces of a volcano's rim – Santoríni and its attendant islets – form a multicoloured circle around a seemingly bottomless lagoon that, before the volcano's eruption (*c*.1625 BC), was a hummocky volcanic plateau. Thíra, or Thera, are the island's official and ancient name respectively. Foreigners and most Greeks, however, prefer its medieval name, Santoríni, possibly after St Irene, one of three sisters martyred by Diocletian in 304. **Firá**, the capital, sits high on the rim along with its northern suburbs Firostefáni and Imerovígli, their white houses (many antiseismically barrel-vaulted) much rebuilt after a catastrophic 1956 earthquake. East of Firá, the land drops more gradually, with fertile fields leading to the east coast and dark-sand beaches. A few bare cliffs rise again in the southeast. On one of them sits 9th century BC **Ancient Thera** (Tue–Sun 8am–3pm), a most evocative setting even if little remains standing. **Akrotiri** in the far south, a large Minoan town preserved in volcanic ash like Pompeii, is fully excavated and visitable (Apr–Oct daily

Firá, Santoríni.

8am–8pm, Nov–Mar Tue–Sun 8am–3pm). But many of its best artefacts – pots and original frescoes – are in Firá's **Museum of Prehistoric Thera** (Tue–Sun 8am–3pm).

Though Firá, Firostefáni and Imerovígli are highly developed, many other places offer plentiful accommodation, with less density and/or tackiness. **Ía** (**Oia**), on the island's northernmost peninsula, is perhaps Greece's most photographed village. As at Imerovígli, **skaftá** ("dug-out") houses in the volcanic cliffs converted into highly sought-after accommodation, are a local speciality. More conventional accommodation beckons at **Kamári** and **Périssa**, busy resorts on the east coast. Both have roasting hot black pebble beaches; either make a good starting point from which to climb up to Ancient Thera, then down the other side, with boats available to shuttle you back.

Cruise ships put in below Firá at **Skála Firá**, from where you ascend by donkey, by funicular or by foot up the stone stairway. Big ferries anchor at **Athiniós**, 10km (6 miles) further

south. The most popular boat excursions offered are to **Thirassía**, Santoríni's sleepy and beachless satellite islet opposite Ía; and to the volcanic islets of **Paleá** and **Néa Kaméni** in the middle of the submerged caldera, where passengers have the opportunity to bathe in marine hot springs or clamber over a still-steaming cinder cone.

Anáfi

About 250 people live on **Anáfi** ⑳ in winter, surviving mainly by fishing and subsistence farming. Summer tourism has boosted the economy, but development is slow despite the island figuring regularly on ferry lines between Santoríni, Crete and the Dodecanese.

The south-facing harbour, **Ágios Nikólaos**, has few amenities – best walk briefly east to palm-tree-tufted Klisídi beach, with rooms and tavernas. A short bus ride or half-hour walk up, the **Hóra** offers a wider choice of both, and life in the streets is still fairly untouristy. Both a road (seasonal bus) and maintained path head east via the south coast to

TIP

The Little Cyclades have two to three main-line summer ferry services from Piraeus, plus a regular small local boat (the *Express Skopelitis*) that calls daily from Amorgós and Náxos.

Dinner with a view, Santoríni.

Zoödóhou Pigís Monastery (Tue, Thu, Sun 8am–1pm, 2–4pm), erected over the ancient shrine to Apollo. Extensive courses of marble masonry in its walls are believed to be remnants of the old temple. Above the monastery soars the massive pinnacle, claimed larger than Gibraltar, that is Anáfi's most distinctive feature. Under an hour's climb from the lower monastery brings you to smaller, blindingly white **Panagía Kalamiótissa** on the summit, a popular sunrise vantage for those prepared to sleep out here. The church is not open, but you can get water from the cistern outside. Between the pinnacle and Klisídi are various outstanding beaches, best of these **Katsoúni** and **Roúkounas**.

The Back Islands (Little Cyclades)

Small fishing boats still play their part in the economy of the Cyclades.

The so-called "Back Islands" or Little Cyclades beyond Náxos – **Donoússa**, **Irakliá**, **Skhinoússa** and **Koufonísi** – have permanent populations of 100 to 200 each. They're hardly secret (or cheap) destinations now, with ample tourist facilities including bank ATMs on each one.

Hilly **Donoússa** ㉛ has lovely south-coast beaches popular with campers, and some walking opportunities; views southwest from the port village take in the barren Makáres islets and the grand profile of Náxos. **Koufonísi** ㉜ (technically Áno Koufonísi) is the flattest of the quartet, and the busiest with a Páros-Mýkonos-type clientele, thanks to excellent beaches and a charming main village. The entire south coast looks across to Káto Koufonísi (day-trip accessible, with another beach and taverna) and hulking Kéros (off-limits), which was a third-millennium BC burial site and source of much of the Cycladic material in Greek museums. **Skhinoússa** ㉝ has no less than 16 beaches, few with facilities, fringing the coast, while its hilltop Hóra has an adjacent medieval fortress. **Irakliá** ㉞ has two settlements: the harbour, Ágios Geórgios, and Hóra, just over an hour's hike above, plus a visitable cave, but the fewest beaches of the group.

Ancient Delos

Extensive Greco-Roman ruins occupying much of minuscule Delos (Dílos), southwest of Mýkonos, make the four-square-kilometre (1.5-sq-mile) islet the near-equal of Delphi and Olympia.

If you suffer from seasickness, be forewarned: the island occupies one of the most turbulent reaches of the Aegean. The boat trip takes about 40 minutes; in windy conditions (the norm), breakfast should be a dry bread-roll or two, nothing more. In summer, there are also daily trips to Delos from Tínos.

Delos became a shrine because Leto, a nymph pregnant by Zeus, gave birth there first to Artemis and then, clutching a palm tree, to Apollo. A floating rock, Delos was rewarded for braving Hera's jealous wrath by four diamond pillars that anchored it to the seabed.

Most of the ruins occupy a broad area on the island's west coast. To the south is the theatre quarter, with various domestic buildings. On the north of the site are the sanctuaries to which pilgrims from all over the Mediterranean came with votive offerings and sacrificial animals.

For nearly a thousand years, Delos was the political and religious centre of the Aegean, and host to the Delian Festival, held every four years and, until the 4th century BC, Greece's greatest religious gathering. The Romans turned it into a grand trade fair, and made Delos a free port. It also became Greece's main slave market, where as many as 10,000 slaves (as against 25,000 local residents) were said to be sold daily. In 88 BC, Mithridates, king of Pontus, sacked Delos, followed by the pirate Athenodoros in 69 BC; it never recovered, and fell into disuse.

The Sanctuaries of Apollo and Dionysos

Follow the pilgrim route from the Sacred Harbour to a ruined, monumental gateway leading into the Sanctuary of Apollo. Within are three temples dedicated to Apollo and one to Artemis, and the remains of a colossal marble statue of the god. Close by is the Sanctuary of Dionysus, with several Dionysic friezes and outsized phalli standing on pedestals – including a marble phallic bird, symbolising the body's immortality. Continue to the stunning Lion Terrace, where five Archaic lions squat. (These are copies; the weathered originals, carved from Naxian marble, are in the museum.) Below this is the Sacred Lake, and a palm tree which marks the spot of Apollo's birth.

Most visitors delight in the residential portion of Delos, occupied by merchants rather than gods. Their houses, close to the commercial port, form a warren separated by narrow lanes equipped with Roman drains and niches for oil-burning street-lamps. The main street leads to the modest theatre, which seated 5,500, with superb views from the uppermost of its 43 rows. Either side of the theatre are grander mansions named for the subjects of their still-exquisite courtyard mosaics: Dionysos, Trident, Dolphin, Masks.

From the theatre quarter, a gentle stroll leads to the summit of Mount Kýnthos (110 metres/360ft), offering memorable views of the ruins and the Cyclades. Finish off your tour by descending first past the Hellenistic grotto of Hercules, and then stopping at the terrace of shrines to the Foreign Gods. During the town's prime, practically the entire Levant traded here, under the tutelage of shrines erected to their own divinities.

One of the lean lions, carved in the 7th century BC, which guard Delos' Sacred Lake.

The aquamarine waters of the Gulf of Mirabello.

CRETE

Greece's largest and southernmost island is characterised by soaring mountains, Venetian townscapes, a proudly independent people and unique remains of Europe's first great civilisation.

Megalónisos (Great Island) is what Cretans call their home, and "great" refers to far more than size. It certainly applies to the Minoan civilisation, the first in Europe and the core of Cretan history. Visitors by the thousands pour into the ruins of Knossos, Phaistos, Malia and Agía Triáda, before heading towards one of the scores of excellent beaches. With two major international airports, Crete cannot be classified as undiscovered, but through its sheer scale it manages to contain the crowds and to please visitors with widely divergent tastes. While a car is essential for discovering the best of the island, car hire is, unfortunately, comparatively expensive unless you book well in advance on-line.

For four months of the year, snow lies on the highest peaks which provide a dramatic backdrop to verdant spring meadows ablaze with flowers. This, as botanists and ornithologists know well, is by far the best time to visit. The former arrive to view more than 150 species which are unique to the island, while the latter are thrilled by more than 250 types of bird heading north. In spring, the island is redolent with sage, savory, thyme, oregano – and dittany, the endemic Cretan herb. It has long been reputed to be aphrodisiac – the

dialect name for the plant is *érondas*, as in erotic.

Crete, much more than other Greek islands, is a place both for sightseeing and for being on the beach. Minoan ruins are the major magnets, but there are also Greek, Roman and Venetian remains, and a score of museums. There are hundreds of Byzantine churches, many with rare and precious frescoes. If the church is locked, enquire at the nearest café. Even if you don't track down the key, you will enjoy the encounter with local people.

Main Attractions

Iráklio Archaeological Museum
Hrysí islet excursion
Phaistos Palace
Arkádi Monastery
Réthymno old town
Haniá old town
Falásarna beach
Samariá Gorge hike

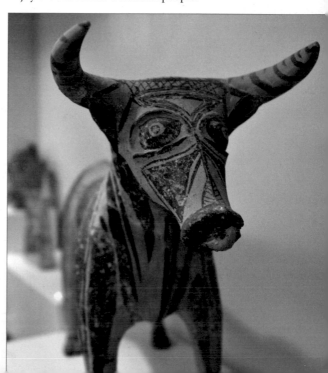

Minoan bull at the Iráklio Archaeological Museum.

Iráklio (Heráklion)

Crete's capital since 1971, **Iráklio ❶** has nearly a third of the island's population and is Greece's fifth-largest city. Once among the wealthiest Greek towns, it – like most of the country – has fallen on hard times since 2008, with unemployment above the national average. Extensive World War II damage was compounded by poor (or rather, no) urban planning choices thereafter. Despite this, attempts are ongoing to remedy a scruffy civic infrastructure, with the old quarter and Venetian monuments getting as much conservationist attention as scarce funds allow.

Most tourists head first for the Minoan site of **Knossos ❷** (daily Apr–Sept 8am–8pm, Oct–Mar 8am–3pm). To fully appreciate the site, this should be combined with a visit to Iráklio's outstanding **Archaeological Museum ❹** (Apr–Oct daily 8am–8pm, Nov–Mar Mon 11am–5pm, Tue–Sun 8am–3pm). The museum reopened in 2014 after extensive renovations, and now includes video installations and interactive exhibitions, with 27 rooms

displaying the "greatest hits" from a collection of more than 5,000 objects, which include the famous Phaistos Disc and the delicate bee pendant from Malia. The tourist office is just opposite, and both are moments from the cafés of **Platía Eleftherías ❸** (Freedom Square).

Iráklio's other major attractions date from the Venetian era, Crete's most prosperous period in historical times. Head seawards towards the old harbour, guarded by the **Koulés fortress ❸** (closed for restoration until further notice), whose three external reliefs of the Lion of St Mark confirm its provenance. From here, stroll westwards along shorefront Sofokéous Venizélou to the excellent **Historical Museum ❹** (www.historical-museum.gr; Mon–Sat 9am–5pm, until 3.30pm in winter), which covers Cretan history and ethnography from the Byzantine Empire to the present. Inside are fine icons and fresco fragments, stone relief carvings, documentation of the local Jewish, Muslim and Armenian communities, folk textiles and a recreation of a traditional Cretan home. Models and prints across the centuries show how Iráklio has developed, as does an interactive model of the medieval city. Due prominence is given to the struggle for Cretan independence and World War II resistance.

Return to the city centre at **Platía Venizélou** (Lion or Fountain Square), which takes its popular names from the stylish 17th-century **Morosíni fountain** E and guardian marble lions 300 years older. Overlooking the square is the handsome Venetian *loggia* F (now the city hall), flanked by the churches of **Ágios Márkos** G (today the municipal art gallery; Mon–Fri 9am–1.30pm, 6–9pm, Sat 9am–1pm) and **Ágios Títos** H (irregular opening). Since 1966, when it was returned from Venice, the skull of St Titus, St Paul's apostle to Crete and its first bishop, has been housed in Ágios Títos.

Walk south along noisy Odós 1866, "market street", redolent with tantalising smells, jammed with people but now very touristy. Admire the Venetian **Bembo Fountain** I and the adjacent Turkish pumphouse (now a café) at the far end before turning

west towards the **Icon and Sacred Art Museum** (daily 8.30am–3pm), inside 15th-century **Agía Ekateríni** J church. Stars of the collection are six icons by 16th-century master Mihaïl Damaskinos.

Finally, walk along the 15th-century **city walls,** in their day the most formidable in the Mediterranean, once besieged for 21 years. They stretch for nearly 4km (2.5 miles) and in parts are 29 metres (95ft) thick. En route, pause a moment at the tomb of the great Cretan author and iconoclast **Nikos Kazantzakis** and enjoy the spectacular views.

Around Iráklio

In and around the village of **Arhánes** 3, 12km (8 miles) south of Knossos, are two churches with interesting frescoes, a good archaeological museum and three Minoan sites the Anemospilia sanctuary, the Gioukhtas peak sanctuary and the caves. Evidence suggests that when the **Anemospiliá** temple was destroyed by an earthquake, a priest was in the ritual act of sacrificing a youth. This conjecture

The Venetian church of Ágios Títos.

Morosíni fountain.

Váï's palm-fringed beach.

has outraged some scholars as much as Nikos Kazantzakis's books outraged the established Orthodox Church.

A drivable track from Arhánes leads up **Mount Gioúkhtas** (811 metres/ 2,660ft), from where you can admire the panorama while griffin vultures soar overhead. Resembling a recumbent figure, said to be Zeus, the mountain top has a Minoan peak sanctuary and inaccessible caves in which Zeus is supposedly buried. Perhaps this proves the truth of the aphorism that "all Cretans are liars" because to most ancient Greeks, Zeus was, after all, immortal.

Týlissos ❹, 13km (8 miles) southwest of Iráklio, one of the few modern villages to retain its original pre-Hellenic name, offers three well-preserved Minoan manor houses (daily 9am–4pm). 20 km (13 miles) further along the same road, **Anógia ❺** is a weaving and embroidery centre. Many locals wear native dress but this is not touristic folklore: Anógia has a long tradition of resistance – the village was razed and the menfolk massacred in 1944 – and its people are among the proudest and most musical in Crete.

From Anógia, another road climbs to the magnificent **Nída plateau,** from where it is a 20-minute uphill stroll to the **Ideon Cave,** which was the nursery, if not the birthplace, of Zeus. Here, the infant god was hidden by the Kouretes, who clashed their weapons to drown the sound of his cries, while the nymph Amalthea fed him goat's milk. Strong walkers might wish to push on along the marked E4 path to the summit of **Mount Psilorítis,** at 2,456 metres (8,060ft) the highest point on Crete.

Return to Iráklio and continue eastwards along the coastal highway for 24km (15 miles) to the so-called Cretan Riviera – reminiscent of Blackpool or Coney Island – and its resorts of **Hersónisos**, **Stalída** (Stalís) and **Mália**. These are neither elegant nor ethnic: bars, loud music, and fast-food outlets abound. Beaches are not always brilliant, and development is best explained by proximity to Iráklio airport.

The palace at **ancient Mália ❻** (daily 8.30am–3pm), traditionally associated with King Sarpedon, brother of

Minos, is contemporary with Knossos. The ruins are not as extensive as Knossos or Phaistos, but even without reconstruction, they are more comprehensible. Recent excavations have unearthed the **Hrysólakkos** (Golden Pit) from the proto-Palatial period (2000–1700 BC), an enormous necropolis with numerous gold artefacts.

Lasíthi province

From the "Riviera", a twisting mountain road leads up to the **Lasíthi Plain**, 840 metres (2,750ft) above sea level and 57km (36 miles) from Iráklio. This fertile upland used to produce abundant crops of potatoes, grain, apples and pears, but depopulation and unusual rains hampering spring planting has meant agricultural decline. The fabled 10,000 windmills here, now derelict, no longer pump up water from the limestone below, having been replaced by diesel pumps. **Psyhró** ❼ village is closest to the giant **Dikteo** (**Diktian**) **Cave,** another birthplace of Zeus.

Back on the coast (reached by the scenic Lasíthi–Neápoli road), **Ágios** Nikólaos ❽, 69km (43 miles) from Iráklio, is invariably abbreviated by tourists to "Ag Nik". Magnificently situated on the Gulf of Mirabello and overlooked by mountains to the east, this is also the capital of Lasíthi district. Between here and **Eloúnda** (10km/6 miles away) are some of the island's best and most expensive hotels, despite Ag Nik lacking a decent beach, though adequate ones lie a short distance southeast. Tourist facilities cluster around Ag Nik's little harbour and adjacent **Lake Voulisméni,** 64 metres (210ft) deep but once believed to be bottomless. Eloúnda's **Spinalónga Island** ❾ (summer daily 9am–7pm, winter by arrangement), an isolated leper colony until 1957 (the last in Europe), with a massive Venetian fortress and poignant memories, is readily reached from Eloúnda or much closer Pláka by boat.

Clinging to the hillside 12km (7 miles) south of Ag Nik, **Kritsá** ❿ is claimed to be the home of Crete's best weavers. Their brilliantly coloured work hangs everywhere – for sale – complementing the flowers and

FACT

The island of Spinalónga was immortalised in Victoria Hislop's eponymous novel, and the successful Greek TV series based on it – Greek tourists appear here in droves now.

The mountainous interior.

Minoan vases at the Iráklio Archaeological Museum.

than a palace, complete with streets and houses, spread over a ridge that overlooks the sea. In spring, when the site is covered with a riot of wildflowers, even those bored with old stones will appreciate it.

Sitía ⓬, 70km (44 miles) from Ag Nik, looks set to remain a backwater since works for expanding the tiny local airport to accept jets have been suspended indefinitely. Mostly a place to just hang out behind the sandy beach, its specific attractions are few – chiefly the **archaeological museum** (Tue–Sun 8am–3pm), full of finds from Minoan Zákros. After 16km (10 miles), you reach fortified Toploú Monastery (daily 8.30am–3pm), with its famously intricate icon Lord Thou Art Great, though most of the premises are off-limits. About 8km (5 miles) further along, you arrive at **Váï** ⓭, renowned for its myriad palm trees, large sandy beach and tropical ambience. The palm trees are native to Crete, and the beach is usually crowded.

contrasting with the whitewashed homes that line the narrow village alleyways. Below stands the 13th–15th-century church of **Panagía Kyrá** (Tue–Sun 8.30am–3pm), Crete's greatest Byzantine treasure. Although many frescoes are damaged or still uncleaned, the *Presentation of the Virgin* and Last Supper appear in full glory.

Some 19km (12 miles) southeast of Ag Nik, is **Gournia** ⓫ (Tue–Sun 8am–3pm), a Minoan town rather

Zákros ⓮ (daily summer 10.30am–5.30pm, winter 8am–3pm), 43km (27 miles) from Sitía, is another great

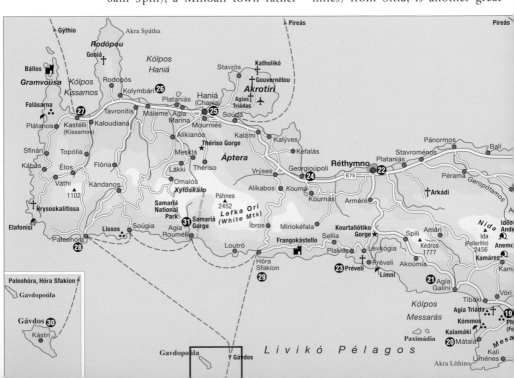

Minoan site, situated below the spectacular **Valley of the Dead,** where caves were used for Minoan burials; the best approach is via the marked path down through the gorge, starting at inland **Zákros** village. The palace-town has the customary central courtyard with royal, religious and domestic buildings and workshops radiating outwards; most date from 1900–1600 BC, the apogee of Minoan civilisation. You may then dine, swim or even stay at adjacent **Káto Zákros** beach hamlet.

Another road from Sitía leads initially south to the low-key resort of **Makrý Gialós** ⓑ, with a long, gently shelving sand beach. Some 29km (18 miles) west, past sheltered coves like Agía Fotiá and Ahliá, lies **Ierápetra** ⓰, the south coast's only real town, and Crete's fourth largest. With little to offer besides a tiny but exquisitely restored Venetian fort (daily summer 8am–3pm) and a small but interesting archaeological "collection" (daily 8am–3pm) inside a former Koranic school, Ierápetra has mostly devoted itself to greenhouse agriculture.

The prime local targets are offshore **Hrysí (Gaïdouronísi)**, graced by idyllic beaches, or the village resort of **Mýrtos**, 15km (9 miles) west, with an enduring "alternative" ambience and more excellent sand.

South from Iráklio

Head south from Iráklio over the island's spine and you reach a breathtaking view of the **Plain of Mesará,** whose rich soil and benign climate make it an agricultural cornucopia. At the edge of the plain, the main enclosed site of **Gortys** ⓱ (modern Górtyna; daily summer 8am–7.30pm) is 41km (26 miles) from Iráklio. This was the capital of the Romans, who came to Crete in 67 BC to settle feuds but who stayed and annexed the island. Outstanding are the Roman *odeon* and a triple-naved basilica of Ágios Títos, the latter by far the best-preserved early church in Crete. But the most renowned artefacts are some stone blocks incorporated into the *odeon*. About 2,500 years ago, a 17,000 character text, the Law Code of Gortys, was incised on these. The script is

The minaret of Ierápetra's Ottoman mosque.

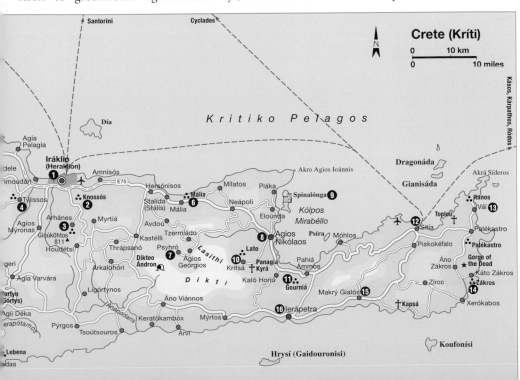

written in ox-plough manner – reading left to right along one line, then right to left along the next.

It's a brief drive south to the long beach at **Léndas** ⑱ (72km/45 miles from Iráklio); nearby **ancient Lebena** was the port for Gortys, and its therapeutic springs made it a renowned sanctuary with a temple to Asklepios, the god of healing. Only traces of this, notably a Hellenistic mosaic, can be seen.

Phaistos ⑲ (modern Festós; daily summer 8am–8pm, winter 8am–3pm), Crete's second great Minoan palace, occupies a magnificent location 16km (10 miles) west of Gortys. State-rooms, religious quarters, workshops, storerooms and functional plumbing can all be identified; those purists who bristle at Knossos's reconstruction will find this site more satisfying, as they will **Agía Triáda** 3km (2 miles) west (daily 10am–4.30pm), a combination of Minoan summer villa and later Dorian town.

The closest beaches are at **Mátala** ⑳, 70km (44 miles) from Iráklio. The resort first gained renown when the caves in the sandstone cliffs flanking the small sandy beach became home to 1960s hippies.

The scenic 30-minute walk south to Red Beach is highly recommended, though **Kómmos** beach to the north is much larger and has a Minoan site, the old port of Phaistos, still being excavated. The larger south-coast resort of **Agía Galíni** ㉑ also lies on the Gulf of Mesará, though a little further west. The harbour, with a short wide quay and a tiny main street jammed with tavernas and bars, is enclosed within a crescent of steep hills covered with modest hotels.

Réthymno and around

From Iráklio, the coastal road runs west towards Réthymno. Leave the expressway 25km (16 miles) from the capital for **Fódele,** a small village rich in orange trees and locally made embroidery. A restored house (www.psfodele.gr; Apr–Oct daily 9am–7pm) here is said to be the 1541 birthplace of Domenikos Theotokopoulos, better known as **El Greco.** Fódele's fame may be fleeting, for the latest word is that El Greco was probably born in Iráklio.

At Stavroménos, turn southeast for the beautifully situated **Arkádi Monastery** (80km/50 miles from Iráklio; Apr–May, Sept–Oct 9am–7pm, June–Aug 9am–8pm, winter until 4/5pm; www.arkadimonastery.gr), Crete's most sacred shrine to its suicidal 1866 resistance to the Turks. The elaborate 16th-century western facade of the church figured on the retired 100-drachma note.

Réthymno ㉒ (Réthimno), which prides itself on being Crete's intellectual capital (reflected in an internationally respected university), has a well-preserved old town with a small, picturesque Venetian harbour; the quayside – choc-a-bloc with restaurants – is guarded by an elegant lighthouse.

On the west, the immense ruined **Fortétsa of 1580** (daily mid-March–mid-Nov dawn–dusk) is claimed to be the largest extant Venetian castle, with excellent views. Inside, almost the only

Busy Réthymno street.

intact structure is the 1647-built Ibrahim Han Mosque, the largest domed structure in Greece.

The town's other main attractions – the **Rimóndi Fountain,** the **archaeological museum** (closed for relocation of exhibition) with a fine collection of painted clay sarcophagi, the **Historical and Folklore** Museum (Mon–Sat 8.30–3pm), with a wealth of rural impedimenta, and the **Nerantzés Mosque** (a converted Venetian church) – all lie between the fortress and the long town beach which starts just past the old port. Venetian and Ottoman houses with unexpected architectural delights line the narrow streets linking these sights, while minarets and wall fountains with ornate calligraphy recall the long Ottoman tenure (and an urban population almost half Muslim before 1898).

Due south from Réthymno, the main road towards Agía Galíni first passes the turnings for **Préveli Monastery** ㉓ (daily Apr–Oct 9am–sunset, winter by appointment), famously active in helping to evacuate stranded Allied servicemen after the fall of

Crete in 1941, and **Plakiás**, with its five distinct beaches and spectacular mountain backdrop, 43km (27 miles) from Réthymno.

The busy E75 coastal expressway continues west from Réthymno towards Haniá, crossing the provincial boundary just before **Georgioúpoli** ㉔ at the mouth of the River Armyrós, which meets the sea at one end of a good long beach. Some, however, may prefer the novelty of nearby Lake

Arkádi Monastery, Crete's most sacred shrine.

Haniá's Venetian-built waterfront.

ICONS AND EL GRECO

The artist El Greco (1541–1614), a Cretan native who studied under Titian, is best known for his portraits and religious pictures painted in Rome and Toledo. His highly distinctive style anticipated modern impressionism by his use of cold white, blue and grey colour schemes, and by his sacrifice of realism to emotional effect. His work also strikingly fuses Byzantine and Renaissance influences, a legacy of his early training as an icon-painter in Iráklio.

These icons were not objects of idolatrous worship, but this was precisely the indictment of the so-called Iconoclasts during the 7th and 8th centuries. In an effort to purify the religion, they proceeded to literally deface thousands of icons throughout Byzantium. Intact pre-9th-century icons are consequently very rare. Iráklio's church of Agía Ekateríni here has a fine collection of icons, including six by Mihaïl Damaskinos, a contemporary of El Greco. Both artists are thought to have studied at the church, all that remains of the Mount Sinai Monastery School, founded by exiles from Constantinople after the fall of "the City".

Two works by El Greco can be viewed on Crete – *View of Mount Sinai and the Monastery of St Catherine* and *Baptism of Christ*, in Iráklio's Historical Museum.

Réthymno's quayside is lined with fish restaurants, but the best dining is in the warren of inland lanes.

Kourná, the only freshwater lake in Crete, with tavernas, idyllic swimming and pedaloes or kayaks to rent.

Haniá and around

Haniá ㉕ (Chaniá), 59km (37 miles) from Réthymno, is Crete's second city and claims to be one of the oldest continuously inhabited places in the world. One of the most vibrant towns in Greece, it has drawn a large population of foreigners and Greeks from elsewhere. At its heart is a delightful old town arrayed around the two Venetian harbours, replete with exquisite Venetian and Ottoman buildings, many of them home to museums. The best two are the **archaeological museum** (Tue–Sun Apr–Oct 8am–8pm, Nov–Mar 8am–3pm), inside a former Venetian monastery, with a collection strongest on painted Minoan larnakes (sarcophagi), Cretan coins with local motifs, Roman statuettes, and Hellenistic mosaics, and the well-designed **Byzantine Museum** (Tue–Sun 8am–3pm) inside San Salvatore church, with icons, jewellery, coins, a floor mosaic and fresco fragments

Agía Rouméli.

rescued from country chapels. A surviving synagogue, **Etz Hayyim** (Fri 10am–3pm, May–Oct Mon–Thu 10am–6pm, Nov–Apr Mon–Thu until 5pm; Sat eve services; www.etz-hayyim-hania.org), has been restored for visits, although 99 percent of Haniá's Jews were deported by the Germans in 1944. Just south of the old-town walls, the **Agorá,** or covered market, was opened in 1913, a copy of Marseille's halles. One of Crete's shopping highlights, its cross-shaped arcades offer shade, a few tavernas and a variety of edible souvenirs.

The closest escape is to the **Akrotíri Peninsula** just east, with several small villages and beaches, plus three important monasteries. Seventeenth-century **Agía Triáda** (alias Zangarolón; daily 8.30am–3pm) is now essentially a museum, with an imposing Venetian facade. **Gouvernétou Monastery** 4km north is a functioning monastery not open to non-Orthodox, but marks the start of a strenuous, two-hour (round trip) hike down to the evocative remains of 11th-century **Katholikó,** Crete's oldest monastery.

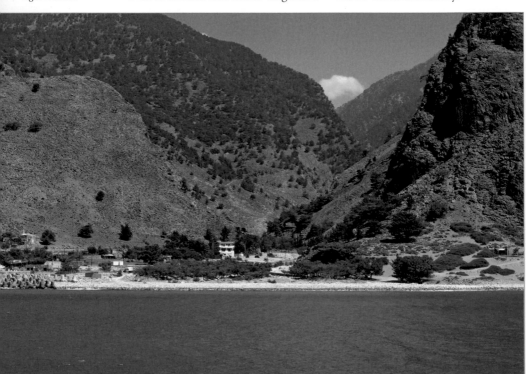

The road west from Haniá hugs the coast, passing several busy small, contiguous resorts, before arriving at **Kolymbári** ㉖, gateway to **Goniá Monastery** (daily 8.30am–3pm) with Ottoman cannonballs stuck in its walls. Beyond, there are memorable views of the plain of Kastéli and the Bay of Kísamos cradled by the peninsulas of Rodopoú and Gramvoúsa. The pleasant but rather characterless town of **Kastéli-Kissámos** ㉗ (42 km/26 miles from Haniá) has an outstanding museum (Tue–Sun 9am–4pm) with Crete's best Roman mosaics. Excursions can be made from here to the "Blue Lagoon" and Venetian island fortress at **Bállos**, at the tip of Gramvoúsa, or to spectacular **Falásarna** beach at the base of the peninsula, complete with ancient city.

From **Plátanos** village above Falásarna, a twisting corniche road leads to Váthi and the turning southwest for 10km (6 miles) more to the **Hrysoskalítissa Convent** (daily 8am–2pm). The name, meaning "Golden Stairway", reflects the legend that one of the 90 steps that lead to a viewpoint is made of solid gold, invisible to sinners. From here, the road continues 5km more to the excellent beaches – hence very busy in season – of shallow **Elafonísi** lagoon. Símos is a highlight. Wade across to the island of the same name, and you are at westernmost Crete.

Different roads from Haniá or Kastéli, both via Kándanos with several frescoed churches on its outskirts, lead to the southwesterly resort of **Paleóhora** ㉘ (76 km/48 miles from Haniá), relatively low-key with a choice of sand and shingle beaches, or to ex-hippie-haven **Soúgia**, with a huge pebble beach and an enjoyable trail-walk to ancient Lissos. Both are linked by daily ferry to **Hóra Sfakíon** (Sfakiá) ㉙, 75km (47 miles) from Haniá, a small, picturesque coastal town with a heroic past. Its main *raison d'être* today – but don't tell this to the macho Sfakians – is as a transfer point for exhausted tourists returning by ferry from their Samariá Gorge excursion. All three resorts also have boats to the remote islet of **Gávdos** ㉚, the southernmost point in Europe (or the northernmost in Africa, as some wags put it).

The cliffs around the Samariá Gorge are the home of the rare and elusive Cretan wild goat, the agrími or krí-krí.

THE SAMARIÁ GORGE

Crete offers an exciting and spectacular walk through the **gorge of Samariá** ㉛, claimed to be the longest (16km/10 miles) in Europe. The walk starts by descending a steep stair-path at Xylóskalo, 1,200 metres (3936ft) above the sea, at the southern end of the vast Omalós plain, itself a 45km (28 miles) tortuous drive from Haniá.

After about 6km (3.5 miles), with most of the steeper descent over, the abandoned **village of Samariá** and its church of Osía María come into view. Stop and admire the church's lovely 14th-century frescoes – an opportunity to regain your breath without loss of face. The going now gets tougher and involves criss-crossing the river-bed (be warned: flash floods can occur and wardens' warnings should be heeded). There is a lot of scree on the way, so you should wear sturdy walking shoes and take great care. As the gorge narrows, the walls soar straight upwards for 300–600 metres (1,000–2,000ft). Soon after passing the church of Aféndis Hristós, the **Sideróportes** (Iron Gates) are reached: here the gorge – scarcely penetrated by sunlight – is little more than 3.5 metres (11ft) wide.

The park is under the strict aegis of the Haniá Forest Service, which specifically forbids certain activities, including singing. While you are walking, the elusive Cretan wild goat, the *agrími*, will probably be nearby, though it is unlikely that you will see any. On the other hand, you may spot bearded vultures overhead.

There is a further 3km (2 miles) of hot and anticlimactic walking before celebrating with a longed-for swim or cold drink at new, coastal **Agía Rouméli** with its tavernas and pensions. In ancient times, this is where Cretan cypress wood, much coveted in the ancient world, was exported to Egypt. Once refreshed, the only practical exit from the gorge – other than more tough hiking east or west along the coast – is by boat eastwards to Hóra Sfakíon or westwards to Soúgia and Paleóhora. There are no roads.

The gorge is open from about May 1 until October 31, exact dates depending on weather and stream conditions (daily dawn–sunset; entrance fee). Allow four to six hours for the walk.

THE PALACE OF KNOSSOS

Until 1894, Crete's Minoan civilisation was little more than a myth. Now its capital is one of the largest and most thoroughly restored sites in Greece.

Knossos (pronounced Knossós in modern Greek) can be a baffling place, difficult to grasp. Some visitors find that the concrete reconstructions and repainted frescoes (often extrapolated from very small existing fragments) aid comprehension. But for many, used to other, more recent ruins that are clearly defensive or overtly religious, the site is mysterious. Can we hope to look back at fragments of a culture from 3,500 years ago and understand its imperatives and subtleties?

In legend, Knossos was the labyrinth of King Minos, where he imprisoned the minotaur, the human-taurine child of his wife Pasiphae. In reality, the place was probably not in the modern sense a palace, but rather an administrative and economic centre, unified by spiritual leadership. The 1,300 rooms of the main complex were used for both sacred and commercial purposes: lustral baths for holy ceremonies; store rooms for agricultural produce; workshops for metallurgy and stone-cutting. Nearby are the Royal Villa and the Little Palace.

Try to visit earlier or later in the day (better yet, visit out of season), to avoid the heat and the worst of the crowds. Look for subtle architectural delights – light wells to illuminate the larger rooms; hydraulic controls providing water for drinking, bathing and flushing away sewage; drains with parabolic curves at the bends to prevent overflow. It is well worth hiring a certified guide to take you around – available ones congregate near the ticket booth.

Combine Knossos with an afternoon visit to the archaeological museum.

The Prince of Lilies or Priest-king Relief, plaster relief at the end of the Corridor of Processions, believed by Arthur Evans to be a priest-king, wearing a crown with peacock feathers and a necklace with lilies on it, leading an unseen animal to sacrifice.

The famous double horns now sitting on the south facade were once regarded as sacred symbols, though perhaps this is an overworking of the bull motif of the site.

Sir Arthur Evans, the English archaeologist whose reconstruction of Knossós, a significant quantity of it based on conjecture, was to prove controversial.

CONTROVERSIAL RESTORATIONS

In 1878, a local merchant, Minos Kalokairinos, uncovered part of Knossos, but the owners of the land prevented further excavation and even the wealthy German Heinrich Schliemann got entangled in unproductive negotiations for purchase of the site.

However, once Crete gained autonomy in 1898, the way was open for the English archaeologist Arthur Evans (later knighted) to buy the land and begin excavating. He worked here from 1900 until 1931, though by 1903 most of the ruins had been uncovered.

Evans' use of reinforced concrete to reconstruct long-vanished timber columns, and his completely speculative upper-storey reconstructions, have received considerable criticism. Moreover, the Minoan frescoes are not only arbitrarily placed, but (those in the Iráklio Museum as well) almost completely modern, painted from scratch by his assistants Piet de Jong and Émile Gilliéron. It's also clear that both the restoration and fresco-retouching was heavily influenced by the Art Nouveau and Art Deco styles prevalent at the time. Others have charged that Evans, a fairly typical Victorian chauvinist, manipulated evidence to fit his theory of the thalassocratic Minoans as prehistoric proto-British imperialists.

Excavation continues to this day, under subtler management.

(The South Propylon) has near life-size frescoes of processionary youths, including the famous slender-waisted cup-bearers. In Minoan art, male figures were coloured red, female white.

A (replica) fresco depicting the capture of a wild bull decorates the ramparts of the north entrance, leading to the road to Knossos' harbour at Amnisos.

The throne room, possibly a court or council room, has a gypsum throne, and frescoes of griffons. These may have symbolised the heavenly, earthly and underworldly aspects of the rulers.

The Palace as it would have looked in its heyday.

RHODES

According to the ancient Greeks, Rhodes was "more beautiful than the sun". Even today's brash resorts cannot dim the appeal of its benign climate, entrancing countryside and unique history.

The largest and best-known of the Dodecanese islands, Rhodes (Ródos; www.rhodesguide.com) is endowed with a balmy climate and a wealth of monuments from many eras. Ancient Rhodes originally consisted of three city-states: Kameiros, Ialysos and Lindos. Following Athenian attacks, they decided to unite, founding the city of Rodos at the island's northeast tip, separated from Asia Minor by a strait just seven nautical miles wide. Fortifications were completed by 408 BC, and the town laid out in the popular grid plan of that era, championed by a certain Hippodamos.

Well-defended by its fleet and strategically positioned, Rhodes prospered as a trading station and led a charmed life despite fickle alliances, as the moment suited, with Athens, Sparta, Alexander the Great, or the Persians. For more on the Rhodes' colourful past, see box.

The Old City

Despite still-visible damage from Allied bombing in early 1945, the Old City of Rhodes ❶ is one of the architectural treasures of the Mediterranean, a remarkably complete walled medieval town. The ramparts themselves (entrance from gate beside Palace of the Grand Masters) give a good perspective over the palm-and-minaret-studded lanes. At the northwest summit stands the **Palace of the Grand Masters** ❶ (May–Oct daily 8am–8pm, Nov–Apr Tue–Sun 8am–3pm), destroyed in 1856 by an ammunition explosion and hastily reconstructed by the Italians during the 1930s. On the ground floor are two excellent galleries detailing medieval and ancient Rhodes, with exemplary layout and labelling.

From outside, the better-restored **Street of the Knights (Odós Ippotón)** ❶, where the chivalric order once housed its members according to

Main Attractions

Palace Of Grand Masters, Rhodes Old Town
Synagogue-Museum, Rhodes Old Town
Modern Greek Art Museum, Rhodes New Town
Líndos Acropolis
Ancient Kameiros
Thárri Monastery Frescoes
Pigés Kallithéas Restored Spa
Tsambíka Monastery & Beach
Paralía Kaláthou Beach
Windsurfing at Prasonísi

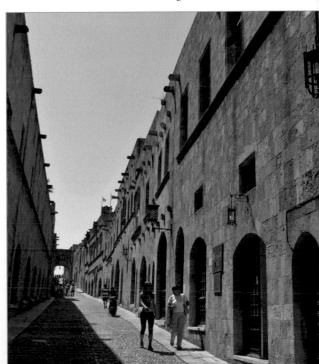

Street of the Knights (Odós Ippotón) in Rhodes Old Town.

Rhodes through the Ages

Rhodes has always been a player – although never yet directed – on the world stage. Too large for outsiders to ignore, too small to be a global power in its own right.

Under Alexander the Great, Rhodes forged links with the Ptolemies; consequently, the Rhodians refused to fight the Egyptians alongside King Antigonos. After Alexander's death, Antigonos sent his son, Demetrios Polyorketes, along with 40,000 men to attack the city in 305 BC; he failed after a year-long siege. The leftover bronze military hardware was melted down to make the island's most famous landmark, the Colossus of Rhodes, a representation of Apollo. A beacon to passing ships, it stood over 30 metres (100ft) tall, somewhere near the harbour entrance, for nearly 70 years before it collapsed during an earthquake in 226 BC.

The city emerged from the siege with its prestige and prosperity significantly enhanced, eclipsing Athens as the cultural beacon of the

Marine Gate, Rhodes Old Town.

east Mediterranean. However, it got ideas above its station when it unwisely tried to reconcile the warring Romans and Macedonians. Rome retaliated in 168 BC by effectively making Rhodes a Roman vassal; involvement in Rome's civil wars a century later saw Rhodes sacked by Cassius and its fleet subsequently destroyed. After Octavius's victory in 42 BC and the establishment of imperial Rome, Rhodes regained a degree of autonomy, and once again served as a finishing school and sybaritic posting for officialdom. But the island's glory days were long gone. In the late Roman and Byzantine times, the island endured second-rate status, prone to barbarian raids.

Early in the 14th century, the Knights Hospitaller of St John – expelled from Palestine and Cyprus – settled on Rhodes, ejecting the Genoese who had been holding the island on sufferance of the Byzantines. They proceeded to occupy and fortify virtually all of the Dodecanese, rebuilding Rhodes Town's rickety Byzantine city walls and acting as a major irritant to the sultan with their depredations of Ottoman shipping. Finally, in mid-1522, Süleyman the Magnificent landed an army of 200,000 on Rhodes to end the problem; Rhodes's second siege was shorter and more conclusive than the first, but only just. The Knights resisted valiantly, but finally were forced to surrender. On New Year's Day 1523, 180 survivors concluded honourable terms of surrender and sailed off to exile on Malta.

The Ottomans suitably appreciated their hard-won possession, at least initially, and instituted the regime common to fortified cities in their empire: Christians were forbidden from staying overnight within the walled old town, although the Jewish community were tolerated in their small quarter to the east. This exclusionary edict gave rise to the *marásia* or Orthodox suburb villages, which hem Rhodes Town on three sides, often bearing the names of their main parish churches. The Ottomans built a few grand mosques from scratch within the city walls, but more usually appropriated small Byzantine and Crusader churches as *mescids* (the Muslim equivalent of a chapel). Even at the zenith of Ottoman power, the Muslim population of the entire island never significantly exceeded 15 percent. Ottoman rule became increasingly desultory and inefficient, resulting in the Italians effectively annexing Rhodes, which they did in the spring of 1912.

their native language, leads downhill to the badly labelled **Archaeological Museum** (Apr–Nov Mon 9am–4pm, Tue–Fri 8am–8pm, Sat–Sun 8am–3pm, Nov–Mar Tue–Sun 8am–3pm), with its "Marine Venus", inspiration for Lawrence Durrell's travel memoir on his two years in Rhodes; the **Byzantine Museum** (Tue–Sun 8.30am–3pm), opposite in the former cathedral of the Knights, with its exhibits of local icons and frescoes; and the nearby ethnographic **Decorative Arts Collection** (temporarily closed), with doors and chests salvaged from Dodecanesian village dwellings.

Despite an enduring resident Turkish minority, Ottoman monuments are not much highlighted except for the **Ottoman Library** (Mon–Sat 9.30am–4pm) and a wonderful **Turkish Bath** (closed for renovations) on Platía Aríonos. The arcaded synagogue of **Kal Kadosh Shalom** (www.rhodesjewish museum.org; Apr–Oct Sun–Fri 10am–3pm; donations welcome), in the former Jewish quarter, can also be visited, as can its adjacent museum (same hours) on the Rhodian Jewish community. The synagogue serves largely as a memorial to the more than 1,800 Jews of Rhodes and Kós who were deported to Nazi death camps in June 1944.

The New Town

Established by the Orthodox Greeks who were banished from the Old City by the Ottomans, and developed by the Italians when they took control in the early 20th century, the New Town (**Neohóri**) is the commercial centre of Rhodes and the administrative capital of the Dodecanese. Here, designer shops abound, peddling Lacoste, Benetton and Trussardi. Watch the world go by and the yachts bobbing from one of the pricey, touristy pavement cafés at **Mandráki** port. Marginally cheaper are the cafés inside the **Néa Agorá** (covered market), though it's largely a tourist-trap of bad restaurants redeemed in part by the Art Deco fish market gazebo at the centre.

Mandráki's quay buzzes night and day with caricature artists, popcorn vendors, sponge-sellers and touts hawking boat trips. Excursion boats leave by 9am for the island of Sými, calling first

Statue of Aphrodite in the Archaeological Museum of Rhodes.

The Palace of the Grand Masters.

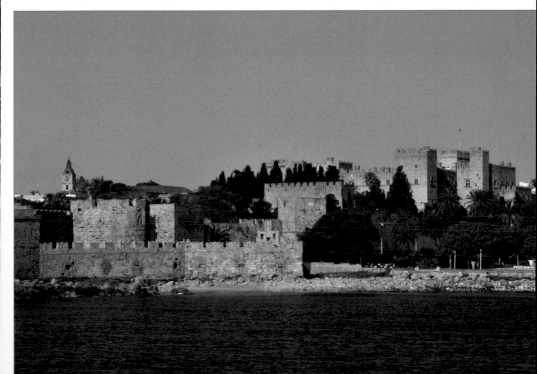

at Panormítis Monastery, or down the east coast to Líndos. Catamarans depart from Kolóna harbour, a 15-minute walk east, while full-sized ferries leave inconveniently from remote Akándia harbour, 1km southeast.

Mandráki, guarded by the round bastion-lighthouse of **Ágios Nikólaos** Ⓗ **(St Nicholas' Fort)**, is also an established port of call for the international yachting circuit, with local charters, too. By the harbour entrance stands a cluster of Italian monuments: the Governor's House with its Gothic arches, the **Cathedral of St John the Evangelist** Ⓘ **(Evangelismós)** next door (with fine Photis Kontoglou frescoes inside; you should be able to visit before or after a service) and, across the way, the post office, Town Hall and Municipal Theatre. Opposite the theatre, the **Mosque of Murad Reis** Ⓙ stands beside one of the island's larger Muslim graveyards. Beyond this is the **Villa Cleobolus** (not open to the public), where Lawrence Durrell lived from 1945 to 1947.

West, on Ekatón Hourmadiés (100 Date-Palms) Plaza, the **Modern Greek Art Museum** Ⓚ (www.mgamuseum.gr; Tue–Sat 8am–2pm) has the richest collection of 20th-century Greek painting outside of Athens. All the big names – semi-abstract Níkos Hadjikyriakos-Ghikas, Spyros Vassiliou, Yiannis Tsarouhis with his trademark portraits of young men, surrealist Nikos Engonopoulos, naïve artist Theophilos, neo-Byzantinist Photis Kontoglou – are well represented. Annexes around the corner and in the old town on Platía Sýmis host temporary exhibits.

Three ancient city-states

One of the original Dorian city-states, **Líndos** ➋, 44km (27 miles) south along the east coast, is the island's other big tourist magnet. Settled early thanks to its fine natural harbour – the island's only one aside from Mandráki at Rhodes Town – its strong acropolis supports a restored Hellenistic Athena temple and another Knights' castle (summer Tue–Fri 8am–8pm, Sat–Mon 8am–3pm, winter Tue–Sun 8am–3pm). Clustered below is the late-medieval village of imposing mansions built by local sea-captains; with

Ancient Kameiros.

Rhodes Town [map]

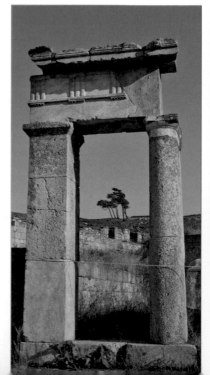

its barren surroundings, the place has always lived from the sea. Italian, German and British bohemians first rediscovered Líndos in the 1960s, attracted by the pellucid light. But it has long since morphed from being an artists' colony to become a package-tour dormitory: midsummer visits, when you can hardly move down the narrow, cobbled streets, are not recommended.

The second of the original city-states, **Kameiros** ❸, 33km (20 miles) down the windswept west coast from Rhodes Town, merits a visit for displaying a perfectly preserved Classical townscape (summer Tue–Fri 8am– 8pm, Sat–Mon 8am–3pm, winter Tue– Sun 8am–3pm), without the usual later accretions. Unlike old Líndos, it was abandoned shortly after 408 BC. At ancient **Ialysos** ❹ (summer Tue– Fri 8am–8pm, Sat–Mon 8am–3pm, winter Tue–Sun 8am–3pm), 12km (7.5 miles) southwest of Rhodes Town, only a Doric fountain and some Hellenistic temple foundations are evident from the ancient city-state. Today, the site is best known for its appealing medieval monastery of **Filérimos**

(same hours as Ialysos), well restored after World War II damage.

Island sights

Superbly sited Knights' castles at **Kritinía** ❺ and **Monólithos** ❻, both beyond Kameiros, make suitable targets to visit, along with the villages of **Siánna** and Monólithos in

Local preserves for sale at a street market.

Knights' Castle at Kritinía.

Tsambíka monastery is a magnet for childless women. If a childless woman conceives after praying there, the child is named Tsambíkos or Tsambíka, names unique to Rhodes.

day) with its glorious, cleaned 14th-century frescoes, hidden amid partly burned pine forest between Líndos and Monólithos.

The best beaches cluster on the more sheltered east coast. The first resort travelling south from Rhodes Town is Kallithéa, which sprang up around the **Pigés Kallithéas Spa 8** (www.kallithea springs.gr; daily 8am–8pm), established there by the Italians. Round the headland is Kallithéa Bay, one of the best beaches on the island and the most energetically exploited for tourism. On the south side of the bay is **Faliráki 9**, one of Greece's more notorious resorts. By day, every form of water sport is available; by night, just a few surviving clubs compete with loud music and improbably alcoholic cocktails.

between, well equipped for visitors, with numerous tavernas. The best Byzantine monuments in the interior are the late Byzantine church of Ágios Nikólaos Foundouklí (always open) with smudged frescoes, just below 798-metre (2,600-ft) Profítis Ilías, and the monastery of **Thárri 7** (daily, all

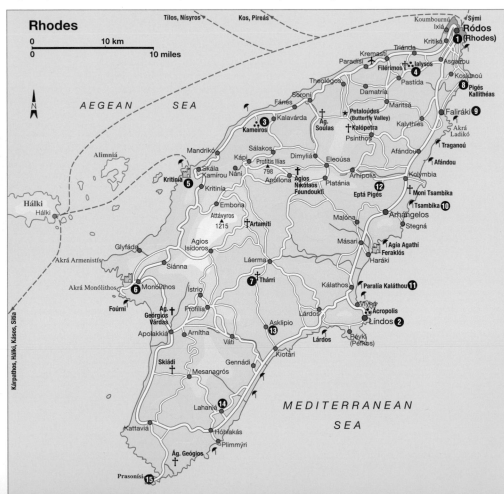

Pebbly **Traganoú,** at the north end of Afándou bay, has caves and overhangs, and is mostly patronised by Rhodians. **Tsambíka beach ⑩** huddles beneath a giant promontory on which stands a tiny, eponymous monastery of the Virgin in her avatar of fertility goddess – hundreds of ex-votos testify to her successful intervention for childless couples. **Paralía Kaláthou ⑪** is the best undeveloped beach on this coast.

Inland from Tsambíka, **Eptá Pigés ⑫** is an enduringly popular oasis, its reservoir an Italian legacy. Northwest of there, the **Petaloúdes** (**Butterfly Valley**) is the seasonal home of millions of Jersey tiger moths, attracted by the Liquidambar orientalis trees in this secluded stream canyon.

Beyond the Líndos promontory, there are few specific sights aside from the wonderfully frescoed 11th-century church (daily 9am–5pm) at **Asklipío ⑬** village, just inland from the burgeoning resort of Kiotári. There are more, usually empty beaches at Gennádi; further south, the ravine-hidden, well-watered village of **Lahaniá ⑭** for some decades attracted a second

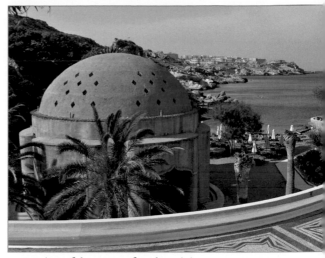

Orientalised Art Deco, complete with palm trees, at Kallithéa.

generation of drop-outs after the original Líndos scene, who renovated traditional houses here under now-expired lease agreements. Land's End for Rhodes is the sandspit-tethered islet of **Prasonísi ⑮**, reached from Kattaviá village. Topography and winds combine to make the broad, flat beach here one of the premier venues for windsurfing and kiteboarding in Greece, with three schools operating every season.

ITALIAN ARCHITECTURE IN THE DODECANESE

The Italians, who occupied the Dodecanese from 1912 until 1943, adorned the historic centres of Rhodes and Kós towns with grandiose public buildings, constructed a huge naval base and the planned town of Porto Lago (Lakkí) on Léros, and did much to reconstruct Kós Town after it was levelled by the 1933 earthquake. Because of its associations with Fascism, any buildings linked to this period, whatever their quality, were until recently disparaged if not deliberately neglected; since the millennium, Italian monuments on all three of the islands cited have benefited from consolidation works.

In Rhodes, a new administrative centre – the Foro Italica – was created, comprising all public services, and centred on Pizza del'Impero with its all-important Fascist Party Headquarters with its tower and speaker's balcony. Beyond lay the city's purpose-built tourist area, which included La Ronda Sea Baths (today a popular bar-restaurant), the Albergo delle Rose (now the casino) and the aquarium at the northerly cape.

Art Deco style featured in the Fascist Youth Building and the football stadium; other buildings, such as the nautical club, the aquarium and the Customs House mixed elements of Art Deco with abstract Ottoman motifs. Out in the countryside, the Pigés Kallithéas spa is the best example of orientalised Art Deco, stylishly blending with its surroundings.

The later phase of Fascist rule, from 1936, coinciding with the harsh tenure of Governor Cesare Maria de Vecchi, stressed the perceived continuity between the Knights Hospitallers and the Italians. Many monuments of the Knights were restored, and new buildings in a "neo-Crusader" style, such as the Bank of Rome, were erected. At the same time, buildings such as the Albergo delle Rose and the Courthouse were "purified" by removing the allegedly superfluous, orientalising features of Art Deco, and replacing these with a cladding of poros stone. In this final stage, Italian architecture in the Dodecanese conformed to Rationalist-Internationalist canons of the decade, with more monumental and rigidly symmetrical structures. The Puccini Theatre (now the Municipal Theatre) on the Piazza del'Impero was the best example of many such around this square.

THE DODECANESE

Closer to Turkey than Greece, the archipelago has enormous variety, from holy Pátmos to busy Kós, from wild Kárpathos to tranquil Lipsí, from fertile Tílos to the volcano that is Nísyros.

reek place names often reveal history, and "Dodecanese" (Dodekánisos), a new name by Greek standards, is no exception. Through four centuries of Ottoman rule, these islands were known as the Southern Sporades, a name still appearing on older maps. During this period, smaller, more barren islands here were granted considerable privileges – in effect, being invited to look after themselves – while larger, more fertile Rhodes and Kós were more strictly governed and colonised by Muslims.

After the establishment of an independent Greece in 1830, and periodic armed hostilities between it and the Ottoman Empire, such privileges were gradually withdrawn. The 12 larger islands (*dódeka nisiá* in Greek) submitted a joint objection against these infringements in 1908; it failed, but the new name stuck, despite there being – depending on how one counts – 18 or even 20 inhabited isles in this chain, extending from northwest to southeast in an arc along the Turkish coast.

In 1912, the Italians, as part of a larger war against the Turks, took this group of islands to cut the Ottoman supply lines to Libya. Despite initial promises to relinquish the archipelago once the Turks left Tripoli, the Italian annexation was consolidated by World War I and the subsequent rise of the

Fascist regime after 1923, when the group was officially renamed the "Italian Islands of the Aegean". The Fascists were busy colonialists, erecting numerous distinctive edifices, planting eucalyptus to drain swamps, building roads and imposing their language, religion and political culture on public life. Repression was stepped up considerably in 1936 when governor Mario Lago was replaced by Cesare Maria de Vecchi, an ardent monarch-Fascist who helped depose Mussolini and was condemned to death by the Salo

Main Attractions

East Coast Beaches, Kárpathos
Ólympos Village, Kárpathos
Sými
Volcanic Caldera, Nísyros
Knights' Castle, Kós
Southwestern Beaches, Kós
Archaeological Museum, Kálymnos
Hóra, Astypálea
Hóra And Its Monastery, Pátmos

Attractive Mandráki, Nísyros.

Secluded Ápella beach, Kárpathos.

Emborió, Hálki.

Republic (though he escaped to South America). In a series of bloody actions against now pro-Allied Italian forces, the Germans assumed control of the Dodecanese in late 1943, but in turn surrendered the islands to the British less than two years later.

Finally, in early 1948, after a 10-month interlude of Greek military rule imposed to weed out local collaborators with the Italians, the Dodecanese were united with Greece to become the country's southeasternmost, and most recent, territorial acquisition. Massive emigration to Australia, South Africa and North America ensued, as in chaotic postwar Greece, union with the "mother" country initially brought little other than freedom of movement. Today, the islanders live – as they always have – largely off the sea, which has brought them a catch of vital importance to the local economy: tourists.

Kárpathos, Kásos and Hálki

The most dramatic way to arrive at **Kárpathos** is by ship from Rhodes, invariably departing at or before dawn. After several hours' journey, the island appears with its imposing, often cloud-flecked summit-ridge. Boats stop at **Diafáni** ❶ (www.diafani.com), the northerly port given a jetty only in 1996. By the mid-morning light, onward passengers have an hour to get acquainted with Kárpathos. Its eastern shore drops steeply to the sea, baby pines sprouting from slopes denuded during the fierce blazes of the 1980s; occasionally, the cliffs stop at large, white, empty beaches.

After these first impressions, the main port of **Pigádia** ❷ in the east is inevitably a disappointment, with little to recommend it other than its fine setting; it dates only from the 19th century, but the islanders themselves – not invading forces – effectively wrecked it with concrete constructions from the 1960s onwards. This lack of distinction also has something to do with Kárpathos's status as a backwater since ancient times; neither the Knights of St John nor the Ottomans bothered

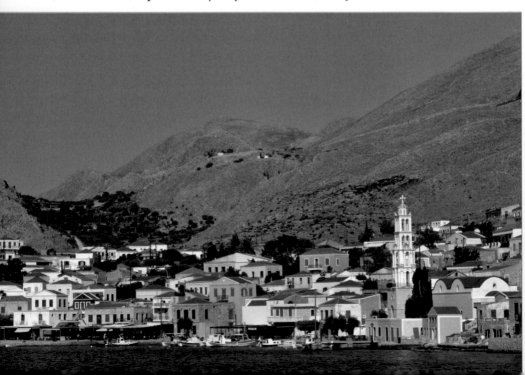

much with it, leaving it to the Genoese and Venetians, who called it Scarpanto.

Getting to a beach is going to be a top priority. An excellent one stretches immediately north for 3km (1.2 miles) along Vróndi Bay. More secluded ones, visible on the ferry ride in, prove close-up to have aquamarine water and white-sand or pebble shores, guarded by half-submerged rock formations. The best of these are Ápella, Aháta and Kyrá Panagiá, accessible either on small-boat excursions or overland – although some Kárpathiot roads are appalling and hire cars are expensive. The west coast is served by good roads but far more exposed, though at remote Levkós, a series of three bays tucked in between headlands, there are excellent beaches and a busy resort.

Most villages are well inland and high up, the standard medieval strategy against pirates, of whom Kárpathos had more than its fair share. The wealthiest settlements are a trio – **Apéri** ❸, Óthos and Voláda – just south of cloud-capped Mount

Kalilímni, 1,215 metres (3,985ft) high, plus **Menetés** near Pigádia, all studded with a variety of traditional and contemporary villas.

Ólympos, draped over a windswept ridge in the northwest of the island, has long been something of a honeypot for anthropologists, academic and amateur, owing to its relict Dorian dialect, its colourful costumes (Easter and Assumption Day are celebrated with special vervc here), music and communal ovens.

But conventional tourism here has been as distorting – and rescuing – as subsidies from abroad have been elsewhere on Kárpathos; the last of several ridgeline windmills stopped working as a real accessory to life late in the 1970s, but one was restored as a (briefly) functioning museum-piece a few years later. It now just makes for a good photo.

If you stay in either Diafáni or (less comfortably) Ólympos, much the best way to spend time is to go for walks on the path network across the north of the island; Avlóna farm hamlet, the beach and ruins at Vrykoúnda,

KARPATHIOT ARCHITECTURE AND DRESS

The source of wealth in Kárpathos seems mysterious at first, since there is little fertile lowland, no industry, and mass tourism began only in the late 1980s. In fact, Kárpathos lives largely off remittances from seamen and emigrants (mostly in the US); this economy has profoundly affected local culture, architecture and attitudes. It has deliberately slowed the development of tourism and, paradoxically, also enhanced the position of women who stayed behind. Overseas values have left their mark on house-building, although even the most vulgar modern pile may sport a date of construction, the owner's initials and a traditional emblem, perhaps a mermaid or double-headed Byzantine eagle.

In its original form, the vernacular Karpathiot house consists of a single, mud-floored space appropriately divided; to one side a raised wooden platform or *dórva*, where the bride's dowry linen, festival clothing and mattresses are kept, the latter rolled out at night. In the centre, a wooden pole – the "pillar of the house" – upholds the ceiling, and to complete the symbolism, a painting or photograph of the couple is pinned to the pole under their

wedding-wreath – a custom perhaps developed to acquaint children with chronically absent fathers. The walls are decked with shelves and plate-racks, containing hundreds of kitsch and near-kitsch ornaments: not local handicrafts, but ethnic dolls, gaudy pottery and other baubles collected by wandering Karpathiot sailors. Even modern, multi-room villas still model their *salóni* (sitting room) on this pattern.

Many Dodecanese islands are matrilineal (as opposed to matriarchal). On Kárpathos, it's merely more evident, at least in the northernmost villages of **Ólympos** ❹ and **Diafáni,** where some women still wear traditional dress; the well-travelled men have worn approximations of Western garb for as long as anyone can remember. The women's waistcoats, blouses, aprons, headscarves and boots are still locally made, but this everyday costume is completed by Irish wool scarves and imported sequins and embroidery, much of it Chinese and Bulgarian. Festival dress is rather more colourful and includes a gold-coin collar, the number of coins signalling a girl's wealth to prospective suitors.

→ Sámos, Agathonisa

Dodecanese

0 _____ 10 km
0 _____ 10 miles

Akköy

Gevrek

Akbük

Ayalik

Milâs

TURKEY

Arkí **28**
Arkí

Lámbi
Kámbos
29 Skála
30 Hóra
Pátmos

Maráthi
L. Geranozú

Platýs Gialós

Lipsí

Katsádiá

Lipsí **27**

Didima

Áltinikum Plaji

Iasos

Koru

Güllük

Hisar

Kyndia

Pesados

Çamköy

Kale

Keramos

Õren

Pirǵos

Levítha

Kínaros

Léros

Partheni

Ag. Marína

Lakkí

Hirókambo

Ákra Tílos

Emborió
Skaliá

Myrtiés

Hório

Arginónda

Vathý

Kálymnos

Póthia
(Kálymnos)

Tingáki

Marmári

Mastihári

Ziá

Paleó
Pylí

Pylí

Andimáhia

Kardámena

Agios Stéfanos

18

Kéfalos

Astypalia

Aspri Pétra

Kós

Ákra Kríkelos

Kablimnos

Psérimos

Lámbi

Kós 16

Asklepeíon **17**

Díkeos
846

19

Brós Thermá

Körmen

Resadiye

Knidos

Cumali

Kargi

Datça

Emecik

Hydas

Bozburun

Taslika

Mandalya
Körfezi

Yalikavak

Myndos

Ortakent

Halikarnassos

Bodrum

Turgutreis

Pserimos

Kerme Körfezi

Vathý
Análipsi
Livádia

23

Astypálea (Hóra)

Astypálea

Giali

Pálii **14**

13 Mandráki

Emborió

Nikiá

Nísyros

15

Gialós (Sými)
Pédi
7

Ag. Vassilíos

Panormítis **8**

Marathoúnda

Sými

Notio   Aigaio

Ag. Pandelímona

10 Mikró Hório

Megálo Horió **11**

Livádia **12**

Tílos

**Ródos
(Rhodes)**

Kremastí
Paradísi
Soroní

Kalavárda

Ialysos

Mandrikó

Kritinia

Kameirós

Apóllona

Émbona

Ág. Isídoros

Dimyliá

Platánia

Láerma

Díkeos

Monólithos

Istrió

Moní Thárri

Lárdos

Líndos

Apolakkiá

Gennádi

Mesanagrós

Lahaniá

Kattaviá

Ákra Prasonísi

6 Hálki

Alimniá

Emborió
(Hálki)

Hório

see Rhodes map

Léros

Arkángelos

Lipsi

0 _____ 5 km
0 _____ 5 miles

Parthéni

26 Alínda

Lakkí

24

Ag. Marína
Plátanos **25**
Vromólithos

Hirókambo

Ákra Tílos

Kálymnos

Emborió
Kolonostílos
22
Télendos

Myrtiés

Kandoúni

Hrýsoheriás

Skálion
Skála

Arginónda

Massoúri

Damos
Hório **21**

Vathýs

Daskalió

Póthia
(Kálymnos) **20**

→ Kós

Pátmos

Sária

Diafáni **1**

4 Ólympos

Mesohóri

Spóa

Levkós

1215

Voláda
Pylés

Othos

Apéri **3**

Menetés

Pigádia (Kárpathos) **2**

Arkása

Kárpathos

Karpáthio Pelágos

Makrá

Agía Marína
Fry

Arvanitohórion

Kásos 5

Áǵ. Geórgios Hadíon

Kriti

0 _____ 5 km
0 _____ 5 miles

TURKEY

Kaş

Kardirler

Rhó

Rhodes

**Kastellórizo
(Megísti)**

9 Kastellórizo

Perastá

Strongylí

more ambitiously to Trístomo inlet, or simply down the canyons to Diafáni are popular targets. Diafáni – something of a beach resort, busy in August – is more geared up for overnight tourism, with a wide selection of facilities.

Kásos and Hálki

Just southwest of Kárpathos, **Kásos ⑤** is its bleak satellite, devastated by an Ottoman massacre in 1824 and totally dependent ever since on seafaring. Effectively protected from conventional tourism by its lack of beaches, it consequently has limited tourist facilities – especially off-season – and is thus frequented mostly by overseas-based Kassiots during the summer festival period.

Hálki ⑥, just off the west coast of Rhodes, is another bare speck of limestone enlivened by the colourful port of **Emborió**. Formerly home to sponge-divers, most of it was restored and it is now packed from April to October with upmarket package tourists. Here, too, beaches are few, mostly pebbly and difficult to access.

Sými

Sými lies northeast of Rhodes, between the outstretched "claws" of Turkey's Datcá Peninsula. Although still retaining some conifer forest, it is waterless and dependent on cisterns or tanker-boats, which means limited tourism. Most visitors come for the day to the photogenic harbour, which at the end of the 19th century supported a greater population (25,000) than Rhodes Town. Prosperity rested on sponge-diving, for which the island long held the Ottoman monopoly, and the related caïque-building industry. Although the Italian takeover of both the Dodecanese and the Libyan coast (where the sponges were harvested) failed to break the Greek hold on the sponge industry, World War II and the rise of synthetic sponges brought down the curtain on an era. War-related privations scattered the population to Rhodes, Athens and overseas, and today fewer than 3,000 call **Gialós ⑦** (the quayside settlement) and Horió (the hillside village) home. Some caïques are still fashioned in the

Gialós greeting featuring traditional dress.

The ferry approaches the port of Gialós.

Haráni boatyards, but the sponges sold from Gialós's souvenir-stalls are mostly imported from Florida and the Philippines.

Pédi, the valley south of Horió ridge, is the only arable patch of land on the island. There is a small waterside hamlet, too, and some scraps of sand beach, flanked on the north by a badly designed yacht marina. Emborió bay, north of Gialós, offers a pebble beach, a Byzantine mosaic floor under a protective shelter, and a small catacomb complex. Indeed, most of the island's beaches are pebbly, and accessible only by arduous hikes or boat excursions; the favourites are Ágios Vassílios, Marathoúnda (with a taverna) and Nanoú. Among rural monasteries, the most artistically distinguished are **Mihaïl Roukouniótis,** due west of town, with its vivid 18th-century frescoes, and (even better) **Agía Marína Nerás** chapel (always open), and **Kokkimídis** monastery (always open), south along (or just off) the paved road to the gargantuan monastery of **Panormítis ❽** (daily; 8.30am–2pm,

Nísyros's semi-active volcano.

3–4pm; free). Being on the sea-lane in from Rhodes, this gets the most visitors, irrespective of merit – a small museum, a large pebble courtyard and a sombre memorial to resistance fighters executed here in 1944 are the main sights.

Kastellórizo (Megísti)

Kastellórizo ❾, some 70 nautical miles east of Rhodes in the shadow of Anatolia, has similarly come down in the world. At the turn of the 19th century, this limestone dot on the map had a population of over 10,000 thanks to the best natural harbour between Piraeus and Beirut, and a schooner fleet based here. But the fleet was sold rather than motorised; the island was heavily shelled during World War I while occupied by the French, then rocked by a 1926 earthquake and a 1944 munitions blast, which together destroyed three-quarters of the houses.

Most "Kassies" emigrated after the war to Rhodes and Western Australia, leaving a virtual ghost town barely clinging to life. The US Government even tried to convince Greece to cede the island to Turkey in 1964, in return for limited hegemony in Cyprus. Geopolitical realities still prevail: the islanders are obliged to get almost everything, from haircuts to fresh vegetables, across the way in Turkish Kaş, where a number of townspeople are of part-Kassie ancestry.

In the end, it was pleasure-yachting and an Oscar-winning film (*Mediterraneo*, filmed here in 1989–90) that probably saved Kastellórizo from desolation. A steady stream of (initially Italian) tourists has revived its fortunes, along with an airport and other government subsidies. There are no beaches and little to see other than rural monasteries, an ancient acropolis, a sea-cave entered only by boat and a tiny red-stone Crusader castle that gives the island its Italianate name. But the social scale of **Kastellórizo Town** is cosy, and the nightlife surprisingly lively.

Tílos and Nísyros

Seahorse-shaped **Tílos**, north of Hálki and west of Rhodes, is the least maritime of these islands. With fertile volcanic soil and sufficient ground water, the islanders instead made Tílos the granary of the Dodecanese. Discerning tourists are attracted by tranquillity, some fine beaches and good hiking opportunities. Historically, there were just two villages, imaginatively named **Mikró Horió** ❿ (Little Village, in the centre) and **Megálo Horió** ⓫ (Big Village, in the west), continually at odds with each other. Mikró was abandoned after World War II in favour of **Livádia** ⓬, the port and main tourist resort. The rivalry supposedly ended with the election in 1998 of a single municipal council – the only sensible solution for a registered population of 500.

The crags above the plains hide seven small castles of the Knights of St John, as well as several medieval chapels (all closed). **Éristos** in the west is the largest and (arguably) best

beach; inland extends a great **kámbos** (fertile plain) planted with citrus, the whole surveyed by Megálo Horió. In the far west, **Agíou Pandelímona** (daily) is the main monastery, and venue for the principal festival (25–27 July, annually).

Circular **Nísyros**, between Tílos and Kós, is not merely "volcanic", as often described, but actually is a volcano – a dormant one that last erupted in 1933. Accordingly, what water exists here is sulphur-tainted, but the island is paradoxically green with oak, almond and other plants that thrive on volcanic soil. Once you're away from the harbour, the capital **Mandráki** ⓭ is attractive with its close-packed houses overawed by Panagí Spilianí monastery, installed in the inevitable Knights' castle, and the even more imposing remains of the 7th-century BC Doric citadel of **Paleókastro** just south. **Pálli** ⓮ is the alternative port for fishermen and yachties, just east of the mineral-water spa. You don't come to Nísyros for beach life, but on the east coast, sandy **Liés** and **Pahiá Ámmos** are more than decent.

Bringing in the catch in Livádia harbour, Tílos.

In Kós's Archaeological Museum.

A quiet backstreet in Mandráki.

hissing steam-vents and sulphurous smell, is deserted.

Kós

The second-largest Dodecanese island in population, **Kós** is also tied for second in size with Kárpathos. It follows the lead of Rhodes in most things: a shared history, give or take a few years; a similar Knights' castle guarding the harbour, plus a skyline of palms and minarets; and an agricultural economy displaced by tourism. However, Kós is much smaller than Rhodes, and much flatter – amazingly so – with only one mountain, Díkeos. The margin of the island is fringed by excellent beaches, many easily reached by motorbike or even pushbike.

There are two inland villages: **Emborió,** essentially abandoned and bought up by outsiders, and the more thriving **Nikiá** ⑮ in the southwest, at the edge of the volcanic caldera created in 1422 when the (originally much taller) island blew its top. Coachloads of tourists based in Kós descend periodically, but otherwise the lifeless crater-floor, with its

A 1933 earthquake devastated most of **Kós Town** ⑯ in the north of the island, but gave Italian archaeologists a perfect excuse to comprehensively excavate the ancient city. Hence much of the town centre is an archaeological park, with the ruins of the **Roman agora** (the eastern excavation) extending up to the 18th-century **Loggia Mosque** and the millennial **Plane**

DIVING FOR SPONGES

In the old days, divers used to submerge themselves by tying heavy stones to their waists. Holding their breath, they could usually get two or three sponges before they had to resurface. Then the "machine" was introduced, a rubber suit with a bronze helmet connected to a rubber hose and a hand-powered air pump. The diver was given enough air-hose for his final depth, where he could stay a long time owing to the constant air supply. Too long, as it soon turned out – compressed air delivered to divers at the new, greater depths bubbled out of solution in their bloodstream as they rose, invariably too rapidly. The results of this nitrogen embolism – "the bends" – included deafness, incontinence, paralysis and often death. By the 1950s, this practice was halted, but it was too late for hundreds of Kalymniot crewmen.

Tree of Hippocrates, not really quite old enough to be contemporary with the great ancient healer. The western digs offer covered mosaics and the colonnade of an indoor running-track; just south stand an odeion (always open) and the **Casa Romana** (Tue–Sun 8.30am–3pm; may close for staff shortages), a restored Roman villa with more mosaics and murals.

The Italian-founded **archaeological museum** (closed for renovation until further notice) has a predictable Latin bias in exhibits, although the highlighted statue, purportedly of Hippocrates the father of medicine, is in fact Hellenistic. Hippocrates himself (*c.*460–370 BC) was born and practised here, but probably died just before the **Asklepeion ⓱**, an ancient medical school 4km (2.5 miles) southwest of town, was established. The site (summer Mon, Sat–Sun 8am–3pm, Tue–Fri 8am–8pm, winter 8am–3pm) impresses more for its position overlooking the straits with Turkey than any structures, for the masonry was thoroughly pilfered by the Knights to build their enormous

Castle in town (Tue–Sun 8am–3pm), which – unlike the one at Rhodes – was strictly military.

Between the Asklepeion and Kós Town, pause at **Plataní,** roughly halfway, to dine at one of three excellent Turkish-run tavernas – although as on Rhodes, most local Muslims have chosen to emigrate to Turkey since the 1960s. There was a small Jewish community here too, wiped out with the Rhodian one in 1944 when all Jews were taken to concentration camps, leaving behind only the marvellous Art Deco **synagogue** by the town agora.

The road east of town dead-ends at **Brós Thermá,** enjoyable hot springs which run directly into the sea. West of town are the package resorts of **Tingáki** and **Marmári**, with long white beaches, and the less frantic **Mastihári**, with a broader beach and a commuter boat to Kálymnos. In the far southeast, facing Nísyros, are the most scenic and sheltered beaches, with names like "Sunny" and "Magic"; at nearby **Ágios Stéfanos ⓲**, twin 6th-century basilicas (unenclosed)

Kós harbour.

are the best of several early Christian monuments on the island. The Kéfalos headland beyond saw the earliest habitation of Kós: Asprí Pétra cave, home to Neolithic man, and Classical Astypalia, birthplace of Hippocrates, with its remaining little theatre.

On the western flank of Mount Díkeos, the Byzantines had their island capital at **Paleó Pýli** 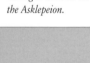, today a jumble of ruins below a castle at the head of a spring-fed canyon. Closer to the 846-metre (2,776-ft) peak cluster the appealing villages collectively known as **Asfendioú,** on the forested north-facing slopes looking to Anatolia. At Ziá, tavernas are more numerous than permanent inhabitants. Asómati's vernacular houses are slowly being bought up and restored by foreigners.

Kálymnos

First impressions of **Kálymnos,** north of Kós, are of an arid, mountainous landmass, and a decidedly masculine energy to the main port town of **Póthia** ⑳, whose biggest attraction is a 2009-opened **archaeological museum** (summer only Tue–Sat 9am–4pm), with excellent Roman-era finds, including a life-size female bronze statue. The now almost-vanished sponge industry has left many reminders: Kálymniot *salónia* crowded with huge sponges and shell-encrusted amphoras, souvenir shops overflowing with smaller sponges, and, more ominously, various crippled old men.

To the northwest loom two castles: Hrysoherías (unenclosed), the Knight's stronghold, and the originally Byzantine fort of Péra Kástro (daily dawn–dusk; free), above the medieval capital of **Horió** ㉑, still the island's second town. Most visitors stay at the beach resorts on the gentler west coast between Kandoúni and Massoúri, with **Myrtiés** the most developed of these, or at the port for the idyllic, car-free islet of **Télendos** ㉒. The east coast is harsh and uninhabited except for the green, citrus-planted valley extending inland from the fjord of Vathýs.

Astypálea

Lonely, butterfly-shaped **Astypálea,** stuck out on a subsidised ferry line

Taking in the view at the Asklepeion.

between the Dodecanese and the Cyclades, would be probably more at home among the latter archipelago. The Knights did not make it this far; a Venetian clan is responsible for the fine castle at the summit of **Hóra** ❷❸, the most dazzling Dodecanese hill-village aside from the Hóra of Pátmos. Houses with colourful wooden *poúndia* (balconies with privies) adorn the steep streets, and until the 1950s there was also a separate hamlet inside the upper castle. Hóra aside, however, Astypálea is rather bleak, with only a few good beaches to the southwest (**Tzanáki, Ágios Konstandínos** and **Vátses**) plus a few more like those at Marmári and Stenó along the island's narrow middle. Most travellers stay at the uninspiring port of Skála, at more congenial **Livádi** each west of Hóra, or at Análipsi (Maltezána) by the airport.

Léros

Léros, with its half-dozen deeply indented bays, looks like a jigsaw-puzzle piece gone astray. The deepest inlet, Lakkí, sheltered an important Italian naval base from 1935 onward, and from here was launched the submarine that torpedoed the Greek battleship *Elli* in Tínos harbour on 15 August 1940.

Today, the main ferry port, **Lakkí** ❷❹ seems incongruous, an Internationalist-Rationalist-style planned town far too grand for the present token population. Its institutional buildings, long neglected as reminders of colonial subjugation, have mostly been restored. The local atmosphere was for years dampened by the presence of three hospitals for handicapped children and mentally ill adults. Substandard conditions in all of these prompted uproar when exposed by the international press; all but one of the institutions has since closed, with a nursing school now operating in their stead.

The rest of Léros is more inviting, particularly **Pandéli** with its waterfront tavernas, just downhill from the capital of **Plátanos** ❷❺, draped over a saddle culminating in a well-preserved Knights' castle. South of both, **Vromólithos** has the best, easily accessible

Plátanos and its Knights' castle, Léros.

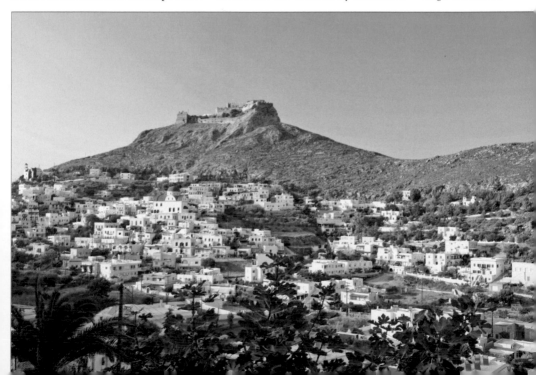

The monastery walls.

car-free beach on an island not known for soft sand. **Ágia Marína,** beyond Plátanos, is the hydrofoil and occasionally catamaran harbour; like Pandéli, it offers good tavernas. **Álinda** 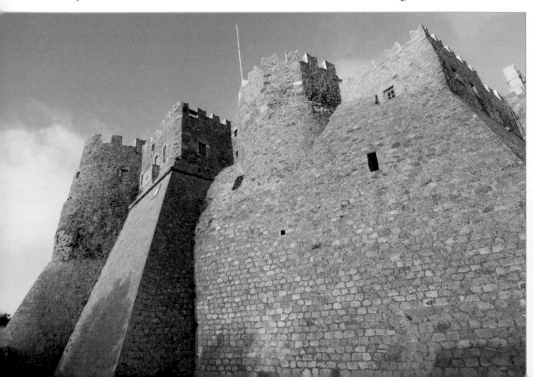,
to the north around the same bay, is the oldest established resort and has a long coarse-sand and gravel beach – plus a poignant Allied cemetery for casualties of the 1943 Battle of Léros.

Lipsí and baby islets

Lipsí ㉗, the small island just north of Léros, has like Tílos awakened to tourism in recent years. It also awoke to unwanted notoriety as the "Island of Terrorism" when Alexandros Giotopoulos, supremo of the notorious November 17 group, was arrested here in 2002 prior to conviction on terrorism charges. The island's fertile appearance is deceptive – there is only one spring, and up to four times the current local community have emigrated (mostly to Tasmania) since the 1950s. All facilities are in the single port town, built around the best natural harbour; smaller bays, with beaches, are at **Katsadiá** in the south,

Platýs Gialós in the northwest and Monodéndri on the east coast.

Beyond Lipsí, other tiny islets see few visitors outside of high summer. **Arkí** ㉘ (pop. 35) clings gamely to life, its scattered houses dependent on solar panels and visits from yachts to the sheltered Port Augusta, with all tourist facilities. Across the way sprawls **Maráthi,** with a long sandy beach and three taverna-rooms. **Agathonísi,** halfway to Sámos, is a metropolis in comparison, with 90 year-round inhabitants scattered in three hamlets. Goats graze the mastic-and-carob-covered hills sloping down to pebble beaches.

Pátmos

Pátmos (www.patmos-island.com) has been indelibly linked to the Bible's Book of Revelations (Apocalypse) ever since tradition placed its authorship here, in AD 95, by John the Evangelist. The volcanic landscape, with its eerie rock formations and sweeping views, seems suitably apocalyptic. **Skála** ㉙ is the port and largest village, best appreciated late at night when crickets serenade

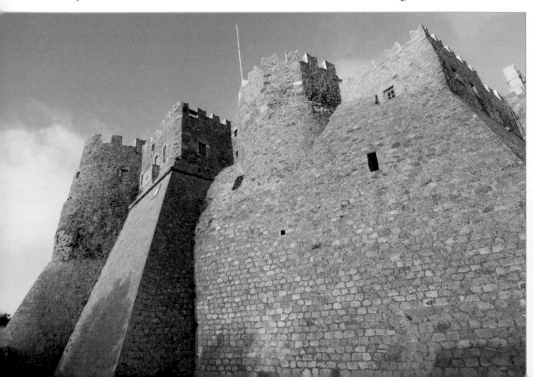

and yacht-masts glimmer against a dark sky. By day, Skála sacrifices any charm to stampeding cruise-ship patrons; all island commerce, whether shops, banks or travel agencies, is here. Buses leave regularly from the quay for the hilltop Hóra ③, but a 40-minute walk along a cobbled path – a short-cut avoiding the road – is preferable.

Just over halfway stands the **Monastery of the Apocalypse** (summer daily 8am–1.30pm, Tue, Thu, Sat 4–6pm; winter 8am–1pm), built on the grotto where John had his Revelation. A silver band on the wall marks the spot where John laid his head to sleep; in the ceiling yawns a great cleft through which the divine voice spoke.

Hóra's core, protected by a huge, pirate-proof fortress and visible from a great distance, is the **Monastery of Agíou Ioánnou Theológou** (same hours as Apocalypse), founded in 1088 by the monk Hristodoulos. A photogenic maze of interlinked courtyards, stairways, chapels and passageways, it occupies the site of an ancient temple to Artemis. The Treasury (entrance fee) houses Greece's most impressive monastic collection outside of Mount Áthos: priceless icons and jewellery are on display, although the prize exhibit is the edict of Emperor Alexios Komnenos granting the island to Hristodoulos. The library, open only to ecclesiastical scholars, contains over 4,000 books and manuscripts.

Away from the tourist-beaten track, Hóra is filled with a pregnant silence, its thick-walled mansions with their pebble courtyards and arcades the preserve of wealthy foreigners. From Platía Lótzia on the north side, one of the finest views in the Aegean takes in at least six islands on clear days.

The rest of the island is inevitably anticlimactic, but the beaches are good. The biggest sandy one is **Psilí Ámmos** in the far south, accessible by boat trip or a 20-minute walk from the road's end, and favoured by naturists. Beaches north of Skála include Melóï, with a good taverna; Agriolivádi; Kámbos, popular with Greek families; isolated Livádi Geranoú, with an islet to swim to; and finally Lámbi, sprinkled with colourful volcanic pebbles, and an excellent taverna.

Monks in the monastery of Agíou Ioánni Theológou.

THE NORTHEAST AEGEAN

While the cosmopolitan eastern islands of Sámos, Híos and Lésvos once played a leading role on the world's stage, the scattered isles of the northeast are still relatively untouched by tourism.

The islands of the northeast Aegean have little in common other than a history of medieval Genoese rule. The northerly group, comprising Thásos, Samothráki and Límnos, has few connections with the south Aegean; indeed Thásos belongs to the Macedonian province of Kavála, and Samothráki to Thracian Évros. These islands, so conveniently close to the mainland, with a short summer season, inevitably attract Greek (and Bulgarian) vacationers more than tourists from further overseas, although Germans are plentiful.

Lésvos, Híos and Sámos to the southeast once played leading roles in antiquity, establishing colonies across the Mediterranean and promoting the arts and sciences, though little tangible evidence of ancient glory remains. All three islands served as bridges between Asia Minor and the rest of the Hellenic world and were, in fact, once joined to the coast of Asia Minor until Ice Age cataclysms isolated them. Turkey is still omnipresent on the horizon, a mere 2km (1.25 miles) across the Mykale straits at Sámos. Historically, relations between the countries have been strained, although recent rapprochement has led to better, cheaper boat connections and more visits by upwardly mobile Turks.

Sunbathing in Lésvos.

Thásos

Just seven nautical miles from mainland Macedonia, mountainous and almost circular **Thásos** is essentially a giant lump of marble, mixed with granite and schist, crumbling into white beach sand at the island's margins. Along with numerous illegal ones scarring the landscape, Greece's largest legal marble quarry provides employment; the cut slabs, lying stacked or being trucked about, are a common sight. In antiquity, gold, silver and precious stones were also mined here.

Main Attractions

Panagía, Thasos
Sanctuary of the Great
    Gods, Samothráki
Evgátis, Límnos
Skála Eressoú, Lésvos
Giustiniani Museum, Híos
Mastihorhoriá, Híos
Néa Moní, Híos
Armenistís, Ikaría
Archaeological Museum,
    Sámos
Seïtáni Beaches, Sámos

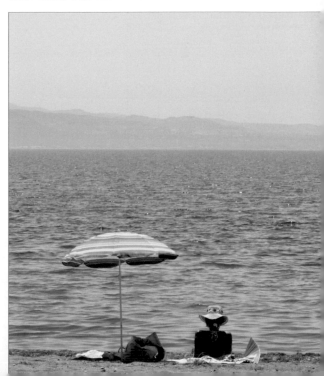

FACT

Due to frequent forest fires during the 1980s and early 1990s, Thásos is now three-quarters denuded of its original pine forest, which survives only in the northeast. It takes forests like these about 50 or 60 years to grow back.

Stunning cove near Alykí.

Ferries and hydrofoils for Thásos leave regularly from Kavála; there are even more RO-RO services for drivers from Keramotí further east. Bus services around the coastal ring road are adequate, though most visitors hire motorbikes – Thásos is small enough for a long day tour – or cars. The east and south coasts have the better beaches; the west coast has access to most inland villages. Honey, preserved walnuts and *tsípouro*, the northern Greek firewater, are favourite souvenirs.

Thásos's past glory as a wealthy mining island and regional seafaring power is most evident at the harbour capital of **Liménas** (or **Thásos Town**) ❶, where substantial remnants of the ancient town have been excavated by the French School; choice bits of the ancient acropolis overhead are nocturnally illuminated. The biggest area, behind the picturesque fishing harbour, is the agora; the nearby **archaeological museum** (summer Tue–Sun 8am–8pm, winter Tue–Sun 9am–3pm) displays a 4-metre (13-ft) kouros (standing statue of a man) carrying a ram.

Beginning at the **Temple of Dionysos,** a good path allows you to explore the ancient acropolis. First stop is the Hellenistic **theatre** (closed for reconstruction); continue to the medieval **fortress,** built by a succession of occupiers from the masonry of an Apollo temple. Tracing the course of massive 5th-century BC walls brings you next to the foundations of an **Athena temple,** beyond which a rock outcrop bears a shrine of Pan, visible in badly-eroded relief. From here, a vertiginous "secret" stairway plunges to the **Gate of Parmenon** – the only ancient entry still intact – at the southern extreme of town.

The first village south from Liménas, slate-roofed **Panagía** ❷ is a busy place whose life revolves around the plane-tree-filled square with its four-spouted fountain. **Potamiá,** further down the valley, is less architecturally distinguished. Visitors come mainly for the **Polygnotos Vagis Museum** (May–Sept Tue–Sat 8.30am–noon, 6–8pm, Sun 8.30am–noon), featuring the work of this locally born sculptor. Beyond, the road plunges to the

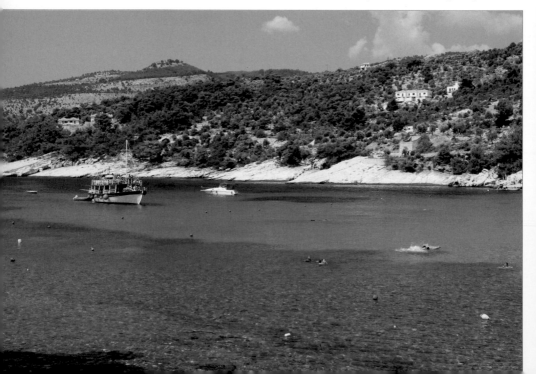

coast at Potamiá Bay. **Skála Potamiás,** at its south end, is purely lodging and tavernas, with more of that just north at Hryssí Ammoudiá; in between stretches a fine, blonde-sand beach. There are even better strands at **Kínyra,** 24km (15 miles) from Liménas, but most one-day tourists schedule a lunch stop at the several beach front tavernas in the hamlet of **Alykí** ❸, architecturally preserved thanks to adjacent ruins: an ancient temple and two atmospheric Byzantine basilicas.

Rounding the southern tip of Thásos, you pass three beach resorts at Astrída, Potós and Pefkári. Only **Astrída** remains attractive, Potós in particular being an overbuilt package dormitory. At **Limenária** ❹, now the island's second town, mansions of the departed German mining executives who used to work here survive. More intriguingly perhaps, it's the starting point for a safari up to hilltop Kástro, the most naturally pirate-proof of the inland villages. Beyond Limenária, there's little to compel a stop on the coast.

Theológos ❺, actually reached from Potós, was the island's Ottoman capital, a linear place where most houses have walled gardens. **Mariés** sits piled up at the top of a wooded valley, just glimpsing the sea. By contrast, **Sotíros** enjoys phenomenal sunsets, best enjoyed from its central taverna shaded by enormous plane trees. Of all the inland settlements, **Megálo Kazavíti** ❻ (officially Megálo Prínos) has the grandest **platía** and the most numerous traditional houses, snapped up and restored in variable taste by outsiders.

Samothráki (Samothrace)

Samothráki raises forbidding granite heights above stony shores and storm-lashed waters, both offering poor natural anchorage. Homer had Poseidon perched on top of 1,611-metre (5,285-ft) **Mount Fengári,** the Aegean's highest summit, to watch the action of the Trojan War to the east. Over time, the forest cover has receded from the now-barren peak, where modern climbers – on rare occasions – still have the same view, extending from northwestern Turkey to Mount Áthos.

Fengári (Mount Moon) and its foothills occupy much of the island,

Lésvos claims to produce the finest olive oil in all Greece. The olives are harvested in November and December, and pressed within 24 hours of being picked.

The Sanctuary of the Great Gods, Samothráki.

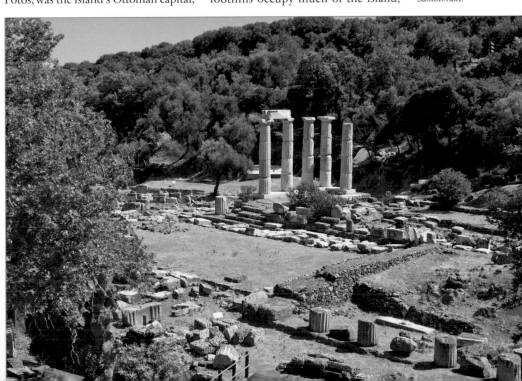

with little level terrain except in the far west. Tourism is barely developed, and the remaining islanders prefer it that way; in its absence, the permanent population has dipped below 3,000, as farming can support only so many. Certainly an overpriced car-ferry from Alexandroúpoli on the Thracian mainland does not help matters. Boats dock at **Kamariótissa,** the functional port where hire vehicles are in short supply, and although most roads are now paved, only the west of the island has a rudimentary bus service. **Samothráki (Hóra)** ❼, 5km (3 miles) east, is more rewarding, nestled almost invisibly in a circular hollow. A cobbled commercial street serpentines past sturdy, basalt-built houses. From outdoor tables at the two tavernas on

Hóra's large platía, you glimpse the sea beyond a crumbled Byzantine-Genoese fort at the edge of town.

Samothráki's other great sight is the **Sanctuary of the Great Gods** ❽, tucked into a ravine some 6km (4 miles) from Kamariótissa along the north-coast road. From the late Bronze Age until the coming of Christianity, this was the major religious centre of the Aegean. Local deities of the original Thracian settlers were easily syncretised with the Olympian gods of the later Aeolian colonists, in particular the Kabiri, or divine twins Castor and Pollux, patrons of seafarers – who needed all the help they could get in the rough seas hereabouts.

The sanctuary ruins (daily 8.30am–3pm; museum closed Mon) visible today are mostly late Hellenistic, and still eerily impressive if overgrown. Obvious monuments include a partly re-erected temple of the second initiation; the odd, round **Arsinoeion,** used for sacrifices; a round theatre area for performances during the summer festival; and the fountain niche where the celebrated Winged Victory of Samothrace (now in the Louvre) was discovered.

About 6km (4 miles) further east, hot springs, cool cascades and a dense canopy of plane trees make the spa hamlet of **Thermá ❾**, the most popular base on the island, patronised by an unlikely mix of the elderly infirm and young bohemian types from several nations. Hot baths come in three temperatures and styles – including outdoor pools under a wooden shelter – while cold-plunge fanatics make for **Gría Váthra** canyon to the east. Thermá is also the base camp for the climb of Mount Fengári, a six-hour round trip.

Villages south of Hóra see few visitors, though they lie astride the route to **Pahiá Ámmos ❿,** the island's only sandy beach. From **Lákoma** village,

it's about 8km (5 miles) by unpaved road to the beach, where a single seasonal taverna operates. Beyond Pahiá Ámmos, you can walk to smaller **Vátos** nudist beach, but you'll need a boat – or to drive clockwise around Samothráki – to reach the gravel beach of **Kípos** in the far southeast.

Límnos

Nowhere in the Aegean does legend match landscape so closely as here. In mythology, Zeus cast hapless Hephaestos from Mount Olympos (Ólymbos) onto Límnos with such force that the fall lamed him permanently. The islanders rescued the god, revering him as a fire deity and patron of metallurgy, an understandable allegiance given the overtly volcanic terrain of Límnos. Hephaestos re-established his forge here; now-solidified lava crags in the west oozed forth as late as the Classical period, reassuring Limnians that Hephaestos was at work.

Dominating the sea approaches to the Dardanelles, Límnos has been occupied since Neolithic times, and has always prospered as a trading

FACT

The 3rd-century BC statue of Victory (Athena Nike) was discovered on Samothráki in 1863 by a French diplomat, Charles Champoiseau, who immediately sent it to Paris. The Greek government has long demanded its return, but so far has had to settle for a plaster copy.

View of Mýrina from the ruined kastró.

station and military outpost, rather than a major political power. The Greek military still controls much of the island's extent, including half of the huge airport, belying an otherwise peaceful atmosphere. The volcanic soil crumbles to form excellent sandy beaches, and produces excellent wine and a variety of other farm products; the surrounding seas yield plenty of fish, thanks to periodic migrations through the Dardanelles.

Most things of interest are found in the port-capital, **Mýrina** ⓫, or a short distance to either side – luckily, since the bus service is appalling. Volcanic stone has been put to good use in the older houses and street cobbles of Mýrina, while elaborate Ottoman mansions face the northerly town beach of Romeïkós Gialós with its cafés; the southerly beach of Néa Máditos abuts the fishing port and seafood tavernas. Public evidence of the Ottoman period is limited to an inscribed fountain and a dilapidated octagonal structure – probably a dervish tekke (lodge) – behind a supermarket, both near the harbour end of the long market street.

Pottery shop on Lésvos.

Festooned engagingly over the headland above town, the ruined **kástro** (always open) is worth the climb for sunset views. Mýrina's admirably presented **archaeological museum** (Tue–Sun 8.30am–3pm) holds finds from the island's major ancient sites: Kabeirio (Kavírio), Hephaestia (Ifestía) and Polyokhni (Polyóhni). These are all a long trip away in the far east of Límnos, and of essentially specialist interest.

Sadder relics of more recent history flank the drab port town of **Moúdros** ⓬ – two Allied cemeteries maintained by the Commonwealth War Graves Commission. During World War I, Moúdros was the principal base for the disastrous Gallipoli campaign; hundreds of war casualties are interred outside Moúdros on the way to Roussopoúli, and behind the village church at **Portianoú**, across the bay.

The road north from Mýrina passes the Italian-dominated Aktí Mýrina resort en route to good beaches at **Avlónas** and **Ágios Ioánnis.** Further north lie the spectacular **dunes of Gomáti**, a protected natural environment beyond a bird-rich marshy area.

THE GARDEN OF THE AEGEAN

Early inhabitants of **Lésvos** were related to the Trojans; in Homer's *The Iliad*, the Achaeans punished Lesbos for siding with Troy. Natives were later supplemented by Aeolian colonists, who – in a convoluted topography created by two penetrating gulfs – founded six city-states, the most important being Eressos, Mithymna, Antissa and Mytilene. Although they vied for political supremacy, Lesbos developed a uniform culture, nurturing such bards as Terpander and Arion well before Alkeos and Sappho in the 6th century pushed lyric poetry to new heights, while their contemporary Pittakos (no friend of aristocrats like Alkeos or Sappho) initiated democratic reforms.

With its thick southern forests and idyllic orchards, Lésvos was a preferred Roman holiday spot; the Byzantines considered it a humane exile for deposed nobility, while the Genoese Gattilusi clan kept a thriving court here for a century. To the Ottomans it was "The Garden of the Aegean", their most productive, strictly governed and heavily colonised Aegean island. Following 18th-century reforms within the empire, a Christian land-owning aristocracy developed, served by a large population of labouring peasants. This quasi-feudal system made Lésvos fertile ground for post-1912 Leftist movements, and its habit of returning left wing MPs since the junta fell has earned it the epithet of "Red Island" among fellow Greeks.

In the opposite direction lie even better ones at **Platý** and **Thános,** with tiered namesake villages on the hillsides just above; continuing southeast from Thános brings you to **Evgátis,** justifiably acclaimed as the island's best beach.

Ágios Evstrátios (Aï Strátis)

A tiny wedge of land south of Límnos, **Ágios Evstrátios** (Aï Strátis; off map) is doubtless the most desolate spot in the northeast Aegean – all the more so since a 1968 earthquake devastated the single village. Thanks to junta-era corruption, reparable dwellings were bulldozed and the surviving inhabitants (22 were killed) provided with ugly, pre-fab replacement housing laid out on a grid plan. This, plus two dozen surviving older buildings, is all you see as you disembark the regular ferries stopping here on the Lávrio–Límnos–Kavála route, or (in summer) the small Límnos-based ferry. Despite all this, the island has grown in popularity as a summer retreat, and you may just have company at the several beaches; the remotest are a tough 90 minutes' walk north or south of "town".

Lésvos (Mytilíni)

Greece's third-largest island, measuring 70 by 40km (44 by 24 miles) at its extremities, distant, fertile **Lésvos** is the antithesis of the *nisáki,* or quaint little islet. Between its far-flung villages lie 11 million olive trees producing 45,000 liquid tonnes of oil a year. Shipbuilding, carpentry, *oúzo*-distilling and pottery remain important, but none rivals the olive, especially since it complements the second industry, tourism. Nets to catch the "black gold" are spread in autumn, once most of the tourists have packed up and left.

Lésvos has a rich and fascinating history, with familiar names like Homer and Sappho featuring. More recently, the years after 1912 also saw a vital local intelligentsia emerge, among them novelists Stratis Myribilis and Argyris Eftaliotis. Since World War II, however, Lésvos's socioeconomic fabric has shrunk considerably with emigration to Athens, Australia and America. However, the operation here

The harbour at Mytilíni.

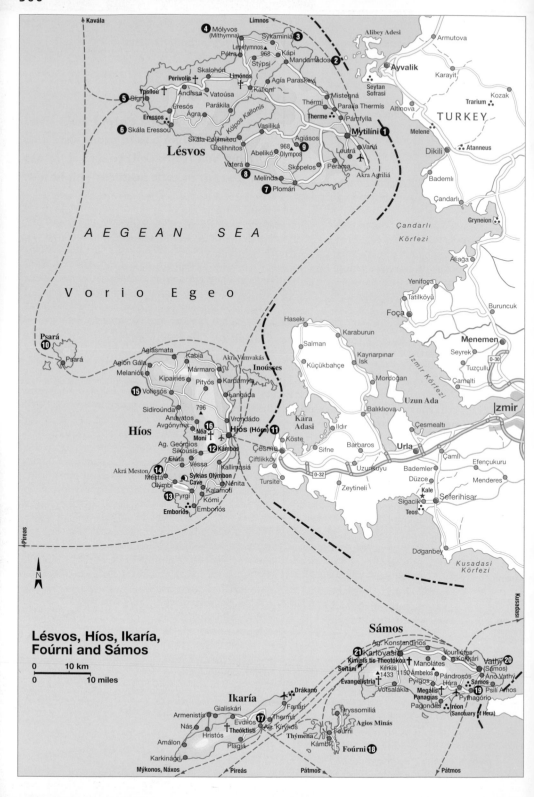

Lésvos, Híos, Ikaría,
Foúrni and Sámos

0   10 km
0   10 miles

AEGEAN SEA

Vorio Egeo

Lésvos

Híos

Ikaría

Sámos

TURKEY

İzmir

since 1987 of the University of the Aegean has stabilised cultural matters.

Mytilíni ❶, the capital (its name is a popular alias for the entire island), has a revved-up, slightly gritty atmosphere, as befits a port town of 30,000 – interesting to stroll around, though few outsiders stay. Behind the waterfront, assorted church domes and spires enliven the skyline, while **Odós Ermoú,** one street inland, threads the entire bazaar, passing a mosque (ruined) and Turkish baths (well restored) en route. Behind the ferry dock stands the **archaeological museum** (Tue–Sun 8.30am–3pm), spread over two premises; the new, uphill annexe features superb mosaics rescued from local Roman villas. Not far away, the **Byzantine Museum** (Mon–Sat 9am–1pm) has been recently renovated, and now features a number of attractive exhibits.

Also noteworthy are a pair of museums in **Variá**, 5km (3 miles) south of town. The **Theophilos Museum** (Mon–Fri 8.30am–2.30pm) contains over 60 paintings by locally born Theophilos Hazimihaïl, Greece's most celebrated naive painter. The nearby **Theriade Museum** (closed for restoration) was founded by another native son who, while an avant-garde art publisher in Paris, assembled this collection, with work by Chagall, Picasso, Rouault, Giacometti, Matisse and Léger.

The road running northwest from Mytilíni follows the coast facing Turkey. **Mandamádos ❷**, 37km (23 miles) from Mytilíni, has on its outskirts the enormous **Taxiárhis Monastery** (daily, all day) with its much-revered black icon. At Kápi, the road divides; the northerly fork is wider, better paved and more scenic as it curls across the flanks of Mount Lepétymnos, passing by the handsome village of **Sykaminiá ❸** and its photogenic, taverna-studded fishing port.

You descend to sea level at **Mólyvos ❹**, linchpin of Lésvos tourism and understandably so: the ranks of sturdy tiled houses climbing to the medieval castle are an appealing sight, as is the

stone-paved fishing harbour. Its days as a colony for bohemian artists and alternative types are over, however, with package tourism now dominant.

Pétra, 5km (3 miles) south, accommodates the overflow on its long beach, while inland at the village centre looms a rock plug crowned with the Panagía Glykofiloússa church. At its foot, the 18th-century **Vareltzídena Mansion** is worth a look, as is the 16th-century frescoed church of **Ágios Nikólaos.**

From Pétra, head 17km (10 miles) south to the turning for **Límonos Monastery**, home to an ecclesiastical museum (daily 9.30am–sunset), before continuing west towards the more rugged half of the island, with its lunar volcanic terrain. Stream valleys foster little oases, such as the one around **Perivolís Monastery** (daily 10am–1pm, 5–6pm; donation welcome), 30km (19 miles) from Limónos, decorated with wonderful frescoes. Some 10km (6 miles) beyond, atop an extinct volcano, the **Monastery of Ypsiloú** (museum inside open 8.30am–3pm) contemplates the abomination of desolation – complete with scattered trunks of the "petrified

Roadside shrine on Lésvos.

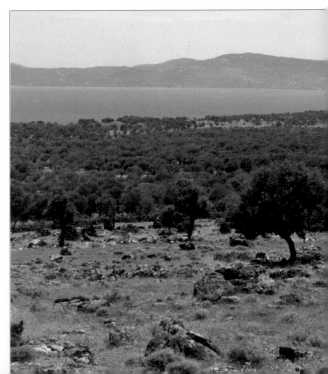

View towards the gulf, southern Lésvos.

Hiking up to the Panagía Glykofiloússa, an 18th-century church in Pétra, Lésvos.

Lésvos mansion.

Ólympos. **Plomári** ❼ on the coast is Lésvos's second town, famous for its oúzo industry; most tourists stay at pebble-beach **Ágios Isídoros** 3km (2 miles) east, though **Melínda**, 6km (4 miles) to the west, is more scenic. **Vaterá** ❽, whose 7-km (4-mile) sand beach is reckoned the best on the island, lies still further west; en route, you can stop for a soak at restored medieval spas outside Lisvóri and Polyhnítos, 45km (28 miles) from Mytilíni.

Inland from Plomári, the remarkable hill village of **Agiásos** ❾ nestles in a wooded valley under Ólympos. Its heart is the major pilgrimage church of Panagía Vrefokratoússa, which comes alive for the 15 August festival, Lésvos's biggest.

forest", a few prehistoric sequoias mineralised by volcanic ash.

Sígri ❺ (90km/56 miles from Mytilíni), a sleepy place flanked by good beaches, is very much the end of the line, guarded by a Turkish-built fort. Most prefer **Skála Eressoú** ❻, 14km (9 miles) south of Ypsiloú, for its beach; in particular, numerous lesbians come to honour Sappho, who was born here.

Southern Lésvos, between the two gulfs, is home to olive groves rolling up to 968-metre (3,175-ft) Mount

Psará

Scarcely 450 inhabitants remain on melancholy **Psará** ❿, its bleakness relieved only by occasional fig trees and the odd cultivated field. Besides the lone port village, there's just one deserted monastery in the far north. Six beaches lie northeast of the port, each better than the preceding, though all catch tide-wrack on this exposed coast. Indeed, the island's main claims to fame are as the site of a massive 1824 massacre by the Ottomans, and being the birthplace of Ioannis Varvakis, hero of the 2012 film *God Loves Caviar*. A few tourists trickle over from Híos, on regular local ferries from Híos Town or Limáni Meston; big ferries call weekly from Lávrio and Kavála.

Híos (Chíos)

Although the island had been important and prosperous since antiquity, the Middle Ages made the **Híos** (www.chios.com) of today. The Genoese seized control here in 1346; the Giustiniani clan established a cartel, the *maona*, which controlled the highly profitable trade in gum mastic. During their rule, which also saw the introduction of mandarin fruit, Híos became one of the wealthiest and most cultured islands in the Mediterranean. Local prowess in navigation was exploited by 150 ships calling here annually and Christopher Columbus apocryphally came to study with Hiot captains prior to his voyages.

In 1566, the Ottomans expelled the Genoese, but granted the islanders numerous privileges, so that Híos continued to flourish until March 1822, when poorly armed agitators from Sámos convinced the reluctant Hiots to participate in the independence uprising. Sultan Mahmut II, enraged at this ingratitude, exacted a terrible revenge: a two-month rampage commanded by Admiral Kara Ali killed 30,000 islanders, enslaved 45,000 more, and saw all settlements except the mastic-producing villages razed. Híos had only partly recovered when a strong earthquake in March 1881 destroyed much of what remained and killed 4,000. Today, Híos and its satellite islet Inoússes are home to some of Greece's wealthiest shipping families.

Its catastrophic 19th-century history ensures that **Híos Town** or **Hóra** ⓫ (pop. 25,000) seems at first off-puttingly modern. Scratch the ferro-concrete surface, however, and you'll find traces of the Genoese and Ottoman years. The most obvious medieval feature is the **kástro** (Venetian style of town planning with all the houses directed inwards). Moated on the landward side, it lacks a seaward rampart, destroyed after the 1881 quake. Just inside the imposing Porta Maggiora stands the outstanding **Giustiniani Museum** (Apr–Oct Tue–Sun 8am–7pm, Nov–May Tue–Sun 8.30am–3pm), a continually changing collection of religious art rescued from rural churches.

Off a small nearby square is a Muslim cemetery with the tomb of Kara Ali – he of the massacres, blown up along with his flagship by one of Admiral Kanaris's fireboats in June 1822. The square itself is lively with the tables of a popular, trendy bar-ouzerí. Further in lies the old Muslim and Jewish quarter with its derelict mosque and overhanging houses; Christians had to settle outside the walls. A hammam at the far end has been carefully restored for use as an exhibition venue.

South of Hóra you pass through **Kámbos** ⓬, a broad plain of high-

Plomári elders.

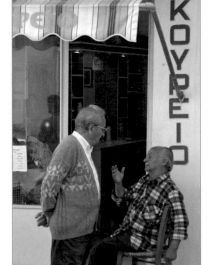

A STICKY BUSINESS

The mastic bushes of southern Híos are the unique source of gum mastic, the basis for many products before petroleum was refined. It was popular in Constantinople as chewing-gum, allegedly freshening the breath of the sultan's concubines. The Romans made mastic toothpicks to keep their teeth white and prevent cavities; Hippocrates praised its therapeutic value for coughs and colds; and lately practitioners of alternative medicine make even more ambitious claims on its behalf.

During the 14th and 15th centuries, the Genoese set up a monopoly in the substance. At its peak, the trade generated enough wealth to support a score of *mastihohoriá* (mastic villages). However, the coming of the Industrial Revolution and the demise of the Ottoman Empire was the end of large-scale mastic production.

Today, smaller amounts are generated in a process which has not really changed since ancient times. In late summer, incisions made in the bark weep resin "tears", which are scraped off and cleaned. Finally, the raw gum is sent to a central processing-plant where it is washed, baked and formed into lozenges of gum. Some 150 tons are produced annually, most of it exported to France, Bulgaria and Saudi Arabia for prices of up to $35 a kilo. However, the severe fire of summer 2012 destroyed nearly 40 percent of the mature mastic bushes, which take 30 years to reach a productive age.

Harvesting resin from the mastic trees, Híos.

Mólyvos surmounted by its medieval castle.

strongholds by the Genoese during the 14th and 15th centuries. Laid out on a dense, rectangular plan, their narrow passages are overarched by earthquake buttresses, with the backs of the outer houses doubling as the perimeter wall. Sadly, an August 2012 fire devastated both the local pines and mastic bushes.

Pyrgí ⓭, 21km (13 miles) from Hóra, is one of the best-preserved *mastihohoriá*, most of its facades adorned with black-and-white geometric patterns called *xystá*. A passageway off the central square leads to the Byzantine Ágii Apóstoli church (rarely open) decorated with later frescoes. In the back alleys, tomatoes are laboriously strung for drying in September by local women.

Some 11km (7 miles) west, **Mestá** ⓮ forms a more sombre, monochrome labyrinth, which retains defensive towers at its corners – several three-storeyed houses have been restored as accommodation. Such quarters are typically claustrophobic, so guests will appreciate the nearby beach resorts of **Kómi** (sand) and **Emboriós** (volcanic pebbles).

walled citrus groves dotted with the imposing sandstone mansions of the medieval aristocracy, standing along narrow, unmarked lanes. Many were destroyed by the earthquake, while a few have been restored as accommodation or restaurants. Irrigation water was originally drawn up by *manganós* or waterwheel; a few survive in ornately paved courtyards.

The onward road heads southwest towards southern Híos, with its 20 **mastihohoriá,** built as pirate-proof

With your own car, the beautiful, deserted west coast with its many coves

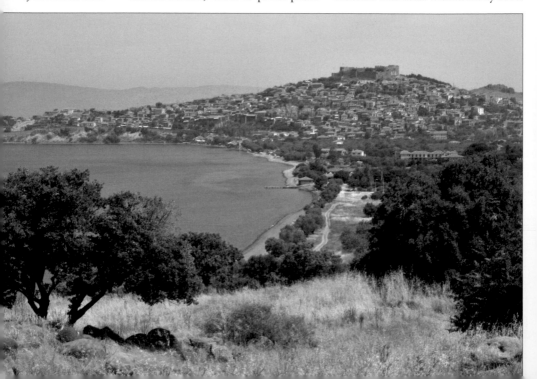

is accessible via attractive **Véssa** and **Sidiroúnda,** the paved road eventually taking you to castle-crowned **Volissós** ⓯ in the far northwest. Around this half-empty village are the island's finest beaches – and scars from a series of recent fires which burnt two-thirds of Híos's forests. The best excursion north of Volissós is to **Ágion Gála** village, with its mysterious cave-church (May–Sept Tue–Sun 11am–6pm; escorted tour only) at the outskirts.

Between Kastélla and Elínda bays, a good road snakes east uphill to **Avgónyma**, a clustered village well restored by returned Greek-Americans. Just 4km (2.5 miles) north perches almost-deserted, crumbling **Anávatos**, well camouflaged against its cliff; from this in 1822, 400 Hiots leapt to their deaths rather than be captured.

Some 5km (3 miles) east, the monastery of **Néa Moní** ⓰ (www.museum teriade.gr; daily sunrise–1pm, 4pm–sunset; museum Tue–Sun 8am–1pm) forms one of the finest surviving examples of mid-Byzantine architecture, founded in 1049 by Emperor Constantine Monomachus IX on a spot where a miraculous icon of the Virgin had appeared. It suffered heavily in 1822 and 1881, first with the murder of its monks and the pillage of its treasures, and then with the collapse of its dome. Despite the damage, its mosaics of scenes from the life of Christ are outstanding and numerous.

Ikaría and Foúrni

The narrow, wing-shaped island of **Ikaría** (www.island-ikaria.com) is named after mythical Icarus, who supposedly fell into the sea nearby when his wax wings melted (the Greek Air Force has adopted him as patron, apparently impervious to the irony). One of the least developed large islands in the Aegean, Ikaría has little to offer anyone intent on ticking off four-star sights, but appeals to those disposed to a decidedly eccentric environment. For three brief months after 17 July 1912, when a certain Dr Malahias declared the island liberated, it was an independent republic, with its own money and stamps. In later decades, Ikaría served as a place of exile for hundreds of Communists; the locals with whom they were billeted thought

An exquisite example of xystá decorations in Pyrgí.

The streets in Mestá can feel a little claustrophobic.

Fishing on Ikaría.

they were the most noble, humanitarian folk they'd ever met and still vote Communist in droves – not quite what Athens intended.

Ágios Kírykos is the capital and main southerly port, its tourist facilities geared to the clientele at the neighbouring spa of Thermá. Taxis are more reliable than the bus for the 41-km (25-mile) drive over the 1,000-metre (3,300-ft) Atherás ridge to **Évdilos**, the north-facing second port. Another 16km (10 miles) takes you past **Kámbos,** with its sandy beach and ruined Byzantine palace, to the tiny port-resort of **Armenistís**. Here only do foreigners congregate, for the sake of excellent beaches – Livádi and Mesakhtí – just east, though the surf can be deadly. **Nás,** 4km (2.5 miles) west, is named for the **naos** or temple of Artemis Tavropolio on the banks of the river draining to a popular pebble cove. **Gialiskári,** a fishing port 4km (2.5 miles) east, is distinguished by its photogenic jetty chapel.

There are few bona fide inland villages, as the proud Ikarians hate to live on top of each other, keeping plenty of room for orchards between their houses. Above Armenistís are four hamlets lost in pine forest, collectively known as **Ráhes;** at Hristós, the largest, people cram the café-bars all night, sleep until noon and carry belongings (or store potent wine) in hairy goatskin bags. The surrounding countryside completes the hobbit-like image, with vertical natural monoliths and troglodytic cottages for livestock made entirely of gigantic granite slabs. One of these, 4km (2.5 miles) above Kámbos, gives dramatic shelter to **Theoskepastí** chapel below which stands **Theóktisti monastery** (usually open) with engaging 17th-century frescoes.

Foúrni , one of several islets southeast of Ikaría, lives from its thriving fishing fleet and boatyards; (expensive) seafood dinners figure high in the ambitions of arriving tourists, who mostly stay in the surprisingly large port town. A road links this with Ágios Ioánnis Hrysóstomos in the south and remote Hryssomiliá in the far north, the only other villages, but path-walking (where possible) and boat-riding are more relaxing ways of getting around – there's no bus, and only seasonal scooter hire.

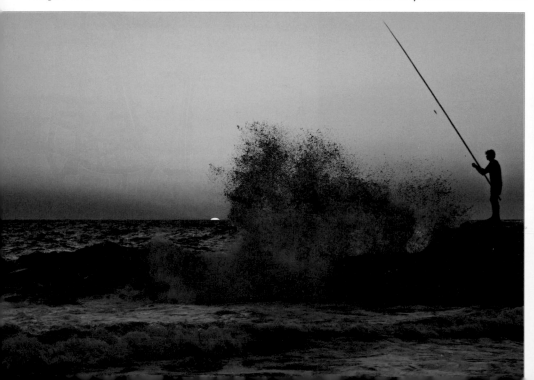

Best of many beaches are at **Kámbi,** one ridge south of port, or at naturist **Áspa,** a tough trail walk beyond.

Sámos

Almost subtropical **Sámos,** with vine terraces, cypress and olive groves, surviving stands of black and Calabrian pine, hillside villages and beaches of every size and consistency, appeals to numerous package tourists. Forest fires – the worst of these in July 2000 – and development have blighted much of the island, but impassable gorges, the Aegean's second-highest mountain, and beaches accessible only on foot hold sway in the far west.

From the immense harbour mole at heavily commercialised **Pythagório** ⑲, constructed by ancient slaves and scarcely changed, you can watch majestic Mount Mykale in Turkey change colour at dusk. The port's shape suggested a frying-pan, hence Tigáni, the town's former name – perhaps too prophetic of what it's become: a casserole of lobster-red Scandinavians fried in suntan-oil. The authorities changed the name in 1955 in honour of native

son Pythagoras. The main attraction in town is the 2010-opened **archaeological museum** (Tue–Sun Apr–Oct 9am–4pm, Nov–Mar 8am–3pm), where highlights include a huge hoard of Byzantine gold coins found in 1984, and monumental Roman statuary.

The 1,040-metre (3,410-ft) **Evpalínio Órygma** (Eupalinos's Tunnel; closed for restoration), an aqueduct built during the rule of the brilliant but unscrupulous tyrant Polykrates (538–522 BC), cuts through the hillside northwest of

The Ottoman viper, Vipera xanthina, a medium-sized viper species, can be found on the Aegean islands. It is by far the most venomous snake of Europe.

Sámos beach resort.

town. It is one of the technological marvels of the ancient world: surveying was so good that two work crews beginning from each end met with no vertical error, and a horizontal one of less than 1 percent. You can visit the first 200m, along the catwalk used to remove spoil from the water channel far below. One re-erected column and sundry foundations – the ruins of what was once a vast **Sanctuary of Hera** (ancient Heraion, Iréon in modern Greek; summer daily 8am–8pm; winter Tue–Sun 8am–3pm) – lie 8km (5 miles) to the west of Pythagório, past coastal Roman baths and the airport.

Vathý or **Sámos Town** ⑳, built along an inlet on the north coast, is the main port, founded in 1832. Tourism is less pervasive here; the principal attraction is the excellent, two-wing **archaeological museum** (Tue–Sun summer 9am–4pm, winter 8am–3pm), with a rich trove of finds from the Sanctuary of Hera. Star exhibit is a 5-metre (16-ft) high, nearly intact kouros (male votive statue), the largest ever found. The small-objects collection confirms the temple's Middle

Eastern slant of worship and clientele: orientalised ivories and locally cast griffin's heads.

Áno Vathý, the large hillside village 1.5km (1 mile) southeast, existed for almost two centuries before the harbour settlement; a stroll will take you through steep cobbled streets separating 200-year-old houses, their overhanging second stories and plaster-lath construction akin to those of northern Greece and Anatolia, though many are senselessly destroyed annually.

First stop of note on the north-coast road (12km/7 miles) is **Kokkári**, a former fishing village now devoted to tourism. The original centre is cradled between twin headlands, while windsurfers launch themselves from a school one cove west of town, the first of several pebble beaches on this coast. Overhead loom the scorched crags of Mount Ámbelos (1,150 metres/3,800 ft), while just past Avlákia a road climbs to the attractive and thriving little village of **Vourliótes**, named after its first inhabitants (who came from Vourla in Asia Minor), and justly famous for its wine production.

Fishing boats in Pythagório harbour.

The coastal highway continues west, sometimes as a sea-level corniche route, to **Karlóvasi** ㉑, 29km (18 miles) from Vathý. It's a sprawling, somewhat dishevelled place, little visited and lumped into five neighbourhoods. Néo, the biggest, houses post-1923 refugees and the university; cavernous, derelict warehouses dominate waterside Ríva district, vestiges of a leather-tanning trade which thrived here before 1970. In one such former warehouse, the excellent **Mousío Vyrsodepsías/Tanning Museum** (Mon–Fri 9am–2pm; free) gives a fascinating overview of the vanished industry, including massive machinery in situ. Meséo is more village-y, as is Paleó, lining a green valley behind the sentinel church of Ágia Triáda. Limín, below Áno, has most local tourist facilities, including the ferry port. The shore west of here has some of Sámos's best beaches, including sand-and-pebble **Potámi**, visited by most of Karlóvasi at weekends. Beyond here, you must walk to a pair of remote, scenic beaches at **Seïtáni**, now a nature reserve to protect its resident monk seals.

Karlóvasi lies roughly halfway around an anticlockwise loop of the island; head south, then east through an interior dotted with small villages of tiled, shuttered houses and stripey-domed churches. At **Ágii Theodóri** junction, choose southwest or east.

Going southwest takes you past Marathókambos and its sleepy, atmospheric port, Órmos, to **Votsalákia**, Sámos's biggest beach resort. Less busy beaches like Psilí Ámmos and Limniónas can be found further west along the road curling around the base of Mount Kérkis (1,437 metres/4,725ft), which forms the west end of the island. The mountain is usually climbed from the uninhabited **Evangelístria convent** on the south or Kosmadéï on the north – either way it is a full day's outing. Returning to Pythagório, schedule stops at the roadside stalls before **Pýrgos** for a jar of local honey, and just below Koumaradéï, at the monastery of **Megális Panagías** (Wed–Mon 10am–1pm, 5.30–8pm), with smudged frescoes dating from after 1586 (there are older, better ones at **Petaloúda** church – always open – near Karlovássi).

Olive grove in Sámos.

GREECE IN BLOOM

The Greek landscape is at its most bountiful in spring and early summer, when every hillside and valley is decorated with glorious colour.

Greece in spring is a botanist's dream and a gardener's despair. Some 6,000 species of wild plant grow in Greece and the islands, and in the spring (March to May), visitors may enjoy a magnificent cornucopia of flowers and fragrances.

Hillsides resemble giant rock gardens, while brilliant patches of untended waste-ground outdo Northern Europe's carefully tended herbaceous borders with ease. Winter rains, followed by a bright, hot, frost-free spring, produce a season's blooming compressed into a few, spectacular weeks before the summer's heat and drought become too much. By late May or early June, the flowers are finished, the seeds for next year's show are ripening, and greens are fading to brown to match the tourists on the beaches.

Summer survival

Except in the cooler, higher mountains, most plants go into semi-dormancy to survive the arid summer. The first rains of autumn, which can come any time between mid-September and late October, tempt a few autumn bulbs into flower, but also initiate the germination of seeds for plants that will grow and build up strength during the winter in preparation for the following spring, when their flowers will again colour in the waiting canvas of the hills and valleys.

The richness and diversity of the flora are due in part to the islands' location between three continents – Europe, Asia and Africa – partly to the Ice Age survival in southern Greece of pre-glacial species, and partly to the wonderful variety of habitats. Limestone, the foundation of much of Greece, is a favourite home for plants, providing the stability, minerals, water supply and protection they need.

Daisies on the east coast.

Wild artichokes are painfully spiny to prepare for the pot; but their flavour is prized by Greek country folk over the spineless cultivated variety, and accordingly they command a price premium.

The hills are alive – sunshine, colour and quantity mark the spring flowering on the islands, as here in the mountains of Crete in mid-April.

Butterflies abound from spring to autumn.

BEETLES, BEES AND BUTTERFLIES

The profusion of flowers and plants provides food for an equal profusion of insects. Butterflies are conspicuous from spring to autumn, including the lovely swallowtail whose colourful caterpillars feed on the leaves of common fennel. Its larger, paler and more angular relative, the scarce swallowtail, despite its name, is actually more abundant.

Look for clouded yellows and paler cleopatras, reddish-brown painted ladies and southern commas, white admirals, and a myriad of smaller blue butterflies.

Butterflies, bees and day-flying hawk moths tend to go for flowers with nectar, while beetles and flies go for the pollen. Some insects even use the heat accumulated in the solar cup of many flowers in order to warm up their sex lives.

The leaves of plants feed armies of insect herbivores, which themselves are eaten by more aggressive insects. Some of the omnivorous Greek grasshoppers and crickets are as happy munching through a caterpillar, or even another grasshopper, as the grass it was sitting on.

The robustness of the native oleander makes it popular as an ornamental roadside hedge; it also colonises stream beds.

According to legend, fire was brought to earth by Prometheus hidden in the smouldering stem of a giant fennel (Ferula communis).

A lovely little chapel awash with colour on Mýkonos.

A lick of fresh paint, Skiáthos Town.

THE SPORADES AND ÉVVIA

The four "scattered islands" (Sporádes) are all
different – Skiáthos lively and busy, Skópelos
quieter and beautiful, Alónisos the least developed,
and Skýros with its own unique culture.

The three northernmost Sporades,
set in one of the more blue-green
reaches of the Aegean, are, with
their lush vegetation and excellent
beaches, a quintessential holiday destination; there's little trace of the ancient
past here, so ruin-spotters may be dis-
appointed. Culturally and administratively, Skýros and Évvia off to the
southeast have had little to do with
their neighbours; Évvia in particular
often feels like part of the mainland.

Skiáthos

The sandy scythe of **Koukounariés**
❶ on **Skiáthos** is used as evidence
on thousands of postcards that the
Aegean can produce the kind of
beach normally associated with the
Caribbean. Propriety would prevent
as many postcards from featuring
Mikrós Krassás (colloquially "Little Banana Beach"), because it caters
for gay nudists. The fact that no one
cares whether bathers at Banana
Beach strip off or not is typical of
the easy-going nature of the people
of Skiáthos as a whole. The island
has beaches for all occasions: some
among the supposed 60 will always
be sheltered whichever direction the
wind is coming from.

Koukounariés and Banana Big
(straight) and Little are near-neighbours
at the end of the twisting, busy 18-km
(11-mile) road that runs along the

Lalária beach, Skiáthos.

south coast of Skiáthos. There are dozens of beaches along it, many with a
taverna or at least a kiosk selling drinks
and sandwiches, and many even with
luxury hotels – Vromólimnos has the
best daytime bar scene. North-coast
beaches like **Mandráki** and **Eliá** are
more pristine. Round-the-island boat
trips pass the rocky and otherwise inaccessible northern shoreline where the
only human construction is the **Kástro**
❷, the abandoned 16th-century capital once connected to the rest of the
island by a single drawbridge. For 300

Main Attractions
Kástro, Skiáthos
Skiáthos Beaches
Skópelos Town
Velanió Beach, Skópelos
Hóra, Skýros
Faltaïts Museum, Skýros
Steni "Hill Station", Évvia
Dimosári Gorge Hike, Évvia
Límni, Évvia

Skópelos Town can lay claim to some distinguished houses, which its inhabitants are proud to adorn.

years, the islanders huddled on this wind-buffeted crag, hoping the pirates would pass them by. In World War II, Allied soldiers hid out here, waiting for evacuation. Today, it is an obligatory stop for the excursion caïques after they have dipped into technicolour grottoes and dropped anchor at **Lalária,** a cove famous for its rock arch, and before proceeding to a beach taverna (usually at Megálos Asélinos) for lunch.

The bluff above under-used **Xánemos** beach at the end of the very busy airport runway has produced fragments suggesting a prehistoric settlement, but neither it nor the rest of the island have ever been properly excavated. German bombing of an Italian ammunition dump in September 1943 severely damaged much of the pretty prewar town, burned again in August 1944. But **Skiáthos Town** ❸ makes up in liveliness what it may lack in architectural merit. In fact, its nightlife is probably the most important consideration after the beaches for the type of visitor that Skiáthos attracts in intimidating numbers during the summer.

The preferences of the fast-living set change constantly, but it is not difficult to spot which places are in vogue, whether one's preference is for beer and blues, wine and Vivaldi, or tequila and trance. The lights are brightest but also the tackiest along **Papadiamándis,** the paved pedestrian street which bisects the two hills on which the town stands, and along the old harbour. The atmosphere is more Greek-oriented at the designer clubs on the water past the yacht marina, somewhat more international at the old-port bars. Expect restaurants, with international flavours as well as Greek, rather than tavernas, and be prepared to pay accordingly, especially along the seafront.

A scooter or hired car is useful to follow the unpaved roads looping through the mountains. They provide stunning views, as well as the chance to pop into monasteries which, with Kástro, are more or less the only buildings of historic interest. Of these, the grandest and closest to town is **Evangelistrías,** with frescoed **Panagías Kehreás** and **Panagías Kounístras**

Sporades

0   10 km

0   10 miles

(all three open daily) also pilgrimage-worthy if the beaches should pall.

Skópelos

Skópelos (www.skopelos.gr) has a distinguished past, which is not so much demonstrated by prominent historical sites as by the exceptionally fine houses in **Skópelos Town ❹**; they form a handsome amphitheatre around a harbour lined with cafés and tavernas under mulberry trees.

The island has escaped earthquakes and Nazi vindictiveness and is therefore the most "authentic" and traditional of the three northern Sporádes (Skýros being in a class by itself). Slate roofs, wooden balconies, hand-painted shop signs and flagstone streets give it a serenity and dignity rarely found in Skiáthos in season. On the other hand, beaches are not as sandy or as numerous as on Skiáthos – mostly on the south-facing coast – though north-facing **Glystéri** is the closest to Hóra. Nudists are welcomed at long, fine-pebble **Velanió** just beyond the family beach of **Stáfylos** (where a gold crown and ornate weapons dating from Minoan

times were found; they are now in the National Archaeological Museum in Athens). Local beaches were, in any case, good enough to serve as locations for the 2007 shooting of the film version of **Mamma Mia!**, a fact the islanders have not been slow to exploit.

Further along the southwest coast, **Agnóndas** serves as an alternative harbour when Skópelos Town is storm-shut; there are good tavernas but not much of a beach. For more of those, carry on down the island "trunk road" to **Pánormos**, the biggest resort after Hóra and environs, with a long gravel beach and yacht shelter at Blo inlet. Better, pine-backed beaches lie just around the corner at **Miliá** and **Kastáni**. The road passes the quake-damaged hamlet of **Paleó Klíma** – now bought up and renovated by outsiders – before ending in the northwest at **Glóssa ❺**, Skópelos' second village whose architecture (like Paleó Klíma's) betrays the strong Thessalian influence tangible on all the northern Sporades. Far below Glóssa to the south is **Loutráki**, another rather nondescript ferry port; some of the very

Cape Kástro, north Skiáthos.

Sailing lesson in the Skiáthos waters.

Card-players, Skópelos Town.

few north-facing Skópelos beaches lie in the other direction, at **Perivolioú** and **Hondrogiórgis**.

Inland and north from the main road, Skópelos has denser forest than Skiáthos, still mostly unburnt and crisscrossed by a mix of dirt tracks and paved lanes. These pass by a reputed 40 monasteries and hundreds of churches (of these, 123 are scattered around Hóra alone). On the side of the island's summit – Mt Délfi – are three ancient cyst-type tombs: the **Sendoúkia**, with their lids ajar. The 15-minute walk there is prominently signposted.

Alónisos

On a hill above **Patitíri** ❻, the last port on the Vólos/Ágios Konstandínos-based ferry, catamaran and hydrofoil routes, is **Hóra,** the former capital of Alónisos, battered by an earthquake in 1965. This quake compounded the blow the islanders had already suffered when all their grapevines died from phylloxera only a decade earlier. Alónisos seems to have been ever thus: the previous capital, Ikos, also the Classical name for the island, literally disappeared when the ground on which it stood sunk into the sea. The submerged remains of Ikos, off **Kokkinókastro** beach, may be explored with a snorkel but not with scuba tanks (a general rule in the Aegean to prevent pilfering and damage).

Alónisos has adjusted to its unrealised potential and bad luck with considerable good grace, attracting a loyal repeat clientele amongst both Greeks and foreigners. Yet it remains the least architecturally distinguished and least developed of the Sporádes, a quiet island surrounded by an interesting collection of islets. Some of them are off-limits to tourists and fishermen alike, protected areas within the National Marine Park reserved for the endangered monk seal and other rare fauna. **Gioúra**, for example, is home to a unique breed of wild goat and also has a cave that in legend sheltered Homer's Cyclops. It and **Pipéri** may not be visited but caïques leave Patitíri on calm days for excursions to the closer islets of **Peristéra** ❼ and **Kyrá Panagía** ❽, where ancient pot-shards can be seen by snorkellers on the sea bed and the eponymous medieval monastery on the latter island still has one monk. Passenger numbers and daylight allowing, trips extend to remote **Psathoúra,** with its huge lighthouse and long sandy beach.

Back on Alónisos, a paved but twisty road links the south and north of the island, including a detour to the little yacht anchorage of **Stení Vála**, with its scuba centre and summer-only information post on the monk seal (the main, all-year information centre is in Patitíri). Otherwise, high-season taxi-boats at Patitíri take bathers to the beach of their choice – the best east-coast ones are **Leftós Gialós**, with two good tavernas, and **Ágios Dimítrios**, with a naturist zone.

Walkers are well catered for with a network of 14 routes, waymarked and maintained with EU funding. One of them leads up pleasantly, in 45 minutes, to the earthquake-shattered **Hóra** ❾, also known as **Paleá Alónisos**. Thanks

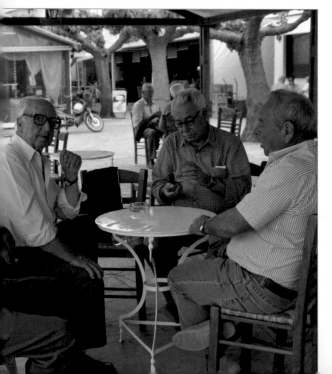

largely to foreigners who spied a bargain and bought damaged houses to fix up, it is now largely inhabited – though overly manicured and not particularly Greek except for one tiny shop selling local dairy products.

Skýros

Skýros (www.greektravel.com/greekislands/skyros) was possibly two islands originally, the halves joining near where there is now a road linking **Lineriá** ⑩, the port, with the little village of Aspoús on the way to Skýros Town. The southern part of the island (Vounó) is mountainous and largely barren, and visitors are unlikely to venture below Kolymbáda beach unless they are heading for Rénes beach or the poet Rupert Brooke's grave in an olive grove at **Trís Boúkes** ⑪. Trís Boúkes is about a 30-minute drive from Kolymbáda, and it's another 15 minutes more to the trailhead for Rénes.

The real appeal of Vounó is from the sea, for cliffs along most of the coast from **Rénes** all the way around to Ahílli Bay near Aspoús fall straight down into the sea. These cliffs are inhabited by a few wild goats and seemingly innumerable Eleanora's falcons, which can be seen darting around the heights all the way over to Skýros Town. Boat excursions can be arranged at Lineriá.

Hóra (Skýros Town) ⑫ is on the northern half of the island (Merói) on the east coast, high above the long sandy beach (better at the south end) that fringes the now-contiguous settlements of **Magaziá** to the south and **Mólos** at the north end. Town life plays out all along the meandering main street, which runs from the main lower square with its nocturnal bars to the elevated plaza at the northern edge of Hóra. Here, the nude statue of Rupert Brooke, which caused a scandal when erected in the 1930s, commands the view beside the excellent, private **Faltaïts Museum** (daily 10am–2pm, 6–9pm) of ethnographic displays, including a tobacco press, a mocked-up Skyrian house interior, antique metalware and local pottery. Traditional costume has more or less disappeared with the last generation, but the carving of mulberry furniture and screens is still practised.

Feline residents, Skópelos Town.

RUPERT BROOKE'S GRAVE

It was quite by chance that Skýros became the burial place of the poet Rupert Brooke. When war broke out in 1914, Brooke first thought of becoming a war correspondent, but soon changed his mind and enlisted as a second lieutenant in the newly formed Royal Naval Division, briefly seeing action at the fall of Antwerp. In the spring of 1915, he arrived on the island of Límnos, where ships and men had begun massing in preparation for the ill-fated assault on Gallipoli.

Moúdros Bay became so crowded that Brooke's detachment was ordered to wait instead off the bay of Trís Boúkes, in the far south of Skýros. Between manoeuvres, he and some fellow officers rested on shore in a small olive grove above the bay which, the others remembered, the poet particularly liked. Several days later, on 23 April, he died on a French hospital ship of blood-poisoning caused by a septic mosquito bite, aged 27; his fellow officers buried him in the olive grove.

Brooke was subsequently beatified in the eyes of a nation mourning its youthful heroes, even though he never lived to see the horrors of trench warfare. Today, the site can be reached by caïque, a long walk from Kolybáda, or by vehicle. There is also a memorial to Brooke in Skýros Town – a highly romanticised bronze statue of "Immortal Poetry".

The Church of Christ, a Skópelos landmark.

Nearby, the worthwhile **archaeological museum** (Tue–Sun 8am–3pm) has choice island finds like a Geometric rhyton (ornate drinking vessel) in the form of a Skyrian pony and an even older faience necklace. A series of small side streets meander up to the **kástro** (closed for repairs), the old Byzantine/Venetian castle on the heights.

Besides the Magaziá-Mólos beach, there are better if more exposed beaches at **Gyrísmata**, **Kareflóu** and **Ágios Pétros** further along the north coast. At **Palamári**, an important Bronze Age town (Mon–Fri 8am–2pm; free) is being excavated. Beyond Palamári, and the turning to scenic Ágios Pétros, pine forest appears, compensating for the mediocrity of west-coast beaches either side of **Atsítsa** and **Ágios Fokás** (each with tavernas). The road loops back all the way to Linariá from Atsítsa, via the stunning viewpoint of **Ágios Pandelímon** and the turn-off for the much better sandy beach of **Pévkos**.

Évvia (Euboea)

Évvia, Greece's second-largest island (after Crete) lies just off the coast of mainland Greece, looking on the map like a large jigsaw-puzzle piece just slightly out of position. The capital, **Halkída ❶**, is close enough to the mainland for a small drawbridge and a newer, far larger suspension bridge to make easy connection. Aristotle is supposed to have been so frustrated in trying to understand the swift tides here in the narrow **Évripos channel**, which reverse direction regularly, that he jumped into the waters.

Halkída is a brash industrial town, but the **kástro** with its mosque and church of **Agía Paraskeví** are worth visiting, as is the archaeological museum (Tue–Sun 8.30am–3pm) in the new town. There is also a synagogue, rebuilt after a fire in 1854 and still used by the small (90-member) but active Romaniote Jewish community. **Erétria ❷** to the south is a crowded, grid-plan resort town where the ferries land from **Skála Oropoú** on the mainland. Like Halkída, Erétria is a town to pass through, but the small **archaeological museum** is very good, as are the adjacent remains of excavated ancient Erétria (Tue–Sun 8am–3pm).

In general, southern Évvia is drier and less green. The coastal road from Erétria is dotted with villages and summer homes until just before **Alivéri** where it turns inland. At Lépoura, turn south for the prosperous seaside town of **Kárystos ❸**, with beaches to either side, and Mount Óhi – with its eminently scenic and hikable **Dimosári Gorge** – overhead. An old cobbled trail traverses the gorge in about three hours from a start-point on the flank of Óhi, finishing at Kallianós beach hamlet.

From Lépoura, the main road forges eastwards through **Háni Avlonaríou**, with the large and unusual 14th-century church of **Ágios Dimítrios**, before continuing through often beautiful hilly farmland to drop down on the east coast to **Stómio** where a small river reaches the sea. The way then hugs the shore through **Platána** to the harbour at **Paralía Kýmis ❹** and the boat to Skýros.

North of Halkída – or west from Kými on a very scenic road – the small village of **Stení ❺** on the slopes of **Mount Dírfys** is a favourite goal for Athenians seeking clean air and grill restaurants. **Límni ❻** on the west coast is the most atmospheric and historic port on the island, its neoclassical houses funded by 19th-century shipping wealth. Just south, in the dense forest of Mt Kandíli, **Galatáki convent** (9am–noon, 5–8pm) is home to several nuns, one of whom will show you 16th-century frescoes in the narthex.

Good pebble beaches begin just north of Límni, appearing intermittently en route to **Loutrá Edipsoú ❼**, with its stunningly refurbished spa-hotel. Beyond, the main road curls around Évvia's northerly Cape Artemísio – where the famous bronze of spear-throwing Poseidon was fished from the sea in 1928. The east coast is mostly mountainous, with rocky shoulders dropping sharply down to the sea, but the road does pass a series of beaches: **Elliniká, Psaropoúli, Paralía Kotsikiás, Angáli**. The first is the smallest and most scenic, the last the most developed. **Agía Ánna ❽**, the hill village inland from Angáli, has an exceptionally well done **Folklore Museum** (Wed–Sun 10am–1pm, Wed 6–8pm).

The bridge to Halkída, Évvia.

Lunch with a view at Boukari
Beach restaurant.

CORFU

Few places have been as exploited and developed for tourism as Corfu. Yet, away from the package-tour resorts, there is much to savour on this beautiful green island.

trategically poised between the Ionian and Adriatic seas, just off the Greek mainland, Corfu (Kérkyra) has an unsurprisingly turbulent history and a long catalogue of invaders. The Venetians in particular left a rich legacy of olive groves, which still form much of the local vegetation. Despite up to a million visitors a year, tourism has not entirely steamrollered the entire island: 10km (6 miles) from the most brazen fleshpots, you can drive along a one-lane potholed road through sleepy villages whose inhabitants stare or wave at you.

Corfu Town

Corfu Town, also known as **Kérkyra ❶**, occupies a central east-coast location. "Corfu" is a corruption of *koryfí*, "peak", of which there are two on a Byzantine-fortified outcrop transformed into the **Paleó Froúrio ❹** (**Old Fort**; daily May–Oct 8am–6pm, Nov–Mar 9am–4pm) by the Venetians during the 15th and 16th centuries, when they cut a canal to make the citadel an island. The Old Fort overlooks Mandráki Harbour, originally a Venetian galley port but now a pleasure-craft marina. The more complete **Néo Froúrio** (**New Fort**) **❸** to the west (same hours as Old Fort) is strictly Venetian and offers wonderful views.

With its tottering, multistoreyed apartments and maze-like lanes ending in quiet plazas, the Old Town constitutes a *flâneur*'s paradise, now listed by Unesco. Vacant bomb sites still yawn near the Néo Froúrio, and many main thoroughfares are brashly commercialised, but the backstreets are surprisingly unspoilt, festooned with washing lines and echoing to pigeon coos. An elegant counterpoint is the **Listón ❻**, to the east, built by the French as a replica of the Parisian Rue de Rivoli. The name refers to local

Main Attractions

Museum Of Asian Art, Kérkyra Town
Byzantine Museum, Kérkyra Town
The Two Forts, Kérkyra Town
National Gallery Annexe, Káto Korakiána
Paleá Períthia Village
Daytrip To Diapóndia Islets
View Of Paleokastrítsa
Halikoúna Beach

The Catholic Cathedral in Corfu Town.

Corfu Town's Listón still buzzes at night.

aristocrats listed in the Venetian Libro d'Oro, who were the only citizens entitled to walk beneath the arcades.

The Listón faces the **Spianáda ⓓ** (Esplanade), a large and grassy open space cleared by the Venetians to deprive attackers of cover. On the southern half of the Esplanade is the plain **Ionian Monument**, which celebrates the island's union with Greece in 1864. It is surrounded by marble reliefs displaying the symbols of the seven Ionian Islands (the *Eptánisa*). Nearby is the Victorian bandstand, where Sunday concerts are held in summer, and the Maitland Rotunda, dedicated to the first, albeit unloved, British High Commissioner. At the far end is the statue of Greece's first president (1827–31) and Corfu's greatest son, Ioannis Kapodistrias. Until the 2008 move to a purpose-built stadium at Gouviá, the Spianáda hosted idiosyncratic cricket matches, an enduring British legacy, as is the enormous Victorian cemetery outside town, and the ginger beer that is still available at some of the Listón's cafés.

Both music and Saint Spyrídon are integral parts of Corfiot life. Until it

was destroyed by Nazi bombs, Kérkyra had the world's largest opera house after Milan's La Scala; there are still regular classical or brass-band performances and thriving conservatories. A few blocks back in the streets behind the Listón is the 16th-century **Church of Ágios Spyrídon ⓔ** (usually open), with sumptuous ceiling murals by local master Panagiotis Doxaras. Spyrídon, after whom seemingly half the male population is named "Spýros", was a 4th-century Cypriot bishop whose remains were taken to Constantinople in the 7th century and then, in 1456, smuggled to Corfu, where he is credited with miraculously saving the island from several disasters. His casket, prominently displayed in the church, is processed around town four times a year.

Across the north side of the Spianáda stands the imposing **Palace of St Michael and St George ⓕ**, erected in 1819–24 as the residence for the British High Commissioners. When the British left, Greek royalty used it as a summer residence. The bronze toga-clad figure who stands above a lily pond in front of the palace is Sir Frederick Adam,

Britain's second High Commissioner. The pool and its water spouts are there to remind people that Adam was the first to ensure Kérkyra Town a reliable water supply, with an aqueduct system still in use today. The palace's state rooms now house the **Museum of Asian Art** (www.matk.gr; Nov–Mar Tue–Sun 9am–4pm, Apr–Oct 8am–8pm). Its collection of almost 11,000 Asian artefacts is one of the most comprehensive collections of its kind in the world, encompassing Buddhist devotional art, Gandhara relief work, Hindu deities and Japanese scrolls.

West of here, the church of Panagía Andivouniótissa accommodates the **Byzantine Museum** G (www.antivouniotissamuseum.gr; Tue–Sun 8.30am–3pm). The *exonarthex* (vestibule) surrounding the single-aisle church on three sides exhibits an impressive array of icons from the 15th to 19th centuries, many of the so-called 'Cretan School'; after the fall of Crete to the Ottomans, many skilled artists came as refugees to Venetian-held Corfu.

Sadly, the **Archaeological Museum** H, with its superb late Archaic artefacts, is closed for repairs until at least late 2016. Most displays came from excavations in Mon Repos estate, 1km (0.6 miles) to the south, the birthplace of Britain's Prince Philip, which has a more modest museum (summer daily 8am–4pm, winter Tue–Sun 8am–3pm) with good temporary exhibits.

Just south of Mon Repos at Kanóni are the photogenic islets of **Vlahérna**, with a little whitewashed monastery (erratic opening times) and causeway to it, and **Pondikonísi**, said to be a local ship petrified by Poseidon in revenge for the ancient Phaecians helping Odysseus.

The north of the island

The coast northwest of town supports busy resorts such as **Kondókali**, **Komméno**, **Dassiá** and **Ýpsos**. Beyond **Barbáti**, the mountains plunge more sharply to the sea and the landscape becomes more stereotypically Mediterranean, mingling cypress with olive trees. To escape the bustle of the resorts, wander inland on an uphill journey past quiet villas and olive groves to **Káto Korakiána**. Here, installed in an

> **FACT**
>
> The Greeks call these west-coast islands the **Eptánisa** – the seven isles. But as Kýthira, the seventh isle, lies off the southern tip of the Peloponnese, it remains quite isolated from the others.

Paleó Froúrio, one of Kérkyra's two Venetian fortresses.

CORFU'S COLONISERS

Habitation dates back 50,000 years, although Corfu enters history as "Corcyra" in the 8th century BC, when it was colonised by ancient Corinth. By the 5th century BC, Corcyra had become a major, independent naval power, siding with Athens against Sparta in the Peloponnesian Wars. Nearly eight centuries of Byzantine tenure from AD 395 brought a measure of stability and prosperity; but latter years saw incursions by the Norman-Angevin Kingdom of the Two Sicilies, the Despotate of Epirus, and the Venetians. Weary of misrule and piracy, in 1386 the Corfiots submitted voluntarily to Venetian rule, which endured for 411 years despite four Ottoman sieges. Napoleon dissolved what remained of the Venetian Empire in 1797, and the French held the island until 1814 (except for the brief reign of the Ottoman-Russian-controlled "Septinsular Republic). The British were occupiers between 1814 and 1864, when all the Ionian Islands were ceded as a sweetener for George I's ascent of the Greek throne. During World War I, Corfu was the final destination of the retreating Serbian army and government-in-exile, and memorials and cemeteries from that era remain. World War II saw Kérkyra Town suffer extensive damage under a German bombardment to displace the Italian occupiers, who had surrendered to the Allies. During a brief but brutal occupation, the Nazis deported Corfu's significant Jewish community.

Locally made lace for sale.

– there are almost no hotels – and enjoy secluded pebble coves. The adjacent villages of **Kalámi** and **Kouloúra** were beloved of the Durrell family.

Mass tourism resumes at **Kassiópi ❹**, once a small fishing village and now a busy resort. The Romans Cicero, Cato and Nero stopped by, but only the crumbled Angevin castle recalls past prominence.

Alternatively, head up the north slopes of 914-metre (2,950-ft) **Mt Pandokrátor** to **Paleá Períthia**, a well-preserved Venetian-era village with several tavernas and innovative lodging. Back on the coast, **Aharávi**, **Róda** and **Sidári ❺** are three over-developed resorts. From Sidári ply the most reliable boats to two of the small inhabited **Diapóndia** islets, Eríkoussa and Othoní (the westernmost point of Greece), popular with Italians. Sidári's finest feature is the series of striking rock formations that rise out of the sea at the western end of the resort.

The west-coast beaches beyond Sidári are calmer, beginning below **Perouládes ❻**, with its superlative sunsets, continuing through Ágios

old, three-storey villa, is the **National Gallery Annexe of Corfu ❷** (www.nationalgallery.gr; Mon, Thu, Sat, Sun 8.30am–3.30pm, Wed, Fri 10am–2pm, 6–9pm), displaying 150 works of prominent Greek painters from all eras since 1830, on permanent loan from the Athens parent collection.

The mini-Riviera between **Kalámi ❸** and **Ágios Stéfanos Sinión** basks in the nickname of "Kensington-on-Sea" after a posh clientele who stay in villas

The 13th-century Angelókastro.

Corfu

0   5 km
0   5 miles

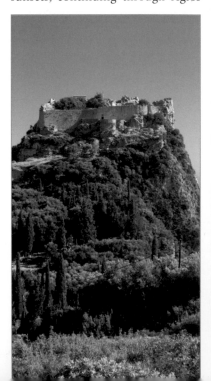

Stéfanos Avliotón, Arílas and Ágios Geórgios Págon. From Ágios Stéfanos Avliotón, boats go to the third Diapóndia islet, **Mathráki**, with its lovely long, uncrowded beaches.

Beyond Makrádes and **Kríni** looms the shattered but still impressive Byzantine-Angevin **Angelókastro** (May–Sept Mon–Fri 8.30am–3pm) guarding the approach to the beautiful double bay of **Paleokastrítsa** ❼, once idyllic but now swamped. The best view of Palcokastrítsa is from the village of **Lákones** above it. Sandy beaches resume at diminuitive **Myrtiótissa** ❽ – beloved of naturists – or much bigger **Glyfáda**, while **Ágios Górdis** is both backpackers' paradise and family resort. Inland, **Pélekas** offers island panoramas from the "Kaiser's Throne", a modified rock formation from which Kaiser Wilhelm II used to watch the sunset.

The south of the island

Inland and south of Kérkyra stands the monstrously kitsch **Achilleion Palace** ❾ (www.achillion-corfu.gr; daily 8am–7pm), built in 1890 for Empress Elisabeth of Austria, then acquired after her 1898 assassination by Kaiser Wilhelm II. It has variously served as a military hospital, casino, film location and conference venue, but the ground floor is now a museum, mostly of Elisabeth and Wilhelm's home furnishings.

Benítses is slowly reinventing itself from downmarket party resort to serious yachtie haven, thanks to its new marina, the largest on Corfu. The main street in **Moraïtika** is an uninterrupted line of restaurants/bars/shops, but the beach is good. The older, inland part of Moraïtika has no tourist development, just an attractive taverna or two as antidotes to the hectic resort below. **Mesongí** ❿ is marginally more pleasant, although the long but very narrow pebble beaches are closely hemmed in. Inland, Mesongí has some of Corfu's oldest olive groves, planted by the Venetians more than 500 years ago.

The main road turns inland here and reaches a crossroads at Áno Mesongí. Continue straight on to excellent Halikoúna beach at the northwest end of the **Korissíon lagoon** ⓫, a protected nature reserve. From the village of **Ágios Matthéos**, you can access long, sandy, scarcely developed **Paramónas** beach.

Turning left instead at Áno Mesongí, then leaving the main road at **Argyrádes** takes you to the coastal hamlet of **Boúkari**, spared exploitation by an utter lack of beaches. On the opposite shore lies **Ágios Geórgios Argyrádon**, a straggling, nondescript resort with only a splendid beach to its credit. The northernmost part of the beach is **Íssos**, which borders the southeast end of the Korissíon Lagoon. The Corfiots have deliberately quarantined the boozing-and-bonking youth element at the far southeast tip of the island, at **Kávos** ⓬, now fallen on hard times. **Levkímmi**, the underrated second-largest town on Corfu, with a picturesque river, goes about its business just inland, seemingly oblivious to its neighbour.

The crystal-clear water at Barbáti beach.

The two-tone waters off Ássos, on the west coast of Kefaloniá.

THE IONIAN ISLANDS

Lushest of all the Greek island chains, the Ionians offer superb beaches, great natural beauty and a distinct culture – including a graceful Venetian influence in the local architecture.

Throughout the Ionian archipelago, as on Corfu, the long Venetian domination (1386–1797) left an indelible mark. Culturally, these islands look west to Europe rather than north to the Balkans or east to Anatolia; only Levkáda had a brief period of Ottoman rule.

A heavy rainfall makes the Ionians among the greenest of Greek island chains. Olive groves and vineyards are reminders that agriculture, rather than tourism, still claim a part in the economy. However, this same unsettled weather has dampened many a traveller's holiday: from mid-September until mid-May, rains can wash out any beach visit quite without warning. The rest of the year, the northwest wind or *máïstros* substitutes for the *meltémi* blowing elsewhere in Greece.

Paxí (Páxos)

Small, hilly and green, **Paxí** (or **Páxos**) ❶ has a rugged west coast with cliffs and sea caves, and various pebble beaches on the gentler east shore. Paxí figures little in ancient history and mythology, and was systematically populated only during the 15th century. Here too the Venetians left a legacy of olive trees, and Paxiot oil ranks among the best in Greece.

All boats dock at the small capital, **Gáïos**, arrayed around its main square and sheltered by the two islets of **Ágios**

Bar sign in Sámi.

Nikólaos (castle) and **Panagía** (small monastery). Gáïos offers narrow streets and a few 19th-century buildings with Venetian-style balconies and shutters, plus most island shops.

Paxí's single main road meanders northwest through olive groves and tiny hamlets consisting of a few houses and perhaps a *kafenío* at lane junctions. Walking is still the best way to explore the maze of old walled paths, dirt tracks and paved lanes crisscrossing the island. **Longós** on the northwest coast is the most exclusive

Main Attractions
Andípaxi, Paxí
Levkáda Town, Levkáda
Pórto Kátsiki, Levkáda
Vathý, Itháki
Petaní, Kefaloniá
Melissáni Cave, Kefaloniá
Ássos, Kefaloniá
Gérakas, Zákynthos
Navágio Bay, Zákynthos
Blue Caves, Zákynthos

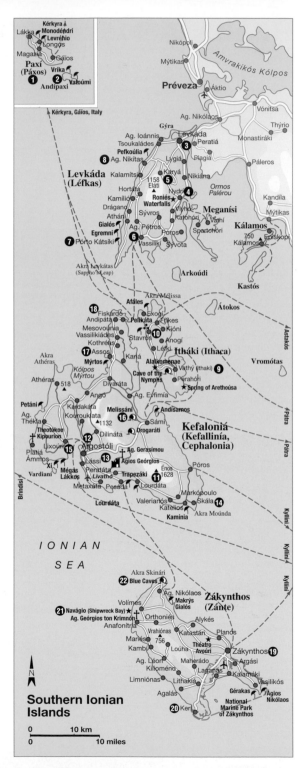

Kérkyra
Lákka ▲ Monodéndri
Levréhio
Longós
Magazá   Gáios
Paxí   Vrika
(Páxos)   Vatoúmi
①   ②
Andípaxi

Kérkyra, Gáïos, Italy

Nikópoli

Mýtikas

Amvrakikós Kólpos

Préveza   Áktio

Vónitsa

Ag. Nikólaos

Gýra   Thýrio

Ag. Ioánnis   Lefkáda   Monastiráki
Tsoukaládes   Peratiá
Pefkoúlia   ③
⑧ Ag. Nikítas   Lygiá   Plagiá
Páleros

Levkáda Kalamítsi   Karyá Nikiána
(Léfkas)   1158 ⑤
Hortáta Eláti   Ormos
Kamíliá   Roniés Nydrí ④ Palérou
Drágano   Waterfalls   Kandíla
Atháni   Sývros   Katohóri **Meganísi**   Mýtikas
Gialós   Ag. Pétros   Vathí
Egremní   Póros Spartohóri   **Kálamos**
⑦ Pórto Kátsíki ⑥   750 Epískopi
Vassilikí Sývota   Kálamos

Akra Lefkátas
(Sappho's Leap)   **Arkoúdi**

Kastós

Akra Mélissa
Aláfes
⑱
Fiskárdo   Exogí
Andipáta   Erikes   **Átokos**
Mesovoúnia   Kióni
Vassilikiádes Stavrós   Anogí
Kothréas   Léfki
⑰ Assos Karriá **Itháki (Ithaca)**
Akra   Mýrtos Alalkomenae
Athéras Kólpos   Vathý (Itháki) ⑨   **Vromótas**
Myrtou Cave of the Perahóri
Athéras 518   Nymphs ★ Spring of Arethoúsa
Divaráta
Petáni Ango
Ag. Efimía
Kardakáta   Melissáni
Ag.   Kouroukláta ⑯ Andísamos
Thékla   Sámi
▲1132
Theotókou   Orogaráti
✝ Kippourion Dilináta **Kefaloniá**
Lixoúri ⑫ Argostóli   **(Kefallinía,**
Platiá ⑮ Ag. Gerasímou **Cephalonia)**
Ámmos ⑬ Lássi **Ágios Geórgios**
Xi   Mégas Peratáta Énos
Vardianí Lákkos Livathó 1628 Póros
Metaxáta Trapezáki ⑪
Pesáda Lourdáta
Markópoulo
Lourdáta   Skála ⑭
Valerianós Katélios Akra Moúnda
Kaminia

IONIAN

SEA

Akra Skinári
⑫ Blue Caves
Volímes   Ag. Nikólaos
Makrýs **Zákynthos**
⑪ Navágio (Shipwreck Bay) Gialós **(Zánte)**
Ag. Geórgios ton Krimnón Orthoniés Alykés
Anafonítria
Vrahiónas Katastári Planós
Maniés 756 Theatro
Kambí Loúha Avoúri Zákynthos ⑲
Ag. Léon Maherádo Argási
Kiliómeno Kalamáki
Limniónas Laganás
Lithakiá Vasilikós
Agalás   Gérakas Ágios
⑳ Kerí National Nikólaos
Marine Park
of Zákynthos

**Southern Ionian
Islands**

0   10 km
0   10 miles

---

resort, flanked by the popular beaches of Levréhio and Monodéndri. The "motorway" ends at **Lákka**, favoured by yachts and the majority of land-bound tourists, with small beaches like Orkós lying nearby.

The satellite islet of **Andípaxi** (**Andípaxos**) ② shelters two excellent beaches mobbed by day-trippers in season, when four tavernas operate. Andípaxi's vineyards produce a heavy red wine favoured for local festivals, and a lighter tawny white.

Levkáda/Levkás

Levkáda is barely an island, joined to the mainland by a floating drawbridge over a canal dredged in ancient times. Yet it feels like one of the Ionians, with predictable Venetian influences on speech and cuisine, plus the imposing fort of Santa Maura by the bridge. Levkáda's rugged landscape has preserved rural lifestyles in the hill villages: older women still wear traditional dress, while local crafts and foodstuffs are avidly promoted.

Levkáda Town ③ faces the canal and the lagoon enclosed by Gíra sandspit, with safe mooring for numerous yachts on the southeast quay. Much of downtown is off-limits to cars.

There are several ornate Italianate churches dating from the late 17th or early 18th century, their Baroque relief work sitting oddly beside antiseismic belfries modelled on oil derricks. The churches (usually open) contain some admirable artwork from the Ionian School painters such as Doxaras, and beautiful iconostases. Secular architectural responses to the 1953 earthquake could be termed "Caribbean-Tudor"; stone-built ground floors are often preserved, supporting lighter, half-timbered upper stories sheathed in corrugated tin.

Heading down Levkáda's east coast, the little port-resorts of **Lygiá** and **Nikiána**, with pebble coves and fish tavernas, are calmer than **Nydrí** ④, 20km (12 miles) south of Levkáda, opposite a mini-archipelago of four islets. Until the 1970s, it was a tiny fishing village, where Aristotle Onassis used to pop over for dinner from Skorpiós, his private island. Now, Nydrí is a busy package resort despite poor beaches. Some 3km (15 miles) inland, the **Roniés Waterfalls** prove surprisingly impressive, revealing abundant water at the heart of Levkáda. Beyond this stretches a fertile upland, studded by churches with Venetian belfries. The main village here is **Karyá** ❺, its vast central *platía* shaded by several giant plane trees.

Beyond Nydrí, Dorpfeld, the German archaeologist, excavated at Stenó and is buried on the far side of sumpy Vlyhó bay. The island ring road curls past **Mikrós Gialós** and **Sývota** bays before descending to **Vassilikí** ❻, 40km (25 miles) from town, one of Europe's premier windsurfing resorts. Beyond Cape Levkátas (Ákra Doukáto) – from where Sappho legendarily leaped to her death – lie spectacular west-coast beaches, accessible by roads of varying steepness. **Pórto Kátsíki** ❼ stars on every third postcard of Levkáda; **Egremní** and **Gialós** are less frequented but nearly as good, while panoramic **Atháni** village has the closest tourist facilities. Further on, **Drymónas** has the best rural architecture, while **Kalamítsi** has an eponymous beach and "shares" **Káthisma**, Levkáda's longest, with **Ágios Nikítas** (**Aï Nikítas**) ❽. The only port actually on the west coast has become its main resort, worth avoiding in peak season.

Itháki (Ithaca)

Most boats dock at the main town, **Vathý** ❾, at the end of a deeply inset bay. The town was badly damaged by an earthquake in 1953, but much has been restored. The attractive harbour front is known for its huge number of tavernas. To the south of the town are a number of sites supposedly associated with events in Homer's Odyssey. These include the **Arethoúsa Spring,** the **Cave of the Nymphs** and, near the port of **Píso Aetós,** ancient **Alalkomenes.** Above Píso Aetós is the

island's deserted medieval capital of **Perahóri** (only a few derelict buildings to see now). The route across the isthmus and along the west coast to the villages of **Léfki** and **Stavrós** in the northern half of the island is particularly beautiful.

Stavrós ❿ is a pleasant but undistinguished town above the west-coast beach and port at **Pólis**. Remains of the island's oldest settlement are on **Pelikáta hill** here. A road winds up past the little hill-village of **Exogí** to a chapel, from where there are spectacular views over the bay of **Afáles**. Another road from Stavrós leads to **Platrithiás,** which also has Mycenean remains. The two lovely port villages of **Fríkes** and **Kióni** are lovely places to stay, but very popular.

Kefaloniá (Cephalonia)

Kefaloniá is the largest and second most mountainous of the Ionian Islands. It holds the highest peak in the island chain, **Mount Énos** ⓫ (1,628 metres/5,340ft), whose summit is set aside as a national park to preserve the native Cephalonian fir.

Italianate church in Levkáda Town.

Argostóli ⓬, the island's capital, is on the west coast on the large Argostóli Gulf. Almost completely destroyed in the huge 1953 earthquake, it has now been rebuilt and is a convenient base from which to explore. The town itself has a few attractions – a small but well-laid-out **archaeological museum** (temporarily closed for renovation), the fascinating **Korgialenios Museum** (Mon 9am–noon, 6–9pm, Tue–Fri 9am–2pm, 6–9pm, Sat 10am–4pm), with its exhibits of bourgeois island life, and the **Fokas-Kosmetatou Foundation** (www.focas-cosmetatos.gr; May–Oct Mon–Fri 10am–2pm), in a beautifully restored neoclassical mansion, displaying mainly antique furniture, paintings and lithographs.

Just south of Argostóli is **Votanókypos Kefaloniás** (Cephalonia Botanica; www.focas-cosmetatos.gr; May–Oct Mon–Sat 9am–2pm), a botanical garden set in an old olive grove which aims to preserve rare species from the island's flora. Further south, across the Livathó plain, are the ruins of the island's Venetian capital, **Ágios Geórgios** (Tue–Sun 8.30am–3.30pm), perched on a hill above the village of Peratáta. The views from the citadel's ramparts are fabulous.

To the north of Argostóli are the ***katavóthres*** ("sea mills"), where seawater runs down holes and under the whole island to Melissáni Cave. Although now just a trickle, before the 1953 earthquake, the flow was strong enough to power flour mills. Heading south from Argostóli, there are more fine beaches, beginning with Makrýs and Platýs Gialós at **Lássi** ⓭, Kefaloniá's largest resort, then round the south coast via Trapezáki and Lourdáta all the way to **Kateliós** and **Skála** ⓮. Here, some impressive mosaics lie within the foundations of a Roman villa (summer Tue–Sun 9am–3pm; free).

Lixoúri ⓯ on the Pallíki Peninsula on the western side of the Argostóli Gulf, can be reached by a frequent car ferry from Argostóli. The town itself is rather sleepy, but the **museum and library** (currently closed for repairs after being damaged by an earthquake) are worth a look. South of Lixoúri, across the earthquake-ruptured plain of Katogís, are the wonderful red sand beaches of **Mégas Lákkos** and **Xí.**

*Popular Andísamos
beach.*

Beyond Xí is **Kounopétra**, the huge boulder that used to rock on its base until the 1953 earthquake set it still. The beautiful fine-pebble beach at **Petaní** is in the northwest of the peninsula.

The spectacular road that crosses the island north of Mount Énos brings you to the monastery of Ágios Gerásimou 16 (daily 7am–1pm, 3–9pm; free), which has an impressive main sanctuary and underground cave where the saint meditated. Next door is the Robola winery, and the road then leads to the port of **Sámi**. The harbour and the wonderful nearby beach of **Andísamos** were used as locations in the filming of *Captain Corelli's Mandolin*, the book of which was set on the island.

Close by Sámi are the caves of **Melissáni** and **Drogaráti**. The **Melissáni Cave** ⑯ (May–Oct daily 9am–7pm, Nov–Apr Thu, Sat, Sun 10am–4pm) is an underground lake with part of the roof open to the sky; when the sun shines down on the water, it becomes a bright translucent blue. The large chamber of **Drogaráti** (summer only daily 8am–8pm) is decorated with hundreds of stalactites and stalagmites. The

A reminder that Captain Corelli's Mandolin was filmed in Kefaloniá.

main road south from Sámi leads to the faded resort of Póros and the excavated Mycenean tholos tomb at **Tzanáta.**

The northern part of Kefaloniá comprises sheer mountains whose cliffs fall precipitously to the sea, as well as pretty villages that largely escaped the 1953 earthquake. The west-coast road is a spectacular, if rather worrying, ride. The famous beach at **Mýrtos** looks impressive from above but consists of coarse pebbles and has a dangerous undertow. Further north is the perfect horseshoe harbour of **Ássos** ⑰. On the

Melissáni is an underground lake.

CORELLI'S MANDOLIN

Set on Kefaloniá during World War II and after, this novel quickly acquired word-of-mouth bestseller status, but is not so popular with the islanders themselves. Greek Left intellectuals and surviving Italian partisans were unimpressed by its anti-Communist stance and disparaging portrayal of ELAS (the Greek People's Liberation Army). The ensuing furore meant that de Bernières had to eat humble pie. It also seems the novel was closely based on the experiences of Amos Pampaloni, an Italian artillery captain on Kefaloniá in 1942–44 who later joined ELAS, and who accused de Bernières of distorting the roles of both Italians and ELAS on the island. The Greek translation was abridged to avoid causing offence, and the film was watered down to a pallid love story as a condition for filming on the island.

isthmus leading to a large hill rising sharply out of the sea is a large 16th-century Venetian fort. However, the island's most upmarket resort is the small port of **Fiskárdo** ⑱, slightly too pretty and popular as a yachting harbour for its own good. There are many wonderful small pebble beaches, many of them backed by cypress trees, all around this northern part of the island.

Zákynthos (Zante)

Dubbed "Zante, Fior di Levante" by the Venetians, the central plain and eastern hills of Zákynthos still support luxuriant vegetation. The south and east coasts shelter excellent beaches, some almost undeveloped, others home to rampant and unsavoury tourism. The once-elegant harbour town of **Zákynthos** ⑲ was rebuilt after the 1953 earthquake in the same style, and though not quite convincingly Venetian, the atmosphere is still pleasant. At the southern end of the harbour is the church of **Ágios Dionýsios** (daily 8am–1pm, 5–10pm), the island's patron saint, rebuilt after an earthquake in 1893 and again in 1948. It

Glitzy Fiskárdo port at dusk.

has a very opulent interior with lots of gold and superb colourful murals.

At the harbour's northern end is Platía Solomoú, surrounding which are the town's other main attractions: the church of **Ágios Nikólaos tou Mólou** (no fixed hours), the huge Byzantine **Museum** (Tue–Sun 8.30am–3pm) with its glorious 17th- and 18th-century paintings; and, tucked behind on Platía Márkou, the **Museum of Solomos and Eminent Zakynthians** (daily 8.30am–3pm), chiefly dedicated to the poet Dionysios Solomos. Above the town is the Venetian fort at **Bóhali** (Tue–Sun July–Oct 8am–7pm, Nov–June 8.30am–3pm) with a very attractive pine-filled interior and wonderful views.

At the southeastern tip of the island is the beautiful **Vasilikós Peninsula,** location of some of the better beaches on the island. The best of these is **Gérakas** on its eastern side. However, the beaches on Laganás Bay are some of the last few nesting sites of the Mediterranean loggerhead turtle. As the majority of visitors to the island are flown into the brash and raucous resort of **Laganás**, there is an agglomeration of hotels, restaurants and bars, fast-food joints and clubs along this coast, severely endangering the survival of the turtles. In response, the **National Marine Park of Zákynthos** has been set up, encompassing the whole gulf between capes Gérakas to Kerí. All affected beaches have wardens to protect the nests, dusk-to-dawn curfews, and boating and land access are restricted.

The broad central plain is the most fertile region in the Ionians and is given over to intensive agriculture. One highlight is the **Skaliá Cultural Centre/ Théatro Avoúri** near Tragáki, a series of stone-built auditoria where storytelling events are held. In the village of Maherádo to the west is the pilgrimage church of Agías Mávras (flexible opening), with its ornate gilded Baroque interior. Over on the east coast are the popular, and slightly tacky, resorts of **Tsiliví** and **Alykés**.

The mountainous west coast is much

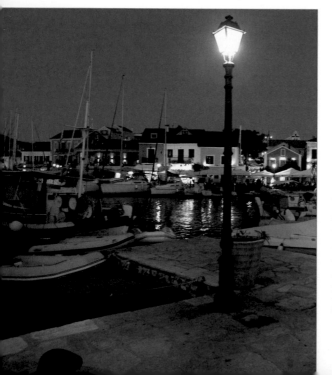

wilder, and sees far fewer tourists. From the cliffs at **Kerí** ⑳, on the southwest peninsula, there are incomparable views of the sea. A string of pretty hill villages runs along the western side of the mountains. The most attractive is **Loúha,** one of the highest settlements on the island, like its neighbours, undamaged by the 1953 tremor. From **Kilioméno,** the road runs north past **Kambí** where a huge cross on a headland commemorates a wartime massacre. Before Kábi, down by the sea is a beautifully situated taverna at **Limniónas** where you can swim off the rocks. Further north, past the monasteries of **Anafonítria** and **Ágios Geórgios ton Krimnón,** is perhaps the Ionians' most iconic tourist sight: the shipwreck at **Navágio Bay** ㉑, surrounded by towering white cliffs. Further on is the mountain village of **Volímes**, noted for its honey and textiles. At the very northern tip of the island (Cape Skinári) are the **Blue Caves** ㉒; sun on the clear water here reflects an iridescent blue on the cave walls (excursions run from the small port of Ágios Nikólaos and Alykés).

Kýthira

The island of **Kýthira** sees at least one ferry boat daily from Gýthion and/or Neápoli, plus occasional sailing from Pireás. Essentially a bleak plateau slashed by well-watered ravines, the island forms part of a sunken landbridge between the Peloponnese and Crete. It shares a history of Venetian and British rule like the other Ionian isles to which it theoretically belongs, although it is now lumped administratively with the Argo-Saronics under Pireás. Architecturally, it's a hybrid of Cycladic and Venetian styles with an Australian accent, courtesy of remittances from the 60,000-odd locals who headed Down Under in the 1950s.

The island does not put itself out for visitors: accommodation is expensive and oversubscribed, the season short, and good tavernas thin on the ground. Yet Kýthira seems increasingly

popular thanks to regular flights from Athens. **Kýthira Town** is also one of the finest island capitals of the Aegean, with medieval mansions and Venetian fortifications. Far below, **Kapsáli** is the yacht berth, though there are better beaches on the east coast, as far as the fishing anchorage of **Avlémonas**. More castles are to be found there and at Venetian **Káto Hóra**, just above **Agía Sofía cavern**, the principal west-coast attraction. In the northeast, the ravine-edge ghost village of **Paleohóra** was the capital from 1248 until 1537, when it failed the pirate-proof test.

The National Marine Park of Zákynthos was set up to protect nesting turtles.

Navágio beach, Zákynthos, is the most photographed in the Ioanians.

Herding sheep in Crete.

TRAVEL TIPS

GREECE

Transport

Getting There **336**
   By Air................................ **336**
   By Sea.............................. **337**
   By Land............................. **337**
Getting Around...................... **337**
   Public Transport **337**
   Private Transport.............. **340**

A – Z

Accommodation **343**
Admission Charges **343**
Budgeting for Your Trip **344**
Business Travellers **344**
Children.................................. **344**
Climate................................... **344**
Crime and Safety.................... **344**
Customs Regulations............. **344**
Disabled Travellers **345**
Embassies and Consulates ... **345**
Entry Requirements **345**
Etiquette **346**
Gay and Lesbian Travellers **346**
Health and Medical Care **346**
Insurance............................... **347**
Internet **347**
Media **347**
Money **348**
Opening Hours........................ **348**
Photography **348**
Postal Services....................... **348**
Religious Services **349**
Student Travellers.................. **349**
Telecoms................................ **349**
Tipping................................... **349**
Toilets.................................... **349**
Tourist Information **349**
Websites **350**
Weights and Measures **350**

What to Bring.......................... **350**
Women Travellers................... **350**

Language

The Greek Language **351**
   Pronunciation tips.............. **351**
Communication **351**
Telephone Calls **352**
In the Hotel **352**
At a Bar or Café..................... **352**
In a Restaurant....................... **352**
Food **352**
   Mezédes/Orektiká............. **352**
   Meat Dishes **353**
   Seafood **353**
   Vegetables.......................... **353**
   Fruit.................................... **353**
   Basic Foods/Desserts **353**
Sightseeing............................ **353**
   At the Shops....................... **353**
Travelling................................ **354**
   Public Transport **354**
   Directions **354**
   On the Road **354**
Times and Dates.................... **354**
Health..................................... **354**

Further Reading

Ancient History and Culture ... **355**
Byzantine History and Culture **355**
Anthropology and Culture **355**
Cuisine **355**
Modern History **355**
Modern Greek Literature........ **356**
Foreign Writers in/on Greece ..**356**
Regional and
   Archaeological Guides....... **357**
Botanical Field Guides **357**
Other Insight Guides **357**

TRANSPORT

GETTING THERE AND GETTING AROUND

Greek customs.

GETTING THERE

By Air

Greece has good air connections with the rest of the world and is serviced by numerous international airlines. Charter flights generally operate from early May to the end of October, even into November to Rhodes and Crete. Nowadays, unless you're on a multi-stop or round-the-world ticket, e-tickets bought online are the norm. The airlines' own websites can be

a good source of discount tickets, matching (or nearly so) the prices offered by general websites like Expedia, Momondo and Fly.com.

The majority of scheduled airline passengers travelling to Greece make Athens' Eleftherios Venizelos Airport their point of entry, though a number of services (from the rest of Europe only) arrive at Thessaloníki's Macedonia Airport, Rhodes, Corfu and Iráklio/Haniá, Crete.

Getting from Athens airport to central Athens and Piraeus

Between Eleftherios Venizelos Airport at Spáta, central Athens and Piraeus, there are various connecting services. Line 3 of the metro takes you – surprisingly slowly, from 6.30am to 11.30pm – into town for €10. Alternatively, take the X95 express bus all the way to central Sýndagma Square (every 15–20 minutes), or the X96 express bus to Pireás port (every 30 minutes). The Piraeus terminus for the X96 bus is all the way anticlockwise around the port, at Aktí Vassiliádi, near gates E1 and E2, however, it does make stops all along the quay in each direction. Tickets for both the X95 and the X96 cost €6 for a single journey; the express buses run around the clock, though with long gaps between midnight and 6am.

A taxi from Venizelos Airport into Athens will cost €35–50 depending on the time of day/night and your final destination, but includes airport supplement and per-bag fee. Even using the Attikí Odós, the toll highway into Athens, the journey time can still amount to over an hour; the same is true for trips to Piraeus via the coastal suburbs.

Getting to Thessaloníki from Macedonia Airport

Macedonia Airport is 15km (9 miles) southeast of Thessaloníki. Regular buses go to the city centre (€1, coin-machine-sold tickets, no change given) and take around 35 minutes. Taxis take 15–20 minutes and cost €10–15.

From Rhodes airport to Rhodes Town

From 6.30am to 11.15pm in season, there is a local bus connection (€2.20) into town. The bus stop is outside the two terminals (turn left out of arrivals). Otherwise, a taxi into town will cost €20–30 depending on number of bags and exact destination.

From Corfu airport to Kérkyra Town

There is no bus service linking the airport with Kérkyra Town. Taxis charge a set, inflated €10 for the short

Useful Airlines Serving Greece from Anglophone Countries

At the moment, there are only guaranteed direct services to Greece from Great Britain and (seasonally) the US. Services from Eire come and go, and there has not been non-stop service from Australia or South Africa in several years.

Aegean Airlines (www.aegeanair.com). Between Athens and London (Heathrow).
British Airways (www.ba.com). Between Athens–Heathrow and Thessaloníki–Gatwick.
Delta Airlines (www.delta.com).

Between New York and Athens, May to October only.
easyJet (www.easyjet.com). Between various UK airports and Athens, Thessaloníki, Rhodes, Corfu, Kos, Zákynthos, Haniá, Iráklio.

run into town. Pre-booked car rental is so advantageously priced that you should forego their blandishments.

From Crete's main airport to Iráklio

A bus service runs the 5km to and from Platía Eleftherías in the centre of town until late at night.

By Sea

Most visitors entering Greece by sea do so from the west, from Italy. You can catch a boat to Greece from Venice, Ancona and Bari, but the most regular service is from Brindisi. Daily ferry lines (less frequent in the low-season) connect Brindisi with the three main western Greek ports: Corfu, Igoumenítsa and Pátras. Corfu is a 6.5-hour trip; Igoumenítsa 8 hours; and Pátras 11–14 hours, depending on whether you take a direct boat or one that makes stops in Corfu and Igoumenítsa. The "Superfast" ferries between Ancona and Pátras offer an efficient 22-hour crossing.

Igoumenítsa is the ideal port of call for those setting off to see central-western Greece. Pátras is best if you want to head directly to Athens or into the Peloponnese. Regular buses and trains connect Pátras and Athens (4 hours by train, a bit less by bus). If you plan to take your car with you on the boat, you should make reservations well in advance. Otherwise, arriving a few hours before the departure time should suffice, except during peak seasons when booking in advance is essential for seats or berths.

By Land

From Europe It is no longer possible to buy a through train ticket from the UK to Greece, and economically it never made much sense. If, as a railpass holder, you're intent on the journey, consult the ultra-useful rail-travel planning website www.seat61.com.

From Asia via Turkey If you are travelling strictly overland to Greece from Asia you will pass through

Italy–Greece Ferries

Agoudimos – www.aferry.co.uk
ANEK – www.anek.gr
Endeavor Lines – no English website
Minoan Lines – www.minoan.gr
Superfast/Blue Star – www.superfast.gr
Ventouris – www.ventouris.gr
www.goferry.gr – a good consolidator/overview site

Landing at Corfu airport.

Istanbul and cross into Greece at the Évros River. The best way to do this is by car or bus. The road is good and the journey from Istanbul to Thessaloníki takes approximately 15 hours; several bus companies serve the route.

The train has the appeal of following the route of the old Orient Express, with better scenery than the road. But, unless you're a great rail fan, the travel time can be off-putting: 17 hours by the timetables, up to 19 hours in practice, including long halts at the border. However, Greek trains currently do not provide international service from neighbouring countries and are unlikely to in future. You will have to get from Turkey to Kastaniés or Kípi, the first stations on the Greek side of the frontier that still have domestic service towards Thessaloníki, though usually with long layovers at Alexandroúpoli.

Another popular option is to take one of the small boats between western Turkish ports and select Greek islands just opposite. Fares are overpriced for the distance involved, but it is undeniably convenient. The most reliable links are from Çesme to Híos (runs all year), Bodrum to Kos (the cheapest crossing) and Kuşadasi to Sámos (no cars carried).

GETTING AROUND

Public Transport

By air

Flying is considerably more expensive than travelling by boat, bus or train, though still reasonable when compared to the price of domestic flights in other countries. For example, the 50-minute propeller-plane flight between Athens and Sámos costs anywhere from €55 to €130 one way – fares are deregulated, and pitched on a demand basis.

There are currently too many airlines in the Greek skies for the size of the market and health of the local economy. In 2013 Olympic Air became a subsidiary of Aegean Airlines. The best, most current sources of discount tickets on extant Greek airlines are the local travel sites www.airtickets.gr, www.travelplanet24.com and www.viva.gr. Foreign credit or debit cards may be viewed with some suspicion, so keep your mobile switched on when booking in case somebody wants to ring you to confirm your identity. Leave plenty of leeway in your domestic flight arrangements if you have to be back in Athens for an international flight. Island flights are often fully booked over the summer, so book these at least a month in advance. Seats bought from a travel agency or one of the very few walk-in offices for any of the airlines listed below are subject to extra surcharges.

By bus

A vast network of bus routes spreads across Greece: the KTEL is a syndicate of bus companies whose buses are cheap and generally punctual, though rural depopulation has meant that schedules on many routes have been thinned or axed completely. KTEL buses on the more idiosyncratic rural routes often have a distinct personal touch, their drivers decorating and treating the bus with great respect. Bus tickets should be secured in advance at the stations for major routes, where seats often sell out. On minor village routes, tickets are dispensed on the bus by the conductor.

In the larger cities, there may be different KTEL stations for different destinations. Travelling from Thessaloníki to Halkidikí, for example, you will leave from a remote eastern station, though all other destinations are served by the more modern unitary terminal. Athens has two terminals, while Iráklio in Crete has three.

City buses

Most of the regular Athens blue-and-white buses are now modern, air-conditioned vehicles, and using them is much less of an ordeal than it used to be. They are still usually overcrowded, and the routes are a mystery even to residents. Trolley buses, with an overhead pantograph, are marginally faster and more frequent. Most services run until nearly midnight. Ticketing can be a trap for the unwary. Plain clothes ticket inspectors will levy fines of 60 times the basic fare for travelling with the wrong ticket, a ticket that hasn't been validated, or no ticket.

There are several kinds of tickets: a 90-minute ticket (€1.40) allowing transfers, which must be validated again before your last journey; a day pass valid for all urban transport methods (currently €4.40, valid 24hr from validation) and a one-week ticket good for seven days from validation. Tickets are only obtainable from a seemingly dwindling network of newsagent kiosks – most can no longer be bothered to sell them – or at booths run by the bus company itself.

The most useful suburban services for tourists are the orange-and-white

Island-hopping by ferry is a popular choice.

KTEL Attica buses going from 14 Mavromatéon Street, Pédio tou Áreos Park, to Rafína (an alternative ferry port for the Cyclades and northeast Aegean), Lávrio (the port for Kéa) and Soúnio (for the famous Poseidon temple there).

Rural buses

In the countryside and on islands, buses can be converted school buses or modern coaches, or even pick-up trucks with seats installed in the payload space to transport tourists. Some drivers ricochet through mountain roads at death-defying speeds; bus accidents, however, appear to be rare. Just stow your luggage carefully to be on the safe side.

On islands, a bus of some description will usually meet arriving ferries (even if a boat is delayed) to transport passengers up the hill to the island's *hóra*, or capital. Bus stops are usually in main squares

or by the waterfront in harbours, and vehicles may or may not run to schedule.

A conductor dispenses tickets on the bus itself; often the fare required and the ticket will not show the same price, with the lower old price over-stamped. This isn't a con, but merely a practice – bus companies use pre-printed tickets until the supply is gone, which may take several years.

By metro, tram and suburban trains

The Athens metro system has halved travel times around the city and made a visible reduction in surface traffic. It runs from 5.30am to 12.30am Sun–Thu, 5.30am–2.30am Fri–Sat, subject to strikes and staff availability. The stations themselves are palatial and squeaky-clean, with advertising placards kept to a minimum. The old ISAP electric line, in existence since the 1930s, has been refurbished and designated Line 1 (green on maps); it links Piraeus with Kifisiá via the city centre. Line 2 (red) links Agios Dimítrios in the south with Agios Andónios in the northwest of town, with extensions works underway down to Glyfáda and up to Thivón. Line 3 (blue) joins Egáleo with the airport at Spáta, via Monastiráki. The main junction stations are Omónia, Sýndagma and Monastiráki.

A single journey on the metro is €1.40 – though it does entitle you to a transfer or two onto above-ground transport within 90 minutes. Alternatively, get a day or week pass

Greek Domestic Airlines

Olympic tel: 801 11 44 444, www.olympicair.com Still possesses the largest route network, including services to obscure islands. 20-kilo baggage allowance.
Aegean tel: 801 11 20 000, www.aegeanair.com/en Cherry-picks the more profitable domestic routes. 20-kilo baggage allowance.
Sky Express tel: 801 11 28 28 88, www.skyexpress.gr Based on Crete, with useful peripheral flights from Iráklio to other islands plus

the mainland. Very expensive, though, and paltry 12-kilo luggage allowance with no carry-ons allowed in principle.
Astra tel: 2310 489390, www.astra-airlines.gr Based in Thessaloníki, with select routes across the country.
Ellinair tel: 2311 224700, www.ellinair.com Based in Thessaloníki, with service to eight domestic airports throughout Greece.

from the attended ticket windows (you're encouraged to use the coin-op machines for simple tickets). As on the buses, plain clothes inspectors do a roaring trade in fines levied against fare dodgers.

There are also three tram lines: Néos Kósmos metro station to Agios Kosmás, Glyfáda to Néo Fáliro, and Sýndagma to Glyfáda. Single tickets on this cost €1.40. Daily and weekly cards are valid on these too.

Thessaloníki has begun construction of its own metro/light rail system, but inauguration is several years away.

Around Athens, there is a network of suburban or proastyakó trains, which most usefully gets you from the town centre to Kiáto in the Peloponnese, where you change platforms for the "real" onward train to Pátra.

By train

We hesitate to write much about Greek trains under present circumstances. Grossly overstaffed, the state railway organisation – OSE in Greek – has been awash in red ink for years, and the troïka of aid lenders would like nothing better than to compel closure of the whole network. Up to now, most Peloponnesian lines (except for Athens–Pátra, with a change at Kiáto, and the rack-and-pinion railway between Diakoftó and Kalávryta) have been axed, as have all mainland peripheral services and international departures to Turkey, FYROM and Bulgaria. Main lines currently running, and likely to survive albeit at reduced

frequencies, are those from Athens to Kalambáka (for the Metéora), Athens to Halkída, and Athens to Thessaloníki, as well as Thessaloníki to Alexandroúpoli.

Train travel is cheaper than the bus, and more comfortable, especially if you get an overnight sleeper to/ from Thessaloníki. In Pátra, the station is conveniently opposite the ferry docks. Trains are usually slower than the equivalent bus route. However, you can speed things up by taking an Intercity express train if you're willing to pay a considerable surcharge. Austerity or no, there should still be a significant discount for round-trip tickets. Students and people under 26 are usually eligible for more discounts. All the common railpasses are honoured in Greece, though you may still have to pay certain supplements and queue for seat reservations.

OSE has a schedule and purchase website – http://tickets.trainose.gr/dromologia/ – though even the English option has plenty of Greek script strewn about it; if you can't find a Greek person to help you, you're best off heading down to the station to buy in person.

By sea

Ferries

Piraeus is the nerve centre of the Greek ferry network, and chances are you will pass through it at least once; in roughly diminishing order of importance, Rafína, Thessaloníki, Lávrio, Vólos, Ágios Konstandínos, Igoumenítsa, Pátra, Kyllíni, Kavála,

Kalamáta and Gýthio are also mainland ferry ports. In high season, routes vary from "milk runs" stopping at five islands en route to your destination, to "express" (semi-) direct ones, so it is worth shopping around before purchasing your ticket. It is also advisable not to purchase your ticket too far in advance: very rarely do tickets for the boat ride actually sell out – this does, however, happen around Easter, from mid-August to early September, and around election times – but there are frequent changes to schedules which may leave you trying to get a refund.

Personalised ticketing for all boats has long been the rule; it is no longer possible to purchase tickets on board, though you can upgrade your class of travel. The only exceptions are a few of the RO-RO short-haul ferries (eg Igoumenítsa-Levkímmi, Páros–Andíparos).

When you buy your ticket, get detailed instructions on how to find its berth – the Piraeus quays are long and convoluted. The staff who take your ticket should make sure you are on the right boat.

Above all, be flexible when travelling the Greek seas. Apart from schedule changes, a bad stretch of weather can keep you island-bound for as long as the wind blows. Strikes, too, are often called during the summer, and usually last for a few days. Out on the islands in particular, the best way to secure accurate, up-to-the-minute information on the erratic ways of ferries is to contact the Port Authority *(limenarhío)*, which monitors the movements of individual boats. Port Authority offices are usually located on the waterfront of each island's principal harbour, away from the cafés. Boats are often very late arriving – to avoid wasting time around the dock, track the real-time progress of your ferry on the live shipping map at www.marinetraffic.com.

If you are travelling by car, especially during the high season, you will have to plan much further ahead because during the peak season, car space is sometimes booked many weeks in advance. The same applies to booking a cabin for an overnight trip during summer.

Gamma class – also known as deck, tourist or third – is the classic, cheap way to voyage the Greek seas. There is usually a seat of one sort or another (you may have to pay a bit extra for a numbered seat) –

Entering Ermoúpli harbour.

though in the newer generations of boats, very limited deck space. If the weather turns bad, you can always go inside to the "low-class" lounge or the snack bar.

Catamarans/"high speeds"

Fleets of sleek new "high speed" ferries or true catamarans, made in France or Scandanavia, are steadily edging out most ordinary craft (as a stroll around the quays at Piraeus will confirm). They have some advantages over hydrofoils – they can be even faster, most of them carry lots of cars, and they're permitted to sail in wind conditions of up to Force 7, whereas "dolphins" are confined to port at 6.

The bad news: there are usually no cabins (because they mostly finish their runs before midnight), food service is even worse than on the old ferries and there are no exterior decks. The aeroplane-seating salons are ruthlessly air-

Ferry/Catamaran/Hydrofoil Timetables

The best schedule resource is the website of the GTP (Greek Travel Pages), www.gtp.gr, which is fairly accurate, with updates at least every few weeks.

Alternatively, major tourist information offices (Rhodes, Iráklio, etc) supply a weekly schedule, and most offices hang a timetable in a conspicuous place so you can look up times even if the branch is closed. This should, however, not

conditioned and subject to a steady, unavoidable barrage of banal Greek TV on overhead monitors (even in *diakikriméni* or "distinguished" class). Cars cost roughly the same to convey as on the old-style boats, but seats are priced at hydrofoil levels. Fuel consumption on such craft is horrendous; they only turn a profit when at least three-quarters full, and

be relied on implicitly – you may miss your boat. In general, for the most complete and up-to-date information on each port's sailings the best source is the Port Police (in Piraeus and most other ports), known as the *limenarhío*.

Be aware that when you enquire about ferries at a travel agent, they will sometimes inform you only of the lines for which they sell tickets.

seem to spend much of their time at half-throttle.

Catamarans come in all shapes and sizes, from the 300-car-carrying behemoths of nel Lines in the north-east Aegean, Cyclades and central Dodecanese, to the tiny Sea Star in the Dodecanese. The far more useful *Dodekanisos Express* and *Dodekanisos Pride* serve more of the Dodecanese, and can take five cars each.

Hydrofoils

Like catamarans, hydrofoils are more than twice as fast as the ferries and about twice as expensive but, as ex-Polish or ex-Russian river craft, are not really designed for the Aegean, and prone to cancellation in bad weather conditions.

Hydrofoils (nicknamed *delfínia* or "dolphins" in Greek) connect Piraeus with most of the Argo-Saronic region (Égina, Angístri, Póros, Ýdra and Spétses), as well as Vólos and the three northerly Sporades (Alónisos, Skiáthos, Skópelos). In the northeast Aegean, there are local, peak-season services between Thásos and the mainland, while in the Dodecanese all the islands between Sámos and Kos, inclusive, are served between May and October only.

Phone numbers for the few surviving hydrofoil companies are constantly engaged, or spew out only pre-recorded information in rapid-fire Greek, so the best strategy is to approach the embarkation booths in person. In Piraeus, these are on Aktí Miaoúli quay, in Kavála right at the kink in the quay. At Vólos, apply to the gatehouse for the harbour precinct; elsewhere, tickets are best obtained from travel agents in towns.

How to Get a Taxi in Greece

Taxis in Greece, especially in Athens, merit a guidebook to themselves. There are three stages to the experience.

First: getting a taxi. It's almost impossible at certain times of the day in Athens, and probably worst before the early afternoon meal. When you hail a taxi, try to get in before stating your destination. The drivers are very picky and often won't let you in unless you're going in their direction. If you see an empty taxi, run for it, be aggressive – otherwise you'll find that some quick Athenian has beaten you to it. Alternatively, you can ask your hotel to book a cab for you.

Second: the ride. Make sure the taxi meter is on "1" when you start out, and not on "2" – that's the double fare, which is only permitted from midnight to 5am, or outside designated city limits. Once inside, you may find yourself with company. Don't be alarmed. It is traditional practice for drivers to pick up two, three, even four individual riders, provided they're going roughly in the same direction. In these cases, make a note of the meter count when you get in. In fact, because taxis are relatively affordable, they can end up functioning as minibus services.

Third: paying up. If you've travelled with other passengers, make sure you aren't paying for

the part of the trip that happened before you got in. You should pay the difference in meter reading between embarking and alighting, subject to a minimum fare of €3.20. Otherwise, the meter will run from €1.20 (not zero) and tell you the straight price, which may be adjusted according to the tariff that should be on a laminated placard clipped to the dashboard. There are extra charges for each piece of luggage in the boot, for leaving or entering an airport or seaport, plus bonuses around Christmas and Easter.

Some drivers will quote you the correct price, but many others will try to rip you off, especially if it seems that you're a novice. If the fare you're charged is clearly above the correct price, don't hesitate to argue your way, in whichever language, back down to a normal price. Coming out of an airport or seaport waving 50- or 100-euro notes is asking for trouble – always keep small bills and coins handy.

These rules apply more to Athens than to the islands, although it's still necessary to be pretty assertive in Thessaloníki or on Crete and Rhodes.

Various radio taxi services exist in Athens and most other larger towns. They can pick you up within a short time of your call to a central booking number, though there are chunky surcharges for this (at least €2).

Private Transport

Cars

Having a car in rural Greece enables you to reach a lot of otherwise

Athens' Rush Hour

Drive at your peril in Athens during its multiple rush hours (7–9.30am, 2–3pm, 4.30–5.30pm, 8–10pm).

inaccessible corners of the country; however, driving a car in Athens or Thessaloníki is unpleasant and confusing. Tempers run short, while road signs, or warnings of mandatory turning lanes, are practically non-existent or obscured by trees.

EU-registered cars are no longer stamped into your passport on entry to the country, can circulate freely for up to six months, and are exempt from road tax as long as this has been paid in the home country – however, you are not allowed to sell the vehicle. Non-EU/EEA nationals will find that a bizarre litany of rules apply to importing cars, chief among them that you must re-export the car when you depart, or have it sealed by Customs in an off-road facility of your choosing.

Car Hire (Rental)

Hiring a car in Greece is not cheap owing to high insurance premiums and import duties. Prices vary with the type of car, season and length of rental and should include CDW (collision damage waiver) and VAT at 23 percent. Payment can, and often must, be made with a major credit card. You must be at least 21 years old and have a full driving licence (EU/EEA residents) or an international driving permit (all others).

From overseas, you can book a car in advance through websites such as www.comparecarrentals.co.uk, www.skycars.co.uk, www.autoeurope. com and www.auto-europe.co.uk. Only if you're a member of some corporate or other affinity group are you likely to get as good a deal (or better) directly through the websites of major rental chains like Hertz, Avis or Budget.

For a walk-in rental in Athens, many small local agencies are along or near Syngroú Avenue in the Makrygiánni district.

Autorent
Syngroú 11, tel: 210 92 20 821, www.autorent.gr

Avance
Syngroú 40, tel: 210 92 00 100, www.avance.gr

Avanti
Syngroú 50, tel: 210 92 33 919, www.avanti.com.gr

Kosmos
Syngroú 9, tel: 210 92 34 696, www.kosmos-carrental.com

Driving in Greece

All EU/EEA licences, and licences held by returning diaspora Greeks irrespective of issuing country, are honoured in Greece. Conversely, all other licences – this includes North American and Australian ones – are invalid, as many tourists from those nations attempting to hire cars have discovered to their cost. These motorists must obtain an international driving permit before departure (issued by the AAA or CAA in North America on the spot for a nominal cost); the Greek Automobile and Touring Club (ELPA) no longer issues them to foreign nationals in Greece. Similarly, with the advent of the single European market, insurance Green Cards are no longer required, though you should check with your home insurer about the need for any supplementary premiums – many policies now include pan-European cover anyway.

Greek traffic control and signals are basically the same as in the rest of continental Europe, though roundabouts are handled bizarrely by French or English standards – in many cases, the traffic entering from the slip road, not that already in the circle, has the right of way – watch for "stop" or "yield" signs or invariably faded pavement markings.

Motorways speeds are routinely in excess of the nominal 100–120 kph (62–75 mph) limits, and drivers overtake with abandon. A red light is often considered not so much an obligation as a suggestion, and oncoming drivers flashing lights at you on one-lane roads means the opposite of what it does in the UK. Here, it means: "I'm coming through" (although sometimes it can mean "Beware! Police checkpoint ahead"). Greece has the highest accident rate in the pre-2004 EU after Portugal, so drive defensively.

Greece has a mandatory seatbelt law (stiff fine for violators), and children under 10 are not allowed to sit in the front seat. It is an offence to drive without your licence on your person (this incurs a stiff fine). Every car must also carry a first-aid kit in the boot (though hire companies tend to skimp on this). Police checkpoints at major (and minor) junctions are frequent, and in addition to the above offences, you can be done for not having evidence of insurance, paid road tax or registration papers in/on the vehicle. If it's clear you've no fixed residence in Greece, your licence may be confiscated and held to ransom at the nearest police station pending

payment of the fine (within 10 working days).

Super and normal unleaded petrol, as well as lead-substitute super and diesel, are readily available throughout Greece, though filling up after dark can be difficult off the main intercity highways. Most filling stations close around 8pm and, although a rota system operates in larger towns, it is often difficult to determine which station is open. Credit cards are widely accepted, but always ask first – card-swiping machines are mysteriously "broken".

Road maps

Gone are the days when visitors had to suffer with mendacious or comical maps which seemed based more on wishful thinking (especially projected but unbuilt roads) than facts on the ground. There are now three commercial Greek companies producing largely accurate maps to the Greek mainland, mountain areas and islands: Terrain (www.terrainmaps.gr), MapGreece (www.mapgreece.gr) and Anavasi (www.anavasi.gr). They can be found country-wide, in tourist-shop racks and better bookshop chains like Newsstand or Papasotiriou. Anavasi has its own convenient shop in central Athens at Voulís 32, selling some of the other two companies' products as well.

Motorcycles, quad-bikes and bicycles

On most Greek islands and in many mainland tourist areas, you'll find agencies that hire small motorcycles, various types of scooters of 50cc to 100cc displacement, and even mountain bikes. These give you the freedom to wander where you will, and weekly rates are reasonable.

Breakdowns

The Greek Automobile Association (ELPA) offers a breakdown service for motorists, which is free to AA/RAC members (production of their membership cards).

Phone 10400 for assistance nationwide. Some car-hire companies have agreements instead with competitors Hellas Service (tel: 1057), Interamerican (tel: 1168) or Express Service (tel: 1154), but these national call centres can be slow to dispatch aid. Always ring a local garage number if this is what the hire company instructs you to do.

For any scooter, even just 50cc, helmets and a motorcycle driving licence are both theoretically required, and increasingly these rules are enforced. The ill-fitting helmets offered are a bit of a joke, but if you refuse them you may have to sign a waiver absolving the dealer of criminal/civil liability – and police checkpoints can be zealous, levying stiff fines (nearly €200) on locals and visitors alike. Having only a car licence while driving a scooter will get you another, steeper fine. Many rental agencies now refuse to give out scooters to folk without the requisite licence, steering them to quad bikes instead – which accounts for their sudden popularity. They are unstable on turns (thus helmets are handed out for riding them too) and arguably the stupidest looking road conveyance ever devised – they're basically modified tractors – but given the two-wheeler licence law, you may not have another choice.

Before you set off, make sure the bike of whichever sort works by taking it for a test spin down the street. Brakes in particular are sometimes badly set (too loose), lights may need new fuses or bulbs, and spark-plugs get fouled. Otherwise, you may get stuck with a lemon, with the added insult of being held responsible for its malfunctioning when you return it.

Reputable agencies now often furnish you with a phone number for a breakdown pick-up service, or will come and fetch you themselves.

Above all, don't take unnecessary chances, like riding two on a bike designed for one. More than one holiday in Greece has been ruined by a serious scooter accident –

Hiring a boat can be an option.

hospital casualty wards are wearily familiar with "road rash". It is strongly suggested that, where possible, you stick with the traditional, manual-transmission Honda/Yamaha/Suzuki scooters of 50–100cc, with skinny, large-radius, well-treaded tyres. The new generation of automatic, button-start *mihanákia/papákia* (as they're called in Greek slang), with their sexy fairings and tiny, fat, no-tread tyres, look the business but are unstable and unsafe once off level asphalt. In particular, if you hit a gravel-strewn curve on one of these, you will go for a spill, and at the very least lose most of the skin on your hands and knees.

Balloon-tire pedal-bike hire is widely practised on flat Kos, with its extensive network of cycle paths. It's also known around Rhodes Town, but not especially recommendable anywhere else. On the more mountainous islands and parts of the mainland, mountain bikes are often hired as part of organised 'safaris'.

Yacht charter

Chartering a yacht is one of the more glamorous ways of island-hopping in Greece. It is by no means cheap, although hiring a boat with a group of friends may not far exceed the price of renting rooms every night for the same number of people.

Depending on your nautical qualifications and your taste for autonomy, you can either take the helm yourself or let a hired crew do so for you. There are over a thousand yachts available for charter in Greece, all of which are registered and inspected by the Ministry of the Merchant Marine. Charter is best done in advance from overseas, through the aegis of agencies like

Cruises

Apparently, one in six of all visitors to Greece embarks on an Aegean cruise. These cruises can range from simple one-day trips to the Saronic Gulf islands close to Athens and Piraeus, to luxury multi-day journeys taking in part of the Turkish coast, Rhodes and Crete. Many people opt for a seven-day excursion, which offers an opportunity to see a couple of islands in the Cyclades, a few of the Dodecanese islands, and a foray over to Istanbul or Ephesus for good measure.

One company that offers a fine alternative to the mega-gin-palaces that ply the Aegean is Seafarer (UK tel: 020 83243117, www.seafarercruises.com), with five thoughtful itineraries, some on 8-passengers yachts, in the Ionian Sea, around the Cyclades, through the Dodecanese, and touching on Turkey. UK-based **Swan Hellenic Cruises** (UK tel: 01858 898 281; www.swanhellenic.com) offer upmarket, all-inclusive holidays on large luxury liners, with guest speakers instructing passengers on anything from archaeology to marine biology.

Nautilus (www.neilson.co.uk) and Sunsail (www.sunsail.com).

Kaïkia and taxi boats

Apart from conventional ferries, most of which carry cars, there are swarms of small *kaïkia* (caïques) which, in season, offer inter-island excursions pitched mostly at day-trippers. Since they are chartered by travel agencies, they are exempt from Ministry of Transport fare controls – as well as the rule that vessels over 35 years old should be scrapped, which is (haphazardly) enforced in Greece for scheduled ferries – and can be very pricey if used as a one-way ticket from, say, Sámos to Pátmos. The stereotypical emergency transfer by friendly fisherman is, alas, largely a thing of the past; never comfortable at the best of times, it is now highly illegal. Knowing this, skippers quote exorbitant prices if approached, and must undertake the journey when the port policeman's gaze is averted.

On many islands where there are remote beaches with poor overland access – most notably Sými, Itháki, Alónisos, Skiáthos, Hálki – local taxi boats provide a fairly pricey shuttle service.

EΛTA
Hellenic Post

A – Z

TRANSPORT

A HANDY SUMMARY
OF PRACTICAL INFORMATION

A

Accommodation

There is a broad range of accommodation in Greece, from deluxe hotels to backpacker hostels. Listed are a sample of different categories across the country.

On the Islands and in many parts of the mainland, the main type of affordable lodging is private rented rooms (*domátia*) and, increasingly common these days, self-catering studios or apartments (*diamerísmata*). These are classified separately from hotels, but also subject to official regulation.

In general, when looking for any kind of accommodation, local tourist offices or the Tourist Police can be of help if you're in a fix – most obviously if no rooms are on offer when you disembark at the dock. "Tourist offices", however, are rarely official and rarely disinterested. The best system, really, is booking a room yourself a few days (or weeks, or months) in advance on the internet.

In popular mass-market resorts like the north coast of Crete, Kos, Corfu, Skiáthos and Zákynthos, many beach side hotels have commitment contracts with overseas package-holiday operators and are barely (if at all) interested in walk-in custom. However, with the demise of many northern European travel companies and the rise of no-frills airlines, smart accommodation proprietors are going back to courting on-spec individual bookings.

Hotel Categories

The Greek authorities have six categories for hotels; this is currently expressed through a star system (no star = basic; five-star = deluxe). This has supposedly replaced an older letter-based categorisation (E to A, plus deluxe), though there are still some hoteliers resisting the change. Although the number of stars is supposed to reflect a hotel's quality, a conference hall, swimming pool or tennis court could place an establishment in the three-star or four-star bracket even though in every other respect – specifically room appointments – it has indifferent facilities. Also, the number of rooms can limit the maximum rating, so you commonly encounter 20-room three-star hotels which are superior in every respect to a nearby 50-room four-star hotel.

Monastery Stays

Monasteries and convents can occasionally provide lodging for travellers of the appropriate gender, though their xenónes (guest lodges) are multi-bedded rooms intended primarily for Orthodox pilgrims. Mt Áthos, of course, has a long tradition of this hospitality – for men only; see page 219 for details on how to obtain a permit to go there. You will have to dress and behave appropriately. The doors may close as early as sunset and some kind of donation may be expected.

Youth Hostels

Greece has a very limited number of official, YHA-affiliated youth hostels for which you theoretically need a youth hostel card. However, you can often buy a YHA card on the spot or just pay an additional charge for the night. There are surviving hostels in Athens, Olymbía and Thessaloníki, and on Santoríni plus Crete at Iráklio, Réthymno, and Plakiás. There is also private, unaffiliated backpacker accommodation of varying quality and repute in Athens, Pátra and on Rhodes and Corfu.

Traditional Settlements

Traditional settlements (*paradosiakí ikismí*) are villages that have been recognised by the Greek government as forming an important part of the national heritage and have been protected from modern intrusions and constructions by law. Almost all of these inns are now in private hands.

Camping

Those who want to stay at organised campsites will find them all over Greece; these are all privately owned. The most beautiful campsites in Greece, however, are usually ones you find on your own. While in most places it is officially illegal just to lay out your sleeping bag or pitch a tent, if you're discreet you will rarely be bothered. That always means asking permission from the owners if you seem to be on private property, patronising nearby businesses and leaving the place looking better than it did when you arrived.

In the mountains, camping is the rule as few alpine refuges are staffed, but even here you should get the local shepherds' consent if they're around.

Admission Charges

Most archaeological sites and museums, public or private, have admission charges varying from €2 for minor affairs up to €20 for stellar attractions. Occasionally (as in Athens and Rhodes) you can get a joint ticket covering several sites and museums at an advantageous price. From November to March, most state-run sites give free admission to EU nationals on Sunday; Monday or Tuesday are the typical days of closure. Students with valid ID get one-third to one-half off entry fees, as do certified teachers, archaeology students and persons 60 or over. On summer full moon evenings, always in August but sometimes July or September too, major archaeological sites like the Parthenon, Lindos or Olympia have free admission for all until about 1.30am – magical. Ask locally, as not all sites have the staff to participate in this programme.

B

Budgeting for Your Trip

Since the advent of the euro, Greece is no longer by any stretch of the imagination an inexpensive country. Travelling as one of a couple, allow a minimum of €30 for a share of accommodation (budget €40–50 each minimum in Athens or Thessaloníki), €15–25 for your half of a sit-down meal, €6–15 each daily for site admissions, and €15–20 for your share of the cheapest small rental car – before petrol costs, which have risen steeply in recent years owing to excise taxes.

Business Travellers

Business travellers are well catered for; most good-standard hotels now have some sort of "business person's corner" with a computer terminal and printer, as well as wi-fi signal for laptops (in the common areas if not in all the rooms). The same hotels tend to have multiple conference/event rooms as well as lounges suitable for semi-formal meetings.

C

Children

Children are adored in Greece, and many families are still highly superstitious about their welfare – don't be surprised to see toddlers with amulets pinned to their clothes to ward off the evil eye. So expect your own kids to be the centre of attention. Children are given quite a bit of leeway in Greece and treated indulgently. They are allowed to stay up late and are routinely taken out to eat in tavernas. You may have to put your foot down when shop owners offer free sweets, or strangers are over-indulgent

towards your own children. There are water parks on several resort islands (Corfu, Rhodes, Crete) but nothing akin to France's Disney World.

Climate

The Greece seen in tourist posters is a perennially warm and sunny place – and it is, by European standards. But this picture does not reflect the considerable climatic variety. The north and inland regions have a modified continental climate, so winters are quite cold and summers extremely hot. In Ioánnina, Trípoli, the Metéora, and Kastoriá, for example, snow and freezing temperatures are not uncommon. In mountainous regions, winters are even more inclement.

The southern islands, the coastal Peloponnese and the Attic Peninsula conform more to the traditional Mediterranean image: a long, warm season of rainless, sunny days extending roughly from late May to mid-October. But here too, the winters can be cool, with rain falling in unpredictable bouts between December and April.

In general, late spring (late April– end June) and autumn (September– October) are the best times to visit. During these periods, you will find mild to warm temperatures, sunny days and fewer tourists. Throughout July and August, Greece is at its most hot and sticky, and most crowded. Still, millions of tourists seem to prefer the heat and the company, choosing this busiest period for their holiday.

Crime and Safety

Sadly, Greece is no longer the crime-free haven of yesteryear. Locking cars and houses is now the norm everywhere, even in the deep countryside where people until recently used to leave a set of keys dangling from the front door.

Central Athens in particular has become hazardous at times. Cars with valuables exposed (or even not) are routinely broken into in such neighbourhoods as Exárhia, Gázi and Keramikós; the thieves, often apparently drug addicts, will steal almost anything irrespective of value, even old CDs or raggedy items of clothing.

Organised gangs of pickpockets and bag-snatchers frequent the metro lines and stations most popular with tourists, in particular Line 3 from the airport, Line 1 from Piraeus, Monastiráki plus Sýndagma stations, and the X95 bus-stop area at Sýndagma. They usually work in teams, and may be plausibly

well dressed. If you are surrounded and pushed up against the carriage wall, or forced to squeeze past them to retrieve your luggage from the rack in the airport-route cars, your wallet, camera or other valuables are about to be (or have been) lifted. Anything in the outside pocket of a daypack or backpack is essentially forfeit. Your cards will be used to obtain cash advances within minutes at exchange booths who are clearly in cahoots with the thieves. Nothing substantive is being done about the problem other than recorded announcements in the metro cars telling you to be aware. If you are new in town, and heavily laden, it's probably worth getting off the metro one station before (Evangelismós) or after (Akrópoli) the central ones and walking back to the centre, or getting an onwards taxi.

Young single females should be alert to the possibility of drugged drinks as a prelude to rape attempts in popular, rowdy beach resorts. Be suspicious of men who offer to bring you cocktails, whose preparation you cannot witness. The perpetrators, it must be said, are as (or more) likely to be other foreigners as Greeks. Use common sense when arranging rides afterwards back to your accommodation.

Because of security considerations, it is unwise to leave luggage unattended anywhere except perhaps in a hotel lobby, under the gaze of the desk staff. Belongings inadvertently left behind in a café will still usually be put aside for you to collect.

Customs Regulations

There are no official restrictions on the movement of goods within the European Union, provided the goods were purchased VAT-paid within the EU. In theory, there are no limitations

CLIMATE CHART

Athens

Maximum temperature
Minimum temperature
Rainfall

to the amount of duty-paid goods that can be moved between EU states. However, cigarettes and most spirits are still cheaper in Greece than in Britain and Ireland, so waiting until you reach your destination to buy these goods will save you money.

Duty-paid goods

If you buy goods in Greece for which you pay tax, there are no restrictions on the amounts you can take home. EU law has set "guidance levels", however, on the following:
Tobacco 3,200 cigarettes, or 400 cigarillos, or 200 cigars or 3kg of tobacco.
Spirits 10 litres
Fortified wine/wine 90 litres
Beer 110 litres
If you exceed these amounts, you must be able to prove the goods are for personal use.

Duty-free goods

For travellers arriving from non-EU countries, allowances for duty-free goods brought into Greece are:
Tobacco 200 cigarettes, or 100 cigarillos, or 50 cigars or 250g of tobacco.
Alcohol 1 litre of spirits or liqueurs over 22 percent volume, or 2 litres of fortified, sparkling or still wine.
Perfume 60cc of perfume, plus 250cc of **eau de toilette.**
Non-EU residents can claim back Value Added Tax (currently between 6 and 23 percent) on any items costing over €120, provided they export the item within 90 days of purchase. Tax-free forms are available at tourist shops and a very few department stores. Keep the receipt and form. Make your claim at the customs area of the airport when departing.

Currency restrictions

There are no limits on the amount of euros visitors can import or export. Cash sums of more than €10,000 or its equivalent should be declared on entry.

Importing cars

Visitors arriving with their own car are allowed to circulate for up to six months without formality; after that the bureaucratic fun begins, and people intending to establish residence will find that it's usually cheaper and easier to buy a Greek-registered car than try to import their overseas motor. Cars detected circulating after the initial six-month period without valid road tax are liable to seizure by customs/tax undercover agents, and are auctioned off if an enormous import duty is not paid.

Police officers in Athens.

Disabled Travellers

Despite nudging from the EU, Greece has some way to go before becoming fully compliant with regulations on facilities for disabled people.
Athens, with lifts in the metro, "kneeling" buses on many routes, recorded announcements of upcoming stops on the metro plus some buses, and ramps (when not blocked by illegally parked cars) at kerbside, is furthest ahead.
Elsewhere, amenities can be poor – there are few or no sound pips for the sight-impaired at pedestrian crossings, and it is common to see the wheelchair-bound tooling down the middle of the asphalt rather than risk the obstacle course of a pedestrian pavement.
Few hotels in the provinces are disabled-friendly, though things are improving slowly, and some are setting aside a few rooms with wide doors and safety handles in the bath – ask when booking.

Embassies and Consulates

Foreign Embassies in Athens

All embassies are open from Monday to Friday only, usually from 8am until 2pm, except for their own national holidays (as well as Greek ones).
Australia Corner Kifissías and Alexándras avenues, Level 6, Thon Building, Ambelókipi; tel: 210-870 4000; www.greece.embassy.gov.au
Canada Ethnikís Antistaseos 48,

Chalandri; tel: 210-727 3400; www.canadainternational.gc.ca/greece-grece
Ireland Vassiléos Konstandínou 7 (by National Gardens); tel: 210-723 2771; www.dfa.ie/irish-embassy/greece
South Africa Kifissiás 60, Maroússi; tel: 210 617 8020
UK Ploutárhou 1, Kolonáki (Evangelismós metro); tel: 210-727 2600, http://ukingreece.fco.gov.uk/en
US Vasilísis Sofías 91, Ambelókipi (Mégaro Mousikís metro); tel: 210-721 2951, http://athens.usembassy.gov

Entry Requirements

Citizens of EU nations and Switzerland have unlimited visitation rights to Greece; your passport will not be stamped on entry or exit. With a valid passport, citizens of the USA, Canada, Australia and New Zealand can stay in the country for up to three months (cumulative) within any six-month period, with no visa necessary. Over-stayers are fined very heavily on exit, to the tune of several hundred euros; it may in fact be cost-effective to have the offending passport "disappear" and be replaced. To stay longer, you must obtain a permit from the nearest Aliens' Bureau; however, this is lately proving nearly impossible (and very expensive) to do. Citizens of all non-EU countries should contact the nearest Greek embassy or consulate about visa and permitted length-of-stay requirements, which are liable to change again in future.

Electricity

220 volts out of double round-pin sockets.

Etiquette

The Greeks are at heart a very traditional nation, protective of their families and their customs. So to avoid giving offence, it is essential to follow their codes of conduct.

Locals rarely drink to excess, so drunken and/or lewd behaviour is treated with at best bewilderment, at worse severe distaste (or criminal prosecution, as many young louts on Rhodes, Zákynthos, Corfu and Crete have learned to their cost).

Nude bathing is legal at only a few beaches (such as on the island of Mýkonos), but it is deeply offensive to most Greeks. Even topless sunbathing is sometimes frowned upon, so watch for signs forbidding it on beaches. The main rule of thumb is this: if it is a secluded beach and/or a beach that has become a commonly accepted locale for nude bathing, you probably won't offend anyone.

On Mýkonos, for example, tourists will shock no one by wearing shorts or a swimsuit in most public places. But this same apparel would be severely alienating in a mountain village in Crete. Observe what other people are wearing and dress accordingly.

To enter a church, men must wear long trousers, and women sleeved dresses. Often dresses or wraps will be provided at the church entrance. Not complying with this code will be taken as insulting irreverence.

Despite assorted scandals and embarrassing espousal of retrograde issues in recent years, the Greek Orthodox Church still commands considerable respect in Greece, so keep any unfavourable comments about the clergy or even Greek civil servants to yourself.

G

Gay and Lesbian Travellers

Overt gay behaviour is not a feature of Greek society. Homosexuality is legal at the age of 17, and bisexual activity fairly common among younger men, but few couples (male or female) are openly gay. Mýkonos is famous as a gay Mecca – Rhodes, Santoríni and Sámos to a lesser degree – while Skála Eressoú on Lésvos (where the poetess Sappho was born) attracts many lesbians. But elsewhere in Greece, single-sex couples are liable to be regarded as odd, although usually as welcome as any other tourists. If discreet, you will attract no attention asking for a double room and will find most people tolerant.

H

Health and Medical Care

Greece has few serious diseases apart from those that you can contract in the US or the rest of Europe. Citizens of the USA, Canada and the EU do not need any immunisations to enter the country.

Drugs and Medicines

Greek pharmacies stock most over-the-counter drugs. The Greeks themselves are enthusiastic hypochondriacs and potion-poppers, and all manner of homeopathic and herbal remedies and premium-ingredient dietary supplements are available – at a price. Many formulas that would be obtainable only on prescription elsewhere, if at all, are freely obtainable in Greece. So you should have no problem obtaining most medicines (except in remote areas and islands).

Essential drugs, made locally under licence, are price-controlled for the moment (though international lenders have their sights trained on this practice), with uniform rates all over the country – eg a tube of 1 percent hydrocortisone cream costs about €4 – but discretional sundries and anything imported can be pricey (eg a packet of four water-resistant French-made bandages for €3.50). If you want to be absolutely sure, pack a supply of your favourite remedies to last out the trip.

Greek authorities take the unauthorised use of drugs very seriously indeed; this is not the country in which to carry cannabis.

Medical Treatment

For minor ailments, your best port of call is a pharmacy. Greek chemists usually speak good English and are well-trained and helpful, and pharmacies stock a good range of medicines (including contraceptives) as well as bandages and dressings for minor wounds.

Certain pharmacies are open outside of normal shop hours and at weekends, on a rotating basis. You can find out which are open either by looking at the bilingual (Greek/English) card posted in pharmacy windows or by consulting a local newspaper. In big cities, and major tourist resorts such as Crete or Rhodes, one or two pharmacies will be open 24 hours a day.

There are English-speaking GPs in all the bigger towns and resorts, whose

rates are usually reasonable. Ask your hotel or the tourist office for details.

Treatment for broken bones and similar mishaps is given free of charge in the state-run Greek hospitals – go straight to the casualty/emergency ward (epígon peristatiká). Have on you your European Health Insurance Card, obtainable in the UK online at www.ehic.org. Be aware that holders of such cards are only entitled to free treatment in the casualty ward, and at the few still-functioning agrotiká iatría (remote rural clinics). If you make the mistake of attending a hospital's outpatient clinic, you'll pay full whack for everything at private rates, and charges are eye-watering: eg €130 for a full battery of blood tests.

For more serious problems and unimpeded use of outpatient clinics on a private basis, you should have private medical insurance. If you have a serious injury or illness, you are better off travelling home for treatment if you can. Greek public hospitals lag behind northern Europe and the US in both their hygiene and standard of care; the Greeks bring food and bedding when visiting sick relatives, and must bribe nurses and doctors for anything beyond the bare minimum in care. All these conditions have been severely exacerbated by the ongoing crisis, with health-care provision very hard hit.

Drinking Water

People carrying a large plastic bottle of mineral water is a common sight in Greece, but it is not the best way of keeping hydrated, as sunlight releases toxic chemicals from the plastic into the water, and the spent bottles contribute enormously to Greece's litter problem. Buy a sturdy, porcelain-lined canteen and fill it from the cool-water supply of bars and restaurants you've patronised; nobody will begrudge you this. Although unfiltered tap water is generally safe to drink, it may be brackish, and having a private water supply is much

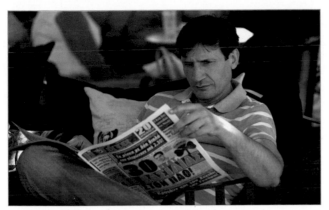

Getting his news fix.

handier. On the mainland and larger islands, certain springs are particularly esteemed by the locals – queues of cars, and people with jerry-cans, tip you off. If you do want bottled water, it can be bought almost anywhere that sells food, even in beach cafés and tavernas, though more conventionally at kiosks and minimarkets. A large bottle should not cost more than about 70 euro-cents, often less.

Animal Hazards

Nearly half the stray dogs in rural areas carry echinococcosis (treatable by surgery only) or kala-azar disease (leishmaniasis), a potentially fatal protozoan blood disease spread by sandflies. So beware of befriending importunate pooches.

Mosquitoes can be a nuisance in some areas of Greece, but topical repellents are readily available in pharmacies. For safeguarding rooms, accommodation proprietors often supply a plug-in electric pad, which vapourises smokeless, odourless rectangular tablets. If you see them by the bed, it's a good bet they'll be needed; refills can be found in any supermarket.

On the islands, poisonous baby pit vipers and scorpions are a problem in spring and summer. They will not strike you unless disturbed, but do not put your hands or feet in places (such as drystone walls) that you haven't checked first. If you swim in the sea, beware jellyfish whose sting is usually harmless but which can swell and hurt for days. A good over-the-counter remedy for this is called Fenistil.

On beaches, it is worth wearing plastic or trekking sandals to avoid sea urchins (those little black pincushions on rocks that can embed their very sharp and tiny spines into unwary feet). A local Greek remedy is

to douse the wound with olive oil and then gently massage the foot until the spines pop out, but this rarely works unless you're willing to perform minor surgery with pen-knife and sewing needle – which should be done, as spine fragments tend to go septic.

Insurance

The benefits of medical insurance coverage for private treatment are noted above. You will have to pay for private treatment up front, so you must keep receipts for any bills or medicines you pay for to make a claim. If you plan to hire a motor scooter in Greece, or engage in any adventure sport, make sure your policy covers such activities.

Internet

Greece has become thoroughly "wired" since the Olympic Games, with bars, cafés, hotels (sometimes only the common areas) and even many tavernas offering a wi-fi signal. Much of the time it is free, or free for the price of a coffee, drink or meal, but usually password protected. Speeds are apt to be moderate rather than blistering – especially in rural areas. With the prevalence of tablet devices and full-sized laptops, internet cafés per se are heading towards extinction, and always were dismal places full of spotty teenagers playing computer games. Should you have to pay for these, assume a maximum of €4 an hour, with 15- or 30-minute increments usually available. Hotel internet charges can be ruinous – we've heard tales of nearly €20 a day – and should be avoided.

Media

Print

Many kiosks throughout Athens and other major resorts receive British newspapers, plus the International Herald Tribune, either late the same afternoon or, more usually, the next day. The English online edition (www.ekathimerini.com) of centre-right Greek newspaper Kathimerini is the best source of Greek news, albeit heavily abridged from the parent publication. Odyssey (www.odyssey.gr) is a glossy, bi-monthly magazine created by and for the wealthy Greek diaspora, somewhat more interesting than the usual airline in-flight mag.

Radio and TV

Ellinikí Radiofonía is the Greek state-owned radio, divided into three different "programmes". The First and (much better) Second (FM 103.70 near Athens, other frequencies regionally) both have abundant Greek popular music, news and talk shows, some foreign pop and occasional jazz and blues. The Third programme (FM 90.9) features classical music. Private station Kanali 1, out of Piraeus (FM 90.4), is also excellent. Additionally, a plethora of private stations broadcast locally from just about every island or provincial town, no matter how tiny.

The BBC World Service no longer beams directly on short-wave to Greece, but has agreements for

Left Luggage

Airport At the far south end, arrivals concourse, Eleftherios Venizelos airport, Pacific Left Luggage offers service; tel: 210-353 0352. They are, however, hideously expensive for anything more than a few hours.
Hotels Most hotels in Greece are willing to store locked suitcases for a week or two if you want to take any short excursions. This is usually a free service, provided you've stayed a night or two, but the hotel will accept no responsibility in the highly unlikely event of theft.
Commercial offices On the islands, there are left-luggage offices in many harbour towns. For a small charge, space can be hired by the hour, day, week or longer. Although the contents will probably be safe, take small valuables with you.

rebroadcast of select programmes with the following local stations: Skaï (100.4 FM) and Antenna (102.7 FM).

There are three state-owned and operated television channels (ET1 and NET, out of Athens, ET3 from Thessaloniki) and a half-dozen private television channels (Antenna, Net, Mega, Star, Skaï (no relation to Rupert Murdoch's Sky) and Alpha). Often they transmit foreign movies and programmes with Greek subtitles rather than being dubbed. Several cable and satellite channels, including Sky and CNN, are also available in the better hotels.

Money

For the moment at least, the Greek currency is the euro (*evró* in Greek), which comes in coins of 1, 2, 5, 10, 20 and 50 cents *(leptá)*, plus 1 and 2 euro, as well as notes of 5, 10, 20, 50, 100, 200 and 500 euro (the latter two denominations rarely seen and viewed with extreme suspicion as likely counterfeits – avoid accepting them at banks).

All banks and most hotels buy foreign currency at the official rate of exchange fixed by the Bank of Greece. Exchange rates go up or down daily. To find the current rate, check displays in bank windows, or the newspapers; you can read the tables even in Greek.

Travellers' cheques are disdained, and very few institutions accept them any longer – or at least not without a 20-minute vetting procedure. It's worth carrying a limited sum of low-denomination banknotes in US dollars or sterling, which are much more

rapidly negotiable at travel agencies and exchange bureaux.

Credit/debit cards

Many of the better-established hotels, restaurants and shops accept major credit cards, as do all airline and ferry-company websites, plus the domestic Greek travel websites www.airtickets.gr and www.travelplanet24.com. Many travel agencies and websites, however, will add a surcharge (typically 3 percent) to credit-card purchases of tickets. The average low-star hotel or taverna does not, however, take cards, or only accepts details as a booking deposit, so enquire before ordering if that is how you intend to pay. You will find that most brands of card are accepted by the numerous autoteller machines, upon entry of your pin number. However, use debit rather than credit cards in ATMs, as the latter tend to have ruinous surcharges, often amounting to over five percent of the transaction value. This caveat aside, you will find that this is the most convenient and least expensive way of getting funds, and most machines operate around the clock. Prepaid cash cards can be an effective way to push down commission charges.

O

Opening Hours

All banks are open 8am–2.30pm Monday to Thursday, and close at 2pm on Friday. ATMs are now everywhere – even the smaller

islands will have at least one – and this is how most travellers obtain cash nowadays, rarely if ever seeing the inside of a bank.

The schedule for business and shop hours is more complicated, varying according to the type of business and the day of the week. The main thing to remember is that businesses generally open at 8.30 or 9am and close on Monday, Wednesday and Saturday at 2.30pm. On Tuesday, Thursday and Friday, most businesses close at 2pm and reopen in the afternoon from 5pm to 8.30pm (winter), 5.30 or 6pm to 9pm (summer).

Supermarkets, both large and small, are the only shops guaranteed to be open all day (Mon–Fri 8.30am–9pm, Sat 8.30am–8pm). Especially on resort islands, there will be at least one open short hours on Sunday too (typically 10am–4pm).

You'll soon learn that schedules are very flexible in Greece (both in business and personal affairs). To avoid disappointment, allow ample time when shopping and doing business. That way, you may also enter into the Greek spirit of negotiation, in which a good chat can be as important as the matter of business itself.

P

Photography

Although Greece is a photographer's paradise, taking photographs at will is not recommended. Cameras are permitted in museums, but to be used without tripod or flash. You may have to pay a fee to use your camcorder at archaeological sites. Watch out for signs showing a bellows camera with a red "X" through it, and do not point your camera at anything in or near airports – most of which double as military bases.

Memory chips for most digital cameras are widely available; photo shops will also happily print from chips, or empty their contents onto a CD for a nominal fee (assume €5).

Postal Services

Most local post offices are open weekdays from 7.30am until 2pm. However, the main post offices in central Athens (on Eólou near Omónia Square and on Sýndagma Square at the corner of Mitropóleos Street) are open longer hours on weekdays, as well as for a few hours on Saturday.

'Greek Time'

Beware Greek schedules. Although shops and businesses generally operate the hours indicated under Opening Hours, there is no guarantee that when you want to book a ferry or buy a gift, the office or shop will actually be open.

Siesta (*mikró ýpno* in Greek) is observed throughout Greece, and even in Athens the majority of people retire behind closed doors between the hours of 3pm and 6pm. Shops and businesses also close, and it is usually impossible to get anything more done until late-afternoon or early evening. To avoid frustration and disappointment, shop and book things between 9.30am and 1.30pm Monday to Friday.

Since 1994, Athens has experimented with "straight" hours

during the winter to bring the country more in line with the EU, but this seems to be discretionary rather than obligatory, with some stores observing the hours and others adhering to traditional schedules – which can be rather confusing. So far it has not caught on across the rest of the country.

During summer, the shops in Athens' Pláka district remain open until 10pm or longer to take advantage of browsers, and tourist shops throughout the country usually trade well into the evening. But butchers and fishmongers are not allowed to open on summer evenings (although a few disregard the law), and pharmacies (except for those on rota duty) are never open in the evenings or on Saturday mornings.

Postal rates are subject to fairly frequent change; currently a postcard or light letter costs 85 euro-cents to any overseas destination. Stamps are available from the post office or from many kiosks *(períptera)* and hotels, which may charge a 10–15 percent commission. But many kiosk owners tend not to be up to date with latest international postal rates. Outbound speeds are reasonable – as little as three days to northern Europe, a week or so to North America.

If you want to send a parcel from Greece, do not to wrap it until a post office clerk has inspected it, unless it's going to another EU country, in which case you can present it sealed. Major post offices stock various sizes of cardboard boxes for sale in which you can pack your material, as well as twine, but you had best bring your own tape and scissors.

Letters from abroad can be sent post restante to any post office. Take your passport or other ID when you go to pick up mail.

R

Religious Services

Most major towns and resort areas with significant foreign patronage or a large expat community – most obviously Corfu, Rhodes, Crete, Sámos, Santoríni, Athens and Thessaloníki – have at least one church dedicated to the Catholic, Anglican or other Protestant (eg Swedish Lutheran) rites, or an agreement for part-time use of an Orthodox premises. There are functioning Catholic parishes for locals on Rhodes, Crete, Corfu, Sýros and Tínos, where foreigners are welcome. Placards posted on the churches themselves, or handouts at the nearest tourist office, give current info on schedules (anything from two Sundays a month to two or three times weekly).

S

Student Travellers

Other than the museum and archaeological site discounts, students and under-26s are eligible for discounted fares and youth passes on ose (the Greek train network) and on some shipping lines, including those operating to and from Italy.

T

Telecoms

For local calls, including to mobiles, buy an OTE (Greek telecoms) telephone card from a kiosk and use a (usually noisy) street-corner booth. Cards come in 100-unit, 500-unit and 1,000-unit denominations; the Hronokarta species is slightly better value. Calls from hotel rooms typically have 200–300 percent surcharges on top of the basic rates – to be avoided for anything other than brief local calls. For overseas calls, almost everyone avoids the truly outrageous OTE rates by buying a code-card, whereby you scratch to reveal a 12-digit code, then ring an 807-prefixed number to enter said code, then the number you want. It may all sound a hassle, but savings can amount to about 70 percent. If you have a laptop, bring a Skype headset along to take advantage of wi-fi zones for calling abroad.

Greece has one of the highest per-capita mobile-phone usage rates in the world, and a mobile is an essential fashion accessory for any self-respecting Greek. Foreign mobile owners will find themselves well catered for, with thorough coverage and reciprocal agreements for most UK-based services. North American users will have to bring a tri-band apparatus to get any joy. In the wake of caps on intra-EU call charges, receiving calls within Greece is affordable if you have an foreign-but-EU-based number, but the costs of calling out adds up quickly. If you're staying for any amount of time, you will find it better to buy a pay-as-you-go SIM card from one of the three Greek providers (Vodaphone, Cosmote, Wind). As an anti-terrorism strategy to keep you from using your phone to set off bombs remotely, you will have to register your identity upon purchase.

Tipping

Menu prices at most cafés, restaurants and *tavérnes* include a

Time Zone

Greece is two hours ahead of GMT and, like the rest of Europe, observes Daylight Savings from 3am on the last Sunday in March until 3am on the last Sunday in October.

service charge, but it is still customary to leave an extra 5–10 percent on the table for the waiters. Taxi drivers are not tipped per se but may "round up" fares to the nearest half-euro. Hotel porters should be given a euro or so per bag.

Toilets

Public conveniences, often subterranean in parks or plazas, or perched on a harbour jetty, are of variable cleanliness and rarely have any paper. Most people just buy a drink in a café and use their facilities. In busy tourist areas, put-upon cafés may post signs saying "toilets for customers only". Elsewhere, establishments are a bit more lenient about those caught short just popping in.

Tourist Information

Tourist offices

If you would like tourist information about Greece during your trip, visit the nearest Greek National Tourist Organisation – GNTO, or EOT in Greek. They provide information on public transport, as well as leaflets and details about sites and museums. There are over a dozen regional GNTO offices across the country. The information booth in Athens can be found at the base of Dionysíou Areopagítou, at the edge of the Pláka district.

In some tourist areas, especially on many islands, there are municipal tourist information centres open from June to September. These are usually prominently sited near the centre of the main town, and provide all the local information you might need. Some can even help with finding accommodation.

Tourist Police

The Greek Tourist Police are a branch of the local police, found in most large towns; sometimes, as on Rhodes, they have separate premises. Each tourist policeman should speak at least one foreign language well. They should be your first port of call in the event of a serious incident involving rogue hoteliers or restauranteurs, and should also be consulted if you are the victim of a serious crime such as assault or robbery, if the regular police seem to be dragging their feet.

Greek National Tourist Organisation Offices

Greek National Tourism Organisation, worldwide (www.visitgreece.gr):

UK and Ireland: 4 Great Portland Street, London W1W 8QJ; tel: (020) 7495 9300.
US & Canada: 800 3rd Avenue, New York, NY 10022; tel: (212) 421 5777.

Websites

Greek weather forecasts are available at:
www.weather.gr
www.poseidon.hcmr.gr/weather_forecast.php?area_id=gr
Windsurfers in particular should consult the Greece page of:
www.windguru.cz
For local journalism in English, try:
www.ekathimerini.com
www.athensnews.com
Reviews and sales of books on all aspects of Greece can be found at:
www.hellenicbookservice.com
Everything about Athens buses is at:
www.oasa.gr
Seagoing schedules are available at:
www.gtp.gr
Buying ferry tickets online and don't just want individual company sites?
www.ticket.gr
www.goferry.gr
For general tourist information and links have a look at:
www.greecetravel.com
The Ministry of Culture site has impressive coverage of most of the country's museums, archaeological sites and remote monuments on:
www.culture.gr
Who's on strike in Greece this week/month? Find out at:

www.apergia.gr
Want to buy CDs of Greek music? Go to:
www.xilouris.gr
All the Greek reptiles and amphibians are at:
www.herpetofauna.gr
All the naturist beaches – which usually happen to be the best ones – are on:
www.barefoot.info/greekgde.html

Weights and Measures

Greece is completely metric, though land is measured and sold in strémmata (1,000 sq metres/10,764 sq ft).

What to Bring

Clothes

Summer visits entail only lightweight, casual clothing. Add a pullover or thin jacket and you will be prepared for the occasional cool night breeze or ferry ride. Lightweight shoes and sandals are ideal in the summer, but you will also need a pair of comfortable walking shoes. If you plan to do any hiking in the mountains or on the islands, bring sturdy, broken-in, over-the-ankle boots with a good tread; leather will be more comfortable in the summer heat than synthetic materials.

In general, both Greeks and tourists dine in casual dress but even in the hottest weather, Athenian men won't wear shorts. Scuffed shoes, ripped jeans, shirt-tails being out or visibly out-of-date clothing are all considered offensive. You will only need formal dress if you plan to go

to fancy establishments, casinos or formal affairs. If you visit Greece during the winter, which can be surprisingly cold, bring the kind of clothes you would wear during spring in the northern US or Central Europe.

Toiletries

Most international brands are widely available, except on the smallest islands. Feminine hygiene products are more likely to be sold in supermarkets than pharmacies.

Sun protection

A hat, sun cream and sunglasses are highly recommended for protection from the intense midday sun (sophisticated sun creams of up to SPF50 are widely available).

Electrical Adaptation

220v AC is the standard electric current throughout Greece. Non-dual-voltage shavers and hair dryers from North America should be left at home in favour of versatile travel models – they can be bought on the spot in Greece. Greek plugs are the standard round, two-pin European continental type, different from those in North America and the UK; plug adaptors for American appliances are easy to find, three-to-two-pin adaptors for UK appliances much less so, so these are best purchased before departure.

Universal plug

Greek basins often aren't equipped with plugs, so if you want water in your sink, a universal plug is essential.

Torch/Flashlight

If you're planning a trip to one of the islands, pack a torch, as walking home from the taverna can be tricky if there's no moon.

Women Travellers

Lone female visitors may still be targeted for attention by predatory Greek males, especially around beach bars and after-hours clubs, but, in general, machismo is no more a problem here than anywhere else in Southern Europe. Greek women have much more sexual freedom than previously, especially in the cities. There is now little controversy in their spending time with their male counterparts, up to and including cohabiting before (or instead of) marriage.

In remote areas, many Greeks are still highly traditional and may find it hard to understand why you are travelling alone. You will not feel comfortable in their all-male cafés.

Tour Operators

Mass-market bucket-and-spade holidays are easy to find on the web. Otherwise, here are a few suggestions for something unusual:
Quality packages and bespoke itineraries on mainland & islands:
Sunvil, UK; tel: 020 85684499, www.sunvil.co.uk
Hidden Greece, UK; tel: 020 87584707, www.hidden-greece.co.uk
Travel à la Carte, UK; tel: 020 72869255, www.travelalacarte.co.uk
Bicycle tours on Crete, Zákynthos, Peloponnese:
Classic Adventures, USA; tel: 1 800 777-8090, www.classicadventures.com
Wildlife tours across the country:
The Travelling Naturalist, UK; tel: 01305 267994, naturalist.co.uk
Sail-and-trek mixed tours:
Explore!, UK; tel: 01252 884296,

www.explore.co.uk
Hellenic Adventures, USA; tel: 1 800 851 6349, www.hellenic adventures.com
Walking holidays, western Crete:
ATG Oxford, UK; tel: 01865 315678, www.atg-oxford.co.uk
Walking and cycling, various parts of Greece:
Exodus London, UK; tel: 020 31317159, www.exodus.co.uk
Ramblers Holidays, UK; tel: 01707 331133, www.ramblersholidays.co.uk
Writing workshops/holistic holidays:
Astra, US; tel: 1303 321-5403, www.astragreece.com
Skyros Centre, UK; tel: 01983 865566, www.skyros.com
Yoga Plus, UK; tel: 01582 724214, www.yogaplus.co.uk

TRANSPORT

LANGUAGE

UNDERSTANDING THE LANGUAGE

THE GREEK LANGUAGE

Modern Greek is the outcome of gradual evolution undergone by the Greek language since the Classical period (5th–4th centuries BC). The language is still relatively close to Ancient Greek: it uses the same alphabet and much of the same vocabulary, though the grammar – other than the retention of the three genders – is considerably streamlined. Many people speak English, some very well, but even attempting a few words in Greek will always be appreciated.

Pronunciation tips

Most of the sounds of Greek aren't difficult to pronounce for English speakers. There are only six vowel sounds: *a, e, i, o, u,* and *y* are consistently pronounced as shown in the table opposite. The letter s is usually pronounced "s", but "z" before an m or g. The sound represented here as *th* is always pronounced as in "thin", not "that"; the first sound in "that" is represented by *d*. Note that "x" is always pronounced as "ks" at the start of a word, not as "z". The "r" is slightly rolled, as in Scottish.

The only difficult sounds are *h,* which is pronounced like the "ch" in Scottish "loch" (we render this as *kh* after "s" so that you don't generate "sh"), and g before e or i, which has no equivalent in English – it's somewhere between the "y" in "yet" and the "g" in "get".

The position of the stress in words is of critical importance, as homonyms abound, and Greeks will often fail to understand you if you don't stress the right syllable (compare *psýllos*, "flea" with *psilós*, "tall"). In this guide, stress

is marked by a simple accent mark (´), except for single-syllable words, which are, however, still stressed.

Greek word order is flexible, so you may often hear phrases in a different order from the one in which they are given here. Like the French, the Greeks use the plural of the second person when addressing someone politely. We have used the polite (formal) form throughout this language section, except where an expression is specified as "informal".

COMMUNICATION

Good morning *kaliméra*
Good evening *kalispéra*
Good night *kaliníhta*

Our Transliteration System

In Greece, all town and village names on road signs, as well as most street names, are written in Greek and the Roman alphabets. There's no universally accepted system of transliteration into Roman, and in any case, the Greek authorities are gradually replacing old signs with new ones that use a slightly different system. This means you will have to get used to seeing different spellings of the same place on maps and signs and in this book.

Below is the transliteration scheme we have used in this book: beside each Greek letter or pair of letters is the Roman letter(s) we have used. Next to that is a rough approximation of the sound in an English word.
NB: the Greek letter have come out wrong here but obviously they have not changed so tell the typesetter to leave them as they are.

A	α		a	cat
B	β		v	vote
Γ	γ		g/y	got *except before* "e" *or* "i", *when it is nearer to* y*acht, but rougher*
Δ	δ		d	then
E	ε		e	egg
Z	ζ		z	zoo
H	η		i	ski
Θ	θ		th	thin
I	ι		i	ski
K	κ		k	kiss
Λ	λ		l	long
M	μ		m	man
N	ν		n	no
Ξ	ξ		x	taxi
O	ο		o	road
Π	π		p	pen
P	ρ		r	room
Σ	σ/ς		s	set *or* charisma
T	τ		t	tea
Y	υ		y	mildly
Φ	φ		f	fish
X	χ		h	loch
Ψ	ψ		ps	maps
Ω	ω		o	road
αι	αι	(ai)	e	hay
αυ	αυ	(au)	av/af	have/raffle
ει	ει	(ei)	i	ski
ευ	ευ	(eu)	ev/ef	ever/left
οι	οι	(oi)	i	ski
ου	ου	(ou)	ou	tourist
γγ	γγ	(gg)	ng	long
γκ	γκ	(gk)	ng	long
γξ	γξ	(gx)	nx	anxious
μπ	μπ	(mp)	b *or* mb	beg / limber
NT	ντ	(nt)	d *or* nd	dog / under
TZ	τζ	(tz)	tz	fads

A – Z

LANGUAGE

Emergencies

Help! *Voíthia!*
Stop! *Stamatíste!*
I've had an accident *Íha éna at'yhíma*
Call a doctor *Fonáxte éna yiatró*
Call an ambulance *Fonáxte éna asthenofóro*
Call the police *Fonáxte tin astynomía*
Call the fire brigade *Fonáxte tous pyrozvéstes*
Where's the telephone? *Pou íne to tiléfono?*
Where's the nearest hospital? *Pou íne to pio kondinó nosokomío?*
There's been a theft *Égine mia klopí*

Hello/Goodbye *yiásas (informal: yiásou)*
Pleased to meet you *hárika*
Yes *ne*
No *óhi*
Thank you *efharistó*
You're welcome *parakaló*
Please *parakaló*
Okay/All right *endáxi*
Excuse me (to get attention) *me synhoríte*
Excuse me (to get past) *syngnómi*
Please write it down for me *Na mou to gráfete parakaló?*
How are you? *Ti kánete? (informal: Ti kánis?)*
Fine, and you? *Kalá, esís?(informal: Kalá, esí?)*
Cheers/Our health! (when drinking) *Yiámas!*
Could you help me? *Boríte na me voithísete?*
Can you show me *Boríte na mou díxete...*
I want... *Thélo...*
I don't know *Den xéro*
I don't understand *Den katálava*
Do you speak English? *Miláte angliká?*
Can you please speak more slowly? *Parakaló, miláte sigá-sigá?*
Please say that again *Parakaló, xanapésteto*
Here *edó*
There *ekí*
What? *ti?*
When? *póte?*
Why? *yiatí?*
Where? *pou?*
How? *pos?*

TELEPHONE CALLS

the telephone *to tiléfono*
phonecard *tilekárta*
May I use the phone, please? *Boró na tilefoníso, parakaló?*
Hello (on the phone) *Embrós/Oríste*

My name is... *Légome...*
Could I speak to... *Boró na milíso me...*
Wait a moment *Periménete mía stigmí*
I didn't hear *Den ákousa*

IN THE HOTEL

Do you have a vacant room? *Éhete domátio?*
I've booked a room *Ého kratísi éna domátio*
I'd like... *Tha íthela...*
a single/double room *éna monóklino/díklino*
double bed *dipló kreváti*
a room with a bath/shower *éna domátio me bánio/dous*
One night *éna vrádi*
Two nights *dyo vradiá*
How much is it? *Póso káni?*
Do you have a room with a sea-view? *Éhete domátio me théa pros ti thálassa?*
Is there a balcony? *Éhi balkóni?*
Is the room heated/air-conditioned? *To domátio éhi thérmansi/klimatismó?*
Is breakfast included? *Mazí me to proinó?*
Can I see the room please? *Boró na do to domátio, parakaló?*
The room is too hot/cold/small *To domátio íne polý zestó/krýo/mikró*
It's too noisy *Éhi polý thóryvo*
Could you show me another room, please? *Boríte na mou díxete állo domátio, parakaló?*
I'll take it *Tha to páro*
Can I have the bill, please? *Na mou kánete to logariasmó, parakaló?*
key *klidí*
towel *petséta*
sheet *sendóni*
blanket *kouvérta*
pillow *maxilári*
soap *sapoúni*
hot water *zestó neró*
toilet paper *hartí toualéttas*

AT A BAR OR CAFÉ

bar/café *bar/kafenío (or kafetéria)*
patisserie *zaharoplastío*
I'd like... *Tha íthela...*
a (Greek) coffee *éna (ellinikó) kafé*
filter coffee *gallikó kafé/kafé fíltro*
instant coffee *neskafé (or nes)*
cappuccino *kapoutsíno*
white (with milk) *me gála*
black (without milk) *horís gála*
with sugar *me záhari*
without sugar *horís záhari*
a cup of tea *éna tsáï*
tea with lemon *éna tsái me lemóni*
orange/lemon soda *mía portokaláda/lemonáda*

Ordering Drinks

býra **beer**
krasí **wine**
áspro **white wine**
kokkinélli **rosé wine**
mávro **red wine**
me to kiló **wine by the kilo**
hýma **bulk, from the barrel**
neró **water**
retsína **resin-flavoured wine**
oúzo **aniseed-flavoured grape-pressing distillate**
rakí **another distilled spirit from vintage crushings**
tsípouro **north-mainland version of rakí**
tsikoudiá **Cretan version of rakí, flavoured with terebinth**
portokaláda **orangeade**
lemonáda **lemonade**

fresh orange juice *éna hymó portokáli*
a glass/bottle of water *éna potíri/boukáli neró*
with ice *me pagáki*
an ouzo/brandy *éna oúzo/koniák*
a beer (draught) *mía býra (apó varélli)*
an ice-cream *éna pagotó*
a pastry, cake *mía pásta (oriental pastries baklavá/kataïfi)*

IN A RESTAURANT

Have you got a table for... *Éhete trapézi yiá...*
There are (four) of us *ímaste (tésseres)*
I'm a vegetarian *íme hortofágos*
Can we see the menu? *Boroúme na doúme ton katálogo?*
We want to order *Théloume na parangíloume*
Have you got wine by the carafe? *Éhete krasí hýma?*
a litre/half-litre *éna kiló/misó kilo of white/red wine áspro/kókkino krasí*
Would you like anything else? *Thélete típot' állo?*
No, thank you *óhi, efharistó*
glass *potíri*
knife/fork/spoon *mahéri/piroúni/koutáli*
plate *piáto*
napkin *hartopetséta*
Where is the toilet? *Pou íne i toualétta?*
The bill, please *to logariasmó, parakaló*

FOOD

Mezédes/Orektiká

taramosaláta **fish-roe dip**
tzatzíki **yoghurt-garlic cucumber dip**
melitzánes **aubergines**

kafterí **tomato and féta dip**
kolokythákia **courgettes**
loukánika **sausages**
tyrokafterí **soft cheese seasoned with hot peppers**
tyropitákia **small cheese pies**
antsoúgies **anchovies**
eliés **olives**
dolmádes **rice-stuffed vine leaves**
saganáki **fried cheese**
fáva **puréed fava beans**

Meat Dishes

kréas **any meat**
arní **lamb**
hirinó **pork**
gourounópoulo **suckling pig**
kotópoulo **chicken**
moskhári **veal, beef**
psitó **roast or grilled**
sto foúrno **roast**
sta kárvouna **grilled**
soúvlas **on the spit**
souvláki **meat cubes on skewers**
kokinistó **stewed in tomato sauce**
avgolémono **egg-lemon sauce**
tiganitó **fried**
kapnistó **smoked**
brizóla **(pork or veal) chop**
paidákia **lamb chops**
pantsétta **pork belly**
sykóti **liver**
kymás **mince**
biftéki **burger (without bun)**
keftédes **meat-balls**
kokorétsi **grilled sheep's entrails**
soutzoukákia **rissoles baked in red sauce**
yiouvarlákia **mince-and-rice balls in egg lemon sauce**
makarónia **spaghetti**
mousakás **lamb and aubergine bake**
piláfi **rice**
me kymá **with minced meat**
me sáltsa **with tomato sauce**
kléftiko **baked lamb**
pastitsáda **braised beef (or cockerel) in spiced tomato sauce**
pastítsio **macaroni with minced meat**
sofríto **veal (or rabbit) in white wine**
spétzofäi **sausage, aubergine and green pepper dish**
stifádo **beef (or rabbit) stewed with small onions**
gýros me pítta **doner kebab**
domátes yemistés **stuffed tomatoes**
piperiés yemistés **stuffed peppers**

Seafood

frésko **fresh**
katapsygméno **frozen**
psári **fish**
óstraka **shellfish**
xifías **swordfish**
koliós **mackerel**
barboúnia **red mullet**

sardélles **sardines**
gávros **fresh anchovy**
marídes **picarel**
mýdia **mussels**
strídia **oysters**
kalamarákia **squid**
soupiés **cuttlefish**
htapódi **octopus**
garídes **prawns**
astakós **lobster**

Vegetables

angináres **artichokes**
arakás **peas**
domátes **tomatoes**
fakés **brown lentils**
fasólia/fasoláda **stewed white beans**
fasolákia (fréska) **green beans, in tomato sauce**
yígandes **stewed butter-beans**
hórta **misc. boiled greens**
hortópitta **vegetable pie**
karóto **carrot**
kolokythákia **courgettes**
kounoupídi **cauliflower**
koukiá **broad beans**
kremídi **onion**
láhano **cabbage**
maroúli **lettuce**
pandzária **beetroot**
patátes(tiganités/sto foúrno) **potatoes (chips/roast)**
revýthia **chickpeas**
skórdo **garlic**
spanáki **spinach**
spanakópitta **spinach pie**
vlíta **boiled greens**
saláta **salad**
domatosaláta **tomato salad**
angourodomáta **tomato and cucumber salad**
horiátiki **Greek salad**

Fruit

míla **apples**
ver'ykoka **apricots**
banánes **bananas**
kerásia **cherries**
sýka **figs**
stafýlia **grapes**
lemónia **lemons**
pepónia **melons**
portokália **oranges**
rodákina **peaches**
ahládia **pears**
fráoules **strawberries**
karpoúzi **watermelon**

Basic Foods/Desserts

psomí **bread**
aláti **salt**
pipéri **pepper**
ládi **(olive) oil**
xýdi **vinegar**
moustárda **mustard**

voútyro **butter**
tyrí **cheese**
avgá (tiganitá) **(fried) eggs**
omelétta **omelette**
marmeláda **jam, marmalade**
rýzi **rice**
yiaoúrti **yoghurt**
méli **honey**
záhari **sugar**
galaktoboúreko **custard pastry**
halvás **semolina and walnut pudding**
ravaní **semolina and syrup cake**

SIGHTSEEING

information plirofories
open/closed anihtó/klistó
Can we see the church/archaeological site? Boroúme na doúme tin eklisía/ta arhéa?
Where can I find the custodian/key? Pou boró na vro to fílaka/klidí?

At the Shops

shop magazí/katástima
What time do you open/close? ti óra aníyete/klínete?

Numbers

1 énas/mía/éna (masc/fem/neut)
2 dýo
3 tris/tría
4 tésseres/téssera
5 pénde
6 éxi
7 eptá
8 októ
9 ennéa
10 déka
11 éndeka
12 dódeka
13 dekatrís/dekatría
14 dekatésseres/dekatéssera
15 dekapénde
16 dekaéxi
17 dekaeptá
18 dekaoktó
19 dekaennéa
20 íkosi
30 triánda
40 saránda
50 penínda
60 exínda
70 evdomínda
80 ogdónda
90 enenínda
100 ekató
200 dyakósia
300 trakósies/trakósia
400 tetrakósies/tetrakósia
500 pendakósia
1,000 hílies/hília
2,000 dýo hiliádes
1 million éna ekatom'yrio

TRANSPORT

A – Z

LANGUAGE

What would you like? *Oríste/ti thélete?*
I'm just looking *Aplós kitázo*
How much is it? *Póso káni?*
Do you take credit cards? *Déheste pistotikés kártes?*
Have you got...? *éhete...?*
size (for clothes) *noúmero*
Can I try it on? *Boró na to dokimáso?*
This is faulty. Can I change it? *Aftó éhi éna elátoma. Boró na to aláxo?*
Can I have a refund? *Boró na páro píso ta leftá?*
a kilo *éna kiló*
half a kilo *misókilo*
a quarter *éna tétarto*
two kilos *d'yo kilá*
100 grams *ekató gramária*
200 grams *dyakósia gramária*
more *perisótero*
less *ligótero*
a little/very little *lígo/polý lígo*
with/without *me/horís*
That's enough *ftáni*
That's all *tipot'állo*

TRAVELLING

airport *aerodrómio*
boarding card *kárta epivívasis*
boat *plío/karávi*
bus *leoforío*
bus station *stathmós leoforíon*
bus stop *stási*
coach *poúlman*
ferry *feribót*
first/second class *próti/défteri thési*
flight *ptísi*
hydrofoil *iptámeno*
motorway *ethnikí odós*
port *limáni*
return ticket *isitírio me epistrofí*
single ticket *apló isitírio*
station *stathmós*
taxi *taxí*
train *tréno*

Public Transport

Can you help me, please? *Boríte na me voithísete, parakaló?*
Where can I buy tickets? *Pou na kópso isitírio?*
At the counter *sto tamío*
Does it stop at... *Káni stási sto...*
You need to change at... *Tha prépi n'aláxete sto...*
When is the next train/bus/ferry to... *Póte févyi to tréno/leoforío/feribót gia...*
How long does the journey take? *Pósi óra káni to taxídi?*
What time will we arrive? *Ti óra tha ftásoume?*
How much is the fare? *Póso káni to isitírio?*
Next stop please *Epómeni stási parakaló*

Can you tell me where to get off? *Tha mou píte pou na katévo?*
Should I get off here? *Edó na katévo?*
delay *kathystérisi*

Directions

right/left *dexiá/aristerá*
Take the first/second right *Párte ton próto/déftero drómo dexiá*
Turn right/left *strípste dexiá/ aristerá*
Go straight on *Tha páte ísia/efthía*
after the traffic lights *metá ta fanária*
Is it near/far away? *Íne kondá/makriá?*
How far is it? *Póso makriá íne?*
It's five minutes' walk *Íne pénde leptá me ta pódia*
It's ten minutes by car *Íne déka leptá me to avtokínito*
100 metres *ekató métra*
opposite/next to *apénandi/dípla*
junction *diastávrosi*
Where is/are... *Pou íne...*
Where can I find... *Pou boró na vro...*
a petrol station *éna venzinádiko*
a bank *mia trápeza*
a bus stop *mia stási*
a hotel? *éna xenodohío?*
How do I get there? *Pos na páo ekí?*
Can you show me where I am on the map? *Boríte na mou díhete sto hárti pou íme?*
Am I on the right road for... *Yia... kalá páo?*
No, you're on the wrong road *Óhi, pírate láthos drómo*

On the Road

Where can I hire a car? *Pou boró na nikiázo avtokínito?*
What is it insured for? *Ti asfália éhi?*
By what time must I return it? *Méhri ti óra prépi na to epistrépso?*
driving licence *díploma*
petrol *venzíni*
oil *ládi*
Fill it up *Yemíste to*
My car has broken down *Hálase to avtokinitó mou*
Can you check... *Boríte na elénhete...*
the brakes *ta fréna*
the clutch *to ambrayáz*
the engine *ti mihaní*
the exhaust *ti exátmisi*
the fanbelt *to imánda*
the gearbox *tis tahítites*
the headlights *ta fanária*
the radiator *to psigío*
the spark plugs *ta boúzia*
the tyre(s) *to lástiho/ta lástiha*

TIMES AND DATES

(in the) morning/afternoon/ evening *to proí/to apógevma/to vrádi*
(at) night *(ti) níhta*

yesterday *htes*
today *símera*
tomorrow *ávrio*
now *tóra*
early *norís*
late *argá*
a minute *éna leptó*
five/ten *pénde/déka*
minutes *leptá*
an hour *mia óra*
half an hour *misí óra*
a quarter of an hour *éna tétarto*
at one/two (o'clock) *stis mia/dýo (i óra)*
a day *mia méra*
a week *mia evdomáda*
(on) Monday *(ti) deftéra*
(on) Tuesday *(tin) tríti*
(on) Wednesday *(tin) tetárti*
(on) Thursday *(tin) pémpti*
(on) Friday *(tin) paraskeví*
(on) Saturday *(to) sávato*
(on) Sunday *(tin) kyriakí*

HEALTH

Is there a chemist's nearby? *Ypárhi éna farmakío edó kondá?*
Which chemist is open all night? *Pio farmakío dianikterévi?*
I don't feel well *Den esthánome kalá*
I'm ill *Íme árostos (feminine árosti)*
He/she's ill *Íne árostos/árosti*
Where does it hurt? *Pou ponái?*
It hurts here *Ponái edó*
I suffer from... *Páskho apo...*
I have a... *Éxo...*
headache *ponokéfalo*
sore throat *ponólemo*

Notices

ΤΟΥΑΛΕΤΕΣ toilets
ΑΝΔΡΩΝ gentlemen
ΓΥΝΑΙΚΩΝ ladies
ΑΝΟΙΚΤΟ open
ΚΛΕΙΣΤΟ closed
ΕΙΣΟΔΟΣ entrance
ΕΞΟΔΟΣ exit
ΑΠΑΓΟΡΕΥΤΑΙ ΕΙΣΟΔΟΣ no entry
ΕΙΣΙΤΗΡΙΑ tickets
ΑΠΑΓΟΡΕΥΤΑΙ ΤΟ ΚΑΠΝΙΣΜΑ
no smoking
ΠΛΗΡΟΦΟΡΙΕΣ information
ΠΡΟΣΟΧΗ caution
ΚΙΝΔΥΝΟΣ danger
ΑΡΓΑ slow
ΔΗΜΟΣΙΑ ΕΡΓΑ road works
ΠΑΡΚΙΝΓ parking
ΧΩΡΟΣ ΣΤΑΘΜΕΥΣΕΩΣ car park
ΑΠΑΓΟΡΕΥΤΑΙ Η ΣΤΑΘΜΕΥΣΗ
no parking
ΤΑΞΙ taxi
ΤΡΑΠΕΖΑ bank
ΤΗΛΕΦΩΝΟ telephone
ΕΚΤΟΣ ΛΕΙΤΟΥΡΓΙΑΣ out of order

FURTHER READING

Books go in and out of print, or change imprints, with such rapidity of late that we've elected not to list the publishers, except for obscure Greek publishers with no internet presence, or one off presses with only internet presence. For most titles, conducting a web search with the author and title should suffice to dredge up its current incarnation (which these days may be a Kindle or print-on-demand edition only, or a used copy for a few pennies).

ANCIENT HISTORY AND CULTURE

Greek Religion: Archaic and Classical, by Walter Burkert. Excellent overview of the gods and goddesses, their attributes, worship and the meaning of major festivals.
The Penguin History of Greece, by A.R Burn. A good, single-volume introduction to ancient Greece.
The Greeks and Greek Love, by James Davidson. This "radical reappraisal of homosexuality in ancient Greece" tries to put queerness back at the centre of the ancient social equation and, despite too many bouts of special pleading, gets some way there.
The World of Odysseus, by M.I. Finley. Reissued 1954 standard on just how well (or not) the Homeric sagas are borne out by archaelogical facts.
Alexander the Great, by Robin Lane Fox. A psychobiography wedded to a conventional history.
Dictionary of Classical Mythology, by Pierre Grimal. Still considered to be tops among a handful of available alphabetical gazetteers.
The Greek World, 479–323 BC, by Simon Hornblower. The eventful period from the end of the Persian Wars to Alexander's demise; the standard university text.

BYZANTINE HISTORY AND CULTURE

The Early Centuries, The Apogee and **The Decline** (3 vols), by John Julius Byzantium Norwich. The most readable and masterful popular history, by the noted Byzantinologist; also available as one massive volume, **A Short History of Byantium**. **Psellus**, Michael Fourteen Byzantine Rulers. That many changes of rule in a single century (10th–11th), as told by a near-contemporary historian.
Art of the Byzantine Era, by David Talbot Rice. Shows how Byzantine sacred craftsmanship extended from the Caucausus into northern Italy, in a variety of media.
Runciman, Steven **The Fall of Constantinople, 1453**. Still the definitive study of an event which continues to exercise modern Greek minds. His **Byzantine Style and Civilization** covers art, culture and monuments.
The Orthodox Church, by Archbishop Kallistos Ware. Good introduction to what was, until recently, the de facto established religion of modern Greece.

ANTHROPOLOGY AND CULTURE

Honor, family and patronage: A study of institutions and moral values in a Greek mountain community, by John Campbell. Classic study of Sarakatsáni shepherds in the Zagorian Píndos, with much wider application to Greece in general, which got the author banned from the area by touchy officialdom.
The Death Rituals of Rural Greece, by Loring H. Danforth and Alexander Tsiaras. Riveting, annotated photo essay on Greek funeral customs.
Portrait of a Greek Mountain Village, by Juliet Du Boulay. Ambéli, a mountain village in Évvia, as it was in the mid-1960s.
Road to Rembetika: Songs of Love, Sorrow and Hashish (Denise Harvey, Límni, Évvia), by Gail Holst. Introduction to the enduringly popular musical form; with translated lyrics and discographies.
The Modern Greek Language, by Peter Mackridge. In-depth analysis by one of the foremost scholars of the tongue's evolution. His more recent Language and National Identity in Greece, 1766–1976 is a masterful yet easily readable study of the language controversy in all its ramifications, especially the mutually reinforcing dynamic of Greek self-perception and how elites and masses chose to express themselves.
Festive Greece: A Calendar of Tradition, by John L. Tomkinson. Copiously photographed calendar of all the extant rites of the Orthodox Church, their pagan substrata erupting frequently and vividly at popular *panigýria*.

CUISINE

Siren Feasts, by Andrew Dalby. Analysis of Classical and Byzantine texts shows just how little Greek food has changed in three millennia.
Mediterranean Seafood, by Alan Davidson. 1972 classic, redone in 2012, that's still the standard reference, guaranteed to end every argument as to just what that fish is on your tavérna plate. Complete with recipes.
Real Greek Food, by Theodore Kyriakou and Charles Campion. The latest cookery book, part authored by the founder of London's Real Greek and Souvlaki restaurants. Beautifully illustrated.
The Wines of Greece, by Konstantinos Lazarakis. An overview, current to late 2005, of what's happening in Greece's eleven recognized wine-producing regions.

MODERN HISTORY

Greece, The Hidden Centuries: Turkish Rule from the Fall of Constantinople to Greek Independence, by David Brewer. Refreshingly revisionist, new work on the "Turkokratia", uniformly dismissed in standard (and nationalist) narratives as a new dark ages but here put in proper perspective.
Twice a Stranger: How Mass Expulsion Forged Modern Greece and Turkey, by Bruce Cark. Nearly a century after the compulsory population exchanges, both nations are

still engaged in digesting the episode – with many on both sides recognising it as a mistake. More thorough on the experience of Orthodox refugees coming to Greece, but still invaluable.

A Concise History of Greece, by Richard Clogg. Clear and lively account of Greece from Byzantine times to 2012, with helpful maps and well-captioned artwork. The best single-volume summary.

Greece: A Jewish History, by K. E. Fleming. The title is carefully chosen; one of the main points here is that local Jews only identified primarily as Greeks after the Nazi deportations – before that, they tended to identify with their hometown and its often idiosyncratic customs.

Greece, the Modern Sequel: From 1831 to the Present, by John Koliopoulos and Thanos Veremis. Thematic and psycho-history of the independent nation, tracing trends, first principles and setbacks.

Salonica: City of Ghosts, by Mark Mazower. A lucid account of this extraordinary city from 1430 to 1950, as Christians, Muslims and Jews came together and prospered, before man and nature tore it apart.

I Was Born Greek, by Melina Mercouri. The tumultuous life and times of Greece's most famous actress, written in 1971 while she was in exile from the junta.

The Greeks: The Land and People Since the War, by James Pettifer. Useful general introduction to politics, family life, food, tourism and other contemporary topics.

Modern Greece: A Short History, by C.M. Woodhouse. Spans the period from early Byzantium to the early 1980s. His classic *The Struggle for Greece, 1941–1949*, reissued by C. Hurst (London), is perhaps the best overview of that turbulent decade.

MODERN GREEK LITERATURE

An Introduction to Modern Greek, by Roderick Beaton. Readable survey of Greek literature since independence.

An Anthology of Modern Greek Poetry, by Nanos Valaoritis and Thanasis Maskaleris. English-only text, but excellent biographical info on the poets and good renditions by two native Greek speakers.

Collected Poems, by C.P. Cavafy, trans. by Edmund Keeley and Philip Sherrard or The Complete Poems of Cavafy, trans. by Rae Dalven. The two "standard" versions available in English; newer 2007 translations by

Evangelos Sachperoglou and Stratis Haviaris will also be of interest but don't break radically new ground.

The Axion Esti, Selected Poems and *The Sovereign Sun*, by Odysseus Elytis. Pretty much the complete works of the Nobel laureate, in translation.

Little Infames, by Panos Karnezis. This collection of short stories is set in his native Peloponnese during the late 1950s and early 1960s; *The Maze* is a darker, more successful novel concerning the Asia Minor Catastrophe. Both display a penchant for old-fashioned plot twists – or excessive whimsical magical realism, depending on point of view. *The Birthday Party* is based on the life of Aristotle Onassis and daughter Christina. Karnezis grew up in Greece, but lives in London, writing in English; however, his concerns remain resolutely Greek.

Zorba the Greek, by Nikos Kazantzakis. This is a surprisingly dark and nihilistic work, worlds away from the crude, two-dimensional character of the film; *The Last Temptation of Christ* provoked riots by Orthodox fanatics in Athens in 1989; *Report to Greco* explores his Cretanness/ Greekness; while *Christ Recrucified* (published in the US as The Greek Passion) encompasses the Easter drama within Christian-Muslim dynamics on Crete. Nobel laureate, woolly Marxist fellow traveller and self-imposed exile, Kazantzakis embodies the old maxim that classics are books praised but generally unread. Whether in intricate, untranslatable Greek or wooden English, Kazantzakis can be hard going.

Red Dyed Hair, by Kostas Mourselas. Politically incorrect picaresque saga of urban life from the 1950s to the 1970s among a particularly feckless paréa; the Greek original still sells well, and formed the basis of popular TV series.

The Murderess, by Alexandros Papadiamantis; trans. Peter Levi. Landmark novel, set on Skiáthos at the turn of the 19th/20th centuries.

Father Dancing (published as A Crowded Heart in the US), by Nick Papandreou. Thinly disguised, page-turning roman-à-clef by the late prime minister's younger son; Papandreou père comes across as an egotistical monster.

Exile and Return, Selected Poems 1967–74, by Yannis Ritsos. The outcome of junta-era internal exile on Sámos for Greece's foremost Communist poet.

Collected Poems 1924–55; Complete Poems, by George Seferis;

trans. Edmund Keeley. The former has Greek-English texts on facing pages and is preferable to the so-called "complete" works of Greece's other Nobel literary laureate.

Farewell Anatolia, by Dido Sotiriou. A best-selling classic since its appearance in 1962, this traces the end of the Greeks in Asia Minor from 1914 to 1922, using a character based on the author's father.

Drifting Cities, by Stratis Tsirkas; trans. Kay Cicellis. Welcome paperback re-issue of this epic novel on wartime leftist intrigue in Alexandria, Cairo and Jerusalem.

An Anthology of Modern Greek Poetry, by Nanos Valaoritis and Thanasis Maskaleris. English-only text, but excellent biographical info on the poets and good renditions by two native Greek speakers.

Z, by Vassilis Vassilikos. Based closely enough on the assassination of leftist MP Grigoris Lambrakis in 1963 by royalist thugs to get the book – and author – banned by the colonels' junta.

FOREIGN WRITERS IN/ON GREECE

The Flight of Ikaros, by Kevin Andrews. An educated, sensitive, Anglo-American archaeologist wanders the back-country in surprising freedom as the civil war winds down. Despite the massive changes since, still one of the best books on the country.

A Foreign Wife, A Fair Exchange and *Aphrodite and the Others*, by Gillian Douras. Scottish-Australian marries Greek-Australian, then consents to return to the "mother" country; the resulting trilogy is about the best of many chronicles of the acculturation experience.

Captain Corelli's Mandolin, by Louis De Bernières. Heart-rending tragicomedy set on occupied Kefaloniá during World War II which has acquired cult status and long-term best-seller-list tenancy since its appearance in 1994.

Prospero's Cell and *Reflections on a Marine Venus*, by Lawrence Durrell. Corfu in the 1930s, and Rhodes in 1945–47, now looking rather old-fashioned, alcohol-fogged and patronising of the "natives", but still entertaining enough.

The Magus, by John Fowles. Best-seller, inspired by author's spell teaching on Spétses during the 1950s, of post-adolescent manipulation, conspiracy and sexual temptation (ie, the usual Fowles obsessions).

North of Ithaka, by Eleni Gage. Eleni is the namesake and granddaughter of the Eleni, whose murder her son Nicholas set out to avenge *(see below)*. A New York journalist, she "took leave" for most of 2002 in her grandmother's village in Epirus, rebuilding the family house and more.
Eleni, by Nicholas Gage. Epirus-born American correspondent returns to Greece to avenge the death of his mother at the hands of a Communist firing squad in 1948.
Falconera, by Alexis Ladas. Ripping good yarn, with plenty of Boy's Own action (but some convincingly well-written un-Boy's Own sex), telling in part of a daring raid to interfere with Germany resupply of Crete by the British-supported Greek Raiding Schooner Flotilla, in which the author served.
Travels in Northern Greece and Mani, by Leigh Fermor and Patrick Roumeli. Written during the late 1950s and early 1960s, before the advent of mass tourism, these remain some of the best compendia of the then already-vanishing customs and relict communities of the mainland.
This Way to Paradise: Dancing on the Tables, by Willard Manus. An American expatriate's affectionate summing-up of 40-plus years living in Líndos, from its innocence to its corruption. Wonderful anecdotes of the hippie days, and walk-on parts for the famous and infamous.
The Colossus of Maroussi, by Henry Miller. Miller takes to Corfu, the Argolid, Athens and Crete of 1939 with the enthusiasm of a first-timer in Greece who's found his element; deserted archaeological sites and larger-than-life personalities.
The Unwritten Places, by Tim Salmon. Veteran Hellenophile describes his love affair with the Greek mountains, and the Vlach pastoral communities of Epirus in particular.
The Summer of my Greek Taverna, by Tom Stone. Set in a thinly disguised Kámbos of early-1980s Pátmos, this is a poignant cautionary tale for all who've ever fantasised about leasing a taverna (or buying a property) in the islands.
Dinner with Persephone, by Patricia Storace. New York poet resident a year in Athens successfully takes the pulse of modern Greece, with all its shibboleths, foundation myths, carefully nurtured self-image and rampant misogyny. Very funny, and spot-on.
Traveller's Greece: Memories of an Enchanted Land, by John Tomkinson. 17th–19th-century traveller's

impressions of islands and mainland, ranging from the enraptured to the appalled.
Eurydice Street, by Sofka Zinovieff. An anthropologist and journalist by training, Zinovieff first came to Greece in the early 1980s (contributing to the first Insight Guide Greece), then returned in 2001 with her Greek husband and two daughters to live in Athens. With sharp insights on nationalism, Orthodoxy, politics, 17 November and leisure (among various topics), this is the best single account of life in contemporary urban Greece – tellingly, translated into Greek. Her more recent debut novel, The House on Paradise Street, is a gripping exploration of the lingering effects of the civil war and its aftermath in contemporary Greece, and a good family drama.

REGIONAL & ARCHAEOLOGICAL GUIDES

Anagnosis Guides (www.anagnosis.gr) Several well-illustrated guides to Athens and surroundings that highlight the obscure, unorthodox and overlooked, with directions to cited sites.
The Living Past of Greece, by A.R. and Mary Burn. Worth toting its oversized format around for the sake of lively text and clear plans; covers most

Send Us Your Thoughts

We do our best to ensure the information in our books is as accurate and up-to-date as possible. The books are updated on a regular basis using local contacts, who painstakingly add, amend and correct as required. However, some details (such as telephone numbers and opening times) are liable to change, and we are ultimately reliant on our readers to put us in the picture.

We welcome your feedback, especially your experience of using the book "on the road". Maybe we recommended a hotel that you liked (or another that you didn't), or you came across a great bar or new attraction we missed.

We will acknowledge all contributions, and we'll offer an Insight Guide to the best letters received.

Please write to us at:
Insight Guides
PO Box 7910
London SE1 1WE
Or email us at:
hello@insightguides.com

major sites from Minoan to medieval.
Byzantine and Medieval Greece, by Paul Hetherington. Erudite and authoritative dissection of the castles and churches of the mainland; his *The Greek Islands: Byzantine and Medieval Buildings* is also invaluable, but has some strange omissions.
The Mountains of Greece: Trekking in the Pindhos Mountains, by Tim Salmon. The best routes on the northern mainland (including Zagóri, and isolated Mt Ólymbos), with schematic maps and some GPS data.
The High Mountains of Crete: White Mountains, Psiloritis & Lassithi Ranges, by Lorraine Wilson. The best of several guides to the island, with nearly 100 hikes of all levels, described by the most experienced foreign trek leader. Sketch maps are minimal – you'll need an additional commercial product from Anavasi Publications.

BOTANICAL FIELD GUIDES

Greek Wildflowers and Plant Lore in Ancient Greece, by Helmut Baumann. As the title says; lots of interesting ethnobotanical trivia, useful photos.
Flowers of Greece and the Aegean, by Anthony Huxley and William Taylor. The only volume dedicated to both islands and mainland, with good photos, though taxonomy is now a bit obsolete.
Flowers of Greece and the Balkans, by Oleg Polunin et al. This book is also showing its age, but again has lots of colour photos to aid identification.
Flowers of the Mediterranean, by Oleg Polunin and Anthony Huxley. Lots of colour plates to aid in identification, and includes flowering shrubs; recent printings have a table of taxonomic changes.

OTHER INSIGHT GUIDES

Insight Guides cover nearly 200 destinations, providing information on culture and all the top sights, as well as superb photography and detailed maps. Other Insight Guides to destinations in the region include Greek Islands and Turkey.

Insight FlexiMaps and TravelMaps are designed to complement our guidebooks. They provide full mapping of major destinations, and their easy-to-fold, laminated finish gives them ease of use and durability. The range of Greek titles include Athens and Crete.

TRANSPORT

A – Z

LANGUAGE

CREDITS

Photo Credits

Acropolis Museum/Nikos Daniilidis 10B, 139B, 140B
akg images 34, 51, 56, 85
Alamy 75, 82, 92, 96MR, 97BR, 165, 203, 291
AWL Images 136, 311BR
Benaki Museum, Photographic Archive 53L, 53R, 57, 81
Bigstock 9BL, 11B, 37, 166T, 166/167B, 172, 177T, 184, 199B, 209, 211, 220, 255, 260B, 261, 263, 269BL, 295B, 297, 305, 306T, 307B, 333T
Britta Jaschinski/Apa Publications 9BR, 18, 19T, 20, 21, 26, 30, 31, 32, 41, 42, 66, 67, 68/69, 70, 71, 72, 73, 76, 79, 88, 89, 93, 98, 99, 100, 101, 103, 104, 108L, 109, 110R, 110L, 115, 116, 120, 124/125, 129T, 157TR, 224/225, 226, 227T, 231, 232, 233, 234T, 234B, 236, 237, 240, 241B, 241T, 243, 244, 245, 246B, 246T, 247, 248, 249, 251T, 252, 253, 254, 257, 259, 260T, 262, 268/269T, 268BR, 268BL, 269ML, 269TR, 270, 271, 272, 273B, 274, 275T, 275B, 276, 277, 278, 279, 280B, 283B, 284, 285, 286T, 286B, 287, 288, 293, 295T, 298, 299, 301T, 301B, 302B, 302T, 303, 304B, 310BR, 310BL,

311ML, 311TR, 312, 313, 314, 315, 316T, 316B, 317, 318, 329, 334, 338, 339, 342, 351
Christof Halbe 222
Corbis 54/55, 61, 84, 94
Design Pics Inc/Rex Features 114
Dreamstime 6ML, 6BL, 6MR, 7MR, 8MR, 8M, 22, 23, 65, 90, 133T, 148B, 168, 169, 171, 173, 174, 176, 177B, 178, 183B, 185T, 186B, 187, 188, 196B, 202, 207, 242B, 250, 256, 266, 304T, 306B, 307T, 309, 319
Ethiniki Pinakothiki 27T
FLPA 118, 119, 121
Fotolia 7TL, 8BL, 39, 45, 129B, 161, 164, 186T, 191, 200, 205, 214, 217, 218, 219, 280T, 294
German Federal Archive 28
Getty Images 4/5, 11T, 12/13, 16/17, 29, 44, 58/59, 62, 63, 64, 74, 87, 96/97T, 97ML, 122/123, 126/127, 128, 196T, 292
Glyn Genin/Apa Publications 7TR, 27B, 91, 107, 112, 132, 137, 139T, 142T, 142B, 143, 144, 145B, 146B, 147T, 147B, 148T, 148/149, 150, 151B, 152, 153, 154T, 154B, 156MR, 156/157T, 156BR, 157ML, 157BL, 157BR, 185B, 228, 229, 230B, 230T, 235B, 235T, 242T, 345

Guglielmo Galvin/Apa Publications 283T
iStock 36, 97BL, 155, 170T, 175, 189B, 193T, 193B, 194, 197, 198T, 208B, 210, 212, 213T, 223, 264, 265B, 265T, 267, 289, 290, 308, 310/311T, 311BL, 324B, 333B, 355
Kevin Cummins/Apa Publications 1, 6MR, 10T, 14/15, 19B, 78, 102, 145T, 227B, 320, 321, 322, 323, 324T, 325, 326, 327, 330, 331T, 331B, 332, 336T, 337, 343, 347
Library of Congress 163T
Nowitz Photography/Apa Publications 7ML, 33, 35, 38, 40, 43, 106, 108R, 111, 113, 133B, 158, 159, 162, 163B, 179, 181, 182, 183T, 336B
Phil Wood/Apa Publications 47, 146T, 199T, 208T, 216
Photoshot 86, 117, 204, 269BR
Princetown University Library 24/25
Public domain 46, 48/49, 50, 273T
Robert Harding 7ML, 198B
Shutterstock 83, 140T, 141, 151T, 170B, 189T, 195, 201, 213B
SuperStock 9TL, 80, 105, 190
Topfoto 52, 60
Travel Pictures Ltd 7B, 95, 96BR, 97TR, 251B

Cover Credits

Front cover: Navagio Beach, Zakynthos *Shutterstock*
Back cover: Parga *iStock*
Front flap: (from top) Ladiko Bay, Rhodes *Britta Jaschinski/Apa*

Publications; Temple of Aphaea, Aegina *Dreamstime*; Bouzouki Player *Britta Jaschinski/Apa Publications*; Beef stifado; *Britta Jaschinski/Apa Publications*

Back flap: The sea from Skiathos Town *Britta Jaschinski/Apa Publications*

Insight Guide Credits

Distribution
UK, Ireland and Europe
Apa Publications (UK) Ltd;
sales@insightguides.com
United States and Canada
Ingram Publisher Services;
ips@ingramcontent.com
Australia and New Zealand
Woodslane; info@woodslane.com.au
Southeast Asia
Apa Publications (SN) Pte;
singaporeoffice@insightguides.com
Hong Kong, Taiwan and China
Apa Publications (HK) Ltd;
hongkongoffice@insightguides.com
Worldwide
Apa Publications (UK) Ltd;
sales@insightguides.com
**Special Sales, Content Licensing
and CoPublishing**
Insight Guides can be purchased in
bulk quantities at discounted prices.
We can create special editions,
personalised jackets and corporate
imprints tailored to your needs.
sales@insightguides.com
www.insightguides.biz

Printed in China by CTPS

First Edition 1987
Seventh Edition 2017

Every effort has been made to
provide accurate information in this
publication, but changes are
inevitable. The publisher cannot be
responsible for any resulting loss,
inconvenience or injury. We would
appreciate it if readers would call our
attention to any errors or outdated
information. We also welcome your
suggestions; please contact us at:
hello@insightguides.com

www.insightguides.com

Editor: Tom Fleming
Author: Marc Dubin
Head of Production: Rebeka Davies
Update Production: AM Services
Picture Editor: Tom Smyth
Cartography: original cartography
Berndtson & Berndtson, updated
by Carte

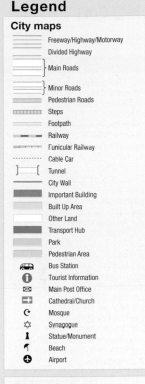

Legend

City maps

	Freeway/Highway/Motorway
	Divided Highway
	Main Roads
	Minor Roads
	Pedestrian Roads
	Steps
	Footpath
	Railway
	Funicular Railway
	Cable Car
	Tunnel
	City Wall
	Important Building
	Built Up Area
	Other Land
	Transport Hub
	Park
	Pedestrian Area
	Bus Station
	Tourist Information
	Main Post Office
	Cathedral/Church
	Mosque
	Synagogue
	Statue/Monument
	Beach
	Airport

Contributors

This brand new edition was
thoroughly updated by Magdalena
Helsztyńska; the update was
managed and copy-edited in-house
by Tom Fleming.

This version builds on the
invaluable contributions of many
earlier editors and writers, such as
Marc Dubin, a well-travelled Londoner
who has a house in Sámos, Maria
Lord, Jeffrey Pike, Professor Richard

Clogg, Dr David Sutton, Professor Gail
Holst-Warhaft, Aglaia Kremezi, Dr
John Lord, Danny Aeberhard, John
Chapple, Lance Chilton, Paul
Hellander and Jeffrey Carson.

The stunning photographs in this
latest edition are the output of Insight
regulars Britta Jaschinski, Glyn Genin
and Richard Nowitz. Tom Smyth was
the in-house picture editor. This guide
was proof read by Darren Longley.

About Insight Guides

Insight Guides have more than
45 years' experience of publishing
high-quality, visual travel guides. We
produce 400 full-colour titles, in both
print and digital form, covering more
than 200 destinations across the
globe, in a variety of formats to meet
your different needs.

Insight Guides are written by
local authors, whose expertise is
evident in the extensive historical
and cultural background features.

Each destination is carefully
researched by regional experts to
ensure our guides provide the very
latest information. All the reviews
in **Insight Guides** are independent;
we strive to maintain an impartial
view. Our reviews are carefully
selected to guide you to the best
places to eat, go out and shop, so
you can be confident that when
we say a place is special, we really
mean it.

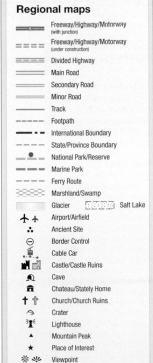

Regional maps

	Freeway/Highway/Motorway (with junction)
	Freeway/Highway/Motorway (under construction)
	Divided Highway
	Main Road
	Secondary Road
	Minor Road
	Track
	Footpath
	International Boundary
	State/Province Boundary
	National Park/Reserve
	Marine Park
	Ferry Route
	Marshland/Swamp
	Glacier Salt Lake
	Airport/Airfield
	Ancient Site
	Border Control
	Cable Car
	Castle/Castle Ruins
	Cave
	Chateau/Stately Home
	Church/Church Ruins
	Crater
	Lighthouse
	Mountain Peak
	Place of Interest
	Viewpoint

INDEX

Main references are in bold type

A

Abdi Efendi Hamam 144
accommodation 343
Achilleion Palace 325
Acropolis 140, 141
Acropolis Museum 139
Adámas 248
Aegina (Egina) **229**
   Christos Kapralos Museum 230
   town **230**
Afáles, bay of 329
Áfyssos 188
Agathonísi 290
Agiá 193
Agía Anárgyri beach 235
Agía Ánna 319
Agía Ánna beach 248
Agía beach 249
Agía Ekateríni church 259
Agía Evpraxía 234
Agía Galíni 264
Agía Iríni 239
Agía Marína 230, 235
Agía Marína 290
Agía Marína beach 239
Agía Marína beach (Batsí) 239
Agía Marína Nerás 284
Agía Paraskeví 318
Agía Paraskeví beach 235
Agía Paraskeví monastery 199
Agía Rouméli 267
Agías Mávras 332
Agía Sofía 208
Agía Sofía cavern 333
Agiásos 302
Agías Triádos 189
Agía Theodóti 251
Agía Triáda 264, 266
Agía Triáda church 248
Ágii Anárgyri 213
Ágii Anárgyriis beach 235
Ágii Theodóri 150, 309
Ágii Theodóri church 217
Ágion Gála 305
Ágion Óros 219
Ágios Ahíllios 215
Ágios Dimítrios 208, 316, 319
Ágios Dionýsios 332
Ágios Evstrátios 299
Ágios Fokás 318
Ágios Geórgios 330
Ágios Geórgios Argyrádon 325
Ágios Geórgios beach 250
Ágios Geórgioschurch 149
Ágios Geórgios ton Krimnón 333
Ágios Geórgios Valsamítis 251
Ágios Gerásimou 331
Ágios Germanós 214
Ágios Górdis 325
Ágios Ioánnis 172, 188, 298
Ágios Ioánnis Détis moastery 246
Ágios Isídoros 302
Ágios Kírykos **306**
Ágios Konstandínos beach 289
Ágios Mámas 235

Ágios Márkos church 259
Ágios Matthéos 325
Ágios Nektários Monastery 231
Ágios Nikítas (Aï Nikítas) 329
Ágios Nikólaos 183, 198, 222, 234,
   253, 261, 274, 301
Ágios Nikólaos beach 250
Ágios Nikólaos (castle) 327
Ágios Nikólaos church 217
Ágios Nikólaos Foundouklí church
   276
Ágios Nikólaos Kasnítsi 213
Ágios Nikólaos Orfanós 209
Ágios Nikólaos (Selenítsa) 173
Ágios Nikólaos tou Mólou 332
Ágios Pandelímon 172, 318
Ágios Pétros 318
Ágios Prokópios beach 248
Ágios Sóstis 240, 243
Ágios Spyrídon cove 155
Ágios Stéfanos 213, 287
Ágios Stéfanos Sinión 324
Ágios Stratigós 172
Ágios Títos 259
Ágios Vassílios 284
Agíou Georgíou Feneoú monastery
   162
Agíou Ioánnou Theológou
   Monastery (Pátmos) 291
Agíou Nikoláou Anápavsa 189
Agíou Nikoláou Filanthropinón 197
Agíou Pandelímona 285
Agíou Stefánou 189
Agnóndas 315
Agora 208
Agorá 266
Agrínio 185
Aháïa **177**
   Diakoftó **177**
   Pátra **177**
Aharávi 324
Aháta 281
Ahílli Bay 317
Ahiropíitos 208
Aigai 216
Akronavpliá 164
Akrotíri 252
Akrotíri 157
Akrotíri Peninsula 266
Áktio 195
Alalkomenes 329
Alatza Imaret Mosque 210
Alexander the Great 39
Alexandroúpoli 223
Aliákmonas River 213
Álinda 290
Ali Pasha 194
Alivéri 319
Alónisos 316
Aloprónia beach 250
Alykés 332
Alykí 247, 295
Alykó beach 248
Ambelákia 188
Amfilohía 185
Ammoudiá 194

Ammoulianí 219
Amorgós 251
Amphipolis 220
Anáfi **253**
Anafonítria 333
Análipsi 289
Anargýrios and Korgialénios
   College 235
Anávatos 305
ancient Erétria 318
Ancient Greek Agora 141
ancient Lebena 264
ancient Mália 260
ancient Olynthos 218
Ancient Thera 252
Andíparos 245
Andíparos Hóra 245
Andípaxi (Andípaxos) 328
Andísamos, beach of 331
Andrítsena 168
Ándros **237**
   Batsí 237
   Gávrio 237
   Goulandris Museum 239
   Hóra Town 237
Anemospiliá temple 259
Angáli 250, 319
Angelókastro 325
Angístri (Agístri) 231
Anógia 260
Áno Merá 242
Áno Meriá 250
Áno Sýros 241
Áno Vathý 308
Ápella 281
Apéri 281
Aphaea Temple (Aegina) 230
Aphrodite (Mílos) 249
Apíranthos 248
Apocalypse Monastery (Pátmos)
   291
Apókroussi beach 240
Apollo Epikourios (Bassae) 168
Apóllonas 247
Apollonía 243
Apollo Temple (Aegina) 230
Aráhova 181
archaeological museum
   Ándros 237
   Árgos 163
   Haniá 266
   Ioánnina 196
   Ionian Islands 330
   Kástro 245
   Kavála 221
   Knossos 258
   Komotiní 223
   Kós 287
   Liménas 294
   Mýkonos 242
   Mýrina 298
   Mytilíni 301
   Návplio 164
   Náxos 247
   Páros 246
   Pláka 248

Póthia 288
Réthymno 265
Rhodes 273
Salamína 229
Sámos 307
Sitía 262
Spárti 169
Thessaloníki 207
Trípoli 166
Vathý 308
Vólos 187
archaeological museum (Corfu) 323
archaeological museum (Évvia (Euboea) 318
archaeological museum (Sporades) 318
architecture 105
Ardittós hills 151
Areópol 172
Arethoúsa Spring 329
Árgos 163
Argostóli 330
Argyrádes 325
Arhánes 259
Arhondikó Tosítsa Museum 198
Arkádi Monastery 264
Arkí 290
Arkteia festival 154
Armenistís 306
Arnádos 240
Arnéa 218
Arsinoeion 297
art 105
Árta 195
Artemis Orthia 169
Artemónas (Sífnos) 243
art galleries
    Hadjikyriakos-Ghikas Gallery 152
    National Art Gallery 149
Asfendioú 288
Asklepeion 287
Asklipío 277
Aslan Pasha Mosque 197
Áspa 307
Ássos 331
Ástakos 185
Astrída 295
Astypálea 288
Astypalia 288
Atelier-Museum Spyros Vassiliou 152
Atháni village 329
Athena Nike Temple 140
Athena temple 294
Athenian stoa (Delphi) 182
Athenian Treasury (Delphi) 182
Athens 137
    Abdi Efendi Hamam 144
    Acropolis 140
    Ágii Theodóri 150
    Ágios Geórgios Church 149
    Ancient Greek Agora 142
    Atelier-Museum Spyros Vassiliou 152
    Attica 154
    beaches 155
    Benáki Museum 143, 148
    Byzantine 151
    Byzantine and Christian Museum 149
    Canellopoulos (Kanellopoulou)
    Museum 144
    Cape Sounion 153
    car rental 341
    Choregic Monument to Lysikratos 142
    Dafní 150
    Fethiye Mosque 144
    Frissiras Museum 152
    Goulandris Natural History Museum 153
    Hadjikyriakos-Ghikas Gallery 152
    Hadrian's Library 144
    Herakleidon 152
    Herodeio or Iródio Theatre 143
    hill of Ardittós 151
    Hill of the Nymphs 151
    hills of 153
    Jewish Museum of Greece 145
    Kapnikaréa Church 147
    Kerameikos Cemetery 142
    Kesarianí 150
    Kifisiá 153
    Kolonáki 150
    Kozáni mansion 148
    Kyriazopoulos Collection of Pottery 144
    Lófos Stréfi 151
    Marathon 154
    metro system 338
    Mitrópolis 146
    Monastiráki 146
    Mount Hymettus 150
    Mount Hymettus (Ymittós) 151
    Mount Lykavitós 149
    Mount Párnitha 153
    Museum of Greek Folk Music Instruments 144
    Museum of Cycladic Art 148
    Museum of Greek Folk Art 145
    National Archaeological Museum 156
    National Art Gallery 149
    National Gallery 165
    National Gardens 147, 148
    National Historical Museum 147
    National Library, University and Academy 147
    Numismatic Museum 147
    Omónia 146
    Parliament Building 147
    Philopappou (Filopáppou) 151
    Piraeus Archaeological Museum 151
    Pláka 145
    Platía Agías Irínis 146
    Platía Karaïskáki 151
    Platía Omónias 146
    Platía Syndágmatos 146
    radio taxi services 340
    Rhamnous 155
    Roman 144
    Roman Agora 144
    Sanctuary of Amphiareion 155
    Sanctuary of Artemis 154
    Stoa of Attalos 142
    Sýndagma Square 147
    Temple of Olympian Zeus 143
    Temple of Poseidon 153
    Theoharakis Foundation 152
    Tower of the Winds 143
    Varvákios Agorá 146
    War Museum 149
    Záppio Park 143
Athinás Street 146
Athiniós 253
Áthos 219
Atsítsa 318
Attica 153
Avdira 223
Avgónyma 305
Avlémonas 333
Avlónas 298

B

Back Islands 254
Balkan Wars 53
Bállos 267
Barbáti 323
Batsí
    Agía Marína beach 239
    Delavóyas beach 239
    Hryssí Ámmos beach 239
    Kyprí beach 239
Batsí (Ándros) 237
beaches
    Mávro Lithári 155
Bembo Fountain 259
Benáki Museum 143, 148
Benáki Museum annexe 152
Benítses 325
Bey Hamam 211
Bezesténi 211
birds 121
Bísti 234
Blue Caves 333
Bóhali 332
botanical garden (Argostóli) 330
Bouboulina, Laskarina 235
Boúkari 325
Brauron 154
breakdown service for motorists 341
Brooke, Rupert 317
Brós Thermá 287
Butterflies Valley 247
Byzantine and Christian Museum 149
Byzantine churches
    Ágios Nikólaos Foundouklí 276
    Panagía Vlahernón 195
Byzantine Empire 41
Byzantine Museum 197, 323, 332
    Haniá 266
    Mytilíni 301
    Rhodes 273
Byzantine Museum (Kastoriá) 213
Byzantine Museum (Véria) 216

C

Canellopoulos (Kanellopoulou) Museum 144
Cape Akrítas 174
Cape Maléa 171
Cape Mátapan (Ténaro) 172
Cape Sounion 153
car hire (rentals) 341
Caribbean-Tudor 328
Casa Romana 287
castles
    Hrysoherías 288

Knights 274
Péra Kástro 288
Cavafy, Constantine 85
Cave of the Nymphs 329
caves 177
  Dikteo (Diktian) 261
  Hryssospiliá (Golden Cave) 250
  Ideon 260
  Katafiki 241
  Pérama 198
  Petrálona 218
  Polyphemus 223
Chain Tower (Thessaloníki) 210
Choregic Monument to Lysikratos 142
Christian catacombs 249
Christianity 48
Christos Kapralos Museum (Aegina) 230
Christ Pandokrátor mosaic 150
churches
  Agía Ekateríni 259
  Agía Sofía 170
  Agía Triáda church 248
  Ágios Geórgios 149
  Ágios Ioánnis 172
  Ágios Márkos 259
  Ágios Nikólaos 301
  Ágios Stéfanos (Kastoriá) 213
  Ekatondapylianí 246
  Ionian Islands 328
  Kapnikaréa 147
  Mitrópolis 146
  Panagía Andivouniótissa 323
  Panagía Armáta 235
  Panagía Kyrá 262
  Panagía Mesosporítissa 155
  Petaloúda 309
  Taxiárhis 172
  Taxiárhis tis Mitropóleos (Kastoriá) 213
Church of Ágios Spyrídon 322
climate 344
climate (Ionian Islands) 327
Constantine, Emperor 39
Constantine I, King 53, 54
Constantinople 41
Corcyra 323
Corfu 321
  archaeological museum 323
  Church of Ágios Spyrídon 322
  Museum of Asian Art 323
Corfu Town 321
Corinth 161
  Trizónia 184
Corinth Canal 159
Crete 257
  Knossos 258
Crete (Kríti) 21
Cyrus, King 35

D

Dadiá Forest Reserve 223
Dafní 150
Damoúhari 188
Dápia 234
Darius, King 35
Dassiá 323
Decorative Arts Collection (Rhodes) 273

Dekoúlou 173
Delavóyas beach (Batsí) 239
Delian League 36
Deligiannis, Theodoros 52
Delos 242
Delphi 181
  Athenian stoa 182
  Athenian Treasury 182
  stadium 183
  theatres 183
Delphi Museum 183
Dervenákia 162
Diafáni 280
Diakoftó (Aháďa) 177
Diapóndia 324
Diavologéfyro (Devil's Bridge) 233
Didymótiho 223
Dikteo (Diktian) Cave 261
Dílofo 199
Dimosári Gorge 319
Dion 215
  village museum 215
Dionysos Temple 294
disabled travellers 345
Dodecanese 279
  Ólympos 281
Dodona 197
Donoússa 254
Dorpfeld 329
Drakólimni 200
Drakólimni (Dragon Lake) 201
Drogaráti, caves of 331
Drymónas 329
Dryopída 241
Durrell, Lawrence 325
Dýo Horiá 240

E

Easter 77
ecclesiastical museum 301
Édessa 216
Edirne 223
Egiáli 252
Eginítissa 231
Egremní 329
Ekatondapylianí church 246
Elafonísi 267
Elafónisos 171
Elefsína 179
Elevtheroúpoli 220
Elgin Marbles 141
El Greco 110, 264
Eliá 313
Eliá beach 242
Elliniká 319
Eloúnda 261
Elytis, Odysseus 85
embassies and consulates 345
Emborió 283
Emborió bay 284
Emboriós 304
Emborió village 286
emergency numbers 346
Epidauros (Epídavros) 165
Epirus 191
  Zagóri 192
Episkopí beach 240
Eptánisa 323
Eptá Pigés 277
Eptapýrgio 210

Erechtheion 140
Erétria 318
Erikoússa 324
Éristos beach 285
Ermoú 147
Ermoúpoli 241
Etolikó 185
Étolo-Akarnanía 184
Etz Hayyim 266
Evangelist 274
Evangelístria convent 309
Evangelistrías 314
Evans, Arthur 269
Évdilos 306
Evgátis 299
Evpalínio Órygma 307
Évripos channel 318
Évros delta 120
Évvia (Euboea) 318
Évzone Guard 147
Exóbourgo 240
Exogí 329

F

facadism 113
Falásarna beach 267
Faliráki 276
Faltaïts Museum 317
Faneroméni Monastery (Salamína) 229
Fengári 295
Féres 223
festivals 96, 97
Fethiye Mosque 144
Fethiye Tzami 197
Filérimos 275
Fínikas 241
Firá 252
Firipláka beach 249
Flea Market 146
Flomohóri 173
flora
  Greece 310
Flórina 215
  Museum of Modern Art 215
Fódele 264
Fokas-Kosmetatou Foundation 330
Fokída 183
Folégandros 250
  Hóra 250
Folk and Ethnological Museum (Macedonia) 211
Folk and Modern Art Museum (Kavála) 221
Folklore Museum 214, 216
  Réthymno 265
Folklore Museum Évvia (Euboea) 319
Folklore Museum (Mýkonos) 242
Folklore Museum (Pláka) 248
Folklore Museum (Stemnítsa) 167
Folk Museum (Komotiní) 223
Folk Museum (Salamína) 229
Food and Drink 98
forests 185
  Skópelos 316
Foúrni 306
Fríkes 329
Frissiras Museum 152
frogs 118

G

Gáïos 327
Galatáki convent 319
Galaxídi 183
Galerius's triumphal arch 207
Galissás 241
Gánema 243
Gastoúni 176
Gate of Parmenon 294
Gávdos 267
Gávrio (Ándros) 237
gay and lesbian travellers 346
gemistá (stuffed tomatoes and peppers) 101
George, King 56
Georgioúpoli 265
Gérakas 332
Geroliménas 172
Giália 239
Gialiskári 306
Gialós 250, 283, 329
Gioúra 316
Gíra sandspit 328
Giustiniani Museum (Híos) 303
Glauke Fountain (Kórinthos) 161
Glóssa 315
Glyfáda 325
Glyfáda beach 248
Glykí 194
Glystéri 315
Gomáti 298
Goniá Monastery 267
Good Friday 96
Gortys 168, 263
Goulandris Museum (Ándros) 239
Goulandris Natural History Museum 153
Gournia 262
Gouvernétou Monastery 266
Governor's House (Mandráki) 274
Grand Masters Palace 271
GreatIdea, the 52
Greece
  flora 310
Greece islands 227
Gría Váthra 297
Gulf of Corinth 21
Gyáros 241
Gyrísmata 318
Gýthio 171

H

Hadjikyriakos-Ghikas Gallery 152
Hadjikyriakos-Gikas, Nikos 150
Hadrian, Emperor 39
Hadrian's Library 144
Halikiáda 231
Halikoúna beach 325
Halkí 248
Hálki 283
Halkída 318
Halkidikí 217
Hamza Bey Mosque 210
Haniá 266
Háni Avlonaríou 319
Haniótis 218
health and medical care 346
Hellenistic Athena temple 274
Hephaisteion 142

Herakleidon 152
Hera temple (Olympia) 175
Hera temple (Perahora Heraion) 159
Herodeio or Iródio Theatre 143
Herodotos 35
Hersónisos, Stalída 260
Hilandaríou 219
Hill of the Nymphs 151
Híos 302
Hippocrates tree 287
Historical Museum
  Crete 258
  Réthymno 265
Hlemoutsi 176
Hondrogiórgis 316
Hóra 240, 249, 289, 291, 303, 316
Hóra (Amorgós) 251
Hóra (Anáfi) 253
Hóra (Folégandros) 250
Hóra (Íos) 251
Hóra (Náxos Town) 247
Hóra Sfakíon (Sfakiá) 267
Hóra (Skýros Town) 317
Hóra Town (Ándros) 237
Hóra Trifylías 175
Horió 250, 283, 288
Hortiátis 211
Hozoviótissa 252
Hristós Monastery (Véria) 216
Hrysí Avgí (Golden Dawn) 62
Hrysí (Gaïdouronísi) 263
Hrysólakkos 261
Hrysoskalítissa Convent 267
Hryssí Ámmos beach (Batsí) 239
Hryssí Ammoudiá 295
Hryssopigís (Golden Wellspring) Monastery (Vathý) 245
Hryssospiliá (Golden Cave) 250

I

Ialysos 275
Ía (Oia) 253
Icon and Sacred Art Museum 259
Ideon Cave 260
Ierá Odós 139
Ierápetra 263
Igoumenítsa 193
Ikaría 305
Imaret 221
Immanouíl arhondiká 214
Internet 347
Ioánnina 196
Ionian Island 327
Ionian Monument 322
Íos 250
Ioulída (Kéa) 239
Irakliá 254
Iráklio (Crete) 258
Iroön 250
Islamic Art Collection 143
Íssos 325
Isthmia 159
Itéa 183
Itháki (Ithaca) 329
Ítylo 173

J

Jason of Pherae 38

Jewish Bath 211
Justinian, Emperor 41

K

Kaiser's Throne 325
Kalafáti beach 242
Kalamáta 173
Kalambáka 188
Kalámi 324
Kalamítsi 249, 329
Kalamítsi beach 218
Kal Kadosh Shalom 273
Kallithéa 276
Kalogriá 177
Kalpáki 201
Kálymnos 288
Kamáres 243
Kamári 253
Kamariótissa 296
Kambí 333
Kámbi 307
Kámbos 303, 306
Kameiros 275
Kaméni Hóra 232
Kamíni 234
Kanatsoúli residences 213
Kandoúni 288
Kapnikaréa church 147
Kapodistrias, Count Ioannis 51
Kapodistrias, Ioannis 230, 322
Kapsáli 333
Karamanlis 59
Karamanlis, Constantine 57
Karamanlis, Kostas 60
Karávi 243
Karavostási (Thesprotía) 193
Kardamýli 173
Kardianí 240
Karefloú 318
Karlóvasi 309
Kárpathos 280
Karpenísi 186
Karpenisiótis valley 186
Karyá 329
Karyádis quarter (Kastoriá) 213
Kárystos 319
Karýtena 167
Kásos 283
Kassándra 218
Kassiópi 324
Kassope 195
Kastáni 315
Kastéli-Kissámos 267
Kastellórizo 284
Kastellórizo Town 285
Kastoriá
  Byzantine Museum 213
  churches 213
  Karyádis quarter 213
  Taxiárhis tis Mitropóleos (Kastoriá) 213
Kastoriá (northern Greece) 213
Kástra 205, 209
Kastráki 189
kástro 245, 246, 250
Kástro 196, 243, 249, 250, 295
Katafíki cave 241
Katápola 251
Katapolianí 240
Katavatí 245

katavóthres (sea mills) 330
Kateliós 330
Káthisma 329
Katholikó 266
Káto Hóra 333
Káto Korakiána 323
Káto Zákros beach 263
Katsadiá 290
Katsoúni 254
Kavála 220
Kávos 325
Kazantzakis, Nikos 85, 259
Kéa 153, 239
    Ioulída 239
Kefalloniá 332
Kefaloniá (Cephalonia) 329
Kelefá 172
Kemal, Mustafa 54
Kerameikos Cemetery 142
Kérkyra. See Corfu Town
Kesarianí 150
Kifisiá 153
Kilioméno, 333
Kilkís 217
Kímolos 249
Kímolos island 227
Kíni 241
Kínyra 295
Kióni 329
Kípi 199
Kípos 297
Klíma 249
Klíma Vale 249
Klisoúra Gorge 185
Knights' castle 274
Knights of St John 45, 48
Knights Street (Odós Ippotón) 271
Knossos 268
Knossos (Crete) 258
Kokkári 308
Kokkinókastro beach 316
Kóllyva 76
Kolóna beach 240
Kolonáki 150
Kolymbári 267
Kolymbíthra beach (Tínos) 240
Kómi 304
Komméno 323
Kómmos 264
Komotiní 222
Kondókal 323
Kónitsa 201
Korgialenios Museum
    Ionian Islands 330
Kórinthos 161
Korissía 239
Korissíon lagoon 325
Koróni 174
Korónia 217
Koronída 247
Kórthi 239
Kós 286
    Loggia Mosque 286
    Roman agora 286
    Town 286
Koufonísi 254
Koukoúli 200
Koukounariés 313
Koulés fortress 258
Kouloúri 229
Koúndouros beach 239

Kounopétra 331
Kozáni mansion 148
Kríni 325
Kritinía 275
Kritsá 261
Kyparíssi 171
Kyprí beach (Batsí) 239
Kyrá Panagiá 281
Kyrá Panagía 316
Kyriakí beach 249
Kyriazopoulos Collection of
    Pottery 144
Kýthira 333
Kýthnos 240

L

Láfkos 188
Laganás 332
Lágia 173
Lahaniá village 277
Lake Doïránis 217
lakes 162
    Megáli (Great) Préspa 120
    Mikrí (Little) Préspa 120
    Trihonída 22
Lake Voulisméni 261
Lakkí 289
Lákoma 297
Lákones 325
Lakonía 169
Lalária 314
Lambrakis, Grigoris 58
Lamía 186
Langáda 173, 252
Langádia 166
Lángeri 246
language
    emergencies, expressions for 352
    pronunciation 351
    use at shops 353
    use in health centers 354
    use in public transport 354
Lasíthi Plain (Crete) 261
Lássi 330
Látomos Monastery 209
Lávrio 153
Lefkádia 216
Léfki 329
Leftós Gialós 316
Léndas 264
Leonidas, King 35
Léros 289
Lésvos 299
Levídi 166
Levkáda/Levkás 328
Lévkes 246
Levkímmi 325
Levkós 281
Levréhio beach 328
Liés 285
Ligonéri 235
limenarhío 340
Limenária 231, 295
Liménas 294
    Panagía village 294
Limín 309
Límni 319
Límni Kerkinis 217
Limniónas 333
Limnióniza 234

Límnos 297
Límonos Monastery 301
Linariá 317
Líndos 274
Lion of Amphipolis 220
Lion of Kéa 239
Lipsí 290
Lipsí island 227
Listón 321
Little Venice 242
Livadákia 243
Livádi 243, 289
Livádia 246, 285
Livadiá (Central Greece) 179
Lixoúri 330
Lófos Stréfi 151
Loggia Mosque (Kós) 286
Longós (resort) 327
Loúha 333
Loúsios Gorge 167
Loutrá 240
Loutrá Edipsoú 319
Loutráki 315
Lygiá 328

M

Macedonia
    Folk and Ethnological Museum 211
    Pella 217
    Vergína 216
    Véria 216
Magaziá 317
Magaziá-Mólos beach 318
Maherádo 332
Makrý Gialós 263
Makrynítsa 188
Mália 260
Mamma Mia! 315
Mandamádos 301
Mandráki 234, 273, 285, 313
Manganári bay 251
Máni 171
    churches 172
    markets (Areópol) 172
    Pýrgos Diroú 172
Manoúsi residences 213
Maráthi 246, 290
Marathon 154
Marathónas 231
Marathoúnda 284
marble horseshoe stadium 151
Mariés 295
Marinatos, Spyridon 157
marine life 118
markets
    Areópol 172
    Flea Market 146
    Xánthi 222
Marmári 287
Marmaria 181
Maroneia 223
Maroúla 241
Mask of Agamemnon 156
Massoúri 288
Mastihári 287
Mátala 264
Mathráki 325
Mávro Lithári beach 155
measures 350
Megáli Evdomáda 96

Megáli Préspa 214
Megáli Préspa lake 214
Megális Panagías 309
Megálo 201
Megálo Horió 285
Megálo Kazavíti 295
Megálo Livádi 243
Megálou Meteórou 189
Mégas Lákkos beaches 330
Megístis Lávras monastery 219
Melissáni, caves of 331
melitzanosaláta (aubergine dip)
    101
Menetés 281
mercenaries 37
Mérihas 240
Mesará plain 263
Meséo 309
Mesolóngi 184
Mesongi (Corfu) 325
Mesopótamos 194
Messinía 173
    Koróni 174
    Voïdokiliá 175
Mestá 304
Metamórfosi tou Sotíra 173
Metaxas, Ioannis 55
Metéora 188
Méthana 231
Méthana Island 21
Methóni 174
Metóhi 231
Métsovo 198
Mihaïl Roukouniótis 284
Mikrí Préspa
    bird life 214
Mikrí Préspa lake 214
Mikró 201
Mikró Horió 285
Mikrós Gialós bay 329
Mikrós Krassás 313
Miliá 315
Mílos 248
Mitrópolis 169
Mitrópolis (Athens' cathedral) 146
Mnesikles 140
moasteries
    Ágios Ioánnis Détis 246
Modern Greek Art Museum 274
Modiáno 211
Mólos 196, 317
Molyvosképastos 201
Mólyvos 301
monasteries
    Agía Paraskeví 199
    Agías Triádos 189
    Ágios Nektários 231
    Agíou Georgíou Feneoú 162
    Agíou Ioánnou Theológou
        (Pátmos) 291
    Agíou Nikoláou Anápavsa 189
    Agíou Stefánou 189
    Apocalypse (Pátmos) 291
    Arkádi 264
    Central Greece 181
    Dafní 151
    Faneroméni Monastery
        (Salamína) 229
    Goniá 267
    Gouvernétou 266
    Hristós Monastery (Véria) 216

Hryssopigís (Golden Wellspring)
    Monastery (Vathý) 245
Límonos 301
Megálou Meteórou 189
Megístis Lávras 219
Néa Filosófou 167
Néa Moní 305
Panagía Mavriótissa 214
Panagía Monastery (Ýdra) 233
Panormítis (Mandráki) 274
Perívleptos 169
Perivolís 301
Préveli 265
Rangóvou 201
Roussánou 189
Stomíou 201
Taxiárhis (Archangel) Monastery
    (Vathý) 245
Taxiárhis (Mandamádos) 301
Taxiárhon Monastery (Sérifos) 243
Theóktisti 306
Timíou Prodrómou 217
Toploú 262
Varlaám 189
Ypsiloú 301
Zoödóhou Pigís Monastery 254
Zoödóhou Pigís (Póros) 232
Monasteries
    Látomos 209
Monastery of Ósios Loukás 181
Monastiráki 146
Monastiráki square 146
Monastiráki Square 146
Monastiriótou synagogue 211
Monemvasiá 170
Moní 231
Monodéndri 199, 290
Monodéndri beach 328
Monólithos 275
Moraïtik 325
Morosíni fountain 259
mosaics 109
mosques 144
Moúdros 298
mountains 181
    Mt Ámbelos 308
    Mt Áthos 219
    Mt Elikónas 181
    Mt Fengári 295
    Mt Gamíla 201
    Mt Gioúkhtas 260
    Mt Hymettus 150, 151
    Mt Lykavitós 149
    Mt Olympos 202
    Mt Panetolikó 186
    Mt Parnassós 181
    Mt Párnitha 153
    Mt Pendéli 153
    Mt Psilorítis 260
    Mt Smólikas 202
    Mt Taÿgetos 169
    Mt Vóras (Kaïmaktsalán) 215
Mount Áthos 218, 219
Mount Dírfys 319
Mount Énos 329
Mount Ménalo 166
Mount Olympos 212
Mount Olympos (Ólymbos) 187, 211
Mount Óros 230
Mount Óssa 187
Mount Pílio (Pelion) 187

Mount Vóras (Kaïmaktsalán) 215
Mousío Vyrsodepsías/Tanning
    Museum 309
Mt Délfi 316
Mt Olympos 22
Mt Pandokrátor 324
Municipal Ethnographic Museum
    197
Murad Reis Mosque 274
museum and library (Líxoúri) 330
Museum of Asian Art (Corfu) 323
Museum of Byzantine Culture
    (Thessaloníki) 207
Museum of Modern Art (Flórina) 215
Museum of Solomos and Eminent
    Zakynthians 332
museums 162, 268
    Acropolis Museum 139
    archaeological museum (Évvia
        (Euboea Évvia)) 318
    Arhondikó Tosítsa 198
    Atelier-Museum Spyros Vassiliou
        152
    Benáki Museum 143, 148
    Benáki Museum annexe 152
    Byzantine Culture (Thessaloníki)
        207
    Byzantine Museum 323
    Byzantine Museum (Kastoriá) 213
    Canellopoulos (Kanellopoulou)
        Museum 144
    Christos Kapralos (Aegina) 230
    ecclesiastical 301
    Environment (Stymfalia) 162
    Folk and Ethnological Museum 211
    Folk and Modern Art (Kavála) 221
    Folklore 214, 216
    Folklore Museum (Mýkonos) 242
    Folklore Museum (Pláka) 248
    Folklore Museum (Sífnos) 243
    Folklore Museum Évvia (Euboea)
        319
    Folklore (Stemnítsa) 167
    Folk Museum (Salamína) 229
    Frissiras Museum 152
    Giustiniani (Híos) 303
    Goulandris Museum (Ándros) 239
    Goulandris Natural History
        Museum 153
    Icon and Sacred Art 259
    Jewish Museum 211
    Jewish Museum of Greece 145
    Modern Greek Art 274
    Municipal Ethnographic 197
    Museum of Greek Folk Art 145
    Museum of Popular Greek
        Musical Instruments 144
    National Archaeological Museum
        146
    National Archaeological Museum
        (Athens) 156
    National Historical Museum 147
    National Museum (Athens) 163
    Numismatic Museum 147
    Open-Air Water 216
    Peloponnesian Folklore
        Foundation (Návplio) 165
    Piraeus Archaeological Museum
        151
    Polygnotos Vagis (Liménas) 294
    Prehistoric Thera Museum 253

War Museum 149
music 89
coast of Asia Minor 91
Mycenae 163
My Family and Other Animals 325
Mykínes 163
Mýkonos 241
Folklore Museum 242
Mylopótamos 188
Mylopótas 251
Mýlos 231
Mýrina 298
ancient sites 298
Myrtiés 288
Myrtiótissa 325
Mýrtos 263
Mýrtos beach 331
Mystrás 165, 169
Mytilíni 301

N

Nanoú 284
Náousa 246
Náoussa 216
Nás 306
National Archaeological Museum 146
National Archaeological Museum (Athens) 156
National Art Gallery 149
National Gallery Annexe of Corfu 324
National Gardens 147
National Historical Museum 147
National Library, University and Academy 147
National Marine Park of Zákynthos 332
Natzís 214
Navaríno Bay (Pýlos) 174
Návpaktos 184
Návplio 164
Náxos 247
Néa Agorá 273
Néa Filosófou monastery 167
Néa Kaméni 253
Néa Moní monastery 305
Neápolis 202
Néa Potídea 218
Necromanteion 194
Negádes 199
Nemea 162
Néo 309
Néo Froúrio (New Fort) 321
Neohóri (Rhodes) 273
Néo Ítylo 173
Néos Marmarás 218
Nerandzópoulos mansion 213
Nerantzés Mosque 265
Nestor 175
Nída plateau 260
Nikiána 328
Nikiá village 286
Nikopolis 195
Nisí 197
Nísyros 285
Nomitsís 173
Norman-Angevin Kingdom 323
northeast Aegean 293
islands 293

Northwest Macedonia 212
Numismatic Museum 147
Nydrí 328

O

OAKA stadium 113
observatory 151
Odós Ermoú 301
Óhi 97
Olympia 175
Hera temple 175
Zeus temple 176
Olympic Games 113, 133, 151
Ólympos (Dodecanese) 281
costume 281
Omónia 146
Open-Air Water Museum 216
Orestiáda lake 213
Ósios Davíd 209
Othoní 324
Óthos 281
Ottoman Library 273
Ouranoúpoli 219
oúzo 103

P

Pahiá Ámmos 285, 297
Palace of St Michael and St George 322
Palaces
Galerius Caesar 207
Palaestra 175
Palamár 318
Palatítsa 216
Paleá 253
Paleá Alónisos 316, 317
Paleá Epídavros 161, 165
Paleá Períthia 324
Paleó 309
Paleó Froúrio 321
Paleohóra 231, 333
Paleóhora 267
Paleohóri 249
Paleokastrítsa 325
Paleokástro 251
Paleókastro 285
Paleó Klíma 315
Paleó Limáni 234
Paleó Pýli 288
Pálli 285
Paloúkia 229
Pamvotídas 197
Pamvótis (Pamvótida) 195
Panagía 221
Panagía Andivouniótissa 323
Panagía Armáta 235
Panagía Drosianí 248
Panagía Eleoússa 215
Panagía Evangelístria 239
Panagía Halkéon 208
Panagía Kalamiótissa 254
Panagía Kosmosótira 223
Panagía Koumbelidíki 213
Panagía Kyrá church 262
Panagía Mavriótissa 214
Panagía Mesosporítissa church 155
Panagía Monastery (Ýdra) 233
Panagía Parigorítissa 195
Panagías Kehreás 314

Panagías Kounístras 314
Panagía (small monastery). 327
Panagía Thalassítra 249
Panagía village (Liménas) 294
Panagía Vlahernón 195
Panahrándou 239
Pandánassa 169
Pandéli 289
Pandelímonos 219
Panórama 211
Panormítis 284
Panormítis Monastery (Mandráki) 274
Pánormos 315
Papademos, Lucas 62
Papadiamándis 314
Papandreou, Andreas 59
Papandreou, George 61
Papandreou, Georgios 58
Pápingo 201
Paradise beach 242
Paralía Kaláthou 277
Paralía Kotsikiás 319
Paralía Kýmis 319
Parálio Ástros 165
Paramónas beach 325
Paraportianí 242
Párga (Epirus) 193
Parikiá (Páros) 246
parks
National Gardens 147
Préspa National Park 120
Parliament Building 147
Parthenónas 218
Passavá 172
passport 345
Pátmos 290
Pátra 177
Paxí (Páxos) 327
Pédi 284
Peirene Fountain (Kórinthos) 161
Pélekas 325
Pelikáta hill 329
Pella (Macedonia) 217
Peloponnese 159
Peloponnesian mountains 21
Pendálofos 212
Perahora Heraion 159
Perahóri 329
Pérama 198
Peráni beach 229
Pérdika 193, 231
Pericles 36
Périssa 253
Peristéra 316
Peristéria beach 229
Perívleptos monastery 169
Perivolioú 316
Perivolís Monastery 301
Perouládes 324
Petaloúda church 309
Petaloúdes (Butterfly Valley) 277
Petaní 331
Pétra 301
Petrálona Cave 218
Pévkos 318
Phaistos 264
Pheidias 108
Philip II of Macedonia, King 38
Philippi 221
Philopappou (Filopáppou) 151

Phylakope 249
Pigádia 280
Pigés Kallithéas spa 276
Pikoulakis Towerhouse 172
Píndos hiking routes 202
Píndos mountains 21, 22
Pipéri 316
Piraeus Archaeological Museum 151
Piraeus (Pireás) 151
Píso Aetós 329
Písses 239
Pláka 145, 248
Pláka beach 248
Plakiás 265
Plakotós 251
Platána 319
Platáni 287
Plataniá 188
Plátanos 267, 289
platía 246
Platía Agías Irínis 146
Platía Aristotélous 206
Platía Avyssinías 146
Platía Eleftherías 258
Platía Karaïskáki 151
Platía Navarínou 207
Platía Omónias 146
Platía Pýrrou 196
Platía Syndágmatos 146
Platía Tríon Navárhon 174
Platía Venizélou 259
Platrithiás 329
Plátsa 173
Platý 299
Platýs Gialós 290
Platýs Gialós beach 242
Pleuron 185
Plomári 302
Pnyx 151
Pólis 329
Pollónia 248
Polygnotos Vagis Museum
   (Liménas) 294
Polýgyros 218
Polyphemus's Cave 223
Pondikonísi 323
Póros 232, 331
   town 232
   Zoödóhou Pigís Monasteries 232
Portára 247
Port Augusta 290
Portianoú 298
Pórto Germenó 179
Pórto Karrás 218
Pórto Kátsíki 329
Pórto Koufós 218
Poseidon Sanctuary 232
Possidonía 241
Potámi 309
Potamiá 294
Póthia 288
Potídea Canal 218
Poulídou 221
Poulikídou residences 213
Prasonísi 277
Prehistoric Thera Museum 253
Préspa Lakes 214
Préspa National Park 120
Préveli Monastery 265
Préveza 195
Promahónas 217

Promýri 188
Propylaia 140
Prousós 186
Provatás beach 249
Psará 302
Psarádes 214
Psaralíki 246
Psaropoúli 319
Psaroú beach 242
Psathí 249
Psáthi beach 251
Psathoúra 316
Psilí Ámmos 291
Psyhró 261
Pýlos 174
   Navaríno Bay 174
Pyrgadíkia 218
Pyrgí 304
Pýrgos 309
Pýrgos Diroú (Máni) 172
Pythagório 307

R

Ráhes 306
Rallis, Ioannis 56
Rangóvou monastery 201
Rénes 317
Réthymno 264
Rhamnous 155
Rhodes 271
   ancient city-states 274
   commercial centre 273
   New Town 273
   old cities 271
Rimóndi Fountain 265
Río-Andírrio straits 184
Ritsos, Giannis 170
Róda 324
Roman Agora 143
Roman agora (Kós) 286
Roman Empire 39, 45
Roman ruins 221
Roniés Waterfalls 329
Rotunda of Ágios Geórgios 208
Roúkounas 254
Roussánou 189

S

Salamína 229
   Faneroméni Monastery 229
   Folk Museum 229
   town 229
Samaras, Antonis 60
Samariá gorge 267
Samariá village 267
Sámi, port of 331
Sámos 307
Sámos Town 308
Samothráki 295
   Sanctuary 296
Samothráki (Hóra) 296
sanctuaries 169, 181
   Apollo (Delphi) 181
Sanctuary (Hera) 308
Sanctuary of Amphiareion 155
Sanctuary of Artemis 154
Sanctuary (Samothráki) 296
Sánta María 246
Santoríni 252

Santoríni (Thera) 157
Sárti 218
schedule resources 340
scooters 342
Seferis, George 84
Seïtáni 309
Sendoúkia 316
Sérifos 243
Sérifos Hóra 243
Sérres 217
Sfaktiría island 174
Siánna 275
Siátista 212
Sidári 324
Sideróportes 267
Sidiroúnda 305
Sífnos 243
   Artemónas 243
   Folklore Museum 243
Sígri 302
Síkinos 250
Simitis, Kostas 60
Síndos 207
Sithonía 218
Sitía 262
Skála 231, 249, 290, 330
Skála Eressoú 302
Skála Firá 253
Skála Oropoú 318
Skála Potamiás 295
Skaliá Cultural Centre/Théatro
   Avoúri 332
Skhinoússa 254
Skiáthos 313
Skiáthos Town 314
Skópelos 315
Skópelos Town 315
Skýros 317
Solomos, Dionysios 83
Sorós 246
Sotíros 295
Souflí 223
Soúgia 267
Spartans 155
Spárti 169
Spétses 234
   towns 234
Spianáda 322
Spílio 245
Spinalónga island 261
Sporades
   archaeological museum 318
Sporádes 313
Stáfylos 315
Stágira 218
Stavrós 329
Stavroupoli 222
Stemnítsa 167
Stení 319
Stení Vála 316
Stoa of Attalos 142
Stómio 319
Stomíou monastery 201
Stoúpa 173
St Paul 205
Stymfalía 162
sun cream and sunglasses 350
Super Paradise beach 242
Sykaminiá 301
Sykí 188
Sými 283

Sýndagma Square 147
Sýros 241
Sývota bay 329

T

tavernas 329
Taxiárhis 172
**Taxiárhis (Archangel) Monastery
(Vathý)** 245
**Taxiárhis Monastery
(Mandamádos)** 301
**Taxiárhis tis Mitropóleos
(Kastoriá)** 213
Taxiárhon Monastery (Sérifos) 243
tekke 144
Télendos 288
temples 182
  Anemospiliá 259
  Aphaea (Aegina) 230
  Aphrodite (Kórinthos) 162
  Apollo (Aegina) 230
  Apollo (Delphi) 182
  Apollo Epikourios (Bassae) 168
  Apollo (Kórinthos) 161
  Athena 294
  Athena Nike 140
  Dionysos 294
  Doric Temple of Poseidon 153
  Hellenistic Athena 274
  Hera temple (Olympia) **175**
  Temple of Zeus 143
  Zeus (Nemea) 162
  Zeus temple (Olympia) **176**
Thános 299
Thárri 276
Thásos **293**
theatres
  Herodeio or Iródio Theatre 143
  Theatre of Dionyso 142
Theodorakis, Mikis 81, 93, 94
The Odyssey 194
Theoharakis Foundation 152
Theóktisti monastery 306
Theológos 295
Theophilos Museum (Variá) 301
Theoskepastí 306
Theriade Museum (Variá) 301
Thermá 297
Thérmo 186
Thermon 186
Thermopylae 187
Theseus 143
Thesprotía
  Karavostási 193
Thessaloníki 205
  Chain Tower 210
  churches 208
  Jewish Museum 211
  Lefkós Pýrgos 210
  museum of Byzantine Culture 207
Thessaloníki (northern Greece) **212**
Thessaly 38
Thirassía 253
Thíva (Thebes) 179
Tholária 252
Tílos 285
Tímiou Prodrómou monastery 217
Tingáki 287
Tínos **239**
  Kolymbíthra beach 240

Tínos Hóra 240
Tiryns 163
toiletries 350
Tombs
  Clytemnestra 163
Toploú Monastery 262
Toróni 218
Tourkovoúnia 151
tour operators 350
Tower of the Winds 143
**traditional settlements
(paradosiakí ikismí)** 343
Traganoú 277
transliteration scheme 351
Treasury (Atreus) 163
Trihonída Lake 22
Tríkala (Zíria) 163
Tríkeri 188
Trípoli 166
Trís Boúkes 317
Trizónia (Corinth) 184
Troezen 233
Tsambíka beach 277
Tsangaráda 188
Tsepélovo 201
Tsilíví 332
Tsizdarákis Mosque 144
Tsolakoglou, General Georgios 56
Turkish Bath 273
turtles 118
Týlissos 260
Tzanáki beach 289
Tzanáta 331

V

Váï 262
Vale of Témbi 187
Vapória 241
Vareltzídena Mansion 301
Vári 241
Variá 301
Varlaám 189
Varvákios Agorá 146
Vasilikós Peninsula 332
Vasilisís Sofías 222
Vassilikí 329
Vaterá 302
Váthia 172
Vathý 245, 308, 329
  Hryssopigís (Golden Wellspring)
    Monastery 245
  Taxiárhis (Archangel) Monastery
    245
Vatopedíou 219
Vátos 297
Vátses beach 289
Vecchi, Cesare Maria de 56
Velanió 315
Venetian fort 263
Venizelos, Eleftherios 53
Vergína (Macedonia) 216
Véria
  Byzantine Museum 216
  Hristós Monastery 216
Véria (Macedonia) **216**
Véssa 305
Via Egnatia 205
Vía Egnatía 191, 193
Víkos Gorge 199
Villa Cleobolus 274

village museum (Dion) 215
visas 345
Vistonída 222
Vítsa 199
Vitsikó (Víkos) 200
Vlahérna 195, 323
Vlatadon 209
Vlyhós 234
Voïdokiliá (Messinía) 175
Voïdomátis River 201
Voláda 281
Vólax 240
Volímes 333
Volissós 305
Vólos 187
Vólvi 217
Vónitsa 185
Votanókypos Kefaloniás 330
Votsalákia 309
Vourkári 239
Vourliótes 308
Vradéto 199
Vromólimnos 313
Vromólithos 289
Vytína 166
Vyzítsa 188

W

War Museum 149
wildlife 116
wine 101

X

Xánemos 314
Xánthi 222
Xerxes's Canal 218
Xí beaches 330
Xiróloutsa pond 200
Xylokériza beach 235

Y

Yahouda Hamam 211
Ýdra **233**
  Panagía Monastery 233
Yeni Cami 211
Yeni Hamam 210
youth hostels 343
Ypsiloú Monastery 301
Ýpsos 323
Ystérnia 240

Z

Zagorá 188
Zagóri (Epirus) 192
Zagóri (Zagorohória) 198
Zagorohória **198**
  national park 199
Zakros 262
Zákros
  village 263
Zákynthos (Zante) 332
Zálongo 194
Zánga beach 174
Zappeio hall 148
Záppio Park 143
Zeus temple (Olympia) 176
Ziá 288

Athens Metro & Tramway

Greece: Physical and Main Ferry Routes

Ancona, Bari	Venezia
Durrës	Tiranë
	Elbasan
Brindisi	
ITALY	Vlorë

MACEDONIA

1179
Mavrovoúni

ALBANIA

Límni Mikrá
Préspa
Florina   Édessa   Langadás
Vérnon
Óros   Thessaloniki
Véria
Bitola

Halk

Kozáni   Kateríni
Aliákmonas

Grevená   Óros
2917
Olympos
Elasóna   Ólympos
Tymfi
2497
Zagori   Kalambáka   GRE
Piniós
Kérkyra   Ioánnina   Tríkala   Lárisa
Kérkyra   Igoumenítsa   Kardítsa   Pílion   Pílio Óros
(Corfu)
Vólos
Fársala

Paxí
(Páxos)
Andípaxi   Árta   Tehnití Límni
Kremastón   Lamía
Preveza   Tymfristós
2315
Levkáda
Levkáda   Meganísi   Agrínio   Ag. Konstandínos
(Léfkas)
Kefaloniá   Aslakós   Náfpaktos   Ámfissa
(Cephalonia)   Itháki   Livadiá
Argostóli   Póros   Pátra   Palovouna
1748
Kórinthiakós Kólpos
Kyllíni   Sálamin
Zákynthos   2224   Kórinthos
(Zante)   Zákynthos   Pýrgos   Árgos
Peloponnisos
(Peloponnese)   Náfplio

IONIAN   Trípoli   Spétses
SEA   Plíaka

Kalamáta   Spárti

Taygetos
Parno

Gýthio

Lakonikós
Kólpos
Neápoli

Kýthira
Kýthira

MEDITERRANEAN SEA

Andikýthira

Ionian Islands

IONIAN SEA

Aráhthos
Notia Pindos
Vória Pindos
Óri Vardoúsia
Argolikós
Kólpos
Thermekós Kólpos

N

Greece: Physical and Main Ferry Routes

0   50 km
0   50 miles